DOUBLEDAY
CELEBRATES
100 YEARS OF
EXCELLENCE

By the same author

Please to the Table
Terrific Pacific

Anya von Bremzen

Photographs by John C. Welchman

DOUBLEDAY

New York London Toronto Sydney Auckland

FIESTA!

A CELEBRATION OF
LATIN HOSPITALITY

PUBLISHED BY DOUBLEDAY
a division of Bantam Doubleday Dell Publishing Group, Inc.
1540 Broadway, New York, New York 10036

DOUBLEDAY and the portrayal of an anchor with a dolphin are
trademarks of Doubleday, a division of Bantam Doubleday
Dell Publishing Group, Inc.

Library of Congress Cataloging-in-Publication Data
Von Bremzen, Anya.
Fiesta!: a celebration of Latin hospitality / Anya von Bremzen.—1st ed.
p.   cm.
Includes index.
1. Cookery, Latin American.   I. Title.
TX716.A1V66   1997
641.598—dc21   97-3641
CIP

ISBN 0-385-47526-8
Text copyright © 1997 by Anya von Bremzen
Photographs copyright © 1997 by John C. Welchman
All Rights Reserved
Printed in the United States of America
November 1997

First Edition

1   3   5   7   9   10   8   6   4   2

To my mother

Ya tebya lyublyu

In any language, I love you more than words can say.

Acknowledgments

My sincere thanks go out to the following people and organizations who have generously helped with recipes, information, and practical assistance, making travel and research in Spain, Portugal, and the Americas a true fiesta.

Rene Acklin, Aerolineas Argentinas, Isabel Álvarez, Clara Maria de Amezúa, El Arrayán restaurant in Queens, Silvina Barroso, Joan Bloom at Hill & Knowlton, Miriam Becker, Eric Basulto at S.O.B.'s nightclub in New York City, Cal'Isidre restaurant in Barcelona, Maurucio Andrade Carneiro, El Comensal restaurant in Lima, De Attucha family, Felix de Jesus, Dorothea Elman–Winston, Cesar Arturo Espinel, Faucett Airlines, Foptour, Alex Gonzalez, Gremio restaurant in Evora, Josie Sison de la Guerra, Inmaculada Guiu, Marisa Guiulfo, Barbara Haber at the Schlessinger Library, Claudio Heckman, Elizabeth Horton at Holt, Hughes & Stamell, Hyatt International, ICEX, Luis Irizar, Tarcila Lazo de la Vega, Maria Lemos, Ana Lineman, Josep Lladonosa, Gabi Llamas, Francis Mallmann, Zulema Martin, Jorje Massey, Jeanne Miserendino at the Tourist Office of Spain, Esteban Modino, Luis Monje at Parador de Segovia, Bertha Palenzuela, Cecilia Parodi, Piedad the "arepa lady," La Porteña restaurant in Queens, Jose Puig, Teresa Quesada at the Embassy of Peru, Steve and Barbara Raichlen, Maria João Ramires at the Portuguese National Tourist Office, Oswald Rivera, Elena Sanchez, Amelia Salgado, Senyor Parellada restaurant in Barcelona, Sheraton Hotels, Laura Tapia, Tempero de Dada restaurant in Bahia, Varig Brazilian Airlines, Pilar Vico at Marketing Ahead, and Victor's Cafe in Miami and New York City.

This project would have never gotten off the ground without the volcanic energy, meteoric dispatch, and rock-solid support of my agent, Alice Martell.

At Doubleday, thanks to my editor, Judy Kern, for her enthusiasm and good cheer, and to Marysarah Quinn for her festive design.

I thank Nancy Novogrod and Barbara Peck at *Travel & Leisure* for giving me the job of my dreams.

My companion, John Welchman—who put me on the road in the first place, literally and metaphorically—shared my travels, sampled my recipes, and lit up the pages of this book with exuberant photographs. There would be no fiesta in my life without him.

The final debt of gratitude goes to my mother, Larisa Frumkin—love, care, and generosity personified.

CONTENTS

Introduction

FIESTA!
A Celebration of Latin Hospitality

This book was born out of my fascination with Latin culture and food, a fascination that grew with time into a compulsion to penetrate this world, to become—as best I could—an insider. It all started in an unlikely place: Moscow in the early 1970s. My neighborhood school, which was attended by children of Latin expatriates and offered Spanish as a second language, was a true Communist showcase for Russo-Latin friendship. We performed Russian dances for the daily streams of visiting dignitaries from Latin America and recited stories about the lives of Allende and Castro. In a classroom where Spanish was taught by a *niña de la guerra* (one of the many Spaniards who were brought to Russia as children during the Spanish Civil War), I shared my desk with students from Havana and Santiago, Buenos Aires, and Bogotá. During class, my friends—forced to subsist on watery borscht and appalled by our habit of eating ice cream in sub-zero temperatures—whispered deliriously delicious stories of soups teeming with meats and tropical vegetables, gigantic steaks, exotic fruit, and pastries steamed in banana leaves. I sat there almost convulsing with hunger and then went home secretly wishing that my mother's *pirozhki* would somehow turn into tamales.

Later in life, I found myself in Jackson Heights, New York, which thousands of Colombian, Peruvian, Argentinian, Ecuadorian, Mexican, and Uruguayan immigrants now call their home. (We also have a Little India, Little Korea, a notable Filipino enclave, and scores of expatriate Russians, but that's another book—or more!) It was there that my childhood fantasies finally came to life.

My Jackson Heights mornings often begin at the counter of my local Chino-Latino luncheonette. There, over a cup of strong aromatic *café con leche* and a savory Cuban sandwich, the Cuban-Cantonese owner, Mr. Elías Chee Chung, reminisces about his youth as a dandy in Batista's Havana. Or, if I am in the mood, I have breakfast at Uruguaya, a tiny pastry shop, every inch of which is festooned with soccer paraphernalia and flashy fiesta gear. I order a flaky empanada and a guava and cream cheese roll, and buy packets of the strong, addictive Argentinian herb tea called *mate*, jars of rich, caramel-flavored condensed milk, called *dulce de leche*, and rare old tapes of the tango idol Carlos Gardel. Afterward, I drop in to our high-tech *botánica*, a ritual herbal store, to get my fortune read. At the local supermarket I buy blue corn and *chuño*—freeze-dried potatoes from the Andes—banana leaves, tropical fruit pulps, yuca (manioc) flour, homemade *chorizo*, and dried avocado leaves. On Sundays I visit Teresa, who roasts guinea pigs in a main street parking lot. If she is out of guinea pigs, as a consolation she offers me a paper cup of centuries-old Inca corn beer called *chicha* and a plate of *mazamorra*, a sweet porridge of purple corn, simmered overnight and perfumed with cinnamon and cloves. I sit on an overturned milk crate and take down her recipe for plantain dumpling soup.

LA CHEEF!..

Late weekend nights I run out of my house at 2 A.M. to greet Piedad, a diminutive Colombian *arepa* vendor, who is my favorite hawker in all of the Americas. She is on her usual street corner, grilling *arepas* and pork kebabs, laughing and drinking beer with Señor César, a chubby Colombian chef who comes out at night to keep her company. We hug, she offers me an *arepa*, and we make a date to get together at her house to make tamales. On the way home I stop by Añoranzas, a dark smoky Colombian salsa club to hear the last set of a great singer, Henri Fiol. On weekend nights my Latin-populated building literally pulsates to the beat of salsa, *cumbia*, and *merengue*, the garlicky perfume of roast pork wafting seductively into the hallway.

Their world has become my world. Like my neighbors, I go out to dance salsa on Mondays, tango on Wednesdays, *charanga* on Thursdays, and *rumba* on Sundays. I make tamales on Sundays, salt cod on Fridays, and crispy suckling pig for the holidays. Seduced by these cultures, I have embarked on long journeys around Latin America to find out more about the people and food I so love, ending up in Spain and Portugal to search for the roots of these cultures and cuisines. While I have traveled quite extensively through Mexico, I am not including Mexican food in this book, as I feel that its richness and individuality is a story unto itself—one that has been well treated in many excellent cookbooks.

Fiesta! is dedicated to the joyous, generous spirit of Latin hospitality. I love the way Latins entertain. I marvel at their hospitality, which so effortlessly blends flair and panache with an easygoing carefree style. They cook in an "open-arms" kitchen, where food is often prepared in large quantities—for immediate and extended family, for neighbors, and for a constant stream of guests. Most of the family-style recipes in this book reflect this tradition. You will always have enough food for everyone, plus leftovers for days to come. *Fiesta!* recipes are straightforward and simple to prepare. Yet they are as spicy, colorful, and flamboyant as the people and cultures that created them.

Fiesta! is not an "encyclopedic" ethnic cookbook, featuring classic recipes from all the Latin countries. It focuses, instead, on style and presentation. It is contemporary rather than classic in that it features honest, easy-to-put-together, inexpensive, and delicious food that answers the demands of American cooks today. At the same time, I have made it as authentic as I can. The recipes and stories come from real people of all kinds, whom I met and often cooked with on my travels. Whether grandmothers from rural villages, well-known chefs, street vendors, artists, or musicians, they all reflect the warm and vibrant way Latins cook today.

The recipes come from the Iberian Peninsula, Latin America, and the Spanish Caribbean, those countries where the fiesta is a dedicated way of life—even when there's not a festival to hand. The countries and traditions are staggeringly diverse, and by using the umbrella term "Latin," I don't mean to downplay the differences between them. Yet there is a common thread: wherever the Iberian colonists went, besides their culinary traditions, they left a legacy of Catholicism with its enormous calendar of holidays, feasts, and fasts. Superimposed upon indigenous traditions, and augmented over the centuries with local customs, music, and foods, these occasions became the very core of the Latin lifestyle. There is hardly a day of the week that passes without a street fair, a block party, a religious procession, a *fiesta patronal* (a patron saint's day), a family reunion, or a community event. Whether it's a Puerto Rican salsa bash, an Argentinian grill party, a Spanish Christmas dinner, a rustic Portuguese village Easter celebration, or a riotous Brazilian carnival, a Latin fiesta is hard to beat for the fun, the music, and, most of all, for the food. On a more modest scale, such is the spirit of Latin hospitality that a neighbor dropping by for coffee or a group of men gathering over a glass of beer and a plate of nibbles will inevitably turn into a festive occasion.

The centuries-long culinary give-and-take between the Old World and the New has been shaped into a natural alliance of great charm and sophistication. The colonists sailed to the New World in search of new treasures, but at first they found just food. Gold and silver turned up too, but all the riches in the Americas combined didn't have as profound and lasting a social impact on the Iberian Peninsula as Native American produce. Ingredients such as potatoes, tomatoes, corn, squash, beans, coffee, and chocolate were imported and now make up the very heart of Spanish and Portuguese cooking. At the same time the colonists brought over livestock, olive oil, olives, capers, salt cod, sausages, and an array of convent sweets, as well as the European culinary methods and techniques that now form the basis of New World cuisine. Anywhere you eat in Latin America you will feel an Iberian legacy. In *Fiesta!*, the Mediterranean flavors of Spain and Portugal mingle naturally and happily with the flavors of Native America, Africa, and the Caribbean.

As salsa (the music) blares from millions of radios from coast to coast, salsa (the sauce) is on its way to becoming the fastest-selling condiment in the country. Latin immigrants unveil bright new versions of ethnic cuisines on an almost daily basis, and each week a new Hispanic foodstuff—yucas, chayotes, jars of multicolored beans and zesty condiments—cross over from the *barrio bodegas* to Grand Unions and A&Ps countrywide. As the Latin communities in the United States are growing apace, I am convinced that Americans will find themselves eating and cooking much more Latin food, as well as enjoying the music, culture, customs, and traditions. I hope *Fiesta!* will pucker the appetite, and help pave the way for the palate into a fabulous world of festive eating.

Festival at Juli, Peru.

Drinks, Dips, Sauces, and Snacks

Drinks

Festival at Juli, Peru.

WITHOUT DOUBT, rum is the most beguiling and romantic of all alcoholic drinks. The soft, amber liquor conjures up images of old sea dogs and pirates, Spanish explorers in search of new conquests, and infamous, Prohibition-era, smugglers and rumrunners. Rum-making is still intimately linked to the checkered histories of the tropical and subtropical cultures where sugarcane prospers: wherever you find sugarcane, you will be sure to run into rum. It was Christopher Columbus himself who first brought sugarcane from the Azores to the Caribbean during his 1493 voyage. Just a few decades later, production was in full swing; and it has formed the backbone of the Spanish Caribbean export industry ever since.

Like all the great liquors of the world, rum has made its own unique contribution to the fine art of mixology: Its masterpieces are the daiquiri and the piña colada. The daiquiri, a potent lime-rum potion, perfumed with fresh mint, is said to have been invented in Cuba by an American engineer, William Cox, at the turn of the century, and named after the small mining town in eastern Cuba where he worked. If you dig a little deeper, though, you will discover that this particular mix actually dates back to the end of the sixteenth century, when the infamous courtier-pirate, Sir Francis Drake, was busy plundering Spanish galleons loaded with New World treasures. Believe it or not, the original function of the drink was purely medicinal! Hundreds of pounds of vitamin C—packed lemons and limes (fruits sturdy enough to prevent spoilage during long voyages) were loaded onto ships adventuring into the Caribbean to prevent outbreaks of scurvy among the crew. The juice was taken daily by the pirates and seawolves as a prophylactic, with a little sugar to sweeten it up and a touch of rum to lift the spirits.

The invention of the piña colada is much more recent. In the early fifties a Puerto Rican entrepreneur named Ramón López Irizarry developed a delicious sweet cream made from the tender meat of young coconuts, which he intended to be used for desserts and drinks. The mixture was marketed as Coco López. A few years later, a spirited bartender named Ramón Marrero, who was working at the Caribe Hilton in San Juan, mixed Coco López with fresh pineapple juice, cracked ice, and rum and came up with the snowy smooth drink, with its irresistible combination of tropical flavors, that we know as the piña colada.

The glamorous decadence of the Cuban tourist industry, coupled with American Prohibition, contributed other rum libations: El Presidente (rum and vermouth); Cuba Libre (rum and Coke); Mary Pickford (rum, pineapple juice, grenadine, and maraschino cherry liqueur); and the exquisite *mojito*, a refreshing cooler of rum, lime, mint, and sparkling water.

On a nonalcoholic note, nothing is more Latino than the brash, poignantly tropical, juice and milkshake bars that dot the streets of Latin American towns and villages. You select your fruit—the beguilingly tart *maracuyá* (passion fruit), white custardy *guanábana*, velvety papaya or mango, refreshingly restrained star fruit, juicy sweet tropical orange, or newly popular (and healthy) combinations of fruit and vegetables such as avocado, carrots, beets, or celery—and it will be blended for you into a frothy nectar that will revive your senses and restore your energy.

Coconut: The Prince of Palms

A famous British naturalist, Alfred Wallace, called the tall, graceful coconut tree "the prince of palms for beauty and utility." And the nut itself, with its refreshing liquid and sweetly fragrant flesh, is a perfect emblem of the tropics. Marco Polo described it as "the Pharaoh's nut," perhaps because it was believed to have been discovered by Egyptian merchants. But when the Iberian adventurers introduced coconut to the European courts in 1674, the Spanish named it coco, as its three "eyes" resembled the funny face of a famous Iberian clown who went by that name.

In its tropical homelands, the coconut palm is a multipurpose tool that knows no boundaries of inventiveness. Under the scorching tropical sun, the palm is a picnic umbrella for shade; the hollowed-out inner shells of the nut make kitchen utensils and musical instruments; mats, ropes, brushes, and even clothes are fashioned from the coir fibers of the husk; furniture is made from the wood; the largest trees are used in construction; the leaves are woven into matting; and the oil is used for candles, cosmetics, or soaps.

The culinary uses of the coconut are likewise legion. The clear liquid inside a green nut makes a lovely refreshing drink, while the oil is sometimes used as cooking fat. A dark, deep-flavored sugar is obtained from the sap of the palm; the flesh makes delicious chips, cakes, confections, and jams; and the nutty, sweet white milk extracted from the grated flesh of a mature coconut is used as a base for stews, soups, flans, and cakes.

The large green-brown coconuts served at tropical beaches are the unripe nuts, still in their husk. Their jelly-like pulp solidifies as the coconut matures to form the firm, juicy, white flesh of a mature, hairy brown coconut. The milky liquid squeezed from the grated flesh, with or without water, produces what we know as coconut milk—not to be confused with the clear "coconut juice" found inside the young coconut. Cream of coconut, such as the famous Puerto Rican Coco López, is a sweetened product, used for tropical drinks.

Handling Coconuts

Coconut palm, street sign, Jackson Heights, New York.

Today, fresh coconuts are easily found at most supermarkets. When choosing one, follow these guidelines: Look for a solid nut that feels heavy for its size, free of cracks and mold, with healthy, shiny brown hairs. Coconuts spoil easily, so once you've cracked the nut, taste the liquid inside. If the taste is rancid, discard the nut and start again. Coconuts are inexpensive, so you might want to buy an extra one just in case. Store coconuts in a cool, dry place for no more than 3 to 4 days.

To crack a coconut, pierce two of its three eyes with an ice pick and drain off the clear liquid inside. To make cracking easier, bake it in a 450 degree F. oven for about 15 minutes. Then whack it hard around the periphery with a hammer or a heavy cleaver. Coconut milk is made by blending grated coconut flesh with hot water and then squeezing out the liquid. The best bet for making milk is to use the pregrated fresh coconut sold frozen and packaged at many markets and is easily found in Asian and Hispanic ones. Goya brand is excellent. Let it defrost, puree it in a blender for a minute or so with 1 cup of boiling water for each cup of grated coconut. Let it stand for 5 minutes and strain it through a sieve, pressing hard on the solids with your fingers. Frozen and thawed coconut flesh is also a good bet for cakes and other desserts. Fresh coconut milk is extremely perishable and should be refrigerated and used within two days. It will keep indefinitely in the freezer packed in Ziploc bags.

Making coconut milk from scratch is a laborious task, and canned coconut milk is an excellent substitute for fresh. It's denser and richer than homemade, and in most cases you will want to thin it out with a little water or broth, especially if you are using it for soups or stews. My favorite brand is Chaokoh, imported from Thailand. Goya and Thai Taste are also reliable.

To grate fresh coconut, crack it as directed on the previous page and break into 5 to 6 pieces with a heavy cleaver. Pry the meat from the shell using a sturdy knife, and peel off the brown outer layer of skin, using a vegetable peeler. Cut the coconut into smallish chunks and grate in a food processor. One coconut will yield about 3 cups grated flesh.

Coconut–Passion Fruit Cocktail

(COCTEL DE COCO Y MARACUYÁ)

To make this exotic tropical cocktail all year round, take advantage of the excellent and inexpensive frozen passion fruit pulp that is available at most Hispanic groceries. Just ask for *maracuyá*!

In a blender, combine the passion fruit pulp, coconut milk, cream of coconut, and rum. Transfer the blended mixture to a pitcher and stir in the ice cubes.

ONE 14-OUNCE BAG (ABOUT 1½ CUPS) FROZEN
    UNSWEETENED PASSION FRUIT PULP, THAWED
    (SEE PAGE 323)
½ CUP CANNED COCONUT MILK, WELL STIRRED
1 CUP CREAM OF COCONUT SUCH AS COCO
    LÓPEZ, WELL STIRRED
1⅔ CUPS LIGHT RUM
3 CUPS ICE CUBES, OR TO TASTE

MAKES 6 TO 7 DRINKS

House painted with ships, La Boca, Buenos Aires, Argentina.

Caipirinhas

Caipirinhas make your mind soar and your body collapse. After three drinks, you can have a conversation about analytical philosophy, but forget walking in a straight line. The name of this drink, so adored in Brazil, comes from the diminutive of the word "*caipira*," a peasant girl. It is made by crushing chunks of fresh lime and its juice, skin and all, sugar, and *cachaça*, a potent liquor made from sugarcane. There are no strict proportions, some prefer their *caipirinhas* sweet, others more sour, some like it strong, others more citrusy. And if you don't have *cachaça*, don't despair, mix up an authentic *caipiroska*—the same libation made with vodka instead of *cachaça*. Unheard of in Siberia, but a hit in Brazil.

3 LARGE JUICY LIMES, HALVED CROSSWISE
3 TO 4 TABLESPOONS SUGAR, OR TO TASTE
1 CUP CACHAÇA OR VODKA
ICE CUBES

1. Squeeze out and reserve some juice from the lime halves, but not so much that they are completely dry. Cut the limes, with their skins, into 1½-inch chunks.

2. In a large mortar and pestle, crush the limes with the sugar. Divide the mixture between 4 short glasses. Add the *cachaça* or vodka. Stir. Add the reserved lime juice and ice cubes to taste.

MAKES 4 DRINKS

Coffee-Rum Cocktail

(BATIDA DE CAFÉ)

This rich and smooth coffee cocktail is one of the many versions of a Brazilian drink called *batida* (which contains *cachaça*), not to be confused with the benign milk shake called *batido*.

In a blender, process the rum, coffee, condensed milk, Kahlúa, and sugar until smooth. Add the desired number of ice cubes, one by one, and blend to crush the ice. Serve in small tumblers over more ice.

1½ CUPS LIGHT RUM
1½ CUPS STRONG COLD COFFEE
3 TABLESPOONS SWEETENED CONDENSED MILK, OR MORE TO TASTE
½ CUP KAHLÚA
2 TABLESPOONS SUGAR
ICE CUBES

MAKES 6 TO 8 DRINKS

Frozen Papaya

(COCTEL DE PAPAYA HELADO)

2 CUPS WHITE RUM

$^1/_2$ CUP MALIBU COCONUT RUM

$^1/_2$ CUP FRESH LIME JUICE

2$^1/_2$ CUPS CHOPPED RIPE PAPAYA

1 TABLESPOON SUGAR, OR MORE, DEPENDING ON
    THE SWEETNESS OF THE PAPAYA

2 CUPS ICE CUBES

Tropical partners rum, papaya, and lime come together in this velvety smooth drink, thick from the freezer. A perfect beach drink!

Blend all the ingredients except the ice in a blender until the papayas are pureed. Add the ice cubes, one at a time, and continue to blend. Transfer the blended drink to a jug or bowl and freeze for 1 hour. Pour into glasses and serve.

MAKES 6 TO 8 DRINKS

Bar Pinochio, market,
Barcelona, Spain.

Rum Fizz with Mint

(MOJITO)

Tangy, fizzy, and perfumed with the heady scent of the Cuban mint called *yerbabuena*, this is one of the most refreshing cocktails imaginable. The recipe is inspired by Victor's Café (a New York restaurant that has a branch in Miami), which makes the best *mojito* I know.

Place the lime slices, lemon juice, sugar, and *yerbabuena* in a tall glass and crush with a long wooden spoon. Add the rum and ice cubes and enough club soda to fill the glass.

2 THIN SLICES FRESH LIME
2 TEASPOONS FRESHLY SQUEEZED LEMON JUICE
2 TEASPOONS SUGAR
1 SPRIG *YERBABUENA,* (AVAILABLE AT GOOD LATIN FRUIT MARKETS), SPEARMINT, PEPPERMINT, OR REGULAR MINT
¼ CUP WHITE RUM
3 TO 4 ICE CUBES
CLUB SODA

MAKES 1 DRINK

Tamarindo

²/₃ CUP TAMARIND PULP (SEE HEADNOTE)
6 CUPS BOILING WATER
¹/₂ CUP SUGAR, OR MORE TO TASTE
ICE CUBES
MINT SPRIGS OR LEAVES, FOR GARNISH

At Latin American and Caribbean *loncherías*, tart, refreshing *tamarindo* (tamarind nectar) is the thirst-quencher of choice. To make it at home, all you need to do is soak tamarind pulp in boiling water and add some sugar. You can find tamarind pulp at Latin, Southeast Asian, or Indian groceries.

1. In a large bowl, combine the tamarind, water, and sugar. Stir and mash the tamarind with a fork to help it dissolve. Let stand until cool.

2. Strain the liquid into a pitcher through a fine sieve, pressing hard on the solids to extract as much juice as possible and scraping the bottom of the sieve with a wooden spoon.

3. Serve in tall glasses, over ice, garnishing each portion with a mint sprig or leaves. If not serving immediately, stir before serving.

MAKES 5 TO 6 DRINKS

Tropical Fruit White Sangría

There are few drinks more playful and charming than the Spanish sangría—light fruity wine, white or red, infused with the flavor and scent of fresh fruit. For me, the fruit, especially when it is allowed to macerate in the alcohol for some time, is the best part of the whole affair. As it's done in tropical Latin countries, I offer a sangría with exotic fruit, such as mango, papaya, cantaloupe, and whatever else is available. Custard apple (cherimoya) and fresh guava would also be wonderful, if you can find them. As for wine, I like the young, slightly effervescent Galician Albariño. If you have a wide-mouthed crock with a good tight lid, it's nice to let the sangría "age" for a couple of days.

½ CUP SUGAR

¼ CUP WATER

1 BOTTLE (750 ML) LIGHT WHITE WINE, SUCH AS ALBARIÑO (SEE HEADNOTE)

1 CUP DICED RIPE BUT FIRM MANGO

½ CUP DICED CANTALOUPE

1 STAR FRUIT, SLICED

½ CUP DICED PAPAYA

1 SMALL ORANGE, SCRUBBED WELL AND DICED

½ CUP MANGO NECTAR

ICE CUBES, OPTIONAL

1. In a small saucepan, combine the sugar and water and heat over medium heat until the sugar is dissolved.

2. In a wide-mouthed crock with a tight-fitting lid, or in a pitcher, combine the syrup, wine, fruit, and nectar. If using a crock, cover tightly and let stand in a cool place for up to 2 days. If serving in a pitcher, serve at once with some ice cubes.

SERVES 4 TO 6

Piña Colada

I was compelled to include this familiar recipe, seeing how many people use a pre-prepared piña colada mix. Making a great fresh-tasting piña colada—to which I add fresh pineapple pulp—from scratch takes almost the same time, with much more uplifting results.

1½ CUPS LIGHT RUM
1 CUP FRESH UNSWEETENED PINEAPPLE JUICE
¾ CUP FINELY DICED FRESH PINEAPPLE
½ CUP CREAM OF COCONUT SUCH AS COCO LÓPEZ, WELL STIRRED, OR MORE TO TASTE
1 SMALL TRAY ICE CUBES
PINEAPPLE WEDGES, FOR GARNISH

In a blender, puree the rum, pineapple juice, fresh pineapple, and Coco López until smooth. Taste and add more Coco López, if desired. Add the ice cubes, several at a time, and blend at high speed until pulverized, about 6 to 8 minutes. Serve, garnished with pineapple wedges.

MAKES 4 DRINKS

Daiquiri

This is the original, pure daiquiri, not frozen or thickened with other fruit. It's simple to make, and you will be enchanted by its classic taste.

Combine the rum, lime juice, sugar, ice, and smashed mint leaves in a cocktail shaker and shake to mix. Pour into a glass and serve, garnished with the unblemished leaf and lime wedge.

MAKES 1 DRINK

3 OUNCES LIGHT RUM

1 OUNCE FRESH LIME JUICE

2 TEASPOONS SUPERFINE SUGAR, OR MORE TO
    TASTE

$\frac{1}{2}$ CUP CRACKED ICE

4 MINT LEAVES, LIGHTLY SMASHED, PLUS AN
    UNBLEMISHED LEAF FOR GARNISH

1 FRESH LIME WEDGE, FOR GARNISH

Soursop Fruit Shake

(GUANÁBANA BATIDO)

Greet your morning, afternoon, or evening, for that matter, with a luscious shake of *guanábana* (soursop), buttermilk, and honey. Of all the tropical fruit for *batidos* (shakes), *guanábana* certainly gets my vote, for its custardy flesh and wonderfully exotic aroma. Frozen *guanábana* pulp is available at any well-stocked Latin grocery. If you can't find it, mango is also excellent.

Process all the ingredients in a blender until the *guanábana* is thoroughly pureed, about 3 minutes. Taste, and blend in more honey if you wish.

ONE 13-OUNCE BAG FROZEN *GUANÁBANA* PULP,
   PARTIALLY THAWED, SEEDS REMOVED, IF ANY
1 CUP BUTTERMILK
$\frac{1}{4}$ CUP MILK (LOW-FAT, IF YOU WISH)
2 TABLESPOONS HONEY, OR MORE TO TASTE

SERVES 4

Dips, Sauces, and Snacks

COCINA LATINA boasts an incredible choice of snacks, hot and cold, sweet and piquant, ample or bite-sized—enjoyed before, after, and in-between meals. Guests are loved and prized in the Latin world. Friends and neighbors often drop by unexpectedly, and casual hospitality is second nature. Every social contact, even if it's a chance encounter on the street, is greeted as an opportunity to share a cup of strong coffee, a *refresco*, a beer, or a hot chocolate, accompanied by a little plate of food—a fritter or a slice of pie, a corn cake or a savory marinated vegetable. From the famous Spanish tapas (born in Andalusian *jerez* bars) to Portuguese *salgadinhos* (salty morsels) and Brazilian *tiro-gostos*, (taste pullers), to Venezuelan *pasapalos*, Cuban *bocaditos* (little bites), and Colombian *aperitivos*—these colorful, little dishes are vibrant arcs in the rainbow of Latin social life.

At every corner and crossing in a Latin country you will bump into vendors selling delicious snacks: *arepas*, the fluffy Colombian cornmeal cakes, topped with shredded cheese; paper bags full of *mariquitas*, Cuban plantain chips; flaky Argentinian empanadas, which invite a multiplicity of filling possibilities; the famous Puerto Rican salt cod fritters and polenta fingers; toasted Cuban sandwiches; little plates of zesty *ceviches*. Throughout the Latin world your taste buds will delight in savory croquettes, crunchy on the outside and silky within; plump tamales, quietly simmering away in their corn husks; griddle cakes filling the streets with an inviting smoky aroma; skewers of meat or seafood with a piquant sauce, corn on the cob, or crispy pork cracklings. The carts and booths that serve up these temptations are the heartbeats of their local neighborhoods. Their flashy, sometimes outrageous signs and logos, the trading calls of their giant-lunged vendors, and the pungent inviting aromas they send into the air make them magnets for the famed vivacity and high spirits of Latin street life.

At home, these snacks do not necessarily signal the beginning of a meal, but are served as nibbles (*algo para picar*) throughout the day. A piece of cheesy cornbread is taken with morning coffee, or a wedge of a plump tortilla at *once*, the second breakfast. A bag of empanadas might be given to children as a school snack; a slice of *pastel* (savory pie) enjoyed by ladies at a *merienda*, afternoon tea; or a plate of salt cod fritters devoured by a group of men after a poker game with a frosty glass of beer or a tumbler of *aguardiente*. In cultures where wasting food is considered a sin, yesterday's boiled yuca, potatoes, or beans are mashed and shaped into all kinds of *croquetas* and fritters. Last night's stew, beefed up with some olives and raisins, is transformed into a filling for empanadas or tamales. Saturday's roast pork, together with some pickles and a slice of cheese, will fill crusty rolls.

For large fiestas, family gatherings, block parties, and saint's day celebrations, these snacks would be turned out *en masse* for the whole neighborhood. The rituals of their preparation are important community events—fiestas in their own right, which bring together daughters, grandmothers, aunts, cousins, neighbors, and maids—who gather over huge kitchen tables to knead dough for pasteles, shape hundreds of tiny empanadas, artfully wrap banana leaves around tamales, roll neat cylindrical *croquetas*.

In more cosmopolitan households, to celebrate important occasions such as christenings, weddings, and coming-out balls, snacks are elaborately presented on silver plates arranged on large tables set with china and crystal, covered with embroidered tablecloths and tropical flower arrangements. Each little bite—the tinier the better—is proudly presented in its own lace doily or

Street vendor, Mendoza, Argentina.

in a tiny cup fashioned from colored paper. At these events you will also encounter foods that will take you right back to the American fifties: white bread tea sandwiches, canapés, deviled eggs, vol-au-vents, little quiches, potted mushrooms, cocktail frankfurters, boiled shrimp in pink mayonnaise sauce, or walnut-crusted cream cheese balls.

Havana Salsa

A spirited black bean dip via Cuban–Puerto Rican chef Eric Basulto. He cooks at SOB's, a Latin club in New York, which delivers the best salsa in town! Serve it with Tropical Chips (page 32), or as a salsa with grilled fish or chicken.

With a slotted spoon scoop the beans from the basic black beans into a bowl. Add 2 tablespoons of the bean liquid. Add all the remaining ingredients and let stand for 30 minutes for the flavors to develop. Garnish with additional yellow and red pepper and cilantro leaves.

MAKES ABOUT 3 CUPS

2 CUPS BASIC BLACK BEANS (PAGE 374)

2 TABLESPOONS FINELY DICED RED BELL PEPPER, PLUS MORE FOR GARNISH

2 TABLESPOONS FINELY DICED YELLOW BELL PEPPER, PLUS MORE FOR GARNISH

2 TABLESPOONS FINELY DICED GREEN BELL PEPPER

1 CLOVE GARLIC, CRUSHED THROUGH A PRESS

3 TABLESPOONS FINELY CHOPPED RED ONION

1 SMALL PLUM TOMATO, FINELY CHOPPED

1½ TABLESPOONS FRESH LIME JUICE

2 TABLESPOONS SHERRY VINEGAR

½ TEASPOON GROUND CUMIN

2 TABLESPOONS VIRGIN OLIVE OIL

⅓ CUP CHOPPED CILANTRO LEAVES, PLUS MORE FOR GARNISH

SALT AND FRESHLY GROUND BLACK PEPPER, TO TASTE

Salsa: A Saucy Mix

Salsa means "sauce" or "liquid" in Spanish. It also happens to be the label attached to a wildly popular musical style—supposedly named after the cry of appreciation from aficionados in the audience following an especially dazzling solo. There is a fierce dispute between Cubans and Puerto Ricans as to whom it belongs. But the greatness of salsa is that it belongs to all. Its foundations are unmistakably Cuban, its identity is Puerto Rican, and its home is New York, the melting pot of Latin cultures. It's a collective art, a dialogue among Africa, Europe, and the Americas, among wood, strings, skin, and metal; singer and chorus; dancers and the band. It's a brash urban hybrid, born out of immigrant life.

A wildly eclectic hodgepodge of influences and styles,

(continued)

and an umbrella term for various kinds of music, yes; but yet, you wouldn't mistake it for anything else.

The New York of the early 1970s played host to the golden days of salsa. This smooth and peppery musical style was a Nuyorican-led rediscovery of various revamped classic Latin styles. Its roots were in the inspirational Cuban genres (*son*, *mambo*, *cha-cha-cha*), and it drew its life-blood from the harmonies and orchestration of American jazz and R&B. (We shouldn't forget that Latino immigrants and African Americans lived side by side in urban ghettos, borrowing and appropriating the sounds of each other's music.) The laboratory for the codification of the modern salsa sound was in the Manhattan studios of Fania Records, which did for salsa what Motown did for rhythm and blues. Its musical director was the Dominican flautist-arranger Johnny Pacheco (who stayed within the Cuban idiom), and its guiding genius, the Nuyorican trombonist, Willie Colón, who introduced more ecclectic touches.

The style that emerged wasn't radical but it was bigger, brasher, brassier, more up-tempo and self-asserting, with lyrics and personalities appealing to larger, more contemporary and varied Latin audiences. A typical gesture of New York salsa is for the soloist to welcome and enumerate all the Latin countries present in the audience: "*Viva Puerto Rico, viva Colombia, viva Cuba*," and so on. This is the true *espíritu de la salsa*.

The new sound caught on like a house afire, developing into a truly pan-Latin urban style, electrifying Hispanic audiences from Miami to Medellín, and conquering a non-Latin following along the way. It is a musical success story that stands for the empowerment of urban Latin immigrants and the consolidation of Latino audiences—a banner of Latin self-respect, dignity, and identity. This was music that developed from the sound of the *barrio*, an immigrant urban ghetto, into a slick, superproduced economic engine, a flashy Latino product and its best-known cultural commodity—a craze in Japan, a hit in Madrid, and a rage in L.A.

The salsa sound is like a pulsing rush, both intensely explosive and tightly controlled, underpinned by the *clave*, the 2-3 or 3-2 syncopated rhythmic pattern that is the beating heart of so much Latin music. It's a shuttling and weaving of cross-rhythms: the thumping of the bass and the conga drums, the rasping pulse of the *güiro* (an instrument made from a hollowed-out gourd), the searing licks of the *cuatro* (a Puerto-Rican guitar) over the riffs of the horns, the anchoring ostinato (the repeated musical pattern) of the piano chords. The salsa vocalist, called *sonero* (after Cuban *son*), is nasal and passionate, working the audience and improvising lyrics in the second half of the song. The singing style invokes the African-derived call and response (much as in American R&B) between the *coro* (chorus), which usually consists of the *orquesta*'s members, and the vocalist.

Salsa dancing is like the music: complex, pulsing, endlessly improvisational, but strictly confined to a rigorous, sinuous regimen of steps, turns, and suave syncopations. The dancing is all in the hips, to the beat of the background figure of the *clave*, which might be all but concealed in the riot of instrumentation, but which every Latino has in his or her blood. The bodies of the best dancers seem to register the polyrhythms of the music, feet to one beat, hips to another, torso to yet a third. Being out on the dance floor, music booming around you like rushing tides, is to experience a disciplined intricacy riding a great organized storm surge of music.

Bahian Coconut-Peanut Dip

(MÔLHO BAHIANO)

This dip was inspired by the tropical Afro-Brazilian flavors of Bahia, where many dishes come in a coconut and ground peanut sauce, with the added zest of tomatoes, garlic, ginger, and often ground dried shrimp. Serve it with strips of grilled chicken or shrimp, or as a sauce with seafood or steak.

1. In a medium-size heavy saucepan heat the annatto oil over medium-low heat. Add the garlic, onion, bell pepper, and chile, and cook, stirring, for 3 minutes. Add the tomatoes, ginger, and paprika and cook, stirring, for 5 minutes. Transfer the mixture to a blender and puree.

2. Return the mixture to the saucepan, add the coconut milk and water, and bring to a simmer over medium-low heat. Cook until it thickens a little, about 5 minutes. Place the peanut butter in a bowl, add about ¼ cup of the simmering mixture, and whisk until smooth. Whisk the mixture back into the saucepan. Cook for another 3 minutes to thicken further. Add the lime juice and hot sauce and season to taste with salt and pepper. Serve slightly warm.

MAKES ABOUT 1 CUP

1 TABLESPOON ANNATTO OIL (PAGE 376)
1 LARGE CLOVE GARLIC, MINCED
¼ CUP CHOPPED ONION
2 TABLESPOONS FINELY DICED RED OR GREEN BELL PEPPER
1 SMALL HOT CHILE OF YOUR CHOICE, SEEDED AND MINCED
4 WELL-DRAINED CANNED TOMATOES, CHOPPED
1½ TEASPOONS CHOPPED FRESH GINGER
1 TEASPOON MILD PAPRIKA
½ CUP CANNED UNSWEETENED COCONUT MILK, WELL STIRRED
⅓ CUP WATER
3 TABLESPOONS CHUNKY NATURAL PEANUT BUTTER
4 TEASPOONS FRESH LIME JUICE, OR MORE TO TASTE
DASH OF HOT SAUCE, TO TASTE
SALT AND FRESHLY GROUND BLACK PEPPER, TO TASTE

Chimichurri Sauce

The recipe for this addictively pungent parsley, garlic, and vinegar sauce comes from my neighborhood Argentinian restaurant called La Porteña. In my view, it even surpasses the many versions of the sauce I've had in Argentina. So addictive is their *chimichurri*, that we usually consume a whole bowl of it with the restaurant's delicious grilled bread long before the arrival of the main course. It is a very simple sauce to make and will keep for a long time, especially if stored in a sterilized jar in the refrigerator. Halve the recipe, if you wish.

2 BUNCHES FLAT-LEAF PARSLEY, CHOPPED
2 LARGE HEADS GARLIC, PEELED AND CHOPPED
1/2 CUP OLIVE OR VEGETABLE OIL, PLUS MORE FOR BLENDING, OPTIONAL
1 TABLESPOON DRIED OREGANO
1 TEASPOON HOT RED PEPPER FLAKES
2 TEASPOONS FRESHLY GROUND BLACK PEPPER
1 TEASPOON GARLIC POWDER
1 TEASPOON GOYA *SAZÓN ADOBO* (*ADOBO SEASONING*), OPTIONAL
1 1/2 CUPS DISTILLED WHITE VINEGAR

1. In a food processor, process the parsley and garlic until finely minced but not pureed. Add a little oil, if necessary, to assist the blending. Scrape into a bowl.

2. Add the rest of the ingredients and mix well. Transfer to an airtight jar with a tight-fitting lid. The sauce will keep in the refrigerator for up to a month.

MAKES ABOUT 3 CUPS

Andalusian Gazpacho Dip

(SALMOREJO)

Enjoyed throughout Andalusia, but a specialty of Córdoba, *salmorejo* is essentially a very thick, garlicky gazpacho, made without the water. Sometimes it's eaten as a soup, at other times it's served as a sauce with batter-fried vegetables. Or it might be placed on the table—fancifully decorated with hard-cooked egg and cubes of good smoked ham—and simply eaten with a spoon alongside a main course. Translated to an American context, this dish shines as an appetizer dip or as a sauce for summer grills—chicken, seafood, or vegetables.

1 CUP CUBED DAY-OLD COUNTRY BREAD (CRUSTS REMOVED)
3 MEDIUM VINE-RIPENED TOMATOES, CHOPPED
1 TABLESPOON CHOPPED RED ONION
2 LARGE CLOVES GARLIC, CHOPPED
3 1/2 TABLESPOONS RED WINE VINEGAR
1/2 CUP VIRGIN OLIVE OIL, PREFERABLY SPANISH
SALT AND FRESHLY GROUND BLACK PEPPER, TO TASTE

1. Soak the bread in water to cover for 10 minutes. Place in a colander and squeeze out all the excess liquid.

2. In a blender combine the bread, tomatoes, onion, garlic, and vinegar and process until smooth. With the motor running, slowly drizzle in the oil until emulsified. Transfer to a bowl, season with salt and pepper, and refrigerate for at least 30 minutes for the flavors to develop.

MAKES ABOUT 1 1/4 CUPS

Ecuadorian Red Chile Dip

(AJÍ CRIOLLO)

This fiery red salsa is a popular table condiment in highland Ecuador, where much of the food tends to be starchy and mellow-flavored. Enjoy it in moderation as a dip, or use it to add a jolt to soups, stews, tamales, and bean dishes. Look for ripe, red, larger chiles such as jalapeños, serranos, or fresnos. The sauce will keep for up to a week in the refrigerator, but you should add the cilantro just before serving.

1/2 CUP CHOPPED RED CHILES, SEEDED ACCORDING TO THE DESIRED DEGREE OF HEAT (MORE SEEDS MEAN MORE HEAT)

1/4 CUP CHOPPED RED BELL PEPPER

2 CLOVES GARLIC, MINCED

2 TABLESPOONS WATER

2 1/2 TABLESPOONS MALT VINEGAR

1/2 TEASPOON SALT

SMALL PINCH OF SUGAR

2 TEASPOONS VEGETABLE OIL

2 TABLESPOONS MINCED RED ONION

2 TABLESPOONS CHOPPED CILANTRO LEAVES

1. In a food processor, pulse the chiles, bell pepper, garlic, and water until finely minced but not pureed.

2. Transfer the processed mixture to a bowl and add all the remaining ingredients. If planning to store the dip, do not add the cilantro until the last minute.

MAKES ABOUT 1 CUP

Lemony Avocado Dip

(AJÍ DE AGUACATE)

As a break from guacamole, try this refreshing
dip, prepared in slightly different versions
throughout South America.

Mash the avocado in a medium bowl. Add all the
other ingredients and refrigerate for 1 hour for the
flavors to develop.

MAKES ABOUT 1 ²/₃ CUPS

1 MEDIUM AVOCADO, PEELED AND PITTED

2 TABLESPOONS MAYONNAISE

2 CLOVES GARLIC, CRUSHED THROUGH A PRESS

¹/₃ CUP FINELY CHOPPED RED ONION

2 SERRANO CHILES, PARTIALLY SEEDED AND
   MINCED

FRESHLY SQUEEZED JUICE OF 1 LARGE LEMON
   (3 TO 4 TABLESPOONS)

1 SMALL BUNCH CILANTRO, TRIMMED AND
   CHOPPED

2 HARD-COOKED EGGS, FINELY CHOPPED

Ajili Mójili Extravagante

Aji-li mójili, as it's properly spelled, is a Puerto Rican dip traditionally prepared from sweet local chiles (*ají dulce*), garlic, vinegar, and lemon juice, and often served as an accompaniment to *frituras* (fritters). But at a San Juan restaurant called Ajili Mójili, it becomes the mother of all salsas, an elaborate relish concocted from more than a dozen ingredients. In fact, it's almost a salad, delicious spooned on meats, grilled fish, rice, or beans.

Combine all the ingredients in a medium-size bowl. Toss gently and refrigerate for at least 1 hour for the flavors to develop. Remove and discard bay leaf before serving.

MAKES ABOUT 2 CUPS

4 MEDIUM PLUM TOMATOES, BLANCHED, PEELED, SEEDED, AND CHOPPED

⅓ CUP FINELY CHOPPED WHITE ONION

3 TABLESPOONS DICED GREEN BELL PEPPER

1 SMALL JALAPEÑO CHILE, FINELY CHOPPED

3 CLOVES GARLIC, MINCED

2 TABLESPOONS SMALL CAPERS, DRAINED

7 PIMIENTO-STUFFED OLIVES, CHOPPED

1 SMALL BOILING POTATO, PEELED, COOKED, AND DICED

½ HARD-COOKED EGG, DICED

2 TABLESPOONS COOKED GREEN PEAS

2½ TABLESPOONS CHOPPED BLANCHED ALMONDS

3 TABLESPOONS FINELY CHOPPED CILANTRO

2 TABLESPOONS FINELY CHOPPED FLAT-LEAF PARSLEY

3 TABLESPOONS RED WINE VINEGAR

FRESHLY SQUEEZED JUICE OF ½ LEMON

1 BAY LEAF

LARGE PINCH OF SUGAR, TO TASTE

SALT AND FRESHLY GROUND BLACK PEPPER, TO TASTE

Cilantro Dip

(MOJO DE CILANTRO)

This spicy dip, just right for most of the snacks in this chapter, will also add zest to soups, grills, boiled root vegetables, and just about anything else.

Place the cilantro, garlic, water, mayonnaise, lemon juice, and vinegar in a blender, and process until finely minced but not pureed. Add all the remaining ingredients and process for several pulses, until just combined but not emulsified. Transfer to a bowl and refrigerate for at least 30 minutes for the flavors to develop.

MAKES ABOUT ³/₄ CUP

1 LARGE BUNCH CILANTRO, TRIMMED AND
   CHOPPED
2 MEDIUM CLOVES GARLIC, CHOPPED
2¹/₂ TABLESPOONS WATER
¹/₂ TABLESPOON MAYONNAISE
3 TABLESPOONS FRESH LEMON JUICE
1¹/₂ TABLESPOONS WHITE OR RED WINE VINEGAR
3 TABLESPOONS FINELY CHOPPED WHITE ONION
PINCH OF SUGAR
3 TABLESPOONS LIGHT OLIVE OIL
1 SMALL DRIED CHILE, CRUMBLED

Tropical Chips

(MARIQUITAS)

Tropical vegetables—plantain, yuca, *boniato* (the white Cuban sweet potato), coconut, yam, and taro root—make the most fashionable new chips around (never mind that the Latinos have been making them for generations!). Serve them with almost any dip in this chapter, and a tropical cocktail.

PEANUT OR CANOLA OIL, FOR DEEP FRYING

COCONUT, YUCA, PLANTAIN, TARO, *BONIATO*, OR YAM CHIPS (SEE BELOW)

COARSE (KOSHER) SALT

Line a large baking sheet with a double thickness of paper towels. In a deep skillet heat the oil over medium heat to 360 degrees F. When the oil is hot enough to sizzle a chip on contact, drop the chips into the oil, a few at a time, and fry until crisp and golden, about 30 seconds (though the exact time will depend on the vegetable and thickness). Drain on paper towels. Sprinkle with salt and cool for at least 10 minutes before serving. The chips can be stored in an airtight container for up to 3 days.

Coconut

With a vegetable peeler, shave enough 3-inch coconut slices to measure 2 cups.

1 MATURE COCONUT (CRACKED AND CLEANED AS DIRECTED ON PAGE 10)

Yuca

Using a mandoline or a swivel vegetable peeler, slice the yuca crosswise into paper-thin slices. With a mandoline, you can also slice the yuca lengthwise to make long chips.

1 POUND YUCA, CUT INTO 3-INCH SECTIONS AND PEELED AS DIRECTED ON PAGE 79.

Plantain

2 GREEN OR SEMIRIPE PLANTAINS (WITH YELLOW AND BLACK SKINS), ABOUT 1 POUND TOTAL, EACH CUT INTO THREE SECTIONS AND PEELED AS DIRECTED ON PAGE 379.

Using a mandoline or the slicing disk of a food processor, slice the plantains crosswise into paper-thin slices. With a mandoline, you can also make long chips by cutting a whole plantain into two pieces, and slicing it lengthwise into paper-thin chips.

Taro, Boniato, or Yam

Using a mandoline or a swivel vegetable peeler, slice the vegetable crosswise into paper-thin slices.

1 POUND TARO (*MALANGA*), *BONIATO*, OR YAM ROOT, PEELED, AND HALVED OR QUARTERED, IF LARGE

Latino Tartar Sauce

(SALSA TARTAR ESTILO LATINO)

A traditional tartar sauce takes on a *sabor latino*, with the addition of green olives, capers, cilantro, hot sauce, and lime juice. Serve it with any fried fish dish, seafood fritters, or empanadas with seafood filling.

In a bowl, whisk the mayonnaise with the broth and lime juice until smooth. Add all the remaining ingredients and let stand for 30 minutes for the flavors to develop.

MAKES ABOUT 1 CUP

⅔ CUP MAYONNAISE

3 TABLESPOONS CHICKEN STOCK (PAGE 372), CANNED LOWER-SALT CHICKEN BROTH, OR WATER

1 TABLESPOON FRESH LIME JUICE

1 TABLESPOON MINCED RED ONION

3 TABLESPOONS CHOPPED CILANTRO

6 PIMIENTO-STUFFED OLIVES, FINELY DICED

1 TABLESPOON DRAINED SMALL CAPERS, PLUS 1 TABLESPOON OF THE BRINE

2 TABLESPOONS FINELY CHOPPED PIMIENTOS

PINCH OF SUGAR, TO TASTE

DASH OF HOT SAUCE OF YOUR CHOICE

Mussel boats, O Grove, Spain.

Tostones

Tostones, the addictive crisp-fried green plantain chips, are a mainstay throughout the Spanish-speaking Caribbean. The proper way to fry *tostones* was demonstrated to me by Oswald Rivera, a dear friend, novelist, and a great authority on Puerto Rican cuisine. For *tostones* to be absolutely crispy and light, they are fried once to cook through, smashed to flatten, and then quickly fried again over higher heat to crisp up. The smashing can be done in a special device called a *tostonera,* but the best result, according to Oswald, is achieved by doing the job with your fist, placing the chip between two pieces of plantain peel. Right before serving, I toss hot *tostones* with oodles of smashed garlic, in the style of New York *cuchifrito* (fritter) joints. They can also be served with almost any dip or sauce in this book; or in the more elegant "Nuevo Latino" style, topped with a dollop of sour cream and smoked salmon or caviar.

3 LARGE GREEN PLANTAINS (ABOUT 1½ POUNDS TOTAL), PEELED AS DIRECTED ON PAGE 379, AND CUT INTO ½-INCH THICK SLICES, SKINS RESERVED

1 TABLESPOON TABLE SALT

PEANUT OR CANOLA OIL, FOR DEEP FRYING

3 LARGE CLOVES GARLIC, CRUSHED THROUGH A PRESS

1½ TABLESPOONS LUKEWARM WATER

2 TEASPOONS COARSE (KOSHER) SALT, FOR SPRINKLING

1. Place the plantains in a large bowl and add enough cold water to cover them by 1 inch. Add 1 tablespoon salt and let the plantains soak for 20 to 30 minutes. Drain and pat them dry as thoroughly as you can with paper towels.

2. In a deep fryer or large deep skillet, heat 1½ inches of oil over medium heat to 325

(continued)

degrees F. In batches, fry the plantains until light golden on both sides and cooked through, about 4 minutes total per batch. Drain the finished batches on paper towels.

3. Place three to four plantain slices between two pieces of the reserved plantain skin and smash hard with your fist, or the bottom of a cup, until they are flattened into $1/8$-inch-thick rounds. Repeat with the remaining plantain slices.

4. Reheat the oil to 375 degrees over medium heat. In batches, fry the plantain slices until deep golden and crispy on both sides, about 3 minutes total per batch. Drain on paper towels.

5. In a small bowl, stir together the garlic and water. Place the plantain slices in a large bowl and quickly toss with the coarse salt and the garlic mixture. Arrange them on a serving platter and serve immediately. Alternatively, the *tostones* can be served with most of the dips in this book, instead of the garlic.

SERVES 4 TO 6

The Immaculate Tortilla

(TORTILLA DE PATATA INMACULADA)

My Madrilenian friend Inma doesn't cook—except for one dish, *tortilla de patata*, the renowned Spanish potato omelet. And like all people who cook only one dish for almost the entire duration of their lives, she makes a flawless potato tortilla, befitting her full name, Inmaculada, "the immaculate." Her secret is to slice the potatoes very thin (preferably in a food processor), fry them in very hot oil, drain them well, mash them together with beaten eggs, and then cook the tortilla *siempre moviéndola*, constantly moving and shaking the skillet. Once it's cooked on one side, Inma freezes for a moment in the pose of a flamenco dancer or a circus animal trainer and exclaims *"¡la vuelta!"* (the flip!) in her low, smoky voice. Then she flips it, cooks it on the other side, and serves it with a side dish of ripe tomato and garlic salad. As a tapa, you can serve it cut into squares, accompanied by toothpicks.

½ CUP PLUS 3 TEASPOONS GOOD OLIVE OIL

3 LARGE BAKING POTATOES, PEELED,
    QUARTERED, AND SLICED ⅛ INCH THICK

1 LARGE RED BELL PEPPER, CORED, SEEDED,
    AND CUT INTO STRIPS

1 LARGE ONION, QUARTERED AND SLICED

6 LARGE EGGS

1 TEASPOON SALT

1 TEASPOON DRIED OREGANO

FRESHLY GROUND BLACK PEPPER, TO TASTE

TOMATO SALAD (RECIPE FOLLOWS), OPTIONAL

1. In a large, preferably cast-iron, skillet heat ½ cup of the oil for 3 minutes over medium-high heat. Reduce the heat to medium and add the potatoes and pepper. Cook, stirring to prevent the potatoes from sticking, until they are half cooked, about 7 minutes. Add the onion and continue cooking until all the vegetables are tender, about 10 more minutes. The potatoes

(continued)

should to be light golden and cooked through. With a slotted spoon, remove the entire contents of the skillet to a colander and let the mixture drain until it is cool.

2. Place the eggs, salt, oregano, and pepper in a large mixing bowl and beat until frothy. Gently stir in the potato mixture. Mash and stir the mixture gently with a fork to crush the potatoes somewhat and mix the vegetables well with the eggs.

3. In a heavy 8- or 9-inch skillet, preferably cast-iron, heat 2 teaspoons of the remaining oil over medium heat until hot but not smoking. Pour the egg mixture into the skillet and spread it with a spatula. Cook, constantly moving and shaking the skillet in light clockwise motions, until the eggs are almost set, 5 to 6 minutes. Invert the omelet into a plate and add the remaining 1 teaspoon of the oil to the pan. Slide the omelet back into the skillet, uncooked side down. Turn the heat to low and cook another 5 minutes until the bottom is set.

4. Transfer to a serving plate, cool, cut into wedges, and serve. The tortilla can be served warm or cold.

SERVES 4 AS A LIGHT ENTREE, OR 8 AS AN APPETIZER

Tomato Salad

2 CLOVES GARLIC, CHOPPED
1/2 TEASPOON COARSE (KOSHER) SALT
1/4 CUP FRUITY EXTRA-VIRGIN OLIVE OIL,
     PREFERABLY SPANISH
6 MEDIUM VINE-RIPENED TOMATOES, DICED
1/4 CUP GOOD RED WINE VINEGAR
FRESHLY GROUND BLACK PEPPER, TO TASTE

1. In a mortar and pestle pound the garlic and salt to a paste. Work in the oil.

2. Place the tomatoes in a bowl and toss with the garlic oil, vinegar, and pepper.

SERVES 4 TO 6

Oregano-Marinated Eggplants

(BERENJENAS ESCABECHADAS CON ORÉGANO)

From Argentina's large Italian community, local cooks learned an impressive repertoire of antipastos and pickles, spicing them generously with their favorite mix of oregano and hot red pepper flakes. In most houses in Buenos Aires you will see large jars of these zesty eggplants marinated in vinegar, herbs, spices, and olive oil, most delicious plucked straight out of the jar for an improvised snack.

DISTILLED WHITE VINEGAR
2 MEDIUM EGGPLANTS (ABOUT 2 POUNDS TOTAL), SLICED ¼ INCH THICK
2 TABLESPOONS DRIED OREGANO
¼ TO ½ TEASPOON HOT RED PEPPER FLAKES
1 TEASPOON FRESHLY GROUND BLACK PEPPER
1 TEASPOON SALT
4 LARGE CLOVES GARLIC, MINCED
⅔ CUP MINCED FLAT-LEAF PARSLEY
OLIVE OIL, FOR DRIZZLING

1. Into a large nonreactive skillet pour equal amounts of vinegar and water to a depth of 3 inches and bring to a simmer over medium heat. Working in batches as necessary, add the eggplant slices in one layer and blanch for 2 minutes on each side. Transfer the finished batches to drain in a nonreactive colander. Squeeze dry between paper towels.

2. In a small bowl, combine the oregano, red pepper flakes, black pepper, and salt.

3. Place a layer of eggplant slices in a medium-sized glass or earthenware rectangular dish. Sprinkle generously with the oregano mixture, some of the garlic, and some of the parsley. Drizzle generously with oil. Repeat the procedure, layering the eggplant slices and seasoning each layer with the oregano mixture, garlic, and parsley, and drizzling generously with oil until all the eggplant slices are used up. Cover with plastic and refrigerate. The eggplants will keep for up to 5 days.

SERVES 6 AS AN APPETIZER

Potato and Salt Cod Puffs

(BOLINHOS DE BACALHAU)

Latin cuisine abounds in various fritters and puffs, both sweet and savory. But none are more beloved than salt cod fritters. Cheap, easy, and full of flavor, in one form or another they appear as a snack from Portugal to Brazil, from Catalonia to the Caribbean. The recipes are legion, but I especially like this very simple one, from my Brazilian friend Ana Lineman. This is the basic recipe, to which you can add minced garlic, finely diced pimientos, diced smoked ham, or other seasonings, if you wish. While Brazilian immigrants on the East Coast drive all the way to Boston for supplies of top-quality salt cod, for this recipe salt cod from the supermarket will do just fine. Start the night before and follow the salt cod soaking instructions on page 377. Latino Tartar Sauce (page 34) makes an excellent accompaniment.

3 MEDIUM RUSSET POTATOES (ABOUT 1¼ POUNDS), PEELED AND CUT INTO LARGE CUBES

½ POUND SALT COD, SOAKED AS DIRECTED ON PAGE 377

2 TABLESPOONS VEGETABLE OIL, PLUS MORE FOR DEEP FRYING THE PUFFS

1 MEDIUM ONION, FINELY CHOPPED

3 TABLESPOONS MINCED FLAT-LEAF PARSLEY

2 LARGE EGGS, BEATEN

1. In a large pot, boil the potatoes in salted water to cover until tender, about 20 minutes. Drain and pat dry with paper towels to get rid of excess moisture. Mash into a fine puree with a potato ricer, and set aside.

2. With your hands, separate the salt cod into very fine shreds. Working in batches, squeeze and rub the shredded cod between paper towels to get rid of as much moisture as possible.

3. In a medium skillet, heat 2 tablespoons of oil over low heat. Add the onion and cook for 5 minutes. Add the salt cod and cook, breaking it up with a fork, for another 5 minutes. Add the parsley and let the mixture cook a little.

4. In a large bowl, stir the salt cod mixture and potatoes together thoroughly with a fork until homogenous. Beat in the eggs, one at a time.

5. In a deep skillet, heat 1½ inches of oil to 375 degrees F. With 2 spoons dipped in cold water, spoon out some of the salt cod mixture and form into balls. Drop the balls into the oil and, in batches, fry on all sides until golden brown, about 3 minutes per batch. Transfer the finished puffs to drain on paper towels. (If you wish, keep the fried puffs warm in a low oven.) Serve at once.

MAKES ABOUT 30 PUFFS

Fish, street sign, Jackson Heights, New York.

Yuca and Goat Cheese Cakes

(FRITURAS DE YUCA CON QUESO DE CABRA)

Although this sounds like a Nuevo Latino recipe, yuca cakes with some sort of tangy fresh cheese are a very traditional offering throughout the Caribbean and parts of South America. This recipe makes very light, fluffy pancakes, excellent either on their own, or with a fresh-tasting sauce such as Salsa Cruda (page 240). Serve them either as an appetizer or as a side dish. This is the basic recipe, to which you can add other flavorings such as garlic, finely diced smoked ham, diced pimientos or chopped olives, herbs, or an additional kind of cheese.

1 ½ POUNDS FRESH YUCA, PEELED AS DIRECTED ON PAGE 79 AND CUT INTO 2-INCH LENGTHS, OR FROZEN AND THAWED

2 QUARTS COLD SALTED WATER

3 LARGE EGGS, BEATEN

1 SMALL ONION, GRATED

1 ¼ CUPS CRUMBLED FRESH GOAT CHEESE

¼ CUP MILK

SALT AND FRESHLY GROUND BLACK PEPPER, TO TASTE

3 TABLESPOONS FLOUR

2 TEASPOONS BAKING POWDER

LIGHT OLIVE OIL, FOR DEEP FRYING

1. In a large saucepan, combine the yuca with the salted water and bring to a boil. Cook over low heat until the yuca is tender, about 25 minutes. Let the yuca cool a little in the liquid.

2. Cut the yuca pieces in half lengthwise and, with a sharp knife, remove the tough stringy fibers that run through its length. In a large bowl, mash the yuca with a potato ricer or a fork.

3. Stir in the eggs, onion, goat cheese, and milk and blend well with two forks. Season the mixture with salt and pepper.

4. Sift the flour with the baking powder into a small bowl and stir it into the yuca. Mix with two forks or with your hands until all the ingredients are well combined, but do not overmix.

5. Wet your hands with cold water and shape the mixture into sixteen flat patties.

6. In a large skillet, heat 1 inch of oil over medium heat to 350 degrees F. Fry the patties in batches until golden brown, about 2 to 3 minutes per side. Transfer the finished batches to drain on paper towels. Serve warm.

MAKES 16 PANCAKES

Plantain Fish Cakes

(TORTITAS DE PLÁTANO Y PESCADO)

Plantains are the potatoes of Ecuador, though the real *papa* is certainly revered just as much. These extraordinary fish cakes are inspired by a popular Ecuadorian snack called *corviche*—grated raw plantain cakes stuffed with fish. I adapted the recipe using cooked, ripe plantains, combined with sautéed snapper, spices, and the tang of lime.

1 LARGE RIPE PLANTAIN (ABOUT 8 OUNCES)

1½ TABLESPOONS ANNATTO OIL (PAGE 376)

¾ POUND SNAPPER, OR OTHER DELICATE WHITE-FLESHED FISH, CUT INTO 1½-INCH CHUNKS

3 TABLESPOONS FINELY DICED RED BELL PEPPER

1 LARGE EGG

1 TABLESPOON FRESH LIME JUICE

2 TEASPOONS MILD PAPRIKA

½ TEASPOON CAYENNE

½ TEASPOON GROUND CUMIN

3 TABLESPOONS FINELY CHOPPED CILANTRO

SALT AND FRESHLY GROUND BLACK PEPPER, TO TASTE

UNFLAVORED BREAD CRUMBS, FOR ROLLING THE CAKES

PEANUT OR CANOLA OIL, FOR FRYING THE CAKES

LIME WEDGES, FOR SERVING

1. Peel the plantain as directed on page 379, and cut into 2-inch chunks. In a saucepan, place the plantain in salted water to cover and cook over medium heat until tender, about 25 minutes. Keep the plantain in the liquid until ready to use.

2. While the plantain is cooking, in a medium skillet heat the annatto oil over medium-low heat. Add the fish and cook on all sides until it flakes easily, about 6 minutes total. Transfer the fish to a bowl and flake it with a fork.

3. Transfer the plantain to a bowl. Mash it thoroughly with a fork, adding 2 tablespoons of the cooking liquid. Into the mashed plantain, stir the fish, and all the remaining ingredients except the bread crumbs, oil, and lime wedges. Mix thoroughly, but without overworking it.

4. With wet hands, shape the mixture into patties 2¼ inches in diameter and roll them in the bread crumbs. In a large skillet, heat ½ inch of oil over medium heat. Fry the fish cakes in batches until golden, about 2 minutes per side. Transfer to drain on paper towels. Serve with the lime wedges.

SERVES 4

Puerto Rican Corn Sticks with Cheese

(SURULLITOS)

These dainty Puerto Rican fried corn sticks, called *surullitos*, are made from cooled, thickened polenta, crispy on the outside and deliciously soft within. They make a lovely snack or accompaniment to soup. I especially like them dipped in a tangy Chimichurri Sauce (page 26). Add pimientos and olives, if you desire extra flavors.

2½ CUPS MILK (SKIM MILK, IF DESIRED)
1¼ CUPS YELLOW CORNMEAL, PREFERABLY STONE-GROUND
SALT TO TASTE
1 TABLESPOON UNSALTED BUTTER
¾ CUP GRATED GOUDA CHEESE
⅔ CUP FINELY DICED WELL-DRAINED PIMIENTOS, OPTIONAL
½ CUP CHOPPED PITTED BLACK OLIVES, OPTIONAL
1 TEASPOON MILD PAPRIKA
PINCH OF CAYENNE
1 TEASPOON SUGAR
CANOLA OIL, FOR DEEP FRYING

1. In a heavy saucepan, bring the milk to a gentle boil. Add the cornmeal in a slow steady stream, stirring with a wooden spoon. Cook, stirring, over low heat until the polenta is thick and smooth, about 5 minutes.

2. Remove from the heat and beat in all the remaining ingredients except the oil. Cool until manageable.

3. With wet hands, break off small pieces of the mixture and shape it into sticks about 3 inches long and ¾ inch wide. Roll them against a flat surface to smooth them.

4. In a deep skillet, heat 2 inches of oil to 360 degrees F. Deep-fry, in batches, until crispy and golden brown on all sides, about 4 minutes total per batch. With a slotted spoon, transfer the fried sticks to drain on paper towels. Serve at once.

MAKES 2 DOZEN CORN STICKS

Corn and Cheese Muffins with Chicken and Pimiento Filling

(PANCITOS DE MAÍZ CON POLLO Y PIMIENTOS)

During our stay in Santiago, our hosts were preparing for their niece's fifteenth birthday, the Chilean equivalent of our sweet sixteen. A huge brigade of cousins, aunts, and maids was in charge of the finger food, and everything was turned out by the hundreds—myriads of little cookies and cakes, savory pastries, canapés, meatballs, and croquettes.

One dish I particularly liked was these miniature corn muffins with a piquant filling of chicken, olives, and pimientos.

1 TABLESPOON UNSALTED BUTTER, PLUS 3 TABLESPOONS, MELTED

¾ CUP FINELY CHOPPED ONION

1 CUP FINELY DICED COOKED CHICKEN

9 PITTED GREEN OLIVES, CHOPPED

3 TABLESPOONS CHOPPED WELL-DRAINED PIMIENTOS

SALT AND FRESHLY GROUND BLACK PEPPER, TO TASTE

1 CUP GRATED MONTEREY JACK OR YELLOW CHEDDAR CHEESE

1 LARGE EGG, LIGHTLY BEATEN

1¼ CUPS MILK

1 CUP YELLOW CORNMEAL, PREFERABLY STONE-GROUND

1 CUP ALL-PURPOSE FLOUR

½ TEASPOON SUGAR

1½ TEASPOONS BAKING POWDER

½ TEASPOON BAKING SODA

1 TABLESPOON ANNATTO OIL (PAGE 376)

1. In a medium-size skillet, melt 1 tablespoon of the butter over medium heat and sauté the onion until wilted, about 5 minutes. In a bowl, combine the onion, chicken, olives, and pimientos and season with salt and pepper. Set aside.

2. In a large bowl, stir together the cheese, egg, milk, and melted butter.

3. Sift the dry ingredients together and stir into the cheese mixture. Blend thoroughly, cover, and let stand for 10 minutes.

4. Preheat the oven to 350 degrees F.

5. Lightly grease three small-cup (1½-inch size) muffin tins. Spoon enough batter into the cups to come one third of the way up the sides. Place a teaspoon of the filling into each cup and spoon enough batter on top so that the cups are just full. Bake for 10 minutes. Remove the muffin tins from the oven and brush the top of each muffin with annatto oil. Return to the oven and continue baking until a toothpick inserted in the center comes out clean, about 10 more minutes.

6. When the muffins have cooled slightly, remove them from their tins, helping yourself with a small spoon. Serve warm.

MAKES 24 MUFFINS

Sea urchins, Chile.

Venezuelan Corn Griddle Cakes

(CACHAPAS)

Sweet, homey, and wonderful, these Venezuelan corn cakes shouldn't be made with anything but fresh, ripe, yellow corn. *Cachapas* have much more corn than flour, and are therefore quite delicate and tricky to flip. When frying them, make sure your heat is quite low and the *cachapas* look almost set before you flip them. The traditional way to eat them is piping hot, with a pat of butter and some grated cheese.

2 CUPS FRESH CORN KERNELS FROM SWEET RIPE
    YELLOW CORN
$^1/_3$ CUP EVAPORATED MILK
1 LARGE EGG
2 TABLESPOONS MELTED UNSALTED BUTTER,
    PLUS 1 PAT OF BUTTER, FOR SERVING
$3^1/_2$ TABLESPOONS FLOUR
2 TABLESPOONS FINE YELLOW CORNMEAL,
    PREFERABLY STONE-GROUND
4 TEASPOONS SUGAR
$^1/_2$ TEASPOON SALT
VEGETABLE OIL, FOR THE GRIDDLE
GRATED PROCESSED MOZZARELLA CHEESE
    (DON'T USE FRESH ITALIAN MOZZARELLA),
    FOR SERVING

1. Combine all the ingredients except the oil, the solid butter for serving, and the mozzarella, in a blender and puree until smooth. Transfer to a mixing bowl and let stand for 10 minutes.

2. Heat a large griddle over high heat and brush lightly with oil. With a ladle, pour enough of the corn mixture onto the griddle to form a 4-inch circle (about $2^1/_2$ tablespoons), spreading it out lightly with a wooden spoon. Turn the heat down to low and cook until the underside is set, 3 to 4 minutes. Flip very carefully and cook until the other side is golden, about $1^1/_2$ minutes more. Repeat with the rest of the batter, keeping the finished *cachapas* warm in a low oven.

3. To serve, spear a pat of butter with a fork and brush the hot *cachapas*. Immediately sprinkle with cheese. Serve at once.

MAKES 6 CAKES

¡¡¡Arepas!!!

It's midnight. My phone rings. I jump. It must be my father from Moscow. "She is here, I found her!" The voice on the other end belongs to my sometime-food-writer, sometime-trombonist friend Jim. Jim is the godfather of the New York underground food scene—he drives miles scouring street corners in search of "the most incredible!!!" *arepas, pombasos, bougasas, papusas,* or whatever else is his latest obsession. But for all the Egyptian grandmothers, mustached souvlaki vendors, and Peruvian guinea pig sellers that he adopts, his heart really belongs to *her,* our angelic-looking diminutive Colombian *arepa* lady, who periodically appears like a heavenly apparition on a not-too-savory street corner between 12 and 3 in the morning, hawking the most luscious *arepas* (white corn cakes) slathered with butter and white cheese. I put my clothes on and run out to meet them. I give her a big kiss, and Jim buys her a *guanábana* milk shake from the juice bar on the corner. We have our ritual *arepa.* Now, everyone in my Colombian neighborhood sells *arepas,* but none come close to hers. Jim doesn't want to know her name, to him she is the saint of street vendors, a creature to be worshiped from afar. I, however, befriended her and went to visit her in the house where she lives with her teenage sons and a big dog. Her name, Piedad (Piety), is fittingly angelic. Here is her *arepa* recipe.

(continued)

2 CUPS MILK

4 TABLESPOONS (1/2 STICK) UNSALTED BUTTER,
 CUT INTO PIECES, PLUS MORE FOR SERVING

1 1/2 CUPS WHITE *AREPA* FLOUR (CALLED
 MASAREPA OR *AREPAHARINA*), AVAILABLE AT
 GOOD HISPANIC MARKETS

1 TEASPOON SALT

1 1/2 TABLESPOONS SUGAR

1 CUP GRATED PROCESSED MOZZARELLA CHEESE
 (DO NOT USE FRESH ITALIAN MOZZARELLA)

VEGETABLE OIL, FOR THE GRIDDLE

1 1/4 CUPS FINELY GRATED *QUESO BLANCO*
 (HISPANIC WHITE CHEESE), FOR SERVING

1. In a small saucepan bring 1 1/2 cups of the milk to a boil. Strain into a bowl and add the 4 tablespoons of butter. Let stand while preparing the next step.

2. In a large bowl, stir together the *masarepa*, salt, sugar, and mozzarella. Make a well in the center and pour in the hot milk. Stir the *masa* and milk together until there are no lumps. Knead the mixture, sprinkling in the remaining 1/2 cup milk, until you have a smooth sticky dough. This should take about 5 minutes.

3. Roll the dough into a 1/2-inch-thick sheet between two pieces of wax paper. With a cookie cutter or the rim of a glass, cut out 3-inch circles. Reroll the scraps and cut out more circles. You should have eight.

4. Brush a griddle or a large cast-iron skillet lightly with oil and preheat over medium-low heat. Fry as many *arepas* as will fit, until they are soft within and golden and slightly crusty on the outside, about 4 minutes per side. Keep separating the *arepas* from the skillet with a metal spatula, or they will stick. Keep the finished *arepas* warm in a low oven.

5. To serve, spear a pat of butter with a fork and brush the *arepas* while still hot. Immediately sprinkle them with a generous coating of grated cheese and serve.

MAKES 8 *AREPAS* TO SERVE AS A SNACK

Empanada:
The Triumph of the Latin Oven

In Spanish, *empanada* means "breaded," though the word refers not to a bread crumb–coated dish, but to a glorious pie—a sweet or savory filling enclosed in bread dough or in flaky pastry. The empanada is an ancient Spanish dish, and when the colonists took off for the New World in the mid-1500s, they carried the recipe with them. The new settlers began to plant and process wheat, and they opened bakeries, selling bread and a variety of savory and sweet empanadas (also known as *pasteles*), fashioned either from bread dough or *hojaldre* (puff pastry). As it is today, the choice of fillings was wide: indigenous wild fowl or Castilian poultry, beef or pork, and both imported and local fresh or salt fish. One can imagine the seasonings: ginger, cumin, caraway and sesame seeds, all prized flavors carried to Europe from Southeast Asia by Portuguese spice traders, and then transported to the colonies.

According to historian Sophie Coe, to guard against the illegal deeds of devious bakers who stinted on ingredients, early colonial municipal laws restricted bread- and empanada-making to Europeans. The preparation had to be done in clear view of the customers, on a clean surface (clear of spiders and dust!), and the empanadas had to be put straight into the ovens after they were made. Still, to be on the safe side, clients often brought their own filling ingredients to be baked into their pies. The early outlaw bakers must have also doubled as hack doctors, as the same laws forbade them to administer medicine and cure wounds.

On the brighter side, we know that the empanada was the *pièce de résistance* at a banquet given by Cortés in Mexico City in 1538. At the end of the meal, huge pies were brought to the table and the ladies were invited to dig in. When they broke the crust, live rabbits and birds leaped out onto the table, to the awestruck response of the chronicler who recorded the event.

The Queen of Empanadas

(LA REINA DE EMPANADAS)

The South American empanadas are the offspring. Their progenitor, the beautiful, large Galician empanada, still remains queen. To Galicians, their empanada is like Pandora's box, concealing an enticing multiplicity of filling possibilities between thin but sturdy layers of crumbly yeast dough. The best Galician empanadas can be found at rustic family-run bakeries, where they are made from dough authentically prepared with beer leavening, the special Galician wheat flour, *harina gallega* (or *fariña galega* in Galician), some cornmeal to add a nice coarse crumbliness, and paprika-hued oil from cooking the filling. For the filling, Galicians have the choice of meat or game, or their spectacular seafood: mussels, octopus, tender scallops, oysters, or fish (though connoisseurs prize small local sardines called *xouba* above the rest). Whatever the filling, it has to be smothered in generous amounts of thinly sliced bell pepper, onion and tomato, cooked down to a mouthwatering melting sweetness, and brightly colored with *pimentón* (paprika) and saffron.

PASTRY

½ CUP LUKEWARM WATER

1 TEASPOON ACTIVE DRY YEAST

LARGE PINCH OF SUGAR

½ CUP OLIVE OIL

½ CUP MILK

1 LARGE EGG, BEATEN

1½ TEASPOONS SALT

3¾ TO 4½ CUPS ALL-PURPOSE FLOUR

FILLING

6 TABLESPOONS VIRGIN OLIVE OIL

1 TABLESPOON CRUSHED GARLIC (CRUSHED THROUGH A PRESS)

14 OUNCES HAKE OR SCROD FILLETS, CUT INTO 1½-INCH CHUNKS

2 LARGE ONIONS, THINLY SLICED

2 RED BELL PEPPERS, CORED, SEEDED, AND JULIENNED

1 GREEN BELL PEPPER, CORED, SEEDED, AND JULIENNED

(continued)

The fish empanada below can easily feed six as a main course, and twelve as an appetizer. The pastry is fabulously versatile: use it for deep-fried pastries, small empanadas, and savory tarts. It freezes beautifully, and the olive oil prevents it from absorbing liquid and getting soggy.

2 CANNED ITALIAN TOMATOES, DRAINED AND
    FINELY CHOPPED
2 BAY LEAVES
PINCH OF SAFFRON THREADS, PULVERIZED
SALT AND FRESHLY GROUND BLACK PEPPER, TO
    TASTE

1 EGG YOLK, MIXED WITH 1½ TEASPOONS MILK,
    FOR THE EGG WASH

1. To make the dough: In a large bowl, stir together the water, yeast, and sugar. Let stand until foamy, about 5 minutes. Whisk in the oil, milk, egg, and salt. Add the 3¾ cups of flour, about 1 cup at a time, until incorporated.

2. Turn the dough out onto a floured surface and knead until it is smooth, elastic, and no longer sticky, about 5 minutes, adding in more flour if the dough continues to stick. Divide the dough in half, shape it into two balls, and place them in a buttered bowl. Cover loosely with plastic wrap and let stand for 30 minutes. (The dough will rise only slightly.)

3. While the dough is rising, prepare the filling: Heat 2 tablespoons of the oil in a large skillet. Add the garlic and fish and cook, stirring, until the fish is opaque throughout, about 5 minutes. Remove the fish from the skillet with a slotted spoon and add the remaining 4 tablespoons of oil. Add the onions, peppers, canned tomatoes, bay leaves, and saffron, cover, and cook over medium-low heat, stirring occasionally, until the vegetables are soft, about 20 minutes. Place the vegetables in a colander for 5 minutes to drain off the excess oil. Discard the bay leaves. In a large bowl, combine the vegetables with the fish, flaking the fish thoroughly with a fork. Season with salt and pepper to taste.

4. Preheat the oven to 375 degrees F.

5. On a floured surface with a floured rolling pin, roll out one ball of dough to a 14-inch circle. Drape the dough over a rolling pin and transfer to a pizza pan or a baking sheet. Spread the filling on the circle, leaving a 1-inch border. Roll out the second ball of dough to a 13-inch circle and place it on top of the first one. Fold the edges of the bottom crust upward and crimp

(continued)

decoratively. With a sharp knife make several slits in the top crust to allow the steam to escape. Brush the top with the egg wash.

6. Bake the empanada until golden brown, about 25 minutes. Let it rest for 10 minutes before slicing and serving.

SERVES 12 AS AN APPETIZER,
6 AS A MAIN COURSE

Market, Barcelona, Spain.

Fried Empanadas

(EMPANADAS FRITAS)

The varieties of empanadas are endless—in Chile the filling might be of local razor clams, called *machas*, or sweet creamed corn; in Brazil they could be stuffed with shrimp and hearts of palm; in coastal Venezuela or Colombia, with fish stewed in a tomato-based sofrito; in Peru, with leftover dark duck meat, and in Spain with fish, peppers, and onions; while the ground beef or shredded cheese filling is certainly universal. Here I offer a good basic pastry and two of my favorite fillings. Picadillo with Sweet Plantain (meats, page 166) also makes an excellent filling.

1. Place the flour and salt in a food processor and process for several pulses to blend. Add the shortening and butter and process until the mixture resembles a coarse meal, about 12 seconds. Add the yolk and rum and process for 3 pulses. Keep adding water, a tablespoon at a time, following with 2 to 3 pulses, until the mixture just sticks together but does not form into a ball around the blades. Turn the pastry out onto a cool, smooth surface, knead briefly, and form it into two balls. (The dough can be prepared ahead of time up to this point and refrigerated overnight.)

2¼ CUPS FLOUR

1 TEASPOON SALT

3 TABLESPOONS SOLID VEGETABLE SHORTENING, CHILLED AND CUT INTO PIECES

5 TABLESPOONS UNSALTED BUTTER, CHILLED AND CUT INTO PIECES

1 EGG YOLK

2 TABLESPOONS WHITE RUM OR VODKA

⅓ CUP ICE WATER

ABOUT 1¾ CUPS COCONUT AND SHRIMP FILLING, OR CHICKEN, RAISIN, AND HEART OF PALM FILLING, SEE RECIPES BELOW, OR ANOTHER FILLING OF YOUR CHOICE

1 LARGE EGG WHITE, BEATEN

VEGETABLE OIL, FOR FRYING

(continued)

2. Flatten one ball of the pastry into a disk. Cover it with wax paper, and roll it out into a rectangle $\frac{1}{16}$ inch thick. With a cookie cutter, cut out $3\frac{1}{2}$-inch circles. Reroll the scraps and cut out more circles. Repeat with second ball of dough.

3. Place a pastry circle on your work surface and put a heaping tablespoon of the filling of your choice on the lower half of the circle. Brush the edges with egg white, and fold the circle in half over the filling to form a crescent. Press the edges with the tines of a fork to seal.

4. Pour $1\frac{1}{2}$ inches of oil into a large, deep skillet and heat to 360 degrees F. Fry the empanadas, a few at a time, until golden brown, about 2 to 3 minutes per side. With a slotted spoon, remove them to drain on paper towels. Keep the finished empanadas warm in a low oven.

MAKES 18 TO 20 EMPANADAS

2 TABLESPOONS UNSALTED BUTTER

2 TEASPOONS ANNATTO OIL (PAGE 376)

1 MEDIUM ONION, FINELY CHOPPED

$\frac{1}{3}$ CUP DICED RED BELL PEPPER

1 LARGE PLUM TOMATO, CHOPPED

$\frac{1}{2}$ TEASPOON MILD PAPRIKA

$\frac{1}{4}$ TEASPOON CHILI POWDER

$\frac{1}{4}$ CUP CANNED UNSWEETENED COCONUT MILK, WELL SHAKEN

$\frac{3}{4}$ POUND SHRIMP (ANY SIZE), PEELED, DEVEINED, AND CUT INTO SMALL PIECES

3 TABLESPOONS DRIED SHREDDED COCONUT

$\frac{1}{4}$ CUP CHOPPED CILANTRO

SALT AND FRESHLY GROUND BLACK PEPPER, TO TASTE

Coconut and Shrimp Filling

(RELLENO DE CAMARÓN Y COCO)

In a medium-size skillet, melt the butter and the annatto oil over medium heat. Add the onion and pepper and sauté, stirring, until softened, about 5 minutes. Add the tomato, paprika, and chili powder, and cook, stirring, for 5 minutes. Add the coconut milk and cook until thickened and reduced, about 3 minutes. Stir in the shrimp and cook until just cooked through, about 2 minutes. Off the heat, stir in the coconut, cilantro, and salt and pepper to taste. Refrigerate for 1 hour to firm up.

MAKES ENOUGH FOR 18 EMPANADAS

Chicken, Raisin, and Heart of Palm Filling

(RELLENO DE POLLO CON PASAS Y PALMITOS)

1. Cover the raisins with boiling water and soak for 10 minutes. Drain well.

2. In a medium-size skillet, melt the butter and annatto oil over medium heat. Add the onion and the garlic and cook, stirring, until the onion wilts, about 5 minutes. Add the chicken and cook, stirring, for another 2 minutes. Stir in the paprika, cayenne, hearts of palm, and pimientos and stir for 1 minute. Stir in the broth and cook for 3 minutes. Season with salt and pepper. Remove from the heat and refrigerate the filling for 1 hour to firm up.

MAKES ENOUGH FOR 18 EMPANADAS

1/4 CUP DARK RAISINS

2 TABLESPOONS UNSALTED BUTTER

2 TEASPOONS ANNATTO OIL (PAGE 376)

2/3 CUP FINELY CHOPPED ONION

1 CLOVE GARLIC, CRUSHED THROUGH A PRESS

2 CUPS DICED COOKED SKINLESS CHICKEN
    BREAST, RINSED WELL AND PATTED DRY

1 TEASPOON MILD PAPRIKA

LARGE PINCH OF CAYENNE

1/2 CUP CHOPPED WELL-DRAINED CANNED
    HEARTS OF PALM

1/3 CUP CHOPPED PIMIENTO

1/3 CUP CHICKEN STOCK OR CANNED LOWER-SALT
    CHICKEN BROTH

SALT AND FRESHLY GROUND BLACK PEPPER, TO
    TASTE

Latin produce, Jackson Heights, New York.

Gaucho Empanadas

(EMPANADAS ARGENTINAS)

The empanada traveled a long route from Spain to find a happy incarnation in the land of the *gauchos*. Although it can be filled with chicken, cheese, or spinach, those in the know wouldn't have it with anything but meat. And as any expert will tell you, the meat has to be finely chopped by hand, never ground. The other secret, which gives the filling a melt-in-your mouth effect, is a large quantity of finely chopped sautéed onion, and a good dose of *aliño* (seasonings). The filling has to be so moist that the juices burst out when you bite into the pie, and the Argentinians laughingly suggest that empanadas should be eaten with your knees open. Good cooks also insist on making the filling the night before—this makes it compact, and infused with the flavor of the seasoning. An authentic village empanada is always made with a lard or pork fat pastry, and baked in a clay oven so hot that the empanada should be ready in the time it takes to say "*padre nuestro.*" If you shy away from lard, you can also use 8 tablespoons chilled butter and 4 tablespoons solid vegetable shortening for this recipe and still achieve a nice flaky crust.

FILLING

- 1¼ POUNDS BONELESS ROUND OR CHUCK STEAK
- 3 TABLESPOONS VEGETABLE OIL
- 3 LARGE ONIONS, FINELY CHOPPED
- 2 CLOVES GARLIC, MINCED
- 2 CANNED TOMATOES, DRAINED AND FINELY CHOPPED
- 1 TEASPOON GROUND CUMIN
- 1 TEASPOON DRIED OREGANO
- 2 TEASPOONS MILD PAPRIKA
- SMALL PINCH OF HOT RED PEPPER FLAKES
- ¼ CUP DARK RAISINS
- 12 PIMIENTO-STUFFED OLIVES, SLICED
- ⅔ CUP WATER
- 2 HARD-COOKED EGGS, CHOPPED
- SALT AND PLENTY OF FRESHLY GROUND BLACK PEPPER

(continued)

1. To make the filling: Place the meat in the freezer for 30 minutes to firm up. Remove from the freezer and, using a large sharp knife, chop the meat as finely as you can. Pat dry with a paper towel.

2. In a large skillet, heat 1 tablespoon of the oil over high heat. Brown the meat in batches, until no longer pink inside, 4 to 5 minutes per batch, tilting the skillet and removing the liquid, if the meat throws off too much juice. Remove the meat to a bowl and drain the skillet. Heat the remaining 2 tablespoons of the oil over medium-low heat and cook the onions, stirring occasionally, until soft, about 7 minutes. Replace the meat in the skillet and add all the other filling ingredients except the eggs, salt, and pepper. Cook for 5 minutes. Remove the filling to a bowl and stir in the egg and salt and pepper to taste. Refrigerate the filling until firmed up, at least 2 hours.

3. To make the pastry: Place the flour and salt in a food processor and process for several pulses to blend. Add the lard and process until the mixture resembles a coarse meal, about 12 seconds. Add 1 tablespoon of the water, the egg yolk, and the vinegar, and process for three pulses. Keep adding water, a tablespoon at a time, following with two to three pulses, until the mixture just sticks together but does not form into a ball around the blades. Turn the pastry out onto a cool, smooth surface, knead briefly, and form it into two balls. (The dough can be prepared ahead of time up to this point and refrigerated overnight.)

4. Flatten one ball into a disk, keeping the other covered with plastic wrap. Cover the pastry disk with wax paper and roll it out into a rectangle $\frac{1}{16}$ inch thick. With a cookie cutter or the rim of a bowl, cut out 5-inch circles. Reroll the scraps and cut out more circles. Work quickly so that the dough does not get warm. Repeat with the rest of the pastry.

5. Place a circle of dough on a work surface, place 2 heaping tablespoons of filling in the center, and brush the edges with the egg white. Bring the edges up over the filling, and pleat in the following way: starting at the bottom, fold $\frac{1}{2}$ inch of the edge toward the center. Keep folding the edges in at $\frac{1}{2}$-inch intervals to form pleats, and seal firmly. Repeat with the rest of the dough and filling.

PASTRY

2¼ CUPS FLOUR

2 TEASPOONS SALT

12 TABLESPOONS CHILLED LARD, OR UNSALTED
   BUTTER CUT INTO SMALL PIECES

6 TO 7 TABLESPOONS ICE WATER

1 LARGE EGG YOLK

1 TABLESPOON WHITE VINEGAR

1 LARGE EGG WHITE, BEATEN

1 LARGE EGG YOLK, MIXED WITH 2 TEASPOONS
   MILK, FOR THE EGG WASH

(continued)

Fiesta!

59

6. Place the empanadas on a baking sheet and brush with the egg wash. Prick each empanada in several places with the tip of a small knife to allow the steam to escape. Bake until the empanadas are golden brown, about 20 minutes. Remove from the oven and let rest for 10 minutes. Serve warm.

MAKES 15 TO 16 EMPANADAS

Political campaign truck, Buenos Aires, Argentina.

Cali-Mío Cheese Breads

(PAN DE YUCA CALI-MÍO)

For anyone with a sweet tooth, my neighborhood Colombian bakery Cali-Mío is paradise. Its shelves are groaning with shiny egg-glazed sweet loaves of cheese-stuffed bread, croquettes and empanadas of all kinds, guava and cream cheese crescents, tamales, *arepas*, and above all, my favorite cheese puffs. When I bit into one for the first time, it was instant *déjà vu*: I immediately recognized the taste of the famous Brazilian Mineiro cheese puffs called *pão de queijo*. While the actual recipes are different, the secret to both is the very fine yuca (manioc) flour (*harina de yuca*), which looks and feels like cornstarch. When mixed with fresh cheese, such as farmer cheese or the Hispanic *requesón*, it produces a very light, chewy, and moist texture, which cannot be achieved with any other flour or starch.

1 POUND FARMER CHEESE OR HISPANIC *REQUESÓN*, CRUMBLED

2 LARGE EGGS, BEATEN

7 TABLESPOONS UNSALTED BUTTER, MELTED AND COOLED TO WARM

⅓ CUP GRATED ROMANO CHEESE

2½ CUPS YUCA FLOUR (*HARINA DE YUCA*)

¼ CUP ALL-PURPOSE FLOUR

2 TEASPOONS BAKING POWDER

½ TEASPOON SALT

1. Preheat the oven to 375 degrees F. Line two baking sheets with lightly greased parchment paper.

2. In a large mixing bowl, combine the farmer cheese, eggs, 6 tablespoons of the butter, and the Romano cheese and mix well with a fork.

(continued)

3. In another bowl, sift together the yuca flour, all-purpose flour, baking powder, and salt. Add it to the cheese mixture and stir well with your hands until the yuca flour is completely incorporated. Knead briefly to combine all the ingredients well. The dough will be moist.

4. Turn the oven temperature down to 325 degrees. Divide the mixture into twenty pieces. Roll each piece into a ball. Place the balls on two greased baking sheets, spacing them at least $1\frac{1}{2}$ inches apart and brush with the remaining butter. Bake in the middle of the oven until they are golden brown and puffed, 25 to 30 minutes. Cool completely on a rack before serving.

MAKES 20 BREADS

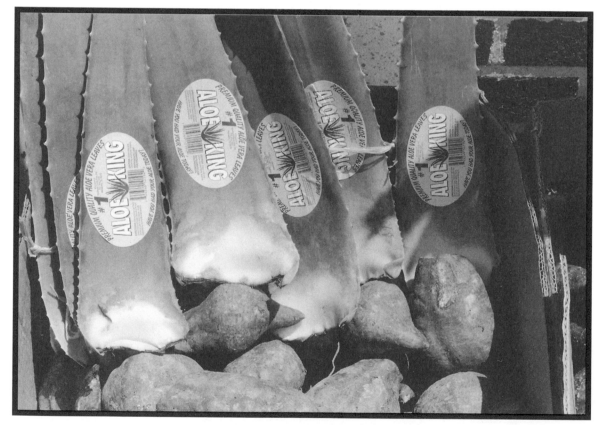

Latin produce, Jackson Heights, New York.

Cuban Tamale Torta

(TORTA DE TAMAL ESTILO CUBANO)

Unlike many other Latin cooks who laboriously fill their tamale dough, the Cubans just mix dough and filling together and steam the tamales in corn husks, thus leaving themselves more time for rumba. But even these "lazy" tamales require the time to stuff them into corn husks and tie them with a string. I simplify the job further by mixing the delicious dough (made from pureed corn kernels) and filling, placing it in a pan lined with banana leaves, covering it with more banana leaves, and cooking the tamal in the oven in a water bath. The result is a moist flavorful tamal cake that can be cut into small squares and served as party food, or cut into large pieces as an accompaniment to a saucy meat or chicken, or served as a luncheon dish. The banana leaves are important as they impart a unique moist tropical sappiness to the tamal. But if you can't get them, substitute fresh corn husks, large leafy greens such as chard, or even blanched cabbage leaves. The bacon and ham filling I suggest is very traditional Cuban, but you can substitute diced chicken, flaked fish, or small shrimp. As it can be quite hard to find fresh corn with just the right starch content for the tamale dough, many Cubans I know agree that canned sweet yellow corn is just right for the job. For a nice presentation, serve the tamal on a platter lined with banana leaves. Halve the recipe if cooking for a small group.

(continued)

6 STRIPS GOOD SMOKY BACON, CHOPPED

3 TABLESPOONS OLIVE OIL

$^2/_3$ CUP FINELY CHOPPED ONION

2 TABLESPOONS MINCED GARLIC

1 LARGE RED BELL PEPPER, CORED, SEEDED,
    AND CUT INTO SMALL DICE

1 SMALL SCOTCH BONNET CHILE, SEEDED AND
    MINCED

$^3/_4$ POUND SMOKY HAM, IN 1 PIECE, CUT INTO
    $^1/_2$-INCH DICE

ONE 16-OUNCE CAN PLUM TOMATOES, DRAINED
    AND CHOPPED

1 TEASPOON GROUND CUMIN

PINCH OF SUGAR

SALT TO TASTE

$4^1/_2$ CUPS WELL-DRAINED CANNED YELLOW CORN

$^2/_3$ CUP MILK

6 TABLESPOONS UNSALTED BUTTER, CUT INTO
    SMALL PIECES

ABOUT $2^1/_3$ CUPS FINE YELLOW CORNMEAL

ONE 1-POUND PACKAGE FROZEN BANANA LEAVES,
    THAWED AND PREPARED AS DIRECTED ON
    PAGE 380, PLUS MORE FOR SERVING,
    OPTIONAL

1. In a large heavy saucepan, cook the bacon until it renders all its fat. Drain off all the fat, leaving the bacon in the pan.

2. Add the oil to the saucepan and heat over medium-low heat. Add the onion, garlic, pepper, chile, and ham and cook, stirring, until the onion is soft, about 7 minutes. Add the tomatoes and cumin. Simmer the mixture until the tomatoes are cooked down to a paste, about 15 minutes. If the mixture begins to stick, add water, 1 tablespoon at a time. Add a pinch of sugar to take the acidic edge off the tomatoes, and salt to taste.

3. While the tomatoes are cooking, process the corn in a food processor with $^1/_4$ cup of the milk and the butter, until you have a very smooth puree, about $2^1/_2$ minutes. You might have to do this in batches.

4. Add the pureed corn and the remaining milk to the saucepan, and cook, stirring, until the mixture begins to thicken, about 3 minutes. Gradually add the cornmeal, stirring constantly, until you have a dough that can easily hold its shape. Take the mixture off the heat and let it cool until just manageable.

5. Preheat the oven to 350 degrees F.

6. Line the bottom of two 8-inch-square baking pans with banana leaves so that you have a 5-inch overhang on all sides. Wet your hands and spread the dough on the banana leaves in both pans, smoothing the top with the back of a wet spoon. Cover the top with more banana leaves so that there is no overhang, trimming them as necessary. Bring the bottom leaves up and fold them over the top. You should have two layers of banana leaves covering the top. Reserve the remaining banana leaves, if any, for serving the tamales, if you wish. Cover the pans tightly with foil.

7. Set the pans in larger baking pans and pour enough simmering water into the outer pans to come two thirds of the way up to the top. Carefully place the pans in the oven and steam, undisturbed, for 2 hours, adding boiling water to the larger baking pans, as necessary.

8. Take the pans from the oven, remove from the water bath and let the tamales cool, without unwrapping them, for 20 minutes.

9. Unwrap the tamales. If serving as a party snack, cut them into 2- to 3-inch squares. Or cut into larger portions if serving as a meal or as a side dish. Line a platter with banana leaves, if desired, and transfer the tamale squares to the platter.

SERVES 16 TO 20 AS SNACK, OR 8 AS A SUBSTANTIAL SIDE DISH OR LIGHT MAIN COURSE

Chilean Fresh Corn Tamales with Basil

(HUMITAS)

I confess, I rarely make tamales: Preparing the dough and the filling, wrapping, tying, and steaming them is just too daunting. But when I do crave the taste, I turn to these easy, unfilled Chilean tamales (called *humitas*), made from ground fresh corn and wrapped in fresh corn husks. They are perfumed with the scent of fresh basil and are usually eaten with a sprinkling of sugar or a dash of hot sauce. Though fresh yellow corn is certainly best, if you feel too lazy to shuck it, used good-quality frozen and thawed corn, plus fresh corn husks for wrapping. I am grateful to El Arrayán, a lovely Chilean restaurant in Queens, for this recipe.

18 EARS FRESH, JUICY, YELLOW CORN, OR 11
    CUPS FROZEN CORN, THAWED
1 TABLESPOON VEGETABLE OIL
1½ CUPS FINELY CHOPPED ONION
SALT AND FRESHLY GROUND BLACK PEPPER, TO
    TASTE
FINE CORNMEAL OR MILK, IF NECESSARY
1 CUP FINELY SLIVERED BASIL

1. Carefully remove the husks from the corn, making sure not to tear them. Rinse the husks under running water and pat them dry with paper towels.

2. Remove the silks and cut the kernels off the corn. You should have about 10 to 11 cups of fresh corn.

3. In a nonstick skillet, heat the oil over medium-low heat and saute the onion, stirring often, until soft but not browned, about 8 minutes. Set aside.

4. Working in batches, process the corn in a food processor until completely smooth, about 3 minutes per batch.

5. Transfer the corn to a large bowl, stir in the onion, season with salt and pepper, and stir thoroughly with a wooden spoon, in a clockwise motion, until the corn turns into a homogenous sticky dough, about 2 minutes. You should have a rather soft dough that easily holds its shape. If it seems too runny, add 2 to 3 tablespoons cornmeal. If it seems too thick, add 2 to 3 tablespoons milk. Add the basil and stir to distribute it evenly. Divide the dough into 6 equal parts.

6. Lay 3 to 4 large corn husks in an overlapping row, all tapered ends facing in one direction. On top of this, place another row of corn husks whose tapered ends face in the opposite direction, the flat ends overlapping with the first row of corn husks by 2 inches. You should have a rough rectangle of corn husks with tapered ends facing in opposite directions.

7. Place ⅙ of the corn mixture in the middle of the corn husk rectangle, and spread it out with a spoon into a much smaller rectangle, about 4½ by 3 inches. Fold in the short ends of the husks to cover the filling completely. Then fold in the long ends so that they overlap. With kitchen string, tie the *humita* securely in the middle. Repeat with the rest of the corn husks and filling.

8. Place the *humitas* in a large, flat saucepan and carefully add water to cover them by 2 to 3 inches. Bring to a boil over high heat, add salt to the water, reduce the heat to medium, and cook the *humitas* for 45 minutes.

9. With a large slotted spoon, remove the *humitas* from the water, gently shaking off the excess. To serve, place the *humitas* on plates and invite your guests to cut off the string and unwrap the *humitas*. Serve with hot sauce or a sprinkling of sugar.

**MAKES 6 LARGE *HUMITAS*,
EACH ONE ENOUGH FOR A LIGHT MEAL**

Chilean Pumpkin Flat Breads with Panela Syrup

(SOPAIPILLAS CON ALMÍBAR DE PANELA)

1½ CUPS FLOUR

2 TEASPOONS BAKING POWDER

½ TEASPOON SALT

1 TEASPOON SUGAR

½ TEASPOON GROUND CINNAMON

¼ TEASPOON GROUND CARDAMOM

1½ CUPS FRESH OR CANNED COOKED PUREED
    PUMPKIN

3 TABLESPOONS UNSALTED BUTTER, MELTED

VEGETABLE OIL, FOR DEEP FRYING

PANELA SYRUP (RECIPE FOLLOWS), FOR SERVING

Sopaipillas, tasty pumpkin fritters, accompanied by a typical South American cane sugar syrup flavored with cinnamon and orange rind, are a common Chilean snack, served up at home, at street corner kiosks, and in markets. Dark cane sugar (*panela, piloncillo, or chancaca* in Chile) can be found at Latin, Indian, and Southeast Asian markets. If the sugar is too hard, break it into pieces with a hammer and grind it in a food processor. Note that these fritters are made from a pumpkin-flavored dough rather than a pourable batter, and have the taste and consistency of soft puffy flat breads. *Sopaipillas* are also delicious with honey.

1. In a large bowl, sift together the flour, baking powder, salt, sugar, cinnamon, and cardamom. Add the pumpkin puree and melted butter and mix well. Turn the dough out onto a lightly floured surface and knead briefly. Divide the dough into fifteen balls.

2. On a piece of wax paper, with a floured rolling pin, roll out each ball into a very thin 5-inch circle. Trim with a knife or a 5-inch cookie cutter. Reroll the scraps. Prick the circles all over with the tines of a fork.

3. In a large skillet, heat 1 inch of oil to 325 degrees F. Fry the flat breads, turning once, until golden brown, about 2 minutes per side. Transfer them to drain on paper towels. Serve with Panela Syrup.

MAKES ABOUT 17 TO 18 *SOPAIPILLAS*

Panela Syrup

Combine all the ingredients in a heavy medium-size saucepan and bring to a simmer over low heat, stirring to dissolve the sugar. Simmer for 10 minutes. Cool to warm or room temperature. Strain.

MAKES ABOUT 1 CUP

1½ CUPS GROUND DARK CANE SUGAR (*PANELA* OR *PILONCILLO*) OR DARK BROWN SUGAR
¾ CUP WATER
ONE 1-INCH PIECE CINNAMON STICK
4 WHOLE CLOVES
RIND OF 1 MEDIUM ORANGE, CUT INTO PIECES

Paulista Sunday Pizza

(PIZZA PAULISTA)

Every Paulista (which is how the 12 million inhabitants of the sprawling metropolis of São Paulo refer to themselves) will proudly inform you that more pizza is consumed on a Sunday in São Paulo than in all of Italy in 1 week. As Paulistas return home from their weekend excursions, they head straight to their neighborhood pizza parlor. But none turns out a better, more authentically Italian pie than the revered pizza joint called Camelo (the Camel). Waiting for a table at Camelo on a Sunday night is a party in its own right—the crowd overflows into the street, sipping Antractica beer or *caipirinhas*, a potent mixture of local sugarcane liquor, lime juice, and sugar, discussing soccer scores, tapping out a samba beat.

While most of the pizzas at Camelo are authentically Italian, their most popular pie comes with a typically Brazilian topping of Swiss chard, green olives, chopped egg, and sliced hearts of palm.

CRUST

1 PACKAGE (2½ TEASPOONS) ACTIVE DRY YEAST
½ TEASPOON SUGAR
1⅓ CUPS LUKEWARM WATER
3 TABLESPOONS VEGETABLE OIL
1 TEASPOON SALT
3¾ TO 4 CUPS ALL-PURPOSE FLOUR
CORNMEAL, FOR SPRINKLING THE PAN

TOPPING

2 TABLESPOONS OLIVE OIL
1 LARGE ONION, FINELY CHOPPED
1 TABLESPOON MINCED GARLIC
6 CUPS CHOPPED SWISS CHARD OR CHICORY LEAVES
1 CUP GRATED MOZZARELLA CHEESE
1 CUP SLICED WELL-DRAINED CANNED HEARTS OF PALM
½ CUP PIMIENTO-STUFFED OLIVES, SLICED
3 HARD-COOKED EGGS, CHOPPED
1 CUP GRATED *QUESO BLANCO* (HISPANIC WHITE CHEESE)
SALT AND FRESHLY GROUND BLACK PEPPER, TO TASTE

1. To make the crust: In a large bowl, stir together the yeast, sugar, and water and let stand until foamy, about 5 minutes. Stir in the oil and the salt.

2. Add 2 cups of the flour and mix well. Continue to add the flour, mixing well with a wooden spoon after each addition, until you have a soft, slightly sticky dough. Transfer the dough to a lightly floured work surface and knead until it is smooth and elastic, about 8 minutes, working in more flour if the dough is still sticky.

3. Shape the dough into a ball and place it in a large buttered bowl. Turn to coat with the butter, cover with plastic wrap, and let it rise in a warm, draft-free place until doubled in bulk, about 1 hour. Lightly oil a 16-inch pizza pan and sprinkle it with cornmeal.

4. While the dough is rising, prepare the topping: In a large skillet, heat the oil over medium heat. Add the onion and garlic and cook until the onion is translucent, about 5 minutes. Add the chard and cook, stirring, until just wilted, about 3 minutes.

5. Preheat the oven to 500 degrees F. for 30 minutes. Position the rack on the lowest shelf of the oven.

6. Flatten the dough into a disk and let it stand, covered, for 5 minutes. On a floured surface with a floured rolling pin, roll out the disk into a circle about 16 inches in diameter.

7. Transfer the dough to the prepared pan. Sprinkle it with the mozzarella, leaving a $\frac{1}{2}$-inch rim. Spread it with the chard mixture, then sprinkle with the hearts of palm, olives, eggs, and the *queso blanco*. Season with salt and pepper to taste.

8. Place the pan on the oven rack, and bake until the crust is golden brown and the cheese is sizzling, 15 to 20 minutes. Remove the pizza from the oven and let it rest for 5 minutes before serving.

MAKES ONE 16-INCH PIZZA

Soups

> I prefer stunning myself with gazpachos to being at the
> mercy of a meddling doctor who kills by hunger.
> — SANCHO PANZA

A HUGE cast-iron caldron or an earthenware *cazuela* bubbling with a hearty, nourishing soup is the true symbol of a Latin family kitchen, the very essence of *comida casera*. For many foreigners (who wonder with bemusement at the absurdly long Latin lunch breaks) it's often difficult to appreciate the cultural significance of an extended, leisurely lunch. But in the ritual-obsessed Latin world, the *comida* is a sacred institution, which gives large families—which often still include the *abuela* (granny), grown up and small children, and assorted other relatives still living under one roof—a chance to gather together over an afternoon meal. This shared meal keeps the identity of the clan alive. It is every family's private daily celebration of coming together. And that meal invariably includes a soup, which may be a steaming bowlful of slow-cooked root vegetables or beans combined with chunks of meats, sausages, or seafood to produce a delicious, fortifying dish.

The basic sustenance of the poor Iberian farmer in days gone by was soup in its purest form: a humble porridge of bread and water, perhaps topped with a single egg. Over the years, these porridges evolved into the famous Spanish gazpachos, and *sopas de ajo*, and the lesser-known but not any less delicious Portuguese *açordas*. Soup as such wasn't known to the Andean pre-Columbian Indians, but they, too, subsisted on soupy stewlike porridges called *locros* (or *rocros*), made with indigenous grains such as maize and quinoa.

The elaborate multi-ingredient soups so central to Latin cooking are believed to have evolved from Spanish *cocidos* (Portuguese *cozidos*) and *pucheros*. As Spanish historians point out, the *cocido* itself derives from a dish called *adafina*—a Sephardic equivalent of *cholent* in which beef, chicken, chickpeas, and eggs were set to cook on a Friday before sunset and allowed to simmer overnight, so that no cooking had to be done on Shabbat. The Iberians transformed the dish—adding pork, bacon, and sausages—to affirm their Catholic faith. From a simple dish—a few ingredients thrown together into a huge family pot, sometimes simmering away for days—the *cocido* evolved into an elaborate multicourse affair, a Sunday day-off meal including different kinds of meat, sausages, vegetables, legumes, and noodles.

As *cocido* went on its voyage around the New World, it picked up many local inflections. The Iberian rice, chickpeas, and cabbage would be replaced or supplemented by indigenous corn, potatoes, yams, yuca, plantains, and squash. While the *cocido* remained *cocido* in its classic Spanish form, in Latin America and the Caribbean, it fused with Argentinian *locros*, Peruvian *chupes*, Colombian and Venezuelan *sancochos*, Chilean *cazuelas*, Cuban *ajiacos*, and Puerto Rican *asopaos*—thick fragrant chowders, soups, and stews that today are the hallmark of Latin American and Caribbean cooking.

As Latin Americans well know, slightly bland starchy tubers and vegetables require a touch of acidity and bite to bring their rich buttery flavor to life. Often these soup-stews are served with a whole array of piquant, fresh-tasting additions and seasoning mixtures: *aliños, encurtidos, refritos,* and *salsitas,* such as pickled onions, avocado slices, spicy sauces, pounded chiles, minced greens, and spiced oils.

Lighter first-course cream soups—which came into middle-class households in the last century as a typically French touch—are still widely enjoyed today. In wealthy households, these would be served from china tureens as a first course at an evening meal or at a formal lunch. In Latin America these classic smooth purees are often flavored with native produce: plantains, yuca, chayote, hearts of palm, or coconut milk. Tropical tubers take excellently to pureeing, having enough starch in them to produce a creamy soup without the addition of flour or cream, and I invite you to experiment with yuca, plantains, *boniatos* (Cuban white sweet potatoes), or taro. Served with piquant garnishes, they make delicious first courses, casual and exotic at the same time.

Most of the soups I present in this chapter are filling enough to be served as one-dish meals. They are nourishing, flavorful, and unusual, equally at home for a special occasion dinner, a large fiesta, or, most important, a family meal.

"El Rey Fritas," Calle Ocho, Miami.

Peruvian Seafood and Potato Chowder

(CHUPE A LA LIMEÑA)

Chupe is a wondrous Peruvian chowder with sweet mellow vegetables such as corn and squash, rice, and seafood or meat, finished with milk and a bit of cheese. The Lima *chupe* is a whole meal, the liquid accompanied by fried fish, enormous poached shrimp (*langostinos*) in their shells, and poached eggs. Here, for the sake of convenience, I add the fish and shrimp right to the soup. If you plan to make the *chupe* ahead of time, boil the rice separately and add it to each serving. There's no need for any other course besides bread and a salad.

4 TABLESPOONS UNSALTED BUTTER

1 MEDIUM ONION, CHOPPED

4 CLOVES GARLIC, CRUSHED THROUGH A PRESS

4 MEDIUM PLUM TOMATOES, PEELED, SEEDED, AND FINELY CHOPPED

1 TEASPOON MINCED SEEDED HOT FRESH CHILE

1 TABLESPOON TOMATO PASTE

9 CUPS FISH STOCK (PAGE 371), OR 5 CUPS CLAM JUICE AND 4 CUPS WATER

2 MEDIUM RUSSET POTATOES, PEELED AND HALVED

SALT AND FRESHLY GROUND BLACK PEPPER, TO TASTE

⅓ CUP LONG-GRAIN RICE

3 MEDIUM BOILING POTATOES (PREFERABLY YUKON GOLD), PEELED AND CUT INTO WEDGES

¾ CUP EVAPORATED MILK

¼ POUND *QUESO BLANCO* (HISPANIC WHITE CHEESE) OR MOZZARELLA CHEESE, CUT INTO SMALL DICE

1½ CUPS FRESH CORN KERNELS

1½ POUNDS FIRM WHITEFISH FILLETS, SUCH AS HALIBUT, CUT INTO 2-INCH CHUNKS

(continued)

1. In a large, heavy soup pot, melt the butter over medium-low heat. Add the onion and garlic and cook until wilted, about 5 minutes. Add the tomatoes and chile and cook, stirring occasionally, until the tomatoes are reduced to a puree, about 12 minutes. Stir in the tomato paste.

2. Add the stock and the halved russet potatoes and bring to a boil. Season with salt and pepper, cover, and cook over medium-low heat for 10 minutes. Add the rice and the boiling potatoes, and cook until the halved potatoes are tender, about 10

minutes. Remove the halved potatoes to a bowl and
mash, adding a little liquid from the soup. Whisk
the mixture back into the soup.

3. Add the milk, cheese, and corn and cook for 10
more minutes, until the rice is tender. Add the
fish, shrimp, and peas, and cook for 5 more minutes.
Stir in the paprika, and adjust the seasoning, if
necessary.

4. Serve, garnishing each portion with egg, if
using, and cilantro leaves.

¾ POUND LARGE SHRIMP, PEELED AND
   DEVEINED
1 CUP GREEN PEAS, THAWED IF FROZEN
1 TEASPOON MILD PAPRIKA
2 HARD-COOKED EGGS, QUARTERED, IF DESIRED
CILANTRO, FOR GARNISH

SERVES 6

Festival at Juli, Peru.

Yuca:
Staple to Half the World

ON HIS first voyage, Columbus was so enchanted by the grace and hospitality of the Taíno Indians he encountered in the Caribbean, that he invited them to his ship, the *Santa María*, for an improvised party the day after Christmas 1492. We know that on this occasion a gift of yuca (also called cassava or manioc) was made to him by a Taíno chief. It's hard to imagine what the Captain General thought of it. Probably not much at all. Obsessed with the idea of finding gold, and not possessing any botanical (or probably gastronomic) talent or curiosity (much to his own dismay), Colón certainly didn't wax lyrical about the new foodstuff. Later colonists, however, were quick to discover the virtues of this tropical tuber: It was a cinch to grow, easy to ship, and could be made into all sorts of sturdy breads and cakes, full of nutrients and calories. As one historian points out, manioc, used as military rations, played a major role in the conquest of the New World by the military and clergy. Hardly an enviable role, but who can blame the poor tuber? When I tell this story to my Latin friends, they react as if I had told them that their favorite nanny was a mass murderer.

It took almost half a millennium for Europeans to take notice and finally delight in the yuca—a staple in South America, the Caribbean, Africa, and parts of Asia. With the newfound popularity of Latin cooking, it's on its way to actually becoming a trendy tuber. Its world production is close to that of the potato, and while in our kitchens it will hardly compete with other New World treasures, for those in the know there is much to appreciate about its comforting slightly nutty taste and buttery texture. In fact, it can be positively addictive.

Yuca was cultivated by the Tupi-Guaraní Indians (the early inhabitants of Brazil) as long as 1,500 years ago. By the time Columbus landed in the West Indies, it was the major supplier of calories for the local population. In the West it's best known as the source for tapioca, but in Latin and Caribbean kitchens it's a blank canvas for inspiration. Dried, dehydrated manioc is known in Brazil as *farofa*, a crunchy meal, usually toasted in butter (looking somewhat like bread crumbs), and served as part of a *feijoada* meal. Very fine yuca starch or flour (*almidón de yuca* or *harina de yuca* in Spanish, and *polvilho* in Portuguese) is turned into delectable chewy breads and cheese puffs throughout South America. Boiled yuca, served with a spicy sauce, is everybody's favorite everyday fare; and when mashed, it can be shaped into all kinds of delicious fritters and croquettes.

Cooking and Handling Yuca By now you would have certainly noticed yuca in an ethnic grocery or in your supermarket: it's that brown cylindrical root, anything from 5 to 20 inches long, covered with a shiny, waxed barklike brown skin. Quality is important, and in Latin American markets, when you chose a yuca, a piece will be hacked off for you to check its quality. (Which is why in Hispanic groceries you will often see yuca with a piece already cut off). The inside should be bright white and crunchy, and the outside free of mold and cracks. To the surprise and great delight of new Latin immigrants, the quality of yuca in the United States tends to be uniformly good.

To handle yuca, working lengthwise, peel off the skin from each section (including the pink part under the skin) with a vegetable peeler or a small sharp knife. Then use a cleaver or heavy knife to hack the bark crosswise into 2- to 3-inch sections. Raw yuca is very starchy, so you should work on a covered surface, as it will leave a chalky white residue.

To cook it, bring the yuca to a boil in plenty of salted water, lower the heat, and simmer it until tender. This should take about 25 minutes. Drain, and when just cool enough to handle, cut the sections in half lengthwise and, with a paring knife, remove the tough stringy core that runs through its center. If not using the yuca immediately, cool it in the liquid in which it cooked. Most Hispanic groceries sell peeled and cored frozen yuca sections, which come in sealed plastic bags. Goya brand is good. Make sure to thaw it thoroughly before cooking, otherwise it will cook unevenly, leaving an unpleasant chalky taste.

Boiled or raw yuca fingers can be deep-fried to compete with french fries; cooked yuca can be mashed, mixed with egg and a bit of flour, and fried into wonderful fluffy fritters, both sweet and savory. Mashed yuca has the consistency of dough and can be used as a shell for filled empanadas, dumplings, and croquettes, as can raw yuca, minced well in a food processor. Chunks of yuca are a mandatory component of the famous Latin tropical tuber stews, such as *sancochos*, and it's a great vegetable for pureed soups because its starchy consistency does not require any other thickener. For salads, treat cooked yuca as you would a potato. Accented with a lively dressing, such as a spicy mayonnaise or a garlicky vinaigrette, it will blend with many flavors, from spicy cooked sausages, to delicate shredded chicken breasts.

However you plan to cook it, yuca has a pleasing blandness that invites strong, bright, acidic flavors. Raw red onions, garlic, cilantro, vinegar, citrus juice, and crushed tomatoes are its natural partners. One of the classic Cuban dishes is *yuca con mojo*, boiled yuca served with citrus- and garlic-flavored melted lard (for which you can, of course, substitute olive oil).

Store, Buenos Aires, Argentina.

Shrimp Bobó (Puree of Yuca with Shrimp, Tomatoes, and Coconut Milk)

(B O B Ó   D E   C A M A R Ã O)

Bobó is a marvelously exotic Afro-Brazilian dish from Bahia. It consists of a velvety puree of cooked yuca mixed with shrimp, broth, and a seasoning mixture of onions, garlic, and tomatoes, all flavored with coconut milk. Traditionally, the yuca and liquid are stirred together really hard so that the resulting puree is thick and starchy, reminiscent of the starchy African mashes called *fufú*. But younger Bahiano cooks often use less yuca and more liquid, making the *bobó* more like a thick and creamy main-course soup that can be eaten with rice.

1½ POUNDS LARGE SHRIMP, IN THEIR SHELLS, PREFERABLY WITH HEADS STILL ON

3 TABLESPOONS OLIVE OIL

3 CUPS WATER

1 TABLESPOON FRESH LEMON JUICE

SALT, TO TASTE

2 POUNDS YUCA (PEELED AS DIRECTED ON PAGE 79), CUT INTO 2-INCH PIECES

2 SMALL ONIONS, CHOPPED

8 LARGE CLOVES GARLIC, CHOPPED

1 SMALL GREEN BELL PEPPER, CORED, SEEDED, AND CHOPPED

6 MEDIUM RIPE TOMATOES, BLANCHED, PEELED, AND CHOPPED

2 TABLESPOONS MINCED FLAT-LEAF PARSLEY

2 TABLESPOONS FINELY SLICED SCALLION GREENS

2 CUPS CANNED COCONUT MILK, WELL STIRRED

1 TABLESPOON ANNATTO OIL (PAGE 376)

2 CUPS BOILED RICE, FOR SERVING

⅓ CUP CHOPPED CILANTRO LEAVES

PIQUANT SAUCE (RECIPE FOLLOWS), AS AN ACCOMPANIMENT

1. Peel and devein the shrimp, reserving the shells and heads. In a heavy saucepan, heat 2 teaspoons of the olive oil over medium heat and sauté the shells and heads, if using them, for 5 minutes, stirring. Add the water, lemon juice, and salt to taste, bring to a boil, and simmer, covered, for 20 minutes. Strain and reserve the broth.

2. Cook the yuca in water to cover by 2 inches until tender, about 25 minutes. Remove the yuca

from the liquid and, when cool enough to handle, remove the stringy core that runs through its center. In a blender, puree the yuca with $1\frac{1}{2}$ cups of the reserved broth until smooth. Do not overblend or the yuca will become gluey. Set aside.

3. In a large, heavy saucepan, heat the remaining olive oil over medium-low heat. Add the onions, garlic, and bell pepper and cook, stirring, until the vegetables are soft, about 10 minutes. Add the tomatoes and cook, stirring, until they are reduced to a puree, about 10 minutes. Add the parsley and scallions and cook for 1 more minute. Transfer the mixture to a blender, add the remaining shrimp broth, and blend to a coarse puree. Return to the saucepan and heat through over medium heat. Slowly stir in the yuca puree, stirring constantly.

4. Stir in the coconut milk, and bring to a simmer. Simmer over medium heat for 5 minutes. Add salt to taste, stir in the shrimp, and cook until they just turn pink, about 4 minutes. Stir in the annatto oil.

5. Divide the rice among six soup plates, add the *bobó*, and garnish each portion with cilantro. Serve the Piquant Sauce on the side.

SERVES 6

Piquant Sauce

Mix all the ingredients together in a bowl and let stand for 30 minutes for the flavors to develop.

MAKES ABOUT $\frac{2}{3}$ CUP

1 LARGE RIPE TOMATO, CUT INTO FINE DICE
$\frac{1}{2}$ GREEN BELL PEPPER, CORED, SEEDED, AND
    CUT INTO FINE DICE
$\frac{1}{2}$ CUP CHOPPED RED ONION
1 TEASPOON MINCED, SEEDED SCOTCH BONNET
    CHILE, OR MORE TO TASTE
3 TABLESPOONS FRESH LEMON JUICE
1 TABLESPOON DISTILLED WHITE VINEGAR
SALT TO TASTE

Three-Potato Chowder from Bogotá

(AJIACO BOGOTANO)

This recipe was given to me by César Arturo Espinel, an esteemed elderly chef from Bogotá. When I asked him to name his favorite dish, his face lit up with a fondness only childhood memories can bring back. "*Ajiaco bogotano*," a soup his mother would prepare with poached chicken and three kinds of potatoes: *papa criolla*, an indigenous yellow Colombian potato; *pastusa*, a creamy white potato that gave the soup its texture; and *habanera*, a waxy red boiling potato. The spiciness in the soup comes from a pureed mixture of chiles, garlic, and cilantro; a tiny touch of cream gives it sweetness, and capers add briny zest. The soup is traditionally garnished with sliced avocado and slivers of red onion.

1 BONE-IN CHICKEN BREAST (ABOUT 1¼ POUNDS), SKINNED AND RINSED

7½ CUPS CHICKEN STOCK (PAGE 372) OR CANNED LOWER-SALT CHICKEN BROTH

1 POUND IDAHO POTATOES, PEELED AND CUT INTO THIN SLICES

1 POUND YUKON GOLD POTATOES, PEELED AND CUT INTO THIN SLICES

1 SMALL ONION, CHOPPED

2 CLOVES GARLIC, CHOPPED

½ CUP DICED RED BELL PEPPER

¼ CUP CHOPPED CELERY

1 SMALL HOT CHILE, SEEDED AND CHOPPED

1 TEASPOON MILD PAPRIKA

½ TEASPOON GROUND CUMIN

1 POUND SMALL RED NEW POTATOES IN THEIR SKINS, SCRUBBED AND HALVED, OR QUARTERED, IF LARGE

SALT TO TASTE

⅓ CUP HEAVY CREAM

1 SMALL AVOCADO, PEELED, PITTED, AND SLICED, FOR GARNISH

2 TO 3 TABLESPOONS SMALL CAPERS, FOR GARNISH

1. In a large soup pot, combine the chicken and stock and bring to a simmer over medium-low, skimming off the foam that rises to the surface. Add the Idaho and Yukon Gold potatoes and simmer, covered, over low heat until the chicken is tender, about 20 minutes. Remove the chicken from the liquid, cool until manageable, bone, shred into bite-size pieces, and reserve. Continue cooking the potatoes until soft, about 10 more minutes.

2. While the potatoes are cooking, combine the onion, garlic, bell pepper, celery, chile, paprika, and cumin in a blender with 1 cup of the broth from the soup pot, and puree until smooth.

3. Add this mixture to the pot, along with the red potatoes. Add salt to taste. Cook the soup until the red potatoes are tender and the other potatoes have almost disintegrated, about 20 minutes more.

4. Stir the cream and the reserved chicken into the soup and simmer for 5 minutes.

5. Ladle the soup into bowls and garnish each portion with capers and avocado slices.

SERVES 6 TO 8

A Dainty Truffle

Here is the account by Gonzalo Jiménez de Quesada of his 1537 expeditions into the dense forest of Magdalena in northern Ecuador. The *Conquistadores* entered a native house. Among maize and beans, they noticed something resembling a truffle: "plants with scanty flowers of a dull purple color and floury roots, a gift acceptable to Indians and a dainty dish even to Spaniards." This was probably a European's first encounter with the potato!

Meatball, Chayote, and Corn Soup

(SOPA DE ALBÓNDIGAS, CHAYOTE, Y CHOCLO)

This is my adaptation of a lovely Ecuadorian main-course soup: beef and rice meatballs, chayote, and corn, floating in a delicious tomato broth flavored with lime and cilantro. Despite the long list of ingredients, it makes an easy and nourishing meal. If you can't find chayote, substitute 1 large zucchini.

MEATBALLS

¾ POUND GROUND BEEF CHUCK

3 TABLESPOONS PLAIN, DRY BREAD CRUMBS

⅓ CUP LONG-GRAIN RICE

1 EGG WHITE, BEATEN

¾ TEASPOON SALT

FRESHLY GROUND BLACK PEPPER, TO TASTE

2 TABLESPOONS ICE WATER

SOUP

5 MEDIUM-SIZE RIPE TOMATOES, BLANCHED,
    PEELED, AND CHOPPED

1 TEASPOON CHOPPED GREEN CHILES

2 CLOVES GARLIC, CHOPPED

¼ CUP CHOPPED ONION

2 TABLESPOONS TOMATO PASTE

1 CUP WATER

1 TABLESPOON ANNATTO OIL (PAGE 376)

1 TEASPOON GROUND CUMIN

7 CUPS CHICKEN STOCK (PAGE 372), CANNED
    LOWER-SALT CHICKEN BROTH, OR WATER

SALT AND FRESHLY GROUND BLACK PEPPER, TO
    TASTE

(continued)

1. To make the meatballs: Combine all the meatball ingredients in a large bowl and set aside.

2. To make the soup: In a blender, puree the tomatoes, chiles, garlic, onion, tomato paste, and water.

3. In a large stockpot, heat the annatto oil over medium-low heat. Add the cumin and stir for 1 minute. Add the pureed tomato mixture and cook, stirring, for 5 minutes. Add the stock and bring to a simmer. Season with salt and pepper to taste.

4. Shape the meatball mixture into balls 1½ inches in diameter, and lower the meatballs into the simmering liquid. Skim the foam that rises to the surface. Add the chayote, cover, and simmer until the chayote is tender, about 20 minutes. Add the corn and simmer for another 5 minutes.

5. Add the lime juice and sugar to the soup and serve, garnished with the red onion and cilantro.

SERVES 6

1 LARGE CHAYOTE, PEELED, CORED, AND CUT
   INTO LARGE DICE
2 CUPS FRESH OR FROZEN AND THAWED CORN
   KERNELS
FRESHLY SQUEEZED JUICE OF ½ LIME
PINCH OF SUGAR
THINLY SLICED RED ONION, FOR GARNISH
CILANTRO LEAVES, FOR GARNISH

Argentinian Hominy and Brisket Soup

(LOCRO CON CARNE DE PECHO)

Almost every Latin American country has its own version of a folksy meal-in-a-bowl soup, thick with various meats and indigenous vegetables such as corn, yuca, pumpkin, and sweet potatoes. These soups are both everyday fare and fiesta food. In Argentina, the Creole classic is a thick soup-stew called *locro*, which, like Mexican *pozole*, is based on hominy, and augmented with a hefty chunk of beef, vegetables, and a spicy Argentinian *sofrito*—a cooked mixture of spices and herbs—that brings the soup to life at the last moment. Traditionally, the *sofrito* is made with lard, for which you can substitute peanut or canola oil.

SOUP

- 3 POUNDS FIRST-CUT BEEF BRISKET, TRIMMED OF ALL FAT
- 11 CUPS WATER
- 1 LARGE ONION, SLICED
- 2 CUPS CHOPPED DRAINED CANNED PLUM TOMATOES
- TWO 1-POUND CANS YELLOW HOMINY
- 1 POUND WINTER SQUASH, CUT INTO 1½-INCH CUBES (ABOUT 2 CUPS)
- 2 MEDIUM BAKING POTATOES, CUT INTO 1½-INCH CUBES
- SALT AND FRESHLY GROUND BLACK PEPPER, TO TASTE
- 3 TABLESPOONS CHOPPED SCALLIONS

(continued)

1. To make the soup: In a large soup pot, combine the brisket and water and bring to a boil, skimming off the foam that rises to the surface. Simmer over low heat, partially covered, until the brisket is tender, about 2 hours.

2. Add the onion, tomatoes, hominy, squash, potatoes, and salt and pepper to taste. Simmer, partially covered until the vegetables are very tender, about 30 minutes.

3. With a slotted spoon, remove the brisket to a bowl. When cool enough to handle, shred the meat by hand into bite-size pieces and return it to the soup. Adjust the seasonings and add the scallions. Keep the soup warm while making the *sofrito*.

4. To make the *sofrito*: In a small saucepan, heat the oil over low heat. Add the remaining ingredients and cook, stirring, for 2 to 3 minutes. Transfer to a sauceboat.

5. Ladle the *locro* into large bowls and swirl some *sofrito* into each portion.

SOFRITO

¼ CUP PEANUT OR CANOLA OIL

2 CLOVES GARLIC, FINELY CHOPPED

2 TABLESPOONS FINELY CHOPPED SCALLIONS

2 HEAPING TEASPOONS MILD PAPRIKA

¾ TEASPOON GROUND CUMIN

1 TEASPOON DRIED OREGANO

1 TABLESPOON MINCED FLAT-LEAF PARSLEY

¼ TO ½ TEASPOON HOT RED PEPPER FLAKES

SERVES 8

Evita's (Eva Perón) Tomb, Recoleta Cemetery, Buenos Aires, Argentina.

Galician White Bean Soup with Greens

(CALDO GALLEGO)

Turnip greens (*grelos*) are the national green of Galicia, a verdant province in northwest Spain. It's not unusual to see old ladies in provincial towns carrying huge baskets of it on their heads to sell at the local market. This is a big family-meal soup containing potatoes, white beans, greens, and sometimes, sausage. Caldo Gallego is not as thick as other classic bean and potato soups, and the intensity of its flavor comes from the rich stock, simmered for a long time with salt pork, ham bone, and veal bone. I use veal shanks here, to give the stock even more depth. Make the stock ahead of time so you can degrease it.

1½ CUPS DRIED WHITE BEANS (SUCH AS GREAT NORTHERN OR NAVY)

10 CUPS WATER, PLUS WATER TO SOAK THE BEANS

1 MEATY SMOKED HAM BONE

1 VEAL SHANK (ABOUT 1 POUND)

ONE 4-OUNCE SLAB SALT PORK

2 SMALL ONIONS

2 SMALL CARROTS, PEELED

SALT AND FRESHLY GROUND BLACK PEPPER, TO TASTE

5 CUPS SHREDDED TURNIP GREENS, KALE, OR SWISS CHARD

3 BOILING POTATOES, PEELED AND CUT INTO 1½-INCH CUBES

½ TEASPOON IMPORTED MILD PAPRIKA

1. Soak the beans in water to cover overnight. Drain and set aside.

2. In a large soup pot, combine the 10 cups water, the beans, ham bone, veal shank, salt pork, onions, and carrots. Bring to a boil, skimming off the foam that rises to the surface. Reduce the heat to low, add salt and pepper to taste, and simmer, covered, until the veal shank is tender, about 1½ to 2 hours.

3. With a slotted spoon, remove and discard the onions, carrots, and salt pork. Remove and set aside the ham bone and veal shank. When cool enough to handle, cut the meat from the veal and ham bones, removing the fat and gristle as you go. Reserve the meat. Cool the stock and skim off the fat.

4. Blanch the turnip greens in boiling salted water to cover for 2 minutes to remove the bitter taste. (Omit this step if using kale or Swiss chard.)

5. Add the potatoes, the turnip greens, and the paprika to the soup and simmer until the potatoes almost disintegrate, about 30 minutes. Add the reserved meats to the soup and cook for 2 minutes to heat through. Adjust the seasoning, ladle the soup into bowls, and serve.

SERVES 8

Galician bagpiper, Spain.

Andean Quinoa Chowder

(CHUPE DE QUINOA)

In Andean countries, quinoa was, and still is, a staple grain—whose cultivation and widespread use predate that of corn. Its popularity is due to the fact that it can sustain the below-freezing temperatures and the low oxygen of the Andes, and is incredibly high in nutrients of all sorts. This is a deliciously filling peasant soup, containing bits of pork, corn, potatoes, and quinoa, thickened with ground roasted peanuts. Vegetarians can omit the pork. Quinoa is available at most health food stores.

1 RED OR GREEN JALAPEÑO CHILE

3 STRIPS BACON, CHOPPED

2 TABLESPOONS PEANUT OR CANOLA OIL

2 BONELESS CENTER-CUT PORK CHOPS (ABOUT
 ½ POUND), CUT INTO ¾-INCH DICE

1 CUP CHOPPED ONION

4 CLOVES GARLIC, SLICED

2 TEASPOONS ANNATTO OIL (PAGE 376)

3 MEDIUM RUSSET POTATOES, PEELED AND CUT
 INTO 1½-INCH CUBES

1 CUP QUINOA, RINSED THOROUGHLY UNDER
 COLD RUNNING WATER

7½ CUPS CHICKEN STOCK (PAGE 372) OR
 CANNED LOWER-SALT CHICKEN BROTH

SALT AND FRESHLY GROUND BLACK PEPPER, TO
 TASTE

⅔ CUP UNSALTED ROASTED PEANUTS

1 LARGE EGG YOLK

½ CUP MILK

1 CUP FRESH CORN KERNELS

CILANTRO SPRIGS, FOR GARNISH

LIME WEDGES, FOR FINISHING THE SOUP

1. In a small, heavy skillet, dry-roast the chile over medium heat until lightly charred. When cool enough to handle, stem and chop the chile and set aside.

2. In a large, heavy stockpot, cook the bacon over medium heat until crisp, about 3 minutes. Add the oil and the pork and brown the pork for about 4 minutes. Drain all but 1 tablespoon of fat from the pot. Stir in the onion and garlic and cook, stirring, until the onion is soft, about 7 minutes. Stir in the annatto oil, potatoes, and quinoa and stir for 2 to 3

minutes. Add the stock, bring to a boil, reduce the heat to low, add salt and pepper to taste, and simmer, covered, until the meat and potatoes are tender, about 35 minutes. The quinoa will swell.

3. Grind the peanuts in a food processor. Add the roasted chile and process with the peanuts to a puree. Add the egg yolk and milk and process until blended. Transfer the mixture to a bowl and slowly whisk in about 1 cup of the hot soup.

4. Slowly stir the mixture back into the soup and add the corn. Simmer for 5 to 7 minutes.

5. Ladle the soup into bowls and serve, garnished with cilantro and a squeeze of lime.

SERVES 6 TO 8

Food Fair in Santarém:
A Carnival of Food

Attracting local producers and restaurateurs from all over Portugal, the Food Festival in Santarém (an hour's drive north of Lisbon) is one of the liveliest, most authentic regional festivals in Europe. A tasting city of dozens of booths, set up to resemble local *tascas* (taverns), springs up for ten days in November. The atmosphere here is not very different from a medieval country fair—straw roofs, rustic clay jugs, wizened old men in traditional black hats, ruddy-faced women in embroidered shawls, hams and sausages suspended from ceilings, wine flowing freely from enormous wooden barrels.

There are sit-down luncheon feasts—one each day from every Portuguese province—as well as music and costumed dancing and crafts exhibitions. Everything is authentic, homemade, and delicious. Cooks, bakers, farmers, and fishermen come to be merry and to display their wares. You can sample Chaves hams from Trás-os-Montes, tangy cheeses from the Serra da Estrela, pork and clams from the Alentejo, lustrous shellfish from the Costa d'Azul, and an incomparable game and "rabbit-rice" from the northern hills—and wash them down with delicious wines and ports from all over the country. There are as many hunters, mushroom pickers, dairy farmers, and wine makers here as there are visitors. It's a carnival, a gastronomic extravaganza, and living anthropology all at the same time.

Red Bean Soup with Pickled Onion Relish

(SOPA DE FRIJOLES COLOMBIANA CON ENCURTIDO DE CEBOLLAS)

1 POUND DRIED RED KIDNEY OR PINTO BEANS

6 CUPS WATER

2 TABLESPOONS OLIVE OIL

2 MEDIUM ONIONS, CHOPPED

2 TABLESPOONS MINCED GARLIC PLUS 1 LARGE
    CLOVE, CRUSHED THROUGH A PRESS

1 LARGE GREEN PLANTAIN (ABOUT 8 OUNCES),
    PEELED AS DIRECTED ON PAGE 379 AND CUT
    INTO LARGE DICE, IF AVAILABLE

1 CUP CHOPPED CARROT

1 TABLESPOON MILD PAPRIKA

1/2 TEASPOON CAYENNE

2 TEASPOONS GROUND CUMIN

PINCH OF GROUND CINNAMON

6 1/2 CUPS CHICKEN STOCK (PAGE 372) OR
    CANNED LOWER-SALT CHICKEN BROTH

1 SMALL RED ONION, HALVED AND SLICED

1 SMALL BUNCH CILANTRO, TRIMMED AND
    CHOPPED

3 TABLESPOONS FINELY DICED RED BELL PEPPER

1 SMALL JALAPEÑO CHILE, SEEDED AND THINLY
    SLICED

2 TABLESPOONS RED WINE VINEGAR

SALT AND FRESHLY GROUND BLACK PEPPER, TO
    TASTE

This is my version of a classic Colombian red bean soup—a thick spicy puree of red beans and green plantains, whose richness is punctuated by a garnish of lightly marinated red onion slices and cilantro leaves. The soup can be made a day ahead, but add some liquid as you reheat it, since it tends to thicken on standing. Add the garnish right before serving.

1. Soak the beans overnight in the 6 cups of water. Do not drain.

2. In a large, heavy stockpot, heat the oil over medium-low heat. Add the chopped onions and minced garlic and cook, stirring, for 5 minutes until the onions wilt. Add the plantain and carrot and cook, stirring, for another 5 minutes until the vegetables begin to soften. Stir in the paprika, cayenne, cumin, and cinnamon and stir for 30 seconds. Add the beans with their soaking liquid and the stock and bring to a boil, skimming.

Reduce the heat to low and simmer, covered, until the beans are very tender, about 1¹/₂ to 1³/₄ hours.

3. While the soup is cooking, prepare the garnish. Blanch the red onion in boiling water for 15 seconds and refresh it under cold running water. Squeeze well and pat dry with paper towels. Place onion in a bowl and add the cilantro, bell pepper, chile, crushed garlic, and vinegar. Toss all the ingredients together and let stand for 25 minutes.

4. With a slotted spoon, remove half of the solids from the soup and puree coarsely in a food processor with about 1 cup of the liquid. Return to the pot and heat for 2 minutes. Add salt and pepper to taste.

5. Ladle the soup into bowls and add some of the onion mixture to each bowl.

SERVES 8 TO 10

Cilantro Soup with Chicken and Rice

(ARROZ AGUADITO)

Cilantro enthusiasts will rejoice at this fragrant, jade soup-stew from Peru, whose name translates as "soupy rice." It belongs to the same family as Puerto Rican *asopao* or Brazilian *canja*—dishes in which the rice swells in the liquid to produce a nourishing, filling meal. In northern Peru, this is a favorite hangover cure.

3 TABLESPOONS PEANUT OR CANOLA OIL

1 LARGE ONION, CHOPPED

1 BOILING CHICKEN (ABOUT 3 POUNDS), RINSED WELL, DRIED, AND CUT INTO 8 SERVING PIECES

2 MEDIUM BUNCHES CILANTRO, TRIMMED AND CHOPPED

1 CUP TIGHTLY PACKED CHOPPED SPINACH

1 LARGE CLOVE GARLIC, CRUSHED THROUGH A PRESS

1 TO 2 SMALL GREEN HOT CHILES OF YOUR CHOICE, SEEDED AND CHOPPED

8 CUPS WATER

SALT AND FRESHLY GROUND PEPPER, TO TASTE

1 CUP LONG-GRAIN RICE

½ CUP DICED RED BELL PEPPER

½ CUP DICED YELLOW OR GREEN BELL PEPPER

1½ CUPS FRESH OR FROZEN AND THAWED GREEN PEAS

FRESHLY SQUEEZED LEMON JUICE, TO TASTE

1. In a large soup pot, heat the oil over medium heat. Add the onion and cook over medium heat until the onion is translucent, about 5 minutes. Add the chicken and sauté until lightly browned on all sides, about 7 minutes total.

2. While the chicken is cooking, process the cilantro, spinach, garlic, and chiles in a food processor with 1 cup of the water until finely minced.

3. Drain all the fat from the pot and add the cilantro mixture to the chicken. Cook for 2 minutes. Add the remaining 7 cups of water and bring to a boil. Season with salt and pepper. Turn the heat to low, cover, and cook until the chicken is tender, 25 to 30 minutes. Add the rice and cook for another 15 minutes.

4. Add the peppers and peas and cook for 5 minutes more. Correct the seasoning and add lemon juice to taste.

SERVES 6

Portuguese Kale Soup

(CALDO VERDE)

This recipe was given to me by Maria Cacilda Penina Rodrigues, who in 1994 represented the northern province of Minho at the annual food fair at Santarém, in central Portugal. The secret is the splash of fruity green olive oil swirled in at the end. The soup (which can also be made without the sausage) is traditionally served with corn bread.

3 TABLESPOONS PLUS 2 TEASPOONS OLIVE OIL

2 MEDIUM ONIONS, FINELY CHOPPED

1 TABLESPOON MINCED GARLIC

7 MEDIUM RUSSET POTATOES (ABOUT 2¼ POUNDS), PEELED AND CUT INTO 2-INCH CUBES

8 CUPS CHICKEN STOCK (PAGE 372) OR CANNED LOWER-SALT CHICKEN BROTH

2 *LINGUIÇA* SAUSAGES, OR 8 OUNCES GOOD KIELBASA, SLICED MEDIUM-THICK

3 CUPS FIRMLY PACKED FINELY SHREDDED GREEN KALE

SALT AND FRESHLY GROUND BLACK PEPPER, TO TASTE

2 TO 3 TABLESPOONS GREEN FRUITY EXTRA-VIRGIN OLIVE OIL, PREFERABLY PORTUGUESE

1. In a large, heavy soup pot, heat 3 tablespoons of the oil over medium heat. Add the onions and garlic and cook, stirring, until the onions wilt, about 5 minutes. Add the potatoes and cook, stirring, for another 5 minutes. Add the stock, bring to a boil, reduce the heat to medium-low, and cook, partially covered, until the potatoes are tender.

2. While the potatoes are cooking, heat the remaining 2 teaspoons of oil in a small skillet over medium heat and brown the sausage slices on all sides for about 5 minutes. Pat dry with paper towels.

3. Remove the solids from the soup, and, when cool enough to handle, pass them through a food mill or puree them medium-fine in a blender with a little of the liquid. Return to the pot and bring to a boil, stirring. Add the sliced sausage and the kale and cook until the kale is soft about 5 minutes. Season with salt and pepper to taste.

4. Ladle the soup into bowls (preferably earthenware) and into each bowl swirl about 1 teaspoon of the extra-virgin olive oil.

SERVES 6 TO 8

Tarcila's Minestrón

(MINESTRÓN DE TARCILA)

Here is a spectacular green soup from my Peruvian friend Tarcila, this one her native rendition of the Italian minestrone. Her version of *minestrón* is a hearty white bean and pasta soup, flavored with a heady basil puree, but with such typical Latin additions as corn, squash, yellow potatoes, and white cheese. This is a great dish to make ahead of time as the flavors will develop on standing. If you do, prepare the soup up to step 3, and complete the last two steps just before serving. This is a large and filling pot of soup that can feed a number of people as a main course, or it can be stretched over several days. Just keep adding liquid, as it tends to thicken on standing.

1 TABLESPOON OLIVE OIL

1 MEDIUM ONION, CHOPPED

1 SMALL STALK CELERY, FINELY CHOPPED

1 MEDIUM CARROT, PEELED AND DICED

10 CUPS CHICKEN STOCK (PAGE 372) OR CANNED LOWER-SALT CHICKEN BROTH

1 POUND *CALABAZA* OR BUTTERNUT SQUASH, PEELED, SEEDED, AND CUT INTO 1½-INCH CUBES (ABOUT 2 CUPS)

3 MEDIUM POTATOES, PREFERABLY YUKON GOLD, PEELED AND CUBED

1 LARGE EAR OF FRESH CORN, CUT INTO 1-INCH SLICES

2 LARGE CABBAGE LEAVES, COARSELY SHREDDED

1½ CUPS COOKED WHITE BEANS, SUCH AS GREAT NORTHERN OR CANNELLINI

¾ CUP DRIED MEDIUM-SIZE TUBULAR PASTA, SUCH AS MACARONI

1 LARGE BUNCH FRESH BASIL, CHOPPED

½ CUP CHOPPED FRESH SPINACH

2 GARLIC CLOVES, CHOPPED

¼ POUND *QUESO BLANCO* (HISPANIC WHITE CHEESE), (IF UNAVAILABLE SUBSTITUTE MOZZARELLA CHEESE), CUT INTO SMALL DICE

(continued)

1. Heat the oil in a large stockpot over medium heat. Add the onion, celery, and carrot. Cook, stirring, for 5 minutes, until the onion wilts.

2. Add the stock, *calabaza,* and potatoes and cook over medium-low heat for 10 minutes. Add the corn, cabbage, beans, and pasta and continue

¼ CUP CANNED EVAPORATED MILK
SALT AND FRESHLY GROUND BLACK PEPPER, TO
TASTE

cooking for another 20 minutes until the vegetables are tender.

3. While the soup is cooking, process the basil, spinach, and garlic with a little liquid from the soup in a food processor until finely minced. Stir the mixture into the soup, and cook for another 5 minutes.

4. Add the cheese and milk and cook for another 5 minutes to heat through. Season with salt and pepper and serve.

SERVES 8

Festival at Juli, Peru.

Castilian Garlic Soup

(SOPA DE AJO)

If you wander in the maze of narrow cobbled streets of old Castilian towns you will inevitably whiff the inviting aromas of fried garlic. Chances are that someone, somewhere, is preparing a *sopa de ajo*, the intensely flavored garlic soup that symbolizes Castilian cuisine.

I learned this recipe in the town of Segovia, from Luis Monje, a famous chef and cooking teacher who cooks at the Parador de Segovia. Fragrant olive oil, day-old rustic bread, and good paprika are the prerequisites of this simple soup. Traditionally, the soup is served with poached eggs, but lazy cooks often just swirl an egg or two into the hot liquid—which tastes even better to me.

- 7 TABLESPOONS GOOD FRUITY VIRGIN OLIVE OIL, PREFERABLY SPANISH
- 1½ TABLESPOONS SLICED GARLIC
- 3 OUNCES FINELY DICED SERRANO HAM OR PROSCIUTTO
- 3 CUPS CUBED DAY-OLD COUNTRY BREAD (CRUSTS REMOVED)
- 1½ TABLESPOONS BEST-QUALITY MILD PAPRIKA
- 5 CUPS WATER
- 1 LARGE EGG, BEATEN
- SALT AND FRESHLY GROUND BLACK PEPPER, TO TASTE
- 1 TABLESPOON FINELY CHOPPED FLAT-LEAF PARSLEY, FOR GARNISH

1. In a medium-size heatproof earthenware casserole or a heavy saucepan, heat the oil over low heat. Add the garlic and ham and cook, stirring, for 5 minutes without letting the garlic brown. Add the bread cubes and paprika and cook, stirring, for 3 minutes. Add the water, turn the heat up to medium, bring to a simmer, and cook for 5 to 7 minutes. The bread should swell but just about hold its shape.

2. Lower the heat to low and drizzle the egg into the liquid, stirring constantly until the egg is cooked, about 2 minutes. Season with salt and pepper to taste.

3. To serve, divide among four bowls (preferably earthenware) and garnish with parsley.

SERVES 4

Portuguese Bread Soup with Olive Oil and Cilantro

(AÇORDA À ALENTEJANA)

This Portuguese cousin of Castilian garlic soup is the most cherished poor man's meal of Portugal. There are countless variations throughout the country, but the tastiest version is from the province of Alentejo, where I learned this recipe. As is sometimes done in Alentejo, I use hard-cooked eggs instead of poached. Although the recipe will be much less authentic, you can omit the eggs altogether. The final flavor of the soup will depend on the quality of the olive oil—the fruity green Portuguese oil is best.

5 CUPS CHICKEN STOCK (PAGE 372) OR CANNED LOWER-SALT CHICKEN BROTH
1 CUP CHOPPED CILANTRO LEAVES
4 CLOVES GARLIC, CHOPPED
½ TEASPOON CHOPPED FRESH RED CHILE
½ TEASPOON COARSE (KOSHER) SALT
½ CUP GREEN FRUITY EXTRA-VIRGIN OLIVE OIL, PREFERABLY PORTUGUESE
1 LARGE EGG YOLK
2½ CUPS 1½-INCH BREAD CUBES, FROM DAY-OLD COUNTRY BREAD (CRUSTS REMOVED)
2 HARD-COOKED EGGS, QUARTERED

1. In a medium-size saucepan, bring the stock to a simmer over low heat.

2. Using a large mortar and pestle, crush the cilantro, garlic, chile, and salt to a coarse paste. Work in the oil, 1 tablespoon at a time, until incorporated. Alternatively, this can be done in a blender, using the on/off button. If using a blender, make sure the oil is incorporated but not emulsified.

3. Transfer this mixture to a large earthenware serving bowl and beat in the egg yolk. Whisk in 1 cup of the simmering stock, then slowly stir in the rest. Add the bread cubes and let stand for 3 minutes. Add the hard-cooked eggs and serve at once.

SERVES 4

Creamed Plantain Soup with Cilantro Swirl

(SOPA DE CREMA DE PLÁTANO CON CILANTRO)

A creamy nourishing soup made from green plantains is enjoyed in various forms throughout the Spanish-speaking Caribbean and Latin America. I tried several recipes and chose this version, which is a lighter variation of a comforting cream soup, with the added zest of minced cilantro, orange rind, and lime juice. Though a totally green plantain is classic, I like using semiripe plantains for their suggestion of sweetness. Choose plantains that are yellow but not blackened. If making the soup ahead of time, add the cilantro mixture right before serving. To make the dish even more fun, you might want to garnish it with Plantain Chips (page 33).

- 3 LARGE SEMIRIPE YELLOW PLANTAINS (ABOUT 1½ POUNDS IN TOTAL)
- FRESHLY SQUEEZED JUICE OF ½ LEMON
- 3 TABLESPOONS UNSALTED BUTTER
- 1 MEDIUM ONION, CHOPPED
- 5 CLOVES GARLIC, MINCED, PLUS 1 LARGE CLOVE, CHOPPED
- 4 CUPS CHICKEN STOCK (PAGE 372) OR CANNED LOWER-SALT CHICKEN BROTH
- SALT AND FRESHLY GROUND BLACK PEPPER, TO TASTE
- ¾ CUP CANNED EVAPORATED MILK
- ½ CUP CANNED COCONUT MILK, WELL STIRRED
- ⅓ CUP CILANTRO LEAVES
- 1 TEASPOON GRATED ORANGE ZEST
- 3½ TABLESPOONS FRESH LIME JUICE

1. Peel the plantains as directed on page 379 and cut into ½-inch slices. Place in a bowl and toss with the lemon juice to prevent them from discoloring.

2. Heat the butter in a large, heavy saucepan over medium heat. Add the onion and minced garlic and sauté until the onion is softened, about 7 minutes.

Add the plantains and stock and bring to a boil. Reduce the heat to low, season with salt and pepper, and simmer, partially covered, until the plantains are soft, about 25 to 30 minutes.

3. Transfer the mixture to a blender, and puree medium-fine, using the on/off button. Do not overpuree or the plantain will become gluey. Return the soup to the saucepan, add the evaporated and coconut milk, and bring to a simmer. Cook over low heat for 5 minutes.

4. In a small food processor or a blender, process the cilantro, chopped garlic, orange zest, and lime juice. Swirl this mixture into the soup and serve at once.

SERVES 6

Roasted Pepper Gazpacho

(GAZPACHO CON PIMIENTOS ASADOS)

A cooling gazpacho—made with ripe summer tomatoes, tangy with vinegar and garlic, and creamy with soaked bread—this is a symbol of the languid Andalusian summer. Today's Andalusian chefs, while retaining the dish's structure (no V-8, please), often augment it with extra ingredients, such as the roasted peppers found here.

4 MEDIUM RED BELL PEPPERS, CORED AND
   SEEDED
2 CUPS CUBED COUNTRY BREAD (CRUSTS
   REMOVED)
1½ CUPS ICE-COLD WATER, OR MORE TO TASTE,
   PLUS EXTRA FOR SOAKING THE BREAD
3 MEDIUM VINE-RIPENED TOMATOES, CHOPPED
½ CUP CHOPPED RED ONION
1 SMALL KIRBY CUCUMBER, PEELED AND DICED
5 LARGE CLOVES GARLIC, CHOPPED
4½ TABLESPOONS SHERRY OR RED WINE
   VINEGAR, OR MORE TO TASTE
⅔ CUP VIRGIN OLIVE OIL, PREFERABLY SPANISH
SALT TO TASTE
DICED RED ONION, CUCUMBER, AND RED BELL
   PEPPER, FOR GARNISH

1. Preheat the oven to 500 degrees F. Roast the peppers until soft and only slightly charred, turning once, about 15 to 20 minutes. Place the peppers in a paper bag and let stand for 10 minutes to steam. Peel the peppers and chop roughly.

2. Soak the bread in the extra water for 5 minutes. Squeeze dry. In a large bowl, combine the soaked bread with the peppers, tomatoes, onion, cucumber, garlic, and vinegar. Working in two batches, puree these ingredients in a blender until smooth. With the motor running, drizzle in the oil until incorporated. Transfer to a bowl and add the 1½ cups of ice water, using slightly more for a thinner gazpacho. Add salt to taste and adjust the amount of vinegar, if desired.

3. Chill the gazpacho for at least 1 hour. Serve garnished with diced onion, cucumber, and red pepper.

SERVES 6

White Gazpacho with Grapes

(GAZPACHO BLANCO)

This version of an Andalusian gazpacho is made from soaked bread and almonds, and garnished with green grapes and cubes of fried country bread. If you feel too lazy to blanch and peel the grapes, use honeydew balls or diced peeled apple.

1. In a medium bowl, soak the 2 cups cubed bread in ½ cup of the water for 5 minutes. Squeeze dry.

2. In a blender, process the soaked bread, garlic, almonds, and salt to a paste, adding a little water if necessary. Drizzle in the olive oil.

3. Scrape the mixture into a bowl and whisk in the vinegar. Whisking constantly, add the remaining 2 cups water, a little at a time, until incorporated. Chill the soup for at least 2 hours.

4. Prepare the garnishes: Blanch the grapes in boiling water for 30 seconds. Drain and refresh them under cold running water. Peel off the skins. In a medium skillet, heat ½ inch of olive oil over medium heat. In batches, fry the bread cubes until deep golden. Drain on paper towels.

5. To serve, ladle the soup into small bowls and garnish each portion with several grapes and a few croutons. Serve immediately.

2 CUPS CUBED COUNTRY BREAD
    (CRUSTS REMOVED)
2½ CUPS ICE COLD WATER
2 LARGE CLOVES GARLIC, FINELY CHOPPED
¾ CUP GROUND RAW ALMONDS
½ TEASPOON SALT
½ CUP FRUITY VIRGIN OLIVE OIL
2½ TABLESPOONS SHERRY VINEGAR

GARNISHES

12 SEEDLESS GREEN GRAPES
OLIVE OIL, FOR FRYING THE BREAD CUBES
1 LARGE THICK SLICE COARSE COUNTRY BREAD,
    CUT INTO ¾-INCH CUBES

SERVES 4 TO 6

Chilled Avocado Soup with Crabmeat Ceviche

(SOPA DE PALTA CON CEVICHE DE CANGREJO)

Velvety, smooth avocado puree punctuated by the tangy flavors of ceviche. The avocado soup is also great by itself, with a simple garnish of diced red onions, tomatoes, and cucumbers.

4 SMALL HAAS AVOCADOS, PEELED, PITTED, AND
   COARSELY CHOPPED

3½ TABLESPOONS FRESH LIME JUICE

1 TABLESPOON RICE VINEGAR

⅔ CUP LOW-FAT PLAIN YOGURT

3 CUPS CHICKEN STOCK (PAGE 372) OR CANNED
   LOWER-SALT CHICKEN BROTH

2 TEASPOONS GRATED FRESH GINGER

2 CLOVES GARLIC, CRUSHED THROUGH A PRESS

PINCH OF SUGAR

½ TEASPOON MINCED SEEDED FRESH CHILE, OR
   MORE TO TASTE

1½ TEASPOONS GRATED LIME ZEST

CRABMEAT CEVICHE (RECIPE FOLLOWS)

CILANTRO LEAVES, FOR GARNISH

1. In a blender, puree all the ingredients except the Crabmeat Ceviche and the cilantro. You might have to do it in two batches. Transfer to a serving bowl and chill for about 1 hour.

2. Ladle the soup into bowls and serve garnished with Crabmeat Ceviche and cilantro leaves.

SERVES 6

Crabmeat Ceviche

Mix all the ingredients in a glass or ceramic bowl and refrigerate for 30 minutes.

MAKES ABOUT 1 ½ CUPS OR SERVES 6 AS A GARNISH FOR SOUP

10 OUNCES LUMP CRABMEAT, PICKED OVER
½ CUP FRESH LIME JUICE
2 TABLESPOONS FRESH ORANGE JUICE
1 SMALL JALAPEÑO CHILE, SEEDED AND THINLY SLICED
1 SMALL PLUM TOMATO, PEELED, SEEDED, AND DICED
½ RED ONION, QUARTERED AND THINLY SLICED
½ LARGE RED BELL PEPPER, CORED, SEEDED, AND SLICED INTO THIN JULIENNE
SALT, TO TASTE

Crustacean sculpture, Barcelona, Spain.

Salads

IN THE Iberian Peninsula, where the seasonal vegetables are so perfect and ripe and the olive oil so fragrant, there is little need for artifice and invention. When it comes to salads, a sprinkling of salt, a splash of aged vinegar and fruity olive oil over wedges of meaty Portuguese tomatoes, a bowl of mayonnaise to accompany the sweet buttery asparagus of La Rioja, or a garlic and oil emulsion to drizzle over the tender baby lettuces of Navarra—are considered *suficiente*. In a pinch, a more substantial tapa-style composed salad might include chunks of tuna or salt cod, a briny touch of olives or capers, a dressing of mashed garlic and anchovies, and a garnish of chopped or sliced egg or strips of red roasted pepper. But not much more.

In Latin America, where raw vegetables are often served with the meal as a fresh counterpoint to the richness of indigenous roots, beans, and long-simmered stews, the *ensalada* is often just a plate of iceberg lettuce leaves, sliced avocados, and red onions—with lemon wedges, vinegar, and oil served on the side. One salad that does enjoy widespread popularity in both South America and Spain is *salpicón*, an artfully composed mélange of cooked chicken, ham, or seafood and cooked and raw vegetables, with a tart mayonnaise-based dressing.

The best way to create a big Latin-style salad is to improvise and experiment in a fun, carefree sort of way. A grain, such as rice or quinoa, can be enlivened with ample amounts of herbs and a few colorful vegetables. Something tangy—pimiento, hearts of palm, green olives, or marinated artichoke hearts—and something buttery—like pieces of avocado or asparagus—plus a shower of tasty olive oil and lemon juice add color and zest.

If you have leftover cooked beans, let them marinate for a while in a mixture of lime juice, vinegar, and a little oil, and then toss in some diced red and yellow pepper, red onion, and perhaps a handful of diced smoked ham or cooked *chorizo*. A whiff of cumin and chili powder in the vinaigrette will complement black beans; crumbled fresh or dried oregano or thyme will bring out the flavor of white beans; buttery cooked lima beans will take well to the fresh sappy flavors of cilantro and a touch of lemon.

Leftover cooked yuca, chayote, or pumpkin are delicious mixed with red onion, garlic, and herbs, and tossed with a simple and very traditional dressing of Seville (sour) orange juice and olive oil. And don't neglect tropical fruit—mangoes, papayas, and pineapple will give your salad a nice touch of sweetness and extra texture. If you dice your vegetables and fruit very fine, they can turn into colorful *salsitas*, to be spooned over grilled fish or poached chicken. These are all Nuevo Latino touches, nuevo in presentation but authentic latino in spirit.

To make salad dressings especially flavorful, I often start by pounding garlic, a little salt, and perhaps a chile in a mortar and pestle, slowly working in the oil and acids, such as red wine or sherry vinegar, sour orange, lime, or lemon juice. For a creamier dressing, basic vinaigrette can be whisked together with a couple of tablespoons of mayonnaise. Chilpotle chile can add smokiness and heat, while lots of minced cilantro will add character and color.

Portuguese Black-Eyed Pea and Tuna Salad

(SALADA DE FEIJÃO FRADE E ATUM)

In Portugal, this type of cooked vegetable or bean salad, marinated with the aromatic local olive oil and good vinegar, is often laid out on restaurant bar counters to be served as a kind of tapa, taken with drinks before a meal. It's very tasty and simple, but to be a success it requires rich, fruity olive oil and excellent-quality, firm canned tuna, preferably imported from Spain or Italy. If you are an aficionado of salt cod, you can substitute it for the tuna (also a classic way of preparing this dish). Soak and cook it as directed on page 377 and tear by hand into bite-size pieces.

½ POUND DRIED BLACK-EYED PEAS, PICKED
    OVER OR 3 CUPS DRAINED CANNED BLACK-
    EYED PEAS
ONE 6½-OUNCE CAN OIL-PACKED TUNA,
    (PREFERABLY IMPORTED FROM SPAIN OR
    ITALY), DRAINED AND FLAKED INTO BITE-SIZE
    CHUNKS
¾ CUP CHOPPED RED ONION
¼ CUP GREEN FRUITY EXTRA-VIRGIN OLIVE OIL,
    PREFERABLY PORTUGUESE
3 TABLESPOONS BEST-QUALITY RED WINE
    VINEGAR
⅔ CUP TORN CILANTRO LEAVES
SALT AND FRESHLY GROUND BLACK PEPPER, TO
    TASTE

1. Omit steps 1 and 2 if using canned beans. In a large bowl, soak the dried peas in water to cover overnight. Drain.

2. In a large saucepan combine the peas with fresh water to cover by 2 inches and simmer until the beans are tender but not mushy, about 45 minutes to 1 hour. Drain and cool.

3. In a large bowl combine the peas with the rest of the ingredients and chill for 2 hours.

SERVES 4

Grilled Tomato and Fresh Tuna Salad

This extraordinary salad from the Portuguese province of the Algarve, is like a tuna tartare—strips of best-quality raw tuna tossed with grilled tomatoes and allowed to marinate lightly in good vinegar and olive oil. You will need sashimi-grade tuna.

3 LARGE RIPE MEATY TOMATOES, HALVED
    CROSSWISE
10 OUNCES TOP-QUALITY RAW TUNA LOIN,
    COARSELY DICED
SALT AND FRESHLY GROUND BLACK PEPPER, TO
    TASTE
2 FRYING (ITALIAN) PEPPERS, CORED, SEEDED,
    AND THINLY SLICED
1 SMALL RED ONION, QUARTERED AND SLICED
3 TABLESPOONS GREEN FRUITY EXTRA-VIRGIN
    OLIVE OIL, PREFERABLY PORTUGUESE
¼ CUP GOOD RED WINE VINEGAR

1. Prepare the grill or preheat the broiler.

2. Place the tomatoes on the rack, cut size down, and grill until they are soft and the skins are lightly charred 10 to 15 minutes. When the tomatoes are cool enough to handle, remove the skin and cut the tomatoes into chunks.

3. Place the tuna in a mixing bowl and massage the salt and pepper into it. Add the tomatoes, peppers, and onion, and toss thoroughly. Toss the mixture with the oil and vinegar, cover with plastic wrap, and refrigerate for 2 to 6 hours before serving.

SERVES 4 AS AN APPETIZER

Escarole Salad with Romesco Sauce

(ROMESCADA)

This is the Catalan equivalent of salade niçoise or Caesar salad. It consists of tender escarole dressed with a richly complex sauce of tomato, marinated red pepper, tuna, bread, oil, and vinegar, all pounded together with a mortar and pestle. While the sauce can be made in a blender, it will taste infinitely better prepared in a mortar and pestle. If you don't have one large enough, make it in batches. The classic sauce is also delicious with grilled seafood or vegetables, or as a party dip.

1. To make the sauce: In a large mortar and pestle or in a blender, crush the garlic, tomatoes, bread, pimiento, tuna, and paprika to a paste. Slowly add the oil and vinegar, whisking until completely incorporated. Strain the mixture through a sieve, set over a large mixing bowl. Stir in the almonds, salt, and pepper. Let the sauce stand for 30 minutes for the flavors to ripen.

2. Arrange the escarole on a large serving platter. Drizzle with some of the sauce. Decorate with the tuna, olives, anchovies, and salt cod.

SERVES 6 AS A LIGHT MAIN COURSE

ROMESCO SAUCE

5 CLOVES GARLIC, CHOPPED

2 RIPE PLUM TOMATOES, BLANCHED, PEELED, AND CHOPPED

3 (3-INCH) SLICES COUNTRY BREAD, FRIED IN OIL, CRUMBLED

1 LARGE VINEGAR-PACKED PIMIENTO, CHOPPED

2 TABLESPOONS FLAKED OR MASHED DRAINED OIL-PACKED CANNED TUNA

1½ TABLESPOONS BEST-QUALITY MILD PAPRIKA

⅔ CUP VIRGIN OLIVE OIL, PREFERABLY SPANISH

⅓ CUP GOOD RED WINE VINEGAR

3½ TABLESPOONS GROUND ALMONDS

SALT AND FRESHLY GROUND BLACK PEPPER, TO TASTE

2 MEDIUM HEADS TENDER YOUNG ESCAROLE, SEPARATED INTO LEAVES, WASHED, AND DRIED

ONE 6½-OUNCE CAN OIL-PACKED TUNA, PREFERABLY IMPORTED FROM SPAIN OR ITALY, DRAINED AND BROKEN INTO CHUNKS

12 TO 15 OLIVES, 2 TO 3 TYPES

12 GOOD-QUALITY ANCHOVY FILLETS, DRAINED

6 OUNCES SALT COD, SOAKED AS DIRECTED ON PAGE 377 AND TORN INTO BITE-SIZE PIECES (OPTIONAL)

New Potato Salad with Anchovies and Roasted Peppers

(ENSALADA DE PAPAS CON ANCHOAS Y PIMIENTOS)

This warm tapa-style potato salad from Spain is very simple and tasty, and the combination of flavors will also work with blanched green beans or cooked cauliflower.

2 MEDIUM CLOVES GARLIC, CHOPPED

5 ANCHOVY FILLETS, PACKED IN OIL, DRAINED AND CHOPPED

6 TABLESPOONS VIRGIN OLIVE OIL, PREFERABLY SPANISH

2½ TABLESPOONS RED WINE VINEGAR

1½ TABLESPOONS FRESH LEMON JUICE

2 POUNDS NEW POTATOES (EITHER RED OR BROWN) IN THEIR SKINS, WELL SCRUBBED

½ CUP ROASTED RED PEPPER STRIPS (ABOUT 2 MEDIUM PEPPERS) (PAGE 375)

2 TABLESPOONS MINCED FLAT-LEAF PARSLEY

1. In a mortar and pestle, mash the garlic and anchovies to a paste. Drizzle in the oil, vinegar, and lemon juice, stirring until incorporated. Alternatively, this can be done in a blender.

2. Cook the potatoes in boiling salted water to cover until just tender, about 18 minutes. When just cool enough to handle, cut the potatoes into medium-thick slices and arrange them on a serving platter. Drizzle with the anchovy dressing, arrange the pepper strips attractively on the potatoes, and sprinkle with parsley. Serve warm.

SERVES 4 TO 6

Watercress and Hearts of Palm Salad

(ENSALADA DE BERRO CON PALMITOS)

At the classiest steak houses of Buenos Aires, the menus usually consist simply of various cuts of grilled beef, an occasional roast kid or suckling pig, crispy rounds of perfectly fried potatoes, and a variety of salads to accompany the beef. While the meats are the domain of the barbecue chef, the salads are the kitchen chef's only chance to show off his culinary skill, and they range from the nostalgic Waldorf to immensely baroque concoctions with elaborate names and prices to match. The real connoisseurs, however, stick to this classic salad of watercress and sliced *palmitos*, whose crispiness, slight bitterness, and acidity provide just the right contrast to the richness of the beef.

3 LARGE BUNCHES WATERCRESS, RINSED AND
    DRIED, TOUGH STEMS REMOVED
1½ CUPS THINLY SLICED DRAINED CANNED
    HEARTS OF PALM
5 TABLESPOONS EXTRA-VIRGIN OLIVE OIL
2½ TABLESPOONS FRESH LEMON JUICE, OR
    MORE TO TASTE
SALT AND FRESHLY GROUND BLACK PEPPER, TO
    TASTE

Tear the watercress into bite-size pieces. In a large salad bowl toss it with the sliced hearts of palm. Toss with the olive oil until all the leaves are evenly coated and then toss with the lemon juice. Season generously with salt and pepper and serve.

SERVES 6

Russian Salad

(E N S A L A D A   R U S A)

Being Russian, I am always amused to encounter this dish at places like railway station restaurants in Turkey, an Iranian dive in Santa Monica, a Korean barbecue house, or a tapas bar in Bilbao. But nowhere is it a bigger hit than in South America, where its popularity surpasses even its fame in its own homeland. By the way, in Russia this salad is called "Olivier," and is said to have been invented in the nineteenth century by a visiting French chef. Essentially, it's just a good all-purpose potato salad (which is what, no doubt, accounts for its international popularity), with the addition of a few cooked vegetables, and sometimes meats. It makes a great picnic dish or accompaniment to cold meats. Don't frown at the canned peas, their slightly mushy texture is an integral part of the classic taste.

4 LARGE RUSSET POTATOES, PEELED AND
    COOKED
2 LARGE CARROTS, PEELED AND COOKED
1½ CUPS DRAINED CANNED GREEN PEAS
1 LARGE DILL PICKLE, CUT INTO SMALL DICE
⅓ CUP SLICED PIMIENTO-STUFFED OLIVES
2 HARD-COOKED EGGS, CHOPPED
1 CUP BEST-QUALITY MAYONNAISE
1 TABLESPOON DIJON-STYLE MUSTARD
2 TABLESPOONS FRESH LEMON JUICE
2 TABLESPOONS WATER
SALT AND FRESHLY GROUND BLACK PEPPER, TO
    TASTE

1. Cut the potatoes into ½-inch dice. Cut the carrots into ¼-inch dice. Place them in a large bowl and toss with the peas, pickles, olives, and eggs.

2. In a bowl, whisk together the mayonnaise, mustard, lemon juice, and water. Toss the dressing gently but thoroughly into the salad. Season with salt and pepper to taste.

SERVES 4 TO 5

The Latino Big Salad

(ENSALADA LATINA)

This vibrant salad of avocado, tomato, hearts of palm, red onion, and roasted peppers is my salad of choice for big Latin-style parties.

1. In a blender, combine the mustard, garlic, lime juice, vinegar, and chili powder. Slowly drizzle in the oil, until the dressing is emulsified. Add sugar and salt to taste. Let stand for 30 minutes.

2. Combine all the salad ingredients in a large salad bowl and toss with the dressing.

SERVES 8

DRESSING

1 TABLESPOON DIJON-STYLE MUSTARD
3 CLOVES GARLIC, CRUSHED THROUGH A PRESS
¼ CUP FRESH LIME JUICE
2 TABLESPOONS WHITE WINE VINEGAR
1 TEASPOON CHILI POWDER
⅔ CUP VIRGIN OLIVE OIL
LARGE PINCH OF SUGAR, OR MORE TO TASTE
SALT AND FRESHLY GROUND BLACK PEPPER TO TASTE

SALAD

1 MEDIUM HEAD ROMAINE LETTUCE, WASHED, DRIED, AND CUT INTO BITE-SIZE PIECES
2 LARGE AVOCADOS, PEELED, PITTED, AND CUT INTO 1-INCH DICE
5 MEDIUM RIPE TOMATOES, CUT INTO LARGE DICE
1½ MEDIUM RED ONION, QUARTERED AND THINLY SLICED
1 CUP SLICED WELL-DRAINED CANNED HEARTS OF PALM
1 CUP ROASTED RED PEPPER STRIPS (FROM 4 MEDIUM PEPPERS) (PAGE 375)
1 CUP TORN CILANTRO LEAVES

Papaya:
The Fruit of Angels

During one of his voyages to the Caribbean, Columbus noted in his journal that the peaceful local Taíno Indians subsisted largely on a tree melon, which they called "the fruit of angels." He was referring to the papaya. Papaya can be as small as a pear or as large as a watermelon, weighing from $1/2$ to 20 pounds, its flesh hued from pale yellow to bright orange. The soft seeds inside are edible and can be crushed into a delicious salad dressing (page 117). Because both the fruit and the leaves contain a protein-digesting enzyme called "papain," many tropical cooks use green papaya as a meat tenderizer, and use the leaves as an edible wrapper for baked food.

Enjoy papaya in salads and salsas; puree it with some water, buttermilk, or cold chicken stock into refreshing cold soups; blend it with yogurt or milk to make tropical shakes; bake slices of it with poultry or firm-fleshed fish; or add it mashed to cake batter, much as you would grated cooked carrot or sweet potato. Papaya is quite bland, so remember to add a squeeze of lemon or lime to bring its lovely taste to life. And if you encounter a green papaya, bring it home and grate it into a delicious slaw.

Avocado and Papaya Salad

(ENSALADA DE AGUACATE Y PAPAYA)

Avocado and papaya are happy tropical partners in this refreshing salad, which can be served alongside many of the hearty stews and casseroles in this book.

1. Peel and halve the papaya, and scoop out the seeds, reserving 1 tablespoon of the seeds for the vinaigrette. Cut the papaya into thin slices.

2. In a large bowl, toss the baby greens and watercress with half the vinaigrette. Arrange the greens on a large serving platter. Arrange the slices of papaya, avocado, onion, and pepper attractively on the greens and pour the remaining vinaigrette over them.

1 SMALL RIPE BUT FIRM PAPAYA
   (ABOUT ½ POUND)
7 CUPS TORN MIXED BABY GREENS
1 SMALL BUNCH WATERCRESS, RINSED AND
   DRIED, TOUGH STEMS REMOVED
PAPAYA SEED VINAIGRETTE (RECIPE FOLLOWS)
2 SMALL RIPE BUT FIRM HAAS AVOCADOS,
   PEELED, HALVED, PITTED, AND SLICED
1 SMALL RED ONION, THINLY SLICED
1 SMALL RED BELL PEPPER, CORED, SEEDED,
   AND THINLY SLICED

SERVES 8

1 TABLESPOON PAPAYA SEEDS (RESERVED FROM
   ABOVE)
2 TEASPOONS DIJON-STYLE MUSTARD
1 SMALL CLOVE GARLIC, CHOPPED
¼ TEASPOON GROUND CUMIN
½ TEASPOON MILD PAPRIKA
SALT AND FRESHLY GROUND BLACK PEPPER, TO TASTE
2 TABLESPOONS FRESH LIME JUICE
2 TABLESPOONS WHITE WINE VINEGAR
2 TEASPOONS HONEY
⅓ CUP LIGHT OLIVE OIL

Papaya Seed Vinaigrette

Combine all the ingredients except the oil in a food processor and process into a coarse puree. Drizzle in the oil through the feed tube until the dressing is emulsified. Let stand for 15 minutes.

MAKES ABOUT ½ CUP

Fiesta!
117

Brazilian Chicken Rainbow Salad

(SALPICÃO DE GALINHA)

Cheerfully colorful salads of cooked diced meats and cooked vegetables, often dressed with a thin coating of mayonnaise, are very popular in Latin America, where they are refered to as *salpicón*, or *salpicão* in Portuguese. This version, from central Brazil, is a particularly attractive combination of chicken, tender corn, beans, apples, raisins, and hearts of palm. The recipe comes from Dora, a cook from Ouro Prêto. She suggests using just enough mayonnaise to lightly coat the ingredients without obscuring their taste.

SALAD

2½ CUPS DICED COOKED SKINLESS CHICKEN
    BREAST
1⅓ CUPS COOKED CORN KERNELS (FROM 4
    LARGE EARS)
1½ CUPS CUT-UP COOKED GREEN BEANS
    (CUT INTO ½-INCH LENGTHS)
2 MEDIUM COOKED CARROTS, CUT INTO ¼-INCH
    DICE
1 LARGE RED BELL PEPPER, CORED, SEEDED,
    AND CUT INTO FINE DICE
1 SMALL RED ONION, FINELY CHOPPED
1 LARGE TART GREEN APPLE (SUCH AS GRANNY
    SMITH), PEELED, CORED, AND DICED
½ CUP DARK RAISINS
1 CUP CHOPPED WELL-DRAINED CANNED HEARTS
    OF PALM

DRESSING

ABOUT ⅓ CUP GOOD-QUALITY MAYONNAISE
6 TABLESPOONS FRESH LEMON JUICE
1 TABLESPOON WATER

SALT AND FRESHLY GROUND BLACK PEPPER, TO
    TASTE

1. To make the salad: Mix the salad ingredients in a large bowl.

2. To make the dressing: In a small bowl whisk together the mayonnaise, lemon juice, and water.

3. Toss the salad with the dressing and season with salt and pepper to taste.

SERVES 4 TO 5

Green Bean Salad with Lemon-Cumin Vinaigrette

(ENSALADA DE JUDÍAS VERDES CON SALSITA DE LIMÓN AMARILLO Y COMINO)

Cumin, which the South Americans inherited from the Arabs via the Iberian colonists, is one of the most widely used spices on the continent. This salad would be a fitting side dish for many of the heartier main courses in this book. In South America, green beans would not usually be cooked al dente, but suit your taste.

2 POUNDS GREEN BEANS, TRIMMED

1 LARGE RED ONION, QUARTERED AND THINLY SLICED

3 CLOVES GARLIC, CHOPPED

1/2 TEASPOON SALT

6 TABLESPOONS FRESH LEMON JUICE

1/4 CUP RED WINE VINEGAR

1/2 CUP OLIVE OIL (DO NOT USE VIRGIN OR EXTRA-VIRGIN)

1 1/2 TEASPOONS GROUND CUMIN

PINCH OF HOT RED PEPPER FLAKES

2/3 CUP TORN CILANTRO LEAVES

1. Bring a large pot of salted water to a boil. Drop the green beans in the water and cook to desired doneness, about 5 minutes for al dente, 8 minutes for softer beans. Drain in a colander and refresh under cold running water. Cool.

2. Place the beans in a large bowl and toss with the onion.

3. In a mortar and pestle, mash the garlic to a paste with the salt. Transfer to a mixing bowl and whisk in the lemon juice and vinegar. Slowly whisk in the oil until the dressing is emulsified. Stir in the cumin and red pepper flakes.

4. Toss the beans with the dressing, cover with foil, and refrigerate for at least 4 hours or overnight.

5. Just before serving, stir in the cilantro.

SERVES 4 TO 6

Yuca and Chorizo Salad with Chilpotle Dressing

(ENSALADA DE YUCA CON CHORIZO)

To a Latin cook, pleasingly bland starchy yuca is a blank canvas for inspiration. In this salad, from my Colombian friend Piedad, it's skillfully combined with sautéed *chorizo*, red onion, and herbs to produce a great picnic salad, similar to American potato and ham salads. In fact, the *chorizo* can be replaced with diced smoky ham, sautéed bacon, or another sausage, such as Portuguese *linguiça* or kielbasa. Use good-quality cooked *chorizo* sausage and drain it well after cooking. The yuca can be served warm or cold. Halve the amount for smaller number of guests.

4 POUNDS FRESH YUCA, PEELED AS DIRECTED ON PAGE 79 AND CUT INTO 2-INCH LENGTHS

3 QUARTS COLD WATER

3 TABLESPOONS OLIVE OIL

2 CUPS SLICED DRY *CHORIZO* SAUSAGE

2 CLOVES GARLIC, CRUSHED THROUGH A PRESS

1½ CUPS DICED RED ONIONS

½ CUP DICED RED BELL PEPPER

½ CUP DICED GREEN BELL PEPPER

¾ CUP GOOD-QUALITY MAYONNAISE

1 LARGE CANNED CHILPOTLE CHILE, PACKED IN *ADOBO*, DRAINED

3 TABLESPOONS WHITE WINE VINEGAR

1½ TABLESPOONS DIJON-STYLE MUSTARD

¼ TEASPOON SUGAR

3 TABLESPOONS WATER

SALT AND FRESHLY GROUND BLACK PEPPER, TO TASTE

½ CUP THINLY SLICED SCALLION GREENS

1. In a large saucepan, combine the yuca with 3 quarts cold salted water and bring to a boil. Cook over low heat until the yuca is tender, about 25 minutes. Let the yuca cool in the liquid.

2. While the yuca is cooking, heat 1 tablespoon of the oil in a large skillet. Sauté the *chorizo* slices on all sides over medium heat until cooked but not browned, about 5 minutes total. With a slotted spoon, transfer the *chorizo* to a double thickness of paper towels to drain.

3. With a slotted spoon, remove the yuca to a bowl. When just cool enough to handle, cut the yuca in half lengthwise. As you are cutting the yuca, remove the tough stringy fibers with a small sharp knife. Cut the yuca into 1-inch cubes.

4. In a large bowl, toss the yuca with the *chorizo*, garlic, onions, bell peppers, and the remaining olive oil.

5. In a blender, combine the mayonnaise, chilpotle, vinegar, mustard, sugar, and water and blend until smooth.

6. Toss the salad with the dressing. Season with salt and pepper and garnish with scallions.

SERVES 8 TO 10

Rice, Artichoke, and Lima Bean Salad with Green Dressing

(ENSALADA DE ARROZ, HABAS, Y ALCACHOFAS CON SALSA VERDE)

An ideal salad for a large party—full of color and zest, yet inexpensive and simple to make. This is a vegetarian version, but it would also taste great if you decided to add some poached shrimp, chicken, or calamari. This recipe will serve 12 at a buffet, but you can halve it for fewer people.

5 CUPS WATER

3 CUPS LONG-GRAIN RICE

TWO 6½-OUNCE JARS MARINATED ARTICHOKE HEARTS WITH THEIR LIQUID

ONE 16-OUNCE CAN GREEN LIMA BEANS, DRAINED

18 PIMIENTO-STUFFED OLIVES, SLICED

1½ CUPS CHOPPED DRAINED CANNED HEARTS OF PALM

ONE 6½-OUNCE JAR PIMIENTOS

2 CUPS CHOPPED RED ONIONS

6 MEDIUM RIPE TOMATOES, DICED

2 MEDIUM RED BELL PEPPERS, CORED, SEEDED, AND DICED

SALT AND FRESHLY GROUND BLACK PEPPER, TO TASTE

1 LARGE BUNCH CILANTRO, TRIMMED AND CHOPPED

½ CUP CHOPPED FLAT-LEAF PARSLEY

½ CUP FRESH LEMON JUICE

¼ CUP RED WINE VINEGAR

1¼ CUPS VIRGIN OLIVE OIL

1. In a large saucepan, bring 5 cups of salted water to a boil. Add the rice and cook, uncovered, over medium heat, stirring twice, until the liquid is almost absorbed and air bubbles appear on the surface of the rice, about 5 minutes. Reduce the heat to low, cover, and cook until the rice is tender, about 12 minutes. Remove from the heat and let stand, covered, for 20 minutes. Fluff the rice with a fork and transfer it to a large mixing bowl.

2. While the rice is still warm, chop the artichokes and stir them into the rice together with their liquid. Stir in the lima beans, olives, hearts of palm, pimientos, onions, tomatoes, and bell peppers. Season with salt and pepper.

3. In a blender, blend the cilantro, parsley, lemon juice, and vinegar. Drizzle in the oil, blending until well combined.

4. Toss the dressing into the salad gently but thoroughly. Taste and correct the seasoning. Serve immediately or refrigerate for several hours.

SERVES 10 TO 12 AS PART OF A BUFFET

Fish and Seafood

FEW GASTRONOMIC experiences are more intensely local and uniquely pleasurable than a meal of perfectly cooked just-caught seafood. Such feasts linger in our memory like precious souvenirs of the senses.

I close my eyes and transport myself to my favorite fishing places. I can almost taste the meaty *machas* (Chilean razor clams), which turn a vibrant bright pink when cooked; I imagine myself enjoying a platter of ethereal fried Spanish *angulas* (baby eels) or biting into Galician goose barnacles so juicy their liquid bursts out in a miniature explosion. In my mind I slowly savor the intriguingly delicate hake cheeks so prized by the Basques, or a simple feast of Portuguese grilled sardines, smelling sweetly of the sea. I picture myself at the fish market of Valparaíso, Chile, prying sea urchins straight out of their prickly shells and devouring them with a sprinkling of lemon juice and minced onion. My mind flicks from the extraordinary *cebiches* of Peru, to tender sweet Portuguese clams in a cilantro-scented broth. My imagination lingers on the remarkable squid-ink-black seafood rices and noodles of Catalonia.

Returning to reality, I realize it's almost impossible to choose my favorite seafood meal. Perhaps it was in the fishing village of Castro Urdiales on the Cantabrian coast of Spain. The restaurant was Mesón Marinero and the meal consisted of briny home-cured anchovies, which came in many guises; snails cooked in smoky chile sauce; an earthy fisherman's stew of lobster and buttery yellow local potatoes; a huge crab called *centolla*; and a garlicky mélange of roasted hake, hake cheeks, and large meaty mushrooms called *setas*, all perfumed with a shower of fruity olive oil and a flourish of minced parsley. The dishes kept arriving in a steady procession, our waiter murmuring sweetly "*una cosita más*" ("just one more").

In Spain and Portugal, seafood is most often prepared with the simplicity and respect its quality demands. Frying and grilling are still the preferred methods, and the accompaniments are often nothing more than a squeeze of lemon or a delicate and simple *salsa verde*. For occasions when the catch of the day has to be stretched to feed a crowd, there are various fisherman's stews, casseroles, and soups, thin or thick, robust or delicate—Castilian casseroles of shellfish and white beans; Basque tuna and potato stew; Portuguese *caldeiradas* in vigorous tomato sauces; Catalan seafood stews called *suquets*, enriched by a *picada* of ground almonds, parsley, and garlic.

I also love the Latin American and Caribbean way with fish and seafood—the endless choice of soupy fish stews: *sancochos* and *ensopados*, *chupes*, *moquecas*, and *mariscadas*. These dishes are the inspiration for some of my favorite seafood recipes in this chapter—laced with flamboyant tropical accents from northeastern Brazil, the Caribbean, or the balmy northern coast of Colombia. If you can't bring back the fish itself, you can at least enjoy the context in which it's served. With their touch of mellow coconut milk, tropical fruit, perky accents of cilantro, fragrant tang of sour orange juice, bright red touch of annatto, or heat of chile—these dishes will startle and surprise even the most jaded palate.

Dada's Zesty Baked Snapper in Banana Leaves

(PEIXE ASSADO, TEMPERO DE DADA)

Here is a recipe for snapper from Dada's famous restaurant in Salvador, Bahia. She bakes it in a banana leaf, but if you can't get banana leaves (found frozen at Latin groceries and some supermarkets), use foil instead.

1. Preheat the oven to 500 degrees F.

2. Make five deep slits diagonally on each side of the fish. Rub the fish with the salt, pepper, and lemon juice and stuff the garlic and cilantro into the slits.

3. In a food processor, process the tomatoes, bell pepper, onion, and peppercorns with the wine and oil, using on/off pulses, until crushed but not pureed.

4. Lay the fish on two overlapping banana leaves and spread the tomato mixture under and over it. Wrap the leaves tightly around the fish, so it is completely enclosed. Tie a piece of kitchen string around the fish, and place it on a baking tray. (Alternatively you can wrap the fish in foil.) Bake for 35 minutes.

5. Carefully transfer the fish to a serving platter, discard the kitchen string, and unwrap the parcel.

1 RED SNAPPER (ABOUT 4 POUNDS), SCALED AND CLEANED, HEAD AND TAIL LEFT ON
1 TEASPOON COARSE (KOSHER) SALT
1 TEASPOON FRESHLY GRATED BLACK PEPPER
1 TABLESPOON FRESH LEMON JUICE
4 CLOVES GARLIC, CRUSHED THROUGH A PRESS
3 TABLESPOONS FINELY CHOPPED CILANTRO
3 MEDIUM RIPE TOMATOES, SEEDED AND CHOPPED
1 LARGE GREEN BELL PEPPER, CORED, SEEDED, AND CHOPPED
1/2 CUP CHOPPED RED ONION
2 1/2 TABLESPOONS GREEN PEPPERCORNS PRESERVED IN BRINE, CRUSHED
1/4 CUP DRY RED WINE
1 1/2 TABLESPOONS FRUITY OLIVE OIL
2 LARGE BANANA LEAVES, THAWED IF FROZEN, AND TENDERIZED AS DIRECTED ON PAGE 380

SERVES 4, OR MORE AS PART OF A BUFFET

Fiesta!

Bahian Shrimp and Snapper Stew

(MOQUECA DE CAMARÃO)

For all their uniqueness, many Bahian dishes derive their flavor base from a typically Iberian seasoning mixture of finely diced onion, bell peppers, tomatoes, garlic, and olive oil, which Dada (see page 127) crushes in a wooden mortar before simmering it slowly with coconut milk. Serve this happy stew for a festive occasion with rice and a big green salad, and follow it with a platter of tropical fruit. I use annatto oil (which gives the dish its orange color) instead of the difficult-to-obtain and peculiarly flavored Bahian palm oil called *dendê*. *Moquecas* are Afro-Brazilian stews, flavored with coconut milk and palm oil, and they can be prepared with a range of ingredients. After you have tasted the snapper, try it with shrimp or lobster, crab, or chicken.

2 SMALL ONIONS, FINELY CHOPPED
5 MEDIUM TOMATOES, FINELY DICED
1 LARGE GREEN BELL PEPPER, CORED, SEEDED, AND DICED
6 CLOVES GARLIC, MINCED
2 TABLESPOONS OLIVE OIL
1 TEASPOON SALT
1½ POUNDS SKINLESS BONELESS RED SNAPPER FILLETS, CUT INTO 2-INCH PIECES
¼ TEASPOON TURMERIC
¼ TEASPOON CAYENNE, OR MORE TO TASTE
1 TEASPOON MILD PAPRIKA
FRESHLY GROUND BLACK PEPPER, TO TASTE
2 CUPS CANNED COCONUT MILK, WELL STIRRED
1 CUP FISH STOCK (PAGE 371), OR ⅔ CUP CLAM JUICE AND ⅓ CUP WATER
1½ POUNDS MEDIUM SHRIMP, PEELED AND DEVEINED
3 TABLESPOONS CHOPPED CILANTRO
1½ TABLESPOONS FRESH LEMON JUICE, OR MORE TO TASTE
DASH OF HOT SAUCE OF YOUR CHOICE, TO TASTE
1 TO 2 TABLESPOONS ANNATTO OIL (PAGE 376)
WHITE RICE (PAGE 247)

1. In a food processor, process the onions, tomatoes, pepper, and garlic with 1 tablespoon of the olive oil and 1 teaspoon of salt, using the on/off button, until the vegetables are crushed but not pureed. Reserve 2 tablespoons of the mixture.

2. Rub the fish with salt and turmeric and set aside.

3. In a large, heavy saucepan, combine all but the reserved 2 tablespoons of the processed mixture, the remaining 1 tablespoon of olive oil, the cayenne, paprika, and salt and pepper to taste, and simmer over low heat, stirring frequently, for 10 minutes until the mixture is thickened and reduced. Add the coconut milk and fish stock and continue simmering for another 10 minutes.

4. Add the fish and the rest of the processed mixture, and cook over low heat for 8 minutes until the fish is almost cooked. Stir in the shrimp and cook 4 more minutes.

5. Stir in the cilantro, lemon juice, hot sauce to taste, and the annatto oil. Serve with white rice.

SERVES 6

Dada's Seasoning

When I explained to Dada, an effervescent Afro-Brazilian lady with a bright yellow headscarf, that I wanted to spend a day in the kitchen of her restaurant watching her cook, she responded with a deep guttural laugh. Somehow it seemed even funnier than my invitation to dance *pagode* (the Bahian cousin of samba) in the main square. Her famous little restaurant, located in Pelourinho, the restored colonial center of Salvador, Bahia, is called Tempero de Dada—"Dada's seasoning." And it is her deft hand with the seasoning, she claims, that is the secret of her success. The other ingredient, she insists, is *alegria*, the explosion of laughter and affection with which she greets her clients.

A little girl growing up in the land of coconut plantations, Dada started cooking at the age of seven, sitting on a special high stool. As a teenager, she made a living catering for rich families in Salvador and dreaming of her own five-star restaurant. As she likes to put it, she settled for a little place with "one and a half stars" in the backyard of a small house. Before she knew it, the picture of her restaurant—with a clothesline stretched right across it, and Gilberto Gil and Caetano Veloso (Brazilian music kings) tucking into her food—was featured in a São Paulo gossip column. All of a sudden the whole town was at her doorstep, lining up for her tasty Bahian food—rich coconut stews, seafood soups, and signature fish grilled in banana leaves—until she moved to more spacious premises in the center of town.

Brazilian Bouillabaisse

(ENSOPADO DE FRUTAS DE MAR À PERNAMBUCANO)

It was in the spectacular colonial town of Olinda, in the state of Pernambuco in northeastern Brazil, that I tasted this robust Portuguese-influenced seafood stew.

It's a whole meal in a bowl, teeming with seafood, a host of vegetables—including whole baby potatoes and chayote—garnished, traditionally, with halved or quartered hard-cooked egg. Serve it with White Rice (page 247), and Watercress and Hearts of Palm Salad (page 113), with Coconut Blancmange with Prune Sauce (page 298) for dessert. The nicest way to serve this stew is in individual earthenware *cazuelas*, which have been warmed in the oven. However, soup plates or deep bowls will also do. I thank Chef Mauricio Andrade Carneiro for the recipe.

4 TABLESPOONS UNSALTED BUTTER

1 LARGE ONION, QUARTERED AND SLICED

4 CLOVES GARLIC, FINELY CHOPPED

2 GREEN BELL PEPPERS, CORED, SEEDED, AND DICED

2 MEDIUM CARROTS, PEELED AND CUT INTO ½-INCH DICE

1 MEDIUM CHAYOTE, PEELED, CORED, AND CUT INTO SMALL DICE

1 LARGE ZUCCHINI, CUT INTO ¾-INCH DICE

4 LARGE MEATY TOMATOES, BLANCHED, PEELED, SEEDED, AND CHOPPED

2 TEASPOONS MILD PAPRIKA

1½ TEASPOONS DRIED OREGANO

4 CUPS FISH STOCK (PAGE 371), OR 3 CUPS CLAM BROTH AND 1 CUP WATER

12 WHITE OR RED TINY NEW POTATOES, WELL SCRUBBED, OR 6 SLIGHTLY LARGER NEW POTATOES, HALVED

SALT AND FRESHLY GROUND BLACK PEPPER, TO TASTE

1½ POUNDS FIRM WHITE-FLESHED FISH FILLETS (SUCH AS SNAPPER, GROUPER, OR HALIBUT), CUT INTO 2-INCH CHUNKS

(continued)

1. In a large, heavy saucepan, melt the butter over medium heat. Add the onion, garlic, and peppers and cook, stirring, for 5 minutes until the onion wilts. Add the carrots, chayote, and zucchini; cover, and cook over low heat for 5 minutes, shaking the saucepan occasionally. Stir in the tomatoes, and cook until they are reduced to a puree, about 7 minutes.

Stir in the paprika and oregano. Add the stock and bring to a simmer. Add the potatoes and salt and pepper to taste, and cook, uncovered, over low heat, until the potatoes and chayote are tender, about 15 minutes.

2. While the liquid is cooking, place the fish, squid, shrimp, and the cooked octopus in separate bowls. Rub each with salt and pepper, and toss each with 1 tablespoon of the lemon juice.

3. Add the fish and octopus to the liquid and cook for 5 minutes, until opaque. Add the shrimp and cook for 1 minute. Add the squid and cook until just tender, about 2 minutes. Do not overcook the squid. Adjust the seasoning and add the scallions, parsley, and additional lemon juice, to taste.

4. Ladle the stew into bowls, garnish with hard-cooked egg and serve at once.

12 OUNCES CLEANED SQUID BODIES, CUT INTO
     RINGS
1 POUND MEDIUM SHRIMP, PEELED AND
     DEVEINED
1 POUND OCTOPUS, COOKED AS DIRECTED IN THE
     NOTE BELOW AND CUT INTO BITE-SIZE PIECES
4 TABLESPOONS FRESH LEMON JUICE, PLUS
     MORE TO TASTE
1/4 CUP SLICED SCALLION GREENS
1 SMALL BUNCH FLAT-LEAF PARSLEY, MINCED
3 HARD-COOKED EGGS, HALVED

SERVES 6

NOTE: Fish stores usually sell whole, frozen, cleaned octopus, weighing 2¹/₂ pounds or more. To cook, thaw the octopus thoroughly; cut off the tentacles and discard the head. Place the octopus pieces in a saucepan with cold water to cover, bring to a boil, add salt, and simmer, covered, over medium-low heat until tender. This should take 45 minutes or more, depending on the exact size of the octopus. Let the octopus cool in the liquid until manageable. Drain and rinse it under cold running water, wiping off the purple outer coating with a paper towel. While octopus is an important element of this dish, you can still have a good *ensopado* without it. If you have any octopus left over, toss it with some cooked white beans or cubed cooked potatoes, a simple vinaigrette, and a shower of parsley. Delicious!

Langosta Exquisita

For more dramatic results, this exotic northern Brazilian lobster dish should be passed under a broiler or salamander to make the top golden and bubbly before serving. The dish will still taste great, however, without this step.

2 LIVE LOBSTERS (ABOUT 1¼ POUNDS EACH)

1 SMALL COCONUT, CRACKED AS DIRECTED ON PAGE 10

1 TABLESPOON OLIVE OIL

¾ CUP FINELY CHOPPED ONION

3 CLOVES GARLIC, MINCED

1 TABLESPOON GRATED FRESH GINGER

¼ TEASPOON GROUND TURMERIC

1 TEASPOON MILD PAPRIKA

½ TEASPOON CAYENNE

½ TEASPOON GROUND CORIANDER

4 MEDIUM RIPE TOMATOES, BLANCHED, PEELED, AND CHOPPED

2⅓ CUPS CANNED COCONUT MILK, WELL STIRRED

3 TABLESPOONS CHOPPED FLAT-LEAF PARSLEY

2 TABLESPOONS MINCED SCALLIONS

SALT AND FRESHLY GROUND BLACK PEPPER, TO TASTE

1. Rinse the lobsters under cold running water and remove the elastic bands from the claws. Bring a large saucepan of salted water to a boil. Lower the lobsters into the water, let it return to the boil, reduce the heat to low, and simmer for 6 to 7 minutes. Let the lobsters stand in the water for 2 minutes, then remove them to a large bowl with a slotted spoon. When cool enough to handle, working in a large strainer set over a bowl to catch the juices, break off the tails and claws, twist off and discard the bodies from the lobsters. Crack the claws and remove the meat, discarding the shells. Remove the meat from the tails and cut it into 1½-inch chunks. Place the lobster meat in the bowl with the lobster juices and set aside.

2. Preheat the oven to 400 degrees F. Using a mandoline peeler or a small sharp knife, slice off very thin strips of the coconut meat to measure about ⅓ cup. Discard the rest of the coconut or save it for making chips (page 32). Place the coconut strips on a baking sheet and bake until light golden, about 10 minutes. Reserve. Increase the oven temperature to 500 degrees.

3. In a medium-size, heavy saucepan, heat the oil over medium heat. Sauté the onion, garlic, and ginger, stirring, until the onion is translucent, about 5 minutes. Add the turmeric, paprika, cayenne, and coriander and stir for 2 minutes. Add the tomatoes and cook, stirring, for 7 to 8 minutes, until thickened and reduced. Stir in the coconut milk, bring to a simmer, and cook for 7 minutes. Stir in the lobster with the accumulated juices, the parsley, and the scallions. Season with salt and pepper.

4. Transfer the stew to a heatproof serving dish and bake until the top is light golden and bubbly, about 5 to 7 minutes. Remove from the oven, top with the toasted coconut strips, and serve at once.

SERVES 2

Tuna in Melting Onion Sauce

(BONITO ENCEBOLLADO)

A beautiful Basque dish of bonito tuna steaks slowly cooked with a melting onion and red pepper sauce. One of the secrets of Basque cuisine is cooking over low heat in an earthenware *cazuela* so that the heat is distributed slowly and evenly, giving the ingredients time to meld and blend without browning.

5 TABLESPOONS VIRGIN OLIVE OIL, PREFERABLY
    SPANISH

4 LARGE CLOVES GARLIC, SLICED

2 CUPS THINLY SLICED ONIONS

1 LARGE RED BELL PEPPER, THINLY SLICED

4 MEDIUM BONITO OR OTHER TUNA STEAKS,
    ABOUT 1 INCH THICK (ABOUT 1³/₄ POUNDS
    TOTAL)

SALT AND FRESHLY GROUND BLACK PEPPER, TO
    TASTE

FLOUR, FOR DUSTING THE FISH

¹/₄ CUP DRY WHITE WINE

¹/₂ CUP FISH STOCK (PAGE 371) OR BOTTLED
    CLAM JUICE

¹/₄ CUP MINCED FLAT-LEAF PARSLEY

1. In a large earthenware *cazuela* or a heavy (preferably enameled cast-iron) skillet, heat the oil with the garlic over medium-low heat. Add the onions and cook until soft, about 10 minutes, shaking the skillet from time to time. Add the bell pepper, and continue cooking over low heat until the onions and pepper are meltingly soft, about 17 minutes, without allowing them to brown. Add water, 1 tablespoon at a time if the mixture begins to stick.

2. Rub the tuna steaks with salt and dust them lightly with flour. Push the onions and pepper to the side of the skillet and add the tuna. Cook for about 6 minutes, until lightly browned, then turn and stir in the wine, stock, and parsley. Spoon the onions and peppers on the fish, season with salt and pepper, cover, and cook, shaking the skillet occasionally, until the tuna looks cooked through, when you flake it with a fork, about 6 minutes more.

SERVES 4

Basque Fisherman Tuna and Potato Stew

(MARMITAKO)

Traditionally, Basque seamen carried with them a supply of potatoes and prepared this classic stew on makeshift stoves with just-caught tuna during their long stints at sea. At home, they were greeted with more *marmitako*, and no one complained.

1. Soak the ancho chile in ½ cup hot water until soft, about 15 minutes. Tear it into pieces and puree it in a blender along with 3 tablespoons of the soaking liquid and the tomato paste.

2. In a heavy soup pot, heat the olive oil with the garlic over medium-low heat. Add the onion and bell peppers and cook, stirring, for 5 minutes. Add the potatoes, tomatoes, and the ancho chile paste, cover, and cook for 10 minutes, stirring once or twice, until the onions and peppers are soft but not browned. Add enough fish stock to barely cover the potatoes, bring to a simmer, season with salt and pepper, and cook until the potatoes are very tender, about 15 to 20 minutes.

3. Add the tuna and cook, shaking the pot, until the fish is just cooked through, about 5 to 7 minutes. Sprinkle with parsley and serve in soup bowls with toasted or grilled country bread.

SERVES 4 TO 6

1 LARGE ANCHO CHILE

½ CUP HOT WATER

2 TEASPOONS TOMATO PASTE

3 TABLESPOONS FRUITY VIRGIN OLIVE OIL, PREFERABLY SPANISH

3 LARGE CLOVES GARLIC, MINCED

1 SMALL ONION, CHOPPED

¾ CUP DICED RED BELL PEPPER

¾ CUP DICED GREEN BELL PEPPER

4 LARGE YELLOW POTATOES (SUCH AS YUKON GOLD), CUT INTO 1¾-INCH CUBES

2 RIPE MEDIUM TOMATOES, BLANCHED, PEELED, AND CHOPPED

ABOUT 2¾ CUPS FISH STOCK (PAGE 371), OR 2 CUPS BOTTLED CLAM BROTH AND ¾ CUP WATER

SALT AND FRESHLY GROUND BLACK PEPPER, TO TASTE

1½ POUNDS BONELESS BONITO OR OTHER TUNA, CUT INTO 1½-INCH CUBES

2 TO 3 TABLESPOONS CHOPPED FLAT-LEAF PARSLEY

Garlicky Hake, Clams, and Mushrooms with Parsley Sauce

(MERLUZA CON ALMEJAS Y SETAS EN SALSA VERDE)

If you can't find large meaty oyster mushrooms, which are an approximation of the Spanish *setas*, substitute sliced shiitake mushroom caps. Actually the star ingredient in the original dish is *kokotas*, highly prized and expensive hake cheeks. If you can find them, you can use fresh halibut cheeks, available in the beginning of summer in the Pacific Northwest. Use about 4 ounces, and they will take about 5 minutes to cook. Ideally this dish should be cooked on the stove top in a heatproof clay *cazuela*. Alternatively, use a heavy enameled cast-iron skillet.

1½ DOZEN SMALL CLAMS, SCRUBBED WELL UNDER COLD RUNNING WATER

2 TABLESPOONS COARSE (KOSHER) SALT

⅔ CUP WATER

¼ CUP FRUITY VIRGIN OLIVE OIL, PREFERABLY SPANISH

2 TABLESPOONS SLICED GARLIC

1½ POUNDS HAKE FILLETS, CUT INTO 6 EQUAL PIECES

FRESHLY GROUND BLACK PEPPER, TO TASTE

¼ CUP FLOUR

4 OUNCES LARGE MEATY OYSTER MUSHROOMS, TRIMMED AND HALVED

⅓ CUP DRY WHITE WINE

¼ CUP MINCED FLAT-LEAF PARSLEY

1. Place the clams in a large bowl, add 2 tablespoons of salt and enough cold water to cover them by 2 inches. Let stand for 1 hour. Drain.

2. In a large skillet, combine the clams with ⅔ cup of water, and bring to a boil. Cover and cook over medium heat, shaking the skillet, until the clams open, about 8 to 10 minutes. Set aside, discarding any clams that do not open.

3. In a large earthenware *cazuela*, or a heavy, enameled cast-iron skillet, heat the oil with the garlic over low heat for 5 minutes, until fragrant but not browned, stirring from time to time.

4. Rub the hake fillets with salt and pepper and roll them in the flour.

5. Add the mushrooms to the *cazuela* and cook, stirring, for 5 minutes. Add the fish and cook until done on one side, about 5 minutes. Turn over, stir in the wine, parsley, and clams with their liquid. Season with salt and pepper to taste. Raise the heat to medium-high and cook until the fish flakes easily when tested with a fork, about 5 minutes. Serve in the *cazuela*, if using it, or carefully transfer to a serving dish. Serve at once.

SERVES 4 TO 6

Market, Barcelona, Spain.

Portuguese Clams in Cilantro and Garlic Sauce

(ALMÊIJOAS BULHÃO PATO)

The coastline of Portugal boasts some of the tastiest shellfish in Europe, and this clam dish, called *Bulhão Pato* (after a nineteenth-century poet-gourmand), is a national classic. Like some of the world's most memorable seafood dishes, it is exceedingly simple: the clams are steamed in their own juice, allowing their sweet taste to stand on its own, then accented with a touch of garlic, lemon, and the earthy taste of cilantro. This dish is usually served in deep bowls with coarse country bread to sop up the juices.

3 DOZEN SMALL CLAMS
2 TABLESPOONS COARSE (KOSHER) SALT
1 1/2 TABLESPOONS GREEN FRUITY EXTRA-VIRGIN
    OLIVE OIL, PREFERABLY PORTUGUESE
3 SMALL CLOVES GARLIC, LIGHTLY SMASHED
1/2 CUP WATER
1/4 CUP MINCED CILANTRO LEAVES
1 TEASPOON GRATED FRESH LEMON ZEST
LEMON WEDGES, FOR SERVING

1. Place the clams in a large bowl, add the salt and enough cold water to cover them by 2 inches. Let stand for 1 hour.

2. Drain the clams and scrub the shells under cold running water.

3. In a large, heavy skillet, heat the oil with the garlic cloves over medium heat. Add the clams and 1/2 cup of water, cover, and steam the clams until they open, about 8 to 10 minutes, shaking the skillet from time to time. Discard any clams that do not open. Stir in the cilantro leaves and lemon zest and cook for 1 more minute.

4. Ladle the clams into soup plates, and serve, accompanied by lemon wedges and crusty peasant bread.

SERVES 3 AS A MAIN COURSE, OR 6 AS AN APPETIZER

Monkfish Gratin with All-i-oli

(RAP AL ALL-I-OLI)

Here, delicious baked monkfish is gratinéed with a Catalan national sauce called *all-i-oli* (or *alioli*), a garlicky mayonnaise, made by painstakingly blending garlic paste and olive oil. Try making it by hand, adding oil literally a drop at a time and whisking constantly. If your sauce breaks, do as the modern Catalan chefs do, use a blender. This dish was prepared for me by a Barcelona restaurateur, Ramón Parellada.

4 THICK PIECES OF BONELESS MONKFISH (ABOUT 6 OUNCES EACH)
3/4 TEASPOON COARSE (KOSHER) SALT
1 TABLESPOON CRACKED BLACK PEPPERCORNS
1 TABLESPOON PLUS 2 TEASPOONS FRUITY VIRGIN OLIVE OIL
3/4 CUP *ALL-I-OLI* (RECIPE FOLLOWS)
1 LARGE BUNCH FRESH SPINACH, STEMMED, RINSED, AND DRIED

1. Preheat the oven to 475 degrees F.

2. Rub the fish with the salt and pepper and place in a small baking dish. Brush it with 1 tablespoon of the olive oil and bake for 10 minutes.

3. Dab about 2 tablespoons of the *all-i-oli* on each fish fillet, return the fish to the oven, and bake until the top is deep golden and bubbly, 7 to 8 minutes.

4. While the fish is browning, heat the remaining 2 teaspoons of the oil in a large skillet. Add the spinach and cook over high heat until wilted, 4 to 5 minutes.

5. To serve, divide the spinach among four plates and top with a fish fillet.

SERVES 4

All-i-oli

4 MEDIUM CLOVES GARLIC, MINCED
¼ TEASPOON SALT
1 SMALL EGG
¾ CUP FRUITY EXTRA-VIRGIN OLIVE OIL,
     PREFERABLY SPANISH

With a mortar and pestle, crush the garlic with the salt to a fine paste. Transfer to a small bowl and whisk in the egg. Whisking constantly, add the oil, drop by drop, making sure each addition is thoroughly incorporated before adding the next. Or, you can transfer the pounded garlic and egg to a blender, and, with the motor running, very slowly drizzle in the oil until it is emulsified. The *all-i-oli* will be quite thick. Scrape it into a small bowl or a jar with a lid. *All-i-oli* will keep in the refrigerator for up to 4 days.

MAKES ABOUT ¾ CUP

Market, Barcelona, Spain.

Marinated Peruvian Swordfish Brochettes

In Peru, the word *anticucho* refers to the unbelievably tasty skewers of beef heart—marinated in cumin, garlic, chile, and vinegar—grilled on braziers on most street corners. However, *anticuchos* are also made with chicken or meaty fish, such as bonito or swordfish.

1. Soak eight short bamboo skewers in cold water for 1 hour.

2. With a mortar and pestle, pound the garlic and salt to a paste. (Alternatively, you can crush the garlic in a press and stir it into the salt.) Transfer the mixture to a glass bowl and add the cumin, paprika, chile, lemon juice, and vinegar. Add the fish, toss to coat it with the mixture, and marinate for 30 minutes in the refrigerator. Remove the fish from the marinade and shake off the excess. Reserve the marinade.

6 LARGE CLOVES GARLIC, CHOPPED
½ TEASPOON SALT
1 TEASPOON GROUND CUMIN
1 TEASPOON SWEET MILD PAPRIKA
1 SMALL DRIED RED CHILE, CRUMBLED
2 TABLESPOONS FRESH LEMON JUICE
1½ TABLESPOONS DISTILLED WHITE VINEGAR
1 POUND BONELESS 1-INCH-THICK SWORDFISH
    STEAKS, CUT INTO 1-INCH CUBES
1 TABLESPOON OLIVE OIL
2 TABLESPOONS ANNATTO OIL (PAGE 376)

3. Prepare coals for grilling or preheat the broiler. Thread the fish on the skewers and brush it with the olive oil. Grill until the fish is lightly charred and cooked through, 4 to 5 minutes per side.

4. While the fish is grilling, place the reserved marinade in a small skillet with the annatto oil, and set it over medium heat until it sizzles, about 3 minutes.

5. Remove the fish from the grill, brush with the hot marinade mixture, and serve at once.

SERVES 4 AS A LIGHT SUPPER, OR 8 AS AN APPETIZER

Brazilian Carnival:
The Greatest Spectacle on Earth

The pre-Lenten Carnival is celebrated by many cultures, but anyone who has experienced the delirious fervor and dazzling ostentation of the Brazilian *Carnaval* will agree that it's the greatest spectacle on earth, a party to end them all. The Carnival tradition itself dates to the decadent Ancient Roman winter festivities called Saturnalias. The hallmark of Saturnalias, which was to become the emblem of the Carnival, was the celebrated reversal of traditional social hierarchies and sex roles: paupers got to be rich, slaves turned into masters, and men dressed up as women—one time a year. Like many Catholic festivities that were born out of pre-Christian traditions, this pagan feast was appropriated by the Catholic Church and made to coincide with the period immediately preceding Lent, thus offering the devout a last opportunity to feast, drink, and be merry before the 40 days of restrictions imposed by Lent.

The *Carnaval* of Brazil is a creative fusion of various festivities—the Catholic Three Kings celebration, medieval shepherd's plays, and festive African folk pageants, the last cleverly adopted by the Portuguese Catholic clergy to offer slaves on the sugar plantations a momentary break from the hardships of everyday life. Over the years, the Brazilian *Carnaval*, with its elaborately symbolic costumes and music, evolved (and is still evolving) into a complex whole, an appropriation of sacred and secular traditions from three continents.

From Thursday noon to the dawn of Ash Wednesday, all other activities in Rio are suspended, and Cariocas pour into the streets, dancing to the orgiastic beat of thousands of drums until, quite literally, everyone drops. Beyond its anarchic appearance, however, the famous *Carnaval* of Rio is a carefully staged event, governed by the complex hierarchies and fierce competition of the neighborhood associations known as *escolas de samba* (samba schools). Months of rehearsals and frantic preparations culminate in the *desfile*, the spectacular parade of the samba schools.

The organization of the Rio Carnival is beyond baroque in its complexity. The samba schools are divided into three groups, the first group comprised of twelve schools, with 2,500 participants, the second group of eighteen, and the third of fourteen, each with a lesser number of participants. There are also parades of other, smaller organizations: *blocos* (blocks), groups of *frêvo* (a genre of music from the northeast), and *banhos de mar à fantasia* (costumed baths by the sea). The *Carnaval* is not only a show but a sport, a contest, the grand finale of which is the announcement of the winner. For each year's Carnival, each samba school invents a theme, reflected in its costumes, dances, and the decoration of its floats. The same is true for the music. Each school issues an outpouring of new songs, which blast from every radio in town before and after the *Carnaval*. The successful ones go on to become Brazil's newest hits.

To experience a real grass-roots street Carnival (which the Brazilians call "Carnival of Participation"), one has to travel to the northeast, to the state of Pernambuco, or to Bahia, Brazil's resplendent former capital and the cradle of Afro-Brazilian popular culture. In the uniquely eclectic world of Bahia, African deities double as Catholic saints, and the music, costumes, and dance are hybrids of European traditions and the rich cultural and religious heritage of the slaves. During *Carnaval*, people of the street, dressed in bizarre fanciful costumes, dance behind decorated trucks, equipped with enormous loudspeakers and bands of drummers and string players known as *tríos eléctricos*, filling the streets with spectacular, otherworldly levels of noise. The music, unlike the carioca samba, is a mix of northeastern genres, such as *frêvo* and *passo*, and other African- and Caribbean-influenced beats.

Most Brazilian feasts, especially those of African origin, feature food prominently, but not the Carnival, which is the antithesis of a cozy family holiday. The foods that fare best at this frantic time are take-out affairs, mostly pizza or lasagna. After all, the word Carnival is derived from the Latin *carne vale*, which means "farewell to flesh," or, more literally, "take away the meat."

Salt Cod in a Shirt

(BACALHAU DE CASACA)

I tasted this heavenly hash of salt-dried fish, plantain, and olives, moistened with coconut milk, at a small family restaurant in the balmy Brazilian town of Manaus, on the banks of the Amazon. There it was prepared with a meaty salted Amazonian fish called *pirarucu* (for which I substitute salt cod), and named *pirarucu de casaca*, "*pirarucu* in a shirt"—I suppose because the fish was "clothed" in a layer of sautéed pepper, plantain, olives, and tomatoes. And, by the way, the recipe also works beautifully with a fresh white, flaky fish, such as haddock or cod.

6 TABLESPOONS OLIVE OIL

1 MEDIUM-RIPE PLANTAIN (ABOUT 8 OUNCES), PEELED AS DIRECTED ON PAGE 379 AND CUT DIAGONALLY INTO ¼-INCH-THICK SLICES

1½ POUNDS SALT COD, SOAKED AS DIRECTED ON PAGE 377

1 LARGE ONION, HALVED AND SLICED

2 CLOVES GARLIC, MINCED

1 LARGE GREEN BELL PEPPER, CORED, SEEDED, AND THINLY SLICED

2 TEASPOONS FLOUR

⅔ CUP FISH STOCK (PAGE 371), SLIGHTLY DILUTED BOTTLED CLAM BROTH, OR WATER

4 CANNED TOMATOES, DRAINED AND CHOPPED

8 PIMIENTO-STUFFED OLIVES, EACH CUT INTO 3 PIECES

⅔ CUP GREEN PEAS, FRESH OR FROZEN AND THAWED

2 TABLESPOONS CHOPPED FLAT-LEAF PARSLEY

2 TABLESPOONS THINLY SLICED SCALLIONS

¼ CUP CANNED COCONUT MILK, WELL STIRRED

1. In a large, nonstick skillet, heat 2 tablespoons of the oil over medium-high heat. Fry the plantain slices until soft and golden, about 5 minutes. With a slotted spoon, transfer them to drain on paper towels.

2. Pat dry the salt cod with paper towels and cut it into 6 to 8 pieces. Add the remaining 4 tablespoons of oil to the skillet and heat it over very low heat. Add the salt cod and sauté gently for about 7 minutes, until it flakes easily. With

a slotted spoon, transfer the fish to drain on paper towels. Drain all but 2 tablespoons of the oil from the skillet.

3. Preheat the oven to 350 degrees F.

4. Reheat the oil over medium heat and add the onion, garlic, and bell pepper to the skillet. Sauté, stirring, until the onion is soft, about 10 minutes. Add the flour and stir for 1 minute. Slowly stir in the fish stock, stirring until the sauce thickens. Stir in the tomatoes and olives and cook the sauce another 5 to 7 minutes, stirring occasionally, until the tomatoes thicken. Add the peas and cook 2 minutes longer. Stir in the parsley and scallions.

5. Arrange half the onion mixture and half the plantain slices on the bottom of a shallow heatproof casserole, preferably earthenware. Arrange the salt cod on top, then spread the rest of the onion mixture and sliced plantain over the fish. Drizzle the coconut milk over and around the fish. Bake until the salt cod is cooked through, and the top is bubbly, about 35 minutes. Serve, accompanied by rice.

SERVES 6

Mussels and Clams in Coconut-Sour Orange Broth

(SANCOCHO DE ALMEJAS Y MEJILLONES CON LECHE DE COCO)

This dish is inspired by Colombian seafood *sancochos* (soup-stews), especially those from the Caribbean coast, where they are prepared with a touch of coconut milk. In Colombia, coconut *sancochos* contain tropical tubers, such as yuca and plantains, but a more elegant preparation is simply to serve the seafood in the coconut broth, flavored with chiles and sour orange juice, and to accompany it with crusty bread or white rice to soak up the juices. It makes a truly special meal, vivid with tropical flavors. You can serve it as an appetizer or a light main course. Traditionally, the mussels and clams are cooked in the spiced broth, but I prefer to cook them separately to avoid having sand in the broth. Accompany the dish with crusty bread or white rice.

3 CUPS FISH STOCK (PAGE 371), OR 2 CUPS BOTTLED CLAM JUICE AND 1 CUP WATER

2 POUNDS SMALL MUSSELS, WELL CLEANED AND BEARDED JUST BEFORE USING

2 POUNDS LITTLENECK CLAMS, SCRUBBED WELL

3 TABLESPOONS UNSALTED BUTTER

1 LARGE ONION, QUARTERED AND SLICED

2 TABLESPOONS MINCED GARLIC

1 SMALL RED BELL PEPPER, CORED, SEEDED, AND SLICED

1 SMALL GREEN BELL PEPPER, CORED, SEEDED, AND SLICED

6 LARGE MEATY PLUM TOMATOES, BLANCHED, PEELED, SEEDED, AND CUT INTO STRIPS

2 CUPS CANNED COCONUT MILK, WELL STIRRED

1 CUP WATER

1 TO 2 MEDIUM DRIED RED CHILES, SEEDED

SALT AND FRESHLY GROUND BLACK PEPPER, TO TASTE

2 TEASPOONS GRATED LIME ZEST

2 TO 3 TABLESPOONS FRESH SOUR ORANGE JUICE (OR A COMBINATION OF LIME AND FRESH ORANGE JUICE)

(continued)

1. In a large saucepan, bring 1½ cups of the fish stock to a simmer over medium-high heat. Add the mussels, cover, and cook, shaking occasionally, until the mussels open, about 5 minutes. With a slotted spoon, remove the mussels from the cooking liquid, discarding any unopened ones.

2. Add the clams to the cooking liquid, cover, and cook, shaking the pan occasionally, until the clams open, about 7 minutes. With a slotted spoon remove the clams from the cooking liquid and reserve. Discard any clams that do not open.

3 TABLESPOONS FINELY SLICED SCALLION GREENS
3 TABLESPOONS MINCED FLAT-LEAF PARSLEY

3. Strain the cooking liquid through a damp cheesecloth into a bowl.

4. In a large, heavy saucepan, heat the butter over medium heat. Add the onion and garlic and cook for 5 minutes. Add the red and green peppers and cook, stirring, for another 5 minutes. Reduce the heat to low, add the tomatoes and cook, shaking the pan occasionally, for 10 minutes, until all the vegetables are softened. Stir in the mussel and clam cooking liquid, the remaining fish stock, the coconut milk, and the water, and bring to a simmer.

5. Toast the chiles in a dry skillet until they turn several shades darker. Add them to the liquid. Season the liquid with salt and pepper and simmer for 5 minutes. Add the lime zest and the sour orange juice. Add the reserved mussels and clams and cook, shaking the pan, to heat through. Add the scallions and parsley.

6. Divide the shellfish and liquid among 4 heated bowls and serve.

SERVES 4

Sour Orange

The sour orange (*naranja agria*) is a large, uncouth-looking orange with bumpy skin, lots of seeds, and orangy-yellow flesh. You wouldn't want to eat it like a fruit, but its juice (highly prized in the Spanish Caribbean and other Latin countries) is aromatic, tangy, and refreshing—excellent for marinades or for dressing starchy tubers, salads, and seafood. It is sold at many Hispanic markets. If unavailable, substitute equal parts of fresh lime and fresh orange juice.

Chilean Salmon and Citrus Escabeche

(ESCABECHE DE SALMÓN)

Ironically, while Chile boasts a phenomenal variety of native fish and seafood, it is the farmed salmon (originally brought over from Scotland) that has become one of its best-known exports. More than simply a recipe, *escabeche* is an ancient Iberian method of preserving fish and fowl in vinegar and oil. When Chileans don't enjoy their salmon prepared in a European manner (which they most often do), they are likely to turn it into this *nuevo chileno escabeche*, a lovely dish for a summer luncheon.

1¼ POUNDS BONELESS SKINLESS SALMON
   FILLETS, CUT INTO 1½-INCH PIECES
SALT AND FRESHLY GROUND BLACK PEPPER, TO
   TASTE
FLOUR, FOR DUSTING THE FISH
2 TABLESPOONS PLUS ½ CUP GOOD OLIVE OIL
7 TABLESPOONS FRESH ORANGE JUICE
7 TABLESPOONS FRESH LIME JUICE
⅓ CUP RED WINE VINEGAR
¼ CUP FISH STOCK (PAGE 371), BOTTLED CLAM
   BROTH, OR WATER
2 SMALL BAY LEAVES
6 SMALL CLOVES GARLIC, SMASHED
12 BLACK PEPPERCORNS, LIGHTLY CRUSHED
¾ CUP THINLY SLICED RED ONION
1 SMALL RED BELL PEPPER, CORED, SEEDED,
   AND THINLY SLICED
1 LONG MILD GREEN CHILE (SUCH AS ANAHEIM),
   THINLY SLICED
1 SMALL ORANGE, SCRUBBED, HALVED, AND
   VERY THINLY SLICED
BOSTON LETTUCE LEAVES, FOR GARNISH
CILANTRO LEAVES, FOR GARNISH

1. Rub the fish generously with salt and pepper and dust it lightly with flour. In a large skillet, heat 2 tablespoons of the oil over medium heat. Add the fish and saute it until very light golden on all sides, about 3 minutes per side. Do not overcook it.

2. In a nonreactive saucepan, combine the orange and lime juices, the vinegar, fish stock, bay leaves, garlic, and peppercorns and bring to a simmer over medium heat. Off the heat, stir in the remaining ½ cup of olive oil, and let the marinade cool to warm.

3. Choose a narrow earthenware covered crock or a lidded glass jar. Place a layer of salmon in the crock, top with some red onion, bell pepper, chile, and orange slices, and pour in some of the marinade. Continue layering the ingredients until all the salmon and vegetables are used up. Pour the remaining marinade into the crock and cover. The fish actually doesn't need to be refrigerated at this point, but you can chill it if you wish. It will be ready after about 6 hours, but will taste better the next day. If the fish is not totally submerged in the marinade, carefully toss it every 2 hours or so, so that the pieces of fish that were at the bottom end up on top. The fish will keep for up to a week in the refrigerator.

4. When ready to serve, discard the bay leaves. Arrange the fish, vegetables, and orange slices on a glass serving dish on a bed of lettuce, and sprinkle with the cilantro leaves.

SERVES 6 AS A LIGHT SALAD OR A FIRST COURSE

Fish café, near
Valparaíso, Chile.

Seared Shrimp Ceviche

In Peru, *ceviche* (there, spelled *cebiche*) comes in myriad varieties, not always with fish, and not always raw. Here, large shrimp are seared in a cast-iron skillet and tossed with the traditional *ceviche* marinade of citrus juices, chiles, red onions, and cilantro. *¡Delicioso!*

1 TABLESPOON OLIVE OIL

1 POUND LARGE SHRIMP, PEELED AND
   DEVEINED, TAILS LEFT ON

¼ CUP FRESH LIME JUICE

3 TABLESPOONS FRESH ORANGE JUICE

2 CLOVES GARLIC, CRUSHED THROUGH A PRESS

½ CUP THINLY SLICED RED BELL PEPPER

1 JALAPEÑO CHILE, SEEDED AND THINLY SLICED

1 SMALL RED ONION, HALVED AND SLICED
   PAPER-THIN

½ CUP TIGHTLY PACKED CILANTRO LEAVES

SALT AND FRESHLY GROUND BLACK PEPPER TO
   TASTE

In a cast-iron skillet or a wok, heat the oil over high heat until almost smoking. Working in batches, sear the shrimp on all sides until just cooked through, about 5 minutes total per batch. Replace all the shrimp in the skillet and toss with all the remaining ingredients. Serve immediately.

SERVES 4 AS A LIGHT MEAL

Cebiche

Peruvian food historians like nothing better than to argue about the origins of *cebiche* (or *ceviche*). It could have arrived from Polynesia with the fearless sailors who crossed the Pacific in their canoes. Or perhaps it was introduced by the Spanish, who in turn inherited the Arab tradition of macerating fish in sour citrus juices. Yet the Andean pre-Columbian Indians also marinated raw fish in fizzy *chicha* (corn beer) or tart passion fruit juice—and served it, accompanied by boiled corn and seaweed.

But whatever the origins, the Peruvians certainly made *cebiche* their own, cooking up a staggering variety of this delicacy. While *corvina* (delicate local sea bass) is classic, meaty local mussels, giant shrimp, octopus and squid, unique black clams; or even vegetables and duck, are just some of the other choices. I had an extraordinary *cebiche* in Lima, prepared by a Chinese-Peruvian cook, Xavier Wong. So fresh was the fish, and so precise the preparation, it could have rivaled the best Japanese sashimi.

Making raw fish *cebiche* is extremely simple. Start with a pound of impeccably fresh raw fish—such as tuna, sea bass, flounder, or red snapper—cut into $1/2$-inch cubes or into very thin slices. Place the fish in a glass or ceramic bowl, massage it lightly with about $1/2$ teaspoon of coarse (kosher) salt, and toss it with $1/3$ cup fresh lime juice and $1/3$ cup of fresh orange juice. To that basic marinade you can add chopped fresh chiles, minced garlic, grated fresh ginger, or a little horseradish to taste.

And it also works with lightly blanched shellfish, such as shrimp, mussels, or clams.

While some insist on marinating the *cebiche* in the refrigerator until the seafood turns opaque throughout (at least 2 hours), contemporary Peruvian cooks often serve it straight away, provided the raw material is sparkling fresh. As for the garnishes, you can choose from thinly sliced red onion, diced tomatoes and avocado, julienned red bell pepper, scallions, and/or cilantro.

In Peru, *cebiche* is a meal all in itself, generously garnished with wedges of cooked sweet potatoes and local corn with giant white kernels, on or off the cob.

Meats

GO OUT to a neighborhood restaurant almost anywhere in South America, and you will think you are a Lilliputian staring at a hundred local Gullivers. All around you, happily preoccupied diners tuck into outsized steaks, *chuletas* (chops) or *milanesas* (fried, breaded, boneless steaks), accompanied by giant piles of french fries and lashings of tasty piquant sauces. But the steaks and the pork chops are reserved for the restaurant. When meat is prepared for families at home, it's usually in the form of a stew or casserole—chunks of beef or lamb cooked to a melting tenderness with beans, yuca, corn, or *calabaza*, and plenty of rich savory liquid accented with cilantro, chiles, and garlic. On weekends these one-pot meals acquire grandiose proportions: the Saturday *feijoada* teams smoked and fresh pork, beef, and sausages; the Sunday boiled dinner is cooked in enormous pots holding a dozen ingredients, and presented in several courses.

For the week that follows the leftovers from these family feasts are lovingly stuffed into empanadas and tamales, molded into *croquetas* and patties, diced into various hashes, or shredded into *ropa vieja*. While grand Latin gestures are reserved for outsiders and special occasions, *comida casera* (home-style cooking) celebrates thriftiness as a prized virtue. A prudent grandmother can transform humble ground beef into a seemingly endless repertoire of mouthwatering dishes. Mixed with a flavorful *sofrito* of tomatoes, garlic, and various seasonings, it's cooked into *picadillos*; stuffed into vegetables; baked between layers of mashed potatoes, grated corn, or pureed plantain; shaped into meatballs, or turned into an *albondigón*, a handsome baked meat loaf.

The Andean pre-Columbian Indians ate little meat, mostly llama, guinea pigs, and wild game, which they consumed raw, dried, cooked into thick stews called *locros*, or *rocros*, or roasted in earth ovens called *pachamanca*. When cows, pigs, sheep, and bulls (the last used for bullfights to entertain the *Conquistadores*) were imported by the Spanish colonists, they brought mixed blessings. The indigenous population was terrified by herds of large animals stomping on their land and destroying their vegetable crops, and their meat—especially their fat—made them violently sick. (So much so that petitions were sent by the colonists back to Spain to prohibit the sale and consumption of meat by the Indians.)

Gradually, over the years, the Indians learned cattle-raising techniques and incorporated the new meats into their cuisines. The vast green pampas of Argentina, southern Brazil, and Uruguay proved to be such extraordinary grazing land that the entire economies of these regions were eventually sustained by cattle-raising—in the case of Argentina, helping to make it the richest country in South America by the middle of the twentieth century.

The pig was, and still remains, the favorite meat, in both the Old and New Latin Worlds. During the Spanish Inquisition pork became a symbol of Christianity, and Jewish and Muslim converts (*conversos*) were forced to hang sausages and hams outside their doors to prove their Catholic allegiance. Suspected infidels carried ham bones with them as protection against the iron hand of the Inquisition. So indispensable was the pig to the early colonists that when Francisco Pizarro's half-brother, Gonzalo, went on a long expedition—chasing after an absurd rumor that cinnamon grew in the Peruvian jungle—he took with him a herd of no less than

6,000 pigs. The highest culinary incarnation of the pig is its appearance on the holiday table in the form of a golden crispy-skinned *lechón* or *cochinillo*—roast suckling pig. Next to *lechón*, the best thing is *pernil*, succulent pork shoulder marinated in a spirited mixture of sour orange or lime juice, spices, and herbs, and slowly roasted until it melts in the mouth. No less cherished are the ubiquitous *chicharrones*,

Sausages at the market, Santiago, Chile.

Parrillada (grilled meat restaurant), Buenos Aires, Argentina.

pork cracklings, and pork ribs. Put on a Latin song, and you will often find yourself recognizing familiar words: *chicharrón*, *lechón*, *pernil*, and all their loving diminutives.

For the most extraordinary lamb dishes, one needs to return to Portugal and Spain with their magnificent festive *asados* (roasts), a whole milk-fed lamb or kid roasted on a spit or in a wood-burning oven; the tiny baby lamb chops of La Rioja grilled over vine-flavored charcoal; or the magnificent deep-flavored wine-braised lamb of central Portugal.

Ofelia's Puchero

Puchero, a scrumptious boiled dinner, is one of the most revered Sunday family rituals in Argentina. We were lucky to have a *puchero* lunch at the house of the noble De Attucha family, once one of the premier ranch owners of Argentina. As is so often the case in many Latin American households, the unofficial matriarch of the clan was the family maid, Ofelia. It was she who prepared the *puchero,* and after lunch I was ceremoniously escorted to her kitchen to pay my respects and express my gratitude for the meal. This is her recipe.

The *puchero* dinner is served in two courses. First comes the rich broth from cooking the meats, served with *fideos,* thin egg vermicelli. The second course is the boiled meats, sausages, and vegetables, served on separate plates and accompanied by the piquant Chimichurri Sauce and various mustards and hot sauces. You will need a very large stockpot for cooking the *puchero;* and remember to soak the chickpeas the night before.

3½ POUNDS FIRST-CUT BEEF BRISKET, TRIMMED OF ALL FAT

5½ QUARTS WATER

1½ CUPS DRIED CHICKPEAS, SOAKED OVERNIGHT

4 MEDIUM CARROTS, PEELED AND CUT INTO 2½-INCH LENGTHS

3 LEEKS, WITH 1 INCH OF GREEN TOPS, WASHED WELL

1 STALK CELERY

6 SMALL ONIONS

1 WHOLE BOILING CHICKEN (3½ POUNDS), WELL RINSED AND PATTED DRY

1½ POUNDS PUMPKIN OR *CALABAZA*, PEELED, SEEDED, AND CUT INTO 1½-INCH CUBES

4 LARGE BOILING POTATOES, PEELED AND QUARTERED

3 EARS OF FRESH CORN, EACH CUT INTO 3 PIECES

1 MEDIUM HEAD CABBAGE (ABOUT 2 POUNDS), CUT INTO 8 WEDGES

4 GOOD-QUALITY FRESH *CHORIZO* SAUSAGES

4 FRESH BLOOD SAUSAGES (*MORCILLA*), OR SUBSTITUTE FRENCH *BOUDIN NOIR,* IF *MORCILLA* IS NOT AVAILABLE

(continued)

Fiesta!
154

1. Place the beef, water, chickpeas, carrots, leeks, celery, and onions in an 8-quart stockpot and bring to a boil, skimming off the foam that rises to the surface. Cook the beef over low heat, partially covered, until almost tender, about 1³/₄ hours.

2. Add the chicken to the pot, bring to a boil, and skim off the foam. Simmer over low heat, covered, for 25 minutes. Add the pumpkin, potatoes, corn, and cabbage. Simmer, covered until the chicken and all the vegetables are tender, about 25 to 30 minutes.

6 OUNCES VERMICELLI OR BROKEN-UP ANGEL-
    HAIR PASTA
CHIMICHURRI SAUCE (PAGE 26)
ASSORTED MUSTARDS AND HOT SAUCES, FOR
    SERVING

3. While the *puchero* is cooking, prick the sausages in several places with the tip of a sharp knife. Place in a large pan with water to cover, bring to a simmer, and cook over low heat until opaque, about 5 minutes. Drain.

4. Cook the vermicelli in boiling salted water until tender, about 3 minutes. Drain.

5. To serve, remove the chicken and beef from the broth with a slotted spoon and, when cool enough to handle, cut both into serving pieces. Cover the meat loosely with foil to keep warm. With a slotted spoon, remove the vegetables from the liquid, discarding the celery, and place them in rows on a large serving platter. Cover them loosely with foil.

6. Divide the cooked vermicelli among eight soup bowls and ladle in the cooking broth. Serve as a first course.

7. Serve the vegetables and meats as a second course, accompanied by the Chimichurri Sauce and assorted mustards.

SERVES 8

Argentina:
Here's the Beef

"*Porteños* would die without their meat," said Señor Villanueva, the proprietor of a famous Buenos Aires grill house, La Chacra. Meat is a way of life in Argentina, where the local cattle, graceful and athletic, roam freely in the vast sweeps of the world's most incredible pasture land—the *pampa húmeda*, (humid pampa), home to the best beef in the world.

Argentinian historians tell an apocryphal story of the arrival of the early colonists to the pampas. When Don Pedro de Mendoza, the second European to set foot in Argentina (the first, Juan Díaz de Solís, was killed by Indians in 1516), arrived in the 1530s, his expedition was accompanied by a dozen

Parrillada (grilled meat restaurant),
Buenos Aires, Argentina.

cows, bulls, and horses. Intimidated by the less-than-friendly reception of the fierce nomadic local Indians, the Spaniards established a makeshift settlement and made a hasty retreat, leaving their cattle behind. When half a century later Don Juan de Garay returned to the site to found the city that was to become Buenos Aires, he discovered that the abandoned cattle had multiplied to produce what he estimated to be a million head.

These wild cattle were considered to be public property and entrusted to the care of the *gauchos*, the fierce, free-spirited lasso-wielding cowboys born to Spanish fathers and Indian mothers. The beef, so abundant and absolutely free, became the main (and sometimes the only) source of food for the colonists. It continues to be cheap, plentiful, and beloved to this day.

Today, at Argentinian *estancias* (cattle ranches), meat is still prepared on traditional huge vertical spits, and the Sunday "roast" on the farm is likely to be an imposing *asado con cuero*, a whole animal with hide on, roasted for over 12 hours over a slow but intense fire made of local hardwood called *quebracho*. Beef is the stuff of weekday meals as well, the monotony broken occasionally by an iguana stew or armadillo in *escabeche*. In the city, the best way to sample an *asado* is to visit one of the many *parrilladas* (grilled meat joints), bastions of tradition and ritual in the quickly modernizing world of contemporary Argentina.

At the entrance of most *parrilladas* you will spot *asadores* (grill chefs) in *gaucho* outfits slowly roasting sheep, goats, and sides of beef on vertical spits positioned in a circle around a wood fire. This welcome is not just for drama. It serves as a living advertisement for the restaurant, giving new customers an opportunity to observe the *asadores* in action, and to check up on the quality of meat and the roasting technique, a matter on which every *Porteño* has strong opinions. The meat roasts slowly and languidly, and when an order is made, an appropriate portion is cut off and finished to the customer's preference. The decoration inside is pretty standard, consisting of the mandatory wood paneling, gaudy paintings of bucolic landscapes and rodeo scenes, plus stuffed deer and cow heads protruding from the walls, interspersed with images of tango legend Carlos Gardel, looking like a cross between Rudolph Valentino and Buster Keaton. This blend of rustic kitsch and cosmopolitan nostalgia captures the true feel of Buenos Aires.

You sit at a long communal table, tango playing softly in the background, and marvel at the appetites of mustached *Porteños* tucking into gargantuan portions of meat. On a busy night a *parrillada* might easily go through 1,000 pounds of beef, with 2 pounds per person considered the average consumption. Many serve up meat from their own cattle farms, perhaps a special breed fed on a secret diet. The real connoisseurs, however, boast that the very first bite will reveal the breed of cow and type of grass on which it grazed.

As soon as you hit your chair, an elderly waiter will rush to your table with a plate of golden empanadas, straight from the wood-burning oven used for roasting meats. Then the grill show begins for real, as you choose your appetizer, perhaps a *provoleta*, a tasty slab of chewy grilled provolone cheese spiced with oregano, or similarly seasoned rounds of grilled eggplant. The next offering from the grill will be a pair of moist crispy-skinned sausages: a paprika-hued spicy *chorizo* and a rich buttery blood sausage called *morcilla*.

And finally, here's the beef. The most relished cuts are *bife de chorizo*, a thin rib cut, and *lomo* (loin), as buttery as an avocado. But the *Porteños* don't frown on more chewy cuts, such as *vacío*, a special cut of flank steak, or *asado de tira*, the ubiquitous short rib steaks. The Argentinians never age their beef, the perfect "resting" time considered to be exactly 24 hours. If you order a *parrillada mixta*, you will get an individual grill, including several cuts of beef: melting chunks of baby goat and suckling pig with crackling skin; offal; crunchy *chinchulines* (intestines); and *mollejas*, tender sweetbreads that melt in your mouth. The way to eat meat is straight from the grill, with nothing more than *chimichurri*, a tangy sauce of parsley, onion, garlic, and vinegar; though with the more expensive, tender cuts, even the sauce is considered *de trop*. The only other accoutrements are crisp, thin rounds of fried potato and a salad.

With so many *parrilladas* to choose from, personal service is all. At the more exclusive establishments of Buenos Aires, such as the famous La Cabaña, when customers arrive, their favorite nibbles will be waiting on the table, the meat order miraculously appearing at the right time, done exactly to their liking. These kinds of places teem with the *gente linda* of Buenos Aires, lean gray-haired men in Armani knock-offs and blond Chanel-clad *señoras* clutching Gucci handbags—elegant, but no less carnivorous than the working class *Porteños*. They will be looked after by quick-witted elderly waiters, who take their art as seriously as if they were the maître d's at the London Ritz. And with good reason. Like the family maids in wealthy households, the *camareros* control the show, and many customers will not go to a restaurant on their waiter's day off. As you exit, your waiter will discreetly hand you his card, and when he changes venue, his customers will often go with him. It's all part of the ritual.

Porteño Mixed Grill

(P A R R I L L A D A   M I X T A)

Unlike more tender cuts, skirt steak and beef flanken benefit from a simple astringent marinade. At home the mixed grill is cooked and served in stages—first the sausages, which are served as a predinner nibble, then the offal (which we are omitting), and then the steak. The meat goes straight from the grill to the plate. The Argentinians believe that letting it sit makes it tough and greasy. Serve the grill with the Chimichurri Sauce and Watercress and Hearts of Palm Salad (page 113).

MARINADE

5 CLOVES GARLIC, CHOPPED

1 TEASPOON FRESHLY GROUND BLACK PEPPER

2 TEASPOONS DRIED OREGANO

½ TEASPOON HOT RED PEPPER FLAKES

2 BAY LEAVES

½ CUP RED WINE VINEGAR

½ CUP WARM WATER

¼ CUP CHOPPED FLAT-LEAF PARSLEY

1 BEEF SKIRT STEAK (ABOUT 1½ POUNDS)

4 SMALL BEEF FLANKEN STEAKS (DO NOT
   CONFUSE WITH FLANK STEAKS), ABOUT 2
   POUNDS IN TOTAL

4 FRESH *CHORIZO* SAUSAGES

4 FRESH BLOOD SAUSAGES (*MORCILLA*) OR
   BOUDIN NOIR, IF *MORCILLA* IS NOT AVAILABLE

OLIVE OIL, FOR BRUSHING THE MEATS

1 LARGE FAT SPRIG OF CURLY PARSLEY

SALT TO TASTE

CHIMICHURRI SAUCE (PAGE 26)

LEMON WEDGES, AS AN ACCOMPANIMENT

1. To make the marinade: Combine all the ingredients in a food processor and process until pureed.

2. Cut the skirt steak across the grain into 4 pieces. Place the meat in a large shallow glass or ceramic dish and pour the marinade over it. Refrigerate for 2 to 6 hours. Bring to room temperature before grilling. Reserve the marinade.

3. Preheat the grill.

4. Prick the *chorizos* and *morcillas* all over with the tip of a small knife. Brush lightly with olive oil and grill over high heat for 10 minutes on each side. Serve at once, as a prelude to dinner. Remove the skirt steak and the beef flanken from the marinade.

5. Brush them lightly with olive oil and place them on the grill. (The meats should grill a maximum of 3 inches away from the heat, but preferably closer.) Grill for 5 minutes, then turn on the other side. Dip the parsley sprig in the marinade and brush the steaks. Grill, brushing with the marinade twice more, for another 5 minutes for medium meat. Remove the steaks from the grill, arrange on a platter, season with salt, and serve at once, with Chimichurri Sauce and lemon wedges.

SERVES 4

Accordionist, San Telmo Market, Buenos Aires, Argentina.

Skirt Steak, Cuban Style

(ROPA NUEVA)

Anyone familiar with Cuban food certainly loves *ropa vieja*, literally "old clothes." Originally from Iberia (the dish is still found in both Spain and Portugal), it was simply meat left over from the meal before, shredded into pieces—hence the name—and cooked in some type of improvised sauce. The Cubans perfected the dish into a classic, preparing it with the grainy boiled skirt or flank steak smothered in piquant tomato sauce. Good recipes for *ropa vieja* abound, but I was taken with the idea suggested to me by a young Cuban-American chef, Gloria Catal. Instead of boiling the meat "to death," as the Cuban tradition dictates, she cuts flank steak into thin slices, sears it, and then adds it to the sauce at the last minute, retaining its natural juiciness. The resulting dish is full of flavor and much faster to prepare. So here we have it, *ropa nueva*—"new clothes"! Green Rice (page 250), Yellow Rice (page 259) or White Rice (page 247) would each make a good accompaniment.

1. Brush a large, heavy cast-iron skillet or wok with oil and heat over high heat. Sear the meat slices, a few at a time, until browned on the outside but rare inside, about 2 to 3 minutes per batch. Transfer the finished batches to a bowl and set aside.

2. In a large, heavy saucepan, heat the 1½ tablespoons of oil over medium heat. Add the onion, garlic, and green and red peppers, and sauté, stirring, until softened, about 7 minutes. Stir in the oregano and cumin and stir for another minute. Stir in the tomato paste and stir until lightly caramelized, about 3 minutes. Stir in the sherry and wine and reduce for 2 minutes.

3. Stir in the tomatoes, stock, olives, and capers. Season with salt and pepper and add enough sugar to take the acidic edge off the dish. Simmer the sauce, uncovered, until flavorful and reduced, about 20 minutes. Stir in the reserved meat and accumulated juices and cook just to heat through. Garnish with parsley and serve over rice.

SERVES 6

1½ TABLESPOONS OLIVE OIL, PLUS ADDITIONAL
    FOR SEARING THE MEAT
1 SKIRT STEAK (ABOUT 1¾ POUNDS), CUT ON
    THE DIAGONAL ACROSS THE GRAIN INTO
    ¼-INCH-THICK SLICES
1 LARGE SPANISH ONION, HALVED AND SLICED
3 CLOVES GARLIC, MINCED
1 SMALL GREEN BELL PEPPER, CORED, SEEDED,
    AND CUT INTO STRIPS
1 MEDIUM RED BELL PEPPER, CORED, SEEDED,
    AND CUT INTO STRIPS
½ TEASPOON DRIED OREGANO
½ TEASPOON GROUND CUMIN
1½ TABLESPOONS TOMATO PASTE
¼ CUP DRY SHERRY
⅓ CUP DRY RED WINE
¾ CUP CANNED CRUSHED TOMATOES WITH THEIR
    LIQUID
1 CUP BEEF STOCK (PAGE 373) OR CANNED
    BROTH
¼ CUP SLICED PIMIENTO-STUFFED OLIVES
3 TABLESPOONS CAPERS
SALT AND FRESHLY GROUND BLACK PEPPER, TO
    TASTE
SUGAR TO TASTE
MINCED FLAT-LEAF PARSLEY, FOR GARNISH
RICE, FOR SERVING (SEE HEADNOTE)

Isabel's Inca Herb-Wrapped Beef

(HUATÍA)

This dish comes from Isabel Álvarez, a former sociologist, who turned her research to the indigenous cooking of Peru—which she presents at her amazing Lima restaurant, La Señoría de Sulco. In pre-Columbian times, she claims, the dish was prepared with wild deer meat wrapped in huge bunches of aromatic herbs, and cooked all night in an underground oven, as a tribute to Mother Earth. Ideally, the herb-wrapped meat should be slowly baked in clay without any water, the herbs slowly releasing their aroma and providing moisture. The perfect vessel would be an unglazed earthenware casserole with a lid, such as a Römertopf. A Le Creuset Dutch oven will work also. For accompaniment Isabel suggests sweet potatoes, also an ancient Inca staple, baked simply in their skins.

4 POUNDS BEEF RUMP WITH SOME FAT,
    IN 1 PIECE

2 TABLESPOONS CRACKED BLACK PEPPER

2 LARGE BUNCHES EACH CILANTRO, BASIL, MINT,
    AND FLAT-LEAF PARSLEY

1 SMALL BUNCH FRESH ROSEMARY, OR 2
    TEASPOONS DRIED ROSEMARY

1 LARGE PINCH DRIED *HUACATAY* (A PERUVIAN
    HERB AVAILABLE AT SOME HISPANIC
    MARKETS), OPTIONAL

12 CLOVES GARLIC, LIGHTLY CRUSHED

1 SMALL DRIED CHILE, CRUMBLED

1 CUP WATER, OPTIONAL

8 SWEET POTATOES, SCRUBBED CLEAN

SALT, TO TASTE

1. Preheat the oven to 400 degrees F. If using an unglazed earthenware casserole, soak it in cold water for 30 minutes. This will help it release extra steam and make the meat juicier.

2. Cut the beef crosswise into six to eight large pieces. Rinse the beef in cold water and rub it with cracked pepper.

3. Untie the bunches of herbs and rinse them in cold water. Do not shake off the liquid. Mix all the herbs together and spread the sprigs on a work surface. Loosely wrap the pieces of meat in the herbs, making sure all the different kinds are evenly distributed. These don't have to be particularly neat bundles, as the herbs will stick to the meat when they begin to cook. Place the bundles in the earthenware pot, or another heavy ovenproof casserole such as Le Creuset. Scatter the *huacatay* (if using), garlic, and the crumbled chile among the beef pieces.

4. Bake for 20 minutes, then reduce the heat to 300 degrees, and bake until the meat is very tender, about 2½ hours longer. You don't need to add liquid, as the meat should release enough juice. However, do check it a couple of times, and if it looks dry, add a cup of water.

5. After the meat has cooked for 1¼ hours, wrap each potato in foil and bake them in the same oven until tender.

6. Season the meat with salt and serve in the same casserole or transfer to a serving platter. Unwrap the potatoes and serve with the meat or on a separate platter.

SERVES 6 TO 8

Fiesta!
163

Plantain "Moussaka"

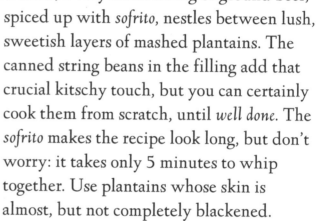

(PASTELÓN DE PLÁTANO)

One of my very favorite Puerto Rican offerings is *pastelón de plátano*, the island's answer to moussaka or shepherd's pie. Here, a very moist filling of ground beef, spiced up with *sofrito*, nestles between lush, sweetish layers of mashed plantains. The canned string beans in the filling add that crucial kitschy touch, but you can certainly cook them from scratch, until *well done*. The *sofrito* makes the recipe look long, but don't worry: it takes only 5 minutes to whip together. Use plantains whose skin is almost, but not completely blackened.

SOFRITO

½ SMALL ONION, CHOPPED

3 CLOVES GARLIC, CHOPPED

¼ CUP CHOPPED GREEN BELL PEPPER

1 SMALL PLUM TOMATO, CHOPPED

½ MEDIUM ANAHEIM CHILE, CHOPPED, OR 2 TEASPOONS CHOPPED JALAPEÑO CHILE

¼ CUP CHOPPED *RECAO* LEAVES (AVAILABLE AT SOME HISPANIC MARKETS) OR CHOPPED CILANTRO LEAVES

⅓ CUP WATER

5 LARGE RIPE PLANTAINS (ABOUT 8 OUNCES EACH), PEELED AS DIRECTED ON PAGE 379

2 TABLESPOONS PLUS 2 TEASPOONS ANNATTO OIL (PAGE 376)

1 LARGE ONION, FINELY CHOPPED

1 POUND GROUND SIRLOIN OR ROUND

½ CUP CANNED CRUSHED TOMATOES WITH THEIR LIQUID

1½ CUPS DRAINED CANNED STRING BEANS

⅔ CUP CHICKEN STOCK (PAGE 372), CANNED LOWER-SALT CHICKEN BROTH, OR WATER

1 TEASPOON GROUND OREGANO

(continued)

1. To make the *sofrito*: Combine all the ingredients in a blender and pulse until crushed, but not pureed.

2. Cut the plantains into 2-inch chunks, place them in a saucepan with enough water to cover them by 1½ inches, and cook over medium heat until soft, about 20 minutes. Leave the plantains in the liquid until ready to use. Do not prepare them more than 15 minutes ahead of time.

3. In a large skillet, heat the 2 tablespoons of annatto oil over medium heat. Add the onion and cook, stirring until it wilts, about 5 minutes. Add the beef, turn the heat up to high, and cook, breaking it up with a fork, until it is no longer pink inside, about 5 minutes. Add the *sofrito*, and all the remaining ingredients except the plantains and the Parmesan and the remaining annatto oil. Turn the heat down to low, and simmer for 10 minutes, stirring occasionally.

1 1/2 TEASPOONS MILD PAPRIKA

LARGE PINCH OF CAYENNE, TO TASTE

SALT AND FRESHLY GROUND BLACK PEPPER, TO TASTE

GRATED PARMESAN CHEESE, FOR SPRINKLING THE *PASTELÓN*

4. While the beef is cooking, remove the plantains to a large bowl with a slotted spoon and add 3/4 cup of the cooking liquid. Quickly mash the plantains with a fork until smooth. Do not overwork, or they will become gluey. Add salt to taste. Do not mash the plantains ahead of time as they become hard as they cool.

5. Preheat the oven to 350 degrees F.

6. To assemble the *pastelón*: Spread half of the plantain mixture in a deep, 8-inch square baking dish. Spread the beef filling on top, and top with a second layer of mashed plantains. Smooth the top with a wet spatula.

7. Brush the top of the *pastelón* with the remaining 2 teaspoons of the annatto oil, and sprinkle generously with Parmesan. Bake until the top is golden, about 20 minutes. Cut into squares and serve.

SERVES 4 TO 6

Picadillo with Sweet Plantain

(PICADILLO CON MADUROS)

One of the most basic and nourishing of everyday Latin meals is *picadillo*, ground meat sautéed in a tomato-based sauce and *sofrito* until moist, flavorful, and delicious. The Cubans like to add a touch of sweetness to their *picadillo*, and traditionally the sweet touch comes from raisins. At the suggestion of chef Eric Basulto, I add diced ripe plantains for their nice lush texture, and a touch of port wine. This dish is great on its own, over rice, or as a filling for empanadas, croquettes, and savory pies. If you like, serve the *picadillo* in a traditional Cuban manner: Place cooked rice in a mold or a cup and invert it into the middle of a dinner plate. Spoon the *picadillo* in a ring around the rice and top the rice with a fried egg. You can turn to most rice recipes in the book for accompaniment.

SOFRITO

½ TABLESPOON OLIVE OIL

2 TEASPOONS ANNATTO OIL (PAGE 376)

1 SMALL ONION, FINELY CHOPPED

2 CLOVES GARLIC, MINCED

½ CUP FINELY DICED RED BELL PEPPER

½ TEASPOON GROUND CUMIN

½ TEASPOON CHILI POWDER

2 MEDIUM RIPE TOMATOES, CHOPPED

BEEF

1 TABLESPOON OLIVE OIL

1 SMALL RIPE PLANTAIN, PEELED AS DIRECTED ON PAGE 379 AND DICED

1¼ POUNDS GROUND BEEF SIRLOIN

2 TABLESPOONS PORT WINE

⅓ CUP DRY RED WINE

⅓ CUP WATER

8 PIMIENTO-STUFFED OLIVES, SLICED

1 TABLESPOON SMALL CAPERS

2 TEASPOONS FRESH LEMON JUICE

SALT AND FRESHLY GROUND BLACK PEPPER, TO TASTE

RICE, FOR SERVING

1. To make the *sofrito*: Heat the olive and annatto oils in a medium-size skillet over medium-low heat. Add the onion, garlic, and red pepper, and cook, stirring, until softened, about 5 minutes. Add the rest of the *sofrito* ingredients and cook over low heat until the tomatoes are reduced to a puree, about 8 minutes. Set aside.

2. To make the meat: Heat the oil over medium-high heat in a deep skillet. Add the plantain and cook, stirring, until soft, about 5 minutes. Add the meat and cook, breaking it up with a fork, until cooked through, about 5 minutes. Tilt the skillet and pour off most of the fat. Add the port and red wine and reduce for 2 minutes. Add the *sofrito*, water, olives, capers, lemon juice, salt, and pepper. Reduce the heat to very low and simmer, stirring occasionally, for 10 minutes. (If using the *picadillo* as a filling for empanadas, raise the heat to high and reduce until the mixture is fairly dry.) Serve over rice.

SERVES 4 TO 6

Carnicería sign, Calle Ocho, Miami.

Creole Beef and Squash Stew with Peaches

(CARBONADA CRIOLLA)

An Argentinian classic, this is a rich, pleasantly sweet, soupy stew. The recipe is from Miriam Becker, one of Argentina's leading food writers. There are many debates about whether to use fresh, dried, or canned peaches. I vote for the dried, as I like the texture of dried fruit with meat.

4½ TABLESPOONS OLIVE OIL

2 POUNDS BONELESS BEEF ROUND, CUT INTO 1½-INCH CUBES

2 MEDIUM ONIONS, CHOPPED

4 CLOVES GARLIC, CHOPPED

2 SLENDER CARROTS, PEELED AND CUT INTO THICK SLICES

ONE 16-OUNCE CAN TOMATOES, CHOPPED, THEIR LIQUID RESERVED

2 BAY LEAVES

2 WHOLE SPRIGS FRESH OREGANO, OR 2 TEASPOONS DRIED OREGANO LEAVES

1½ TABLESPOONS CHOPPED FLAT-LEAF PARSLEY

5½ CUPS BEEF STOCK (PAGE 373)

SALT AND FRESHLY GROUND BLACK PEPPER, TO TASTE

4 MEDIUM BOILING POTATOES, PEELED AND CUT INTO 1¼-INCH CHUNKS

2 MEDIUM EARS OF CORN, EACH CUT INTO 4 SECTIONS

2 TABLESPOONS LONG-GRAIN RICE

10 DRIED PEACHES (AVAILABLE AT HEALTH FOOD STORES AND SOME GOURMET MARKETS), HALVED

¾ POUND *CALABAZA* OR BUTTERNUT SQUASH, PEELED, SEEDED, AND CUT INTO 1½-INCH CUBES (ABOUT 1¾ CUPS)

1. Heat the oil in a large ovenproof casserole and brown the meat in batches over medium-high heat, about 5 to 7 minutes per batch. With a slotted spoon, remove the meat from the casserole and drain off all but 2 tablespoons of the oil.

2. Preheat the oven to 350 degrees F.

3. Add the onions, garlic, and carrots to the casserole and cook over medium heat until the onion is soft, about 7 minutes. Add the tomatoes, bay leaves, oregano, and parsley and replace the beef in the casserole. Add the stock and bring to a simmer. Add salt and pepper to taste. Place the casserole in the oven and cook, covered, until the beef is almost tender, about 1¼ hours.

4. Add the potatoes, corn, rice, and peaches and cook for another 10 minutes. Stir in the squash and cook uncovered for another 25 minutes until the meat and all the vegetables are very tender. Remove bay leaf before serving.

SERVES 6 TO 8

Veal Meatballs with Peas and Artichokes

(ALBÓNDIGAS CON GUISANTES Y ALCACHOFAS)

When the early summer brings tender artichokes and peas, housewives all over the Spanish countryside take to cooking *albóndigas con guisantes*, a delicate stew of ethereal meatballs simmered with tender vegetables, and a bit of serrano ham. This recipe, however, comes from the esteemed Señor Lladonosa, a premier authority on Catalan cuisine, who cooks at the Siete Puertas, one of the oldest and most respected restaurants in Barcelona. In typical Catalan manner, this stew is thickened and enriched with a *picada* of pounded garlic, saffron, almonds, and chiles. Despite the long list of ingredients, the recipe is quite simple. If you feel too lazy, use frozen artichoke hearts instead of making them fresh.

1. To make the *picada*: In a mortar and pestle, crush all the ingredients to a paste. Set aside.

2. To make the meatballs: In a large mixing bowl, combine all the ingredients except the oil and flour and mix gently but thoroughly to

(continued)

PICADA

2 TEASPOONS CHOPPED GARLIC
8 TO 10 SAFFRON THREADS
12 LIGHTLY TOASTED ALMONDS, CHOPPED
1 SMALL DRIED RED CHILE, SEEDED AND
   CRUMBLED
½ TEASPOON SALT

MEATBALLS

¾ POUND GROUND VEAL
½ POUND LEAN GROUND PORK
⅓ CUP FINELY CHOPPED PANCETTA OR SMOKED
   BACON
⅔ CUP SOFT BREAD CRUMBS
1 LARGE EGG, BEATEN
2 TABLESPOONS MINCED FLAT-LEAF PARSLEY
2 TEASPOONS MINCED GARLIC
1 TEASPOON SALT
¼ TEASPOON GROUND CINNAMON
2 TABLESPOONS GOOD FRUITY OLIVE OIL
FLOUR, FOR DUSTING THE MEATBALLS

(continued)

ARTICHOKES

6 LARGE ARTICHOKES, OR 6 FROZEN AND
    THAWED ARTICHOKE HEARTS
LEMON HALVES

SAUCE

1 TABLESPOON GOOD FRUITY OLIVE OIL
1 MEDIUM ONION, FINELY CHOPPED
2 LARGE CLOVES GARLIC, MINCED
$^1/_3$ CUP FINELY DICED SERRANO HAM OR
    PROSCIUTTO
4 MEDIUM PLUM TOMATOES, BLANCHED, PEELED,
    AND FINELY CHOPPED
$^1/_2$ CUP DRY FRUITY WHITE WINE
2 CUPS CHICKEN STOCK (PAGE 372) OR CANNED
    LOWER-SALT CHICKEN BROTH
$1^1/_2$ CUPS GREEN PEAS, PREFERABLY FRESH
SALT AND FRESHLY GROUND BLACK PEPPER, TO
    TASTE

combine. Shape the mixture into balls, about $1^1/_4$ inches in diameter. Set aside.

3. To make the artichokes: Bring a large pot of salted water to a boil. Trim the artichokes and cut off the tough outer leaves. Cut each artichoke in half lengthwise. Rub the cut sides all over with the lemon halves. Drop the artichoke halves and the lemon halves into the water and cook until the artichokes are tender, about 20 minutes or more, depending on the exact size. When cool enough to handle, trim away and discard the leaves, leaving the hearts. Scoop out the fuzzy chokes. Set aside until ready to use.

4. In a heavy saucepan large enough to accommodate all the meatballs and the artichokes, heat the oil over medium heat. Dust the meatballs with flour and fry them in batches until lightly browned, about 6 minutes per batch. Remove with a slotted spoon and set aside.

5. To make the sauce: In the same saucepan, heat the 2 tablespoons oil over medium-low heat. Add the onion, garlic, and ham and cook, stirring until the onion wilts, about 5 minutes. Add the tomatoes and cook, stirring, until they are reduced to a puree, about 8 minutes. Add the wine and reduce over high heat for 5 minutes. Add the broth and the meatballs, and cook over medium heat until the meatballs are cooked through, about 15 to 17 minutes. Add the artichokes and the *picada*, and cook for 5 minutes. Add the peas and cook until just tender, about 3 minutes. Season to taste with salt, if needed, and pepper.

SERVES 6

Meat Loaf in the Style of Matambre

(ALBONDIGÓN ESTILO MATAMBRE)

My Uruguayan neighbor, Amelia Salgado, has a passion for stuffing meats—and the crowning glory of her repertoire is *matambre* (literally "kill hunger"). It's a glorious dish—flank steak rolled around a bright filling of carrots, spinach, and egg—which Uruguay shares with Argentina, though it was originally borrowed from Italian immigrants. When Amelia feels too lazy to fiddle with the flank steak, she produces this handsome *matambre* meat loaf, filled with the same festive *relleno* (stuffing). It's especially delicious cold, accompanied by Russian Salad (page 114) and Chimichurri Sauce (page 26).

3 CUPS TIGHTLY PACKED FRESH SPINACH, RINSED BUT NOT DRAINED
½ CUP CANNED LOWER-SALT CHICKEN BROTH OR WATER
½ CUP SOFT BREAD CRUMBS
1 LARGE EGG
4 TABLESPOONS DIJON-STYLE MUSTARD
1 POUND GROUND BEEF CHUCK OR ROUND
¾ POUND GROUND VEAL OR PORK
1 MEDIUM ONION, GRATED
SALT AND FRESHLY GROUND BLACK PEPPER, TO TASTE
4 HARD-COOKED EGGS
4 SLENDER CARROTS, PEELED AND COOKED
¼ TO ⅓ CUP WELL-DRAINED PIMIENTO STRIPS
MILD PAPRIKA, FOR DUSTING THE MEAT LOAF

1. In a large skillet, cook the spinach in the water clinging to the leaves until wilted, about 5 minutes. When cool enough to handle, squeeze it dry, and chop fine. Set aside.

2. Preheat the oven to 375 degrees F.

(continued)

3. In a food processor, combine the chicken broth, bread crumbs, egg, and 2 tablespoons of the mustard, and process for several pulses. In a large bowl, combine the processed mixture with the beef, veal, and the grated onion. Add salt and pepper to taste. If you wish, fry a small amount of the mixture to check for seasoning.

4. In a jelly-roll pan, spread half of the meat into a rectangle about 6 by 14 inches. Spread 1 tablespoon of the remaining mustard on the rectangle, and line it with the reserved spinach. Lay the hard-cooked eggs in a line in the middle of the rectangle, and place a row of carrots and pimiento strips on each side of the egg.

5. On a piece of wax paper, spread the remaining beef mixture into a rectangle similar in size to the first, and carefully turn it over on top of the first rectangle, peeling off the wax paper. With slightly oiled hands, pat the meat into a neat oval, making sure the edges are securely sealed. Brush the top with the remaining tablespoon of the mustard, and sprinkle with paprika.

6. Bake the meat loaf in the middle of the oven until the juices run clear when you prick it with a fork, about 55 minutes. Remove from the oven, cover loosely with foil, and let stand for 10 minutes. The meat loaf can be served warm, cold, or at room temperature.

SERVES 8

Lamb Stew with Yuca in Cilantro Sauce

(SECO DE CORDERO)

There is a whole class of delectable spiced Peruvian stews called *secos* (dry), to distinguish them from the more soupy stews (*aguaditos*), which are eaten with a spoon. In this cilantro-flavored *seco*, you can substitute whole shoulder lamb chops for the boneless lamb. If you wish, the yuca can be replaced by whole small boiling potatoes, in which case, add them directly to the lamb about halfway through the cooking.

1. In a blender, process the cilantro, chiles, and garlic with a little stock or water until finely minced. Set aside.

2. In a large, heavy casserole, heat the oil over medium-high heat. In batches, brown the lamb on all sides, about 5 minutes per batch. Remove it from the casserole and set aside.

3. Add the onions and cook over medium-low heat, stirring, until soft, about 10 minutes. Add the tomatoes and cook until reduced to a puree, about 8 minutes.

2 MEDIUM BUNCHES CILANTRO, TRIMMED AND CHOPPED

2 YELLOW WAX CHILES, SEEDED AND CHOPPED

2 LARGE CLOVES GARLIC, CHOPPED

2 TABLESPOONS OLIVE OIL

2 POUNDS BONELESS LAMB SHOULDER, CUT INTO 1½-INCH CHUNKS

2 LARGE ONIONS, COARSELY CHOPPED

2 LARGE RIPE TOMATOES, BLANCHED, PEELED, SEEDED, AND CHOPPED

1¾ CUPS CHICKEN STOCK (PAGE 372) OR CANNED LOWER-SALT CHICKEN BROTH

SALT AND FRESHLY GROUND BLACK PEPPER, TO TASTE

2 POUNDS YUCA, PEELED AS DIRECTED ON PAGE 79 AND CUT INTO 2-INCH LENGTHS

RICE, FOR SERVING, IF DESIRED

3 TABLESPOONS DICED RED BELL PEPPER, FOR GARNISH

(continued)

4. Return the lamb to the casserole and add the cilantro mixture. Stir for 5 minutes. Add the stock, and salt and pepper to taste, and bring to a simmer. Reduce the heat to low, cover, and cook over low heat until the lamb is very tender, about 1½ hours.

5. While the lamb is cooking, place the yuca in a pot, add enough water to cover it by 2 inches, and bring to a boil. Add salt, reduce the heat to medium, and cook, partially covered, until the yuca is tender, about 25 minutes. When cool enough to handle, cut the yuca pieces in half lengthwise, removing the tough stringy core that runs through its center.

6. Stir the yuca into the lamb and cook for another 5 minutes. Serve the stew over rice if you wish, garnished with red pepper.

SERVES 4 TO 6

Tango Argentino

Think Argentina, and tango—the seductive, sultry, histrionic dance that conquered Europe and America in the 1920s—will come to mind. But the true tango *Argentino* (as opposed to the glamorously cosmopolitan, marble-floored incarnation popularized by Rudolph Valentino), the tango that is still occasionally danced in small working-class clubs in the back alleys of the San Telmo district in Buenos Aires, is not just a showcase of fancy steps. You will feel the essence of tango as you watch octogenarian *Porteños*, men in sailor suits, wrinkled women in short skirts and fishnet stockings, dancing in close embrace. They enact a melodramatic pantomime—an unfolding story of desire and seduction, of vio-

lence, abandonment, and revenge, fanciful and unpredictable, with abrupt stops, rapid turns, and theatrical dips—performed to the melancholy sound of the famous tango accordion, the *bandoneón*, the heartbreaking strain of the violin, and the slightly dissonant clatter of an out-of-tune upright.

Like other great musical genres that have transcended their cultures—the brooding Portuguese *fado*, the frenetic Brazilian samba, the Cuban rumba, and American jazz—the tango is a bastard child of the slums, born out of poverty and despair. No one can tell the exact origin of tango, but it flourished in the brothels of the port slums around Buenos Aires in the last decade of the nineteenth century. Like any true creation of the port, it bears traces of the many cultures that docked their ships in Argentina. In it you will recognize the sounds of the Andalusian tango, the Cuban habanera, the African ritual percussion beat, popular melodies from Europe, and folk songs of the Argentinian *gauchos* (cowboys).

Jorge Luis Borges writes that in the old days tango was danced by male couples, tramps and thugs, who at night would show it off to the prostitutes in the bordellos. And indeed, with its violent gestures, frivolous lyrics, and dubious pedigree, the tango created an uproar in the straitlaced high society of Buenos Aires. But nothing was to stop it. In fact, its air of eroticism and scandal made it that much more desirable. Soon it was danced in the streets and cafés of Buenos Aires and, more discreetly, in its salons—before it hit Paris in 1920 and became the first Latin dance to take Europe by storm. In Argentina, it was the great tango idol Carlos Gardel, with his suave voice and Hollywood-style charisma, who trans-

Relief of dancing couple, La Boca,
Buenos Aires, Argentina.

formed the tango from a violent erotic dance of the underclasses into a song style (technically known as *tango-balada*), which came to symbolize Argentina and continues to resonate up to this day.

Patagonia Seven-Hour Leg of Lamb

(PIERNA DE CORDERO ASADO POR SIETE HORAS)

This dish was created by Argentina's premier chef, Francis Mallmann. It was inspired by the incredible Patagonian lamb of his childhood, and a traditional French recipe for slowly cooked whole leg of lamb—so tender, you can eat it with a spoon. Francis serves this dish with Argentinian Sweet Potato Gnocchi (page 220). Double the gnocchi recipe if serving with the lamb.

1½ TEASPOONS DRIED THYME
2 TEASPOONS SALT
3 LARGE CLOVES GARLIC, SLICED
1 LEG OF LAMB (ABOUT 6 TO 7 POUNDS)
3 TABLESPOONS UNSALTED BUTTER
2½ TABLESPOONS VEGETABLE OIL
¾ CUP CHOPPED CELERY
4 LARGE LEEKS, WITH ABOUT 1 INCH OF GREEN, CUT INTO CHUNKS
3 CUPS DRY RED WINE, PREFERABLY FROM MENDOZA, SUCH AS TRAPICHE
3 CUPS BEEF STOCK (PAGE 373) OR CANNED BROTH
WATER, AS NEEDED

1. Preheat the oven to 425 degrees F. In a small bowl, combine the thyme and salt. Roll the garlic slices in this mixture. With a sharp knife make slits all over the lamb and stuff the slits with the seasoned garlic.

2. In a heavy casserole or Dutch oven large enough to accommodate the lamb and all the liquid, heat the butter and oil over medium-high heat. Brown the lamb on all sides and remove it from the casserole. Add the celery and leeks and cook, stirring, for about 7 minutes. Replace the lamb in the casserole, add 1 cup of the wine and 1 cup of stock, and bring to a boil.

3.   Place the casserole in the oven and bake, uncovered, for 20 minutes. Reduce the oven temperature to 275 degrees and bake for 3½ hours, basting and adding equal amounts of wine and stock to keep up the level of the liquid. Cover, and continue baking until the lamb is almost falling off the bone, about 2½ to 3 hours more. Keep adding wine and stock until you run out of both. After that, add water. There should always be about 2 cups of liquid in the pan.

4.   Remove the lamb from the liquid to a carving board and cover it with foil. On top of the stove, reduce the braising liquid in half, about 15 minutes over high heat. Puree it in a food mill or food processor together with the vegetables.

5.   Cut the lamb into serving pieces, transfer it to a serving platter, and pour the sauce over it.

SERVES 6 TO 8

Latino Roast Pork Shoulder

(PERNIL)

Nothing titillates the Spanish Caribbean taste buds more than a great plate of *pernil* (picnic pork shoulder), spiced up with a good marinade, and roasted for a long time in a slow oven so that it's almost falling off the bone, but still juicy. To produce a crispy skin, I turn the oven to high at the last stages of cooking. The pork needs to marinate overnight.

MARINADE

1 SMALL HEAD GARLIC, SEPARATED INTO CLOVES,
    PEELED, AND CHOPPED

1 TABLESPOON COARSE (KOSHER) SALT

2 TABLESPOONS CRACKED BLACK PEPPERCORNS

1 TEASPOON HOT RED PEPPER FLAKES

1 TABLESPOON DRIED OREGANO

1 SPRIG FRESH THYME, OR 2 TEASPOONS DRIED
    THYME

1 CUP FRESH SOUR ORANGE JUICE (SEE PAGE
    145) OR A COMBINATION OF ORANGE AND
    LIME JUICE

¼ CUP OLIVE OIL

¼ CUP RED WINE VINEGAR

2 BAY LEAVES, CRUMBLED

4 WHOLE CLOVES, CRUSHED IN A MORTAR

1 PICNIC PORK SHOULDER (ABOUT 7 POUNDS),
    TRIMMED OF ALL BUT A THIN LAYER OF FAT

2 CUPS WATER, PLUS MORE AS NEEDED

½ CUP DRY SHERRY

1 TABLESPOON WORCESTERSHIRE SAUCE

1. To make the marinade: In a food processor, process all the marinade ingredients to a paste.

2. Rub the pork all over with the marinade, place it in a large plastic bag, close the bag tightly, and refrigerate overnight.

3. Preheat the oven to 325 degrees F.

4. Place the pork on a rack in a large baking pan. Pour the 2 cups of water, the sherry, and the Worcestershire sauce into the pan and roast the pork for 4 hours, basting from time to time, until very tender. (Cover it loosely with foil if the crust is browning too much.) Keep adding water, 1 cup at a time, to maintain the same level of liquid in the pan.

5. Increase the oven temperature to 400 degrees. Remove the foil, if using, and roast the pork for another 30 minutes, until the skin is crispy.

6. Transfer the pork to a cutting board, cover it loosely with foil, and let it stand for 15 minutes before carving. Degrease the pan juices and transfer them to a sauceboat.

7. Carve the pork and serve it accompanied by the pan juices.

SERVES 10

Pork Loin with Picadillo Stuffing

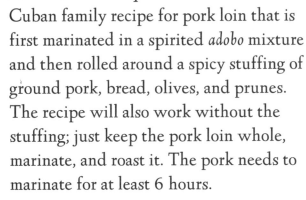

(LOMO DE CERDO RELLENO CON PICADILLO)

Throughout Latin America and the Spanish Caribbean, roast pork in one form or another is the centerpiece at important dinners and banquets. This is an old Cuban family recipe for pork loin that is first marinated in a spirited *adobo* mixture and then rolled around a spicy stuffing of ground pork, bread, olives, and prunes. The recipe will also work without the stuffing; just keep the pork loin whole, marinate, and roast it. The pork needs to marinate for at least 6 hours.

ADOBO MARINADE

- 5 CLOVES GARLIC, CRUSHED THROUGH A PRESS
- 2 TEASPOONS MILD PAPRIKA
- 2 TEASPOONS COARSE (KOSHER) SALT
- 1 TEASPOON HOT RED PEPPER FLAKES
- 2 TEASPOONS DRIED OREGANO
- 1 TEASPOON GROUND CUMIN
- ¼ TEASPOON GROUND CINNAMON
- ½ TABLESPOON FIRMLY PACKED LIGHT BROWN SUGAR
- 2 TABLESPOONS WHITE VINEGAR
- 1 TABLESPOON OLIVE OIL

- 1 BONELESS PORK LOIN (4 TO 5 POUNDS), BUTTERFLIED FOR STUFFING
- *PICADILLO* STUFFING (RECIPE FOLLOWS)
- 1 TABLESPOON OLIVE OIL
- 1¼ CUPS CHICKEN STOCK (PAGE 372) OR CANNED LOWER-SALT CHICKEN BROTH
- ½ CUP DRY WHITE WINE
- ¼ CUP MEDIUM-DRY SHERRY
- ½ CUP WATER, OPTIONAL, PLUS 2 TABLESPOONS COLD WATER
- 1 TABLESPOON FLOUR
- CILANTRO LEAVES, FOR GARNISH

1. To make the marinade: Puree all the marinade ingredients in a blender. Rub the meat all over with this mixture and refrigerate it for at least 6 hours or overnight. Bring to room temperature before roasting.

2. Preheat the oven to 350 degrees F.

3. Open the meat like a book and spread the stuffing all over its surface. Roll it up, jelly-roll style, starting with a long side. Tie it securely with a kitchen string. Set the roast in a baking pan and brush it with the oil. Pour the stock, wine, and sherry over the roast and bake, basting frequently, until the juices run clear when you test the meat with a skewer, about 1½ hours (approximately 20 minutes per pound).

4. Remove the roast from the oven, transfer it to a carving board, and let it stand for 10 minutes, covered loosely with foil.

5. On top of the stove, bring the pan juices to a boil, adding about ½ cup of water if they seem too reduced. In a small bowl, blend the flour with 2 tablespoons of cold water and slowly whisk this into the gravy. Cook, stirring, until the gravy thickens, about 2 minutes.

6. Carve the meat into slices, arrange the slices on a serving platter, and garnish with cilantro. Pass the gravy separately in a sauceboat.

SERVES 8 TO 10

In a large skillet, heat the oil over medium heat. Add the onion and garlic and cook, stirring, until the onion is soft, about 7 minutes. Add the pork, turn the heat to high, and cook, stirring, until lightly browned, about 5 minutes. Stir in the olives, prunes, oregano, thyme, cumin, and chili powder, and stir for 2 minutes. Add the wine and stock and cook for another 2 minutes. Stir in the bread and salt and pepper to taste, and transfer the mixture to a bowl. Cool until manageable.

PICADILLO STUFFING

3 TABLESPOONS OLIVE OIL

1 SMALL ONION, CHOPPED

2 TEASPOONS MINCED GARLIC

¾ POUND LEAN GROUND PORK OR BEEF

¼ CUP THINLY SLICED PIMIENTO-STUFFED OLIVES

⅓ CUP CHOPPED PITTED PRUNES

1 TEASPOON GROUND OREGANO

½ TEASPOON DRIED THYME

½ TEASPOON GROUND CUMIN

¼ TEASPOON CHILI POWDER

⅓ CUP DRY WHITE WINE

⅓ CUP CHICKEN STOCK (PAGE 372) OR CANNED LOWER-SALT CHICKEN BROTH

1½ CUPS CUBED STALE BREAD

SALT AND FRESHLY GROUND BLACK PEPPER, TO TASTE

Feijoada:
Three Cultures in One Pot

In Brazil, *feijoada* is ritual: a celebration of overindulgence, laziness, and *joie de vivre*. Brazilians like to say that *feijoada* is like a *calderão* (the black *feijoada* cauldron) bubbling with three cultures. Originally, the dish was created by slaves on the sugar plantations from black beans and scraps of dried meat from the master's table. The accompanying fried manioc flour (*farofa*) is an Indian touch, while the shredded kale, another mandatory side dish, is decidedly Portuguese, as are the cured meats that go into the *feijoada*.

Traditionally, *feijoada* days are Wednesdays and Saturdays, the weekend one being fuller and more elaborate. For Cariocas, Saturdays begin with a morning on the beach, followed by a long leisurely *feijoada* meal, and a late siesta. Life resumes around ten with a light supper and dancing. Cariocas say that *feijoada* should be eaten the way it cooks, slowly and languidly, a little at a time.

At establishments famous for their *feijoada*, such as the Cesar Park Hotel in Rio, the experience begins even before you enter the restaurant. You are greeted at the door by a lady in Bahian ruffled dress, who offers you a diminutive glass of *batida* (a festive drink of fruit juice and *cachaça*, the Brazilian "white lightning"), and a platter of *toresmos*, sinfully addictive salty pork cracklings. Then you help yourself to the meal. At home the beans and meats are cooked and served together, but at formal restaurants they are laid out separately: dried beef; several kinds of sausage; smoked bacon; tongue, ears, and feet of pig; and perhaps roast pork of some kind. Often the thick dark liquid from cooking the beans is served separately in small cups. (The Cariocas swear by it as the best remedy for a hangover.) The traditional accompaniments are crunchy *farofa* (buttered fried manioc flour), white rice, shredded stir-fried kale, sliced oranges, and plates of pickled chiles of varying degrees of heat, the hottest ones being the tiny *malaguetas*.

Feijoada Completa

What meats should go into a *feijoada*? This is a matter of heated debates even in Brazil. While the southerners swear by a hefty chunk of beef, northern purists adhere to the "pork only" rule. Some like pig's ears, others prefer tail. Things get even more complicated in the United States, where one is forced to make substitutions. American corned beef has its defenders and its detractors; as do Polish kielbasa and Italian sausage. Everyone, however, agrees that—though it will still be delicious—without the dried beef and pig's feet, the dish is not a real *feijoada*. The other matter of consensus is the cooking time: long and slow, to allow the smoky flavors of the meat to meld with the beans.

If you have access to a Brazilian butcher and want an authentic experience, ask for pig's feet, ears, and tail, all of which should be blanched first to get rid of the extra fat. Dried beef (*carne seca*) and cured tongue—which should be soaked overnight—are a must, as are the traditional sausages *linguiça*, and *paio*. Either a pork loin or a beef brisket can fulfill the function of the mandatory "noble" cut. Both will taste better if they are first rubbed with salt and seared in hot oil. And finally, don't forget the smoked meats: a good slab of bacon, and smoked pork butt or chops. This is the *feijoada completa*.

The recipe below—an amalgamation of several given to me by Brazilian cooks in this country—features a slightly shortened but authentic choice of meats. Most of them can be found at a good Hispanic butcher shop, though a German butcher who carries a variety of smoked meats is also a good bet. For a simpler feast, turn to your supermarket for some pig's feet, smoked pork butt, beef brisket, kielbasa, and a slab of bacon. Some meats have to be soaked overnight, so start early. You will also need a very large pot. *Feijoada* is an extravagant meal and the recipe below makes enough for a party, with plenty of leftovers. Kick off with *Caipirinhas* (page 12), and follow the meal with tropical fruit.

(continued)

1 POUND DRIED BEEF (*CARNE SECA, TASAJO, CHARQUI,* OR MEXICAN *CECINA*) OR JERKED BEEF

SMOKED PORK TONGUE, OPTIONAL

2 PIG'S FEET, SPLIT LENGTHWISE

1 POUND SWEET ITALIAN SAUSAGE, PRICKED IN SEVERAL PLACES WITH THE TIP OF A KNIFE

4 TABLESPOONS VEGETABLE OIL

3 POUNDS FIRST-CUT BEEF BRISKET OR BONELESS PORK LOIN

SALT TO TASTE

2 POUNDS DRIED BLACK TURTLE BEANS, PREFERABLY GOYA

½ POUND LEAN SMOKED BACON, IN 1 PIECE

2 POUNDS SMOKED PORK CHOPS OR SMOKED PORK BUTT

1 POUND *LINGUIÇA* OR KIELBASA SAUSAGE

1 LARGE ONION, FINELY CHOPPED

10 CLOVES GARLIC, CRUSHED THROUGH A PRESS

1 LARGE BUNCH CILANTRO, RINSED AND TIED WITH STRING

ACCOMPANIMENTS

DOUBLE RECIPE WHITE RICE (PAGE 247)

FAROFA (RECIPE FOLLOWS)

STIR-FRIED GARLICKY KALE (PAGE 236)

6 JUICY ORANGES, CUT INTO WEDGES

VARIOUS PICKLED CHILE PEPPERS

TRIPLE RECIPE PIQUANT SAUCE (PAGE 81)

1. In separate bowls, soak the dried beef and the smoked tongue (if using) in cold water to cover for at least 6 hours or overnight. Drain and rinse before cooking.

2. In a large pot, blanch the pig's feet in water to cover over medium heat for 15 minutes. Add the Italian sausage, and cook for another 5 minutes. Drain.

3. In a large skillet, heat 2 tablespoons of the oil over high heat. Rub the beef brisket or pork loin generously with salt, and brown it on all sides. Pat dry with paper towels.

4. In a 5-quart stockpot, combine the beans, the reserved dried beef and tongue (if using), the pig's feet, brisket or pork loin, the bacon, and the smoked pork chops or butt. Add enough water to cover the beans and the meats by 2½ inches and bring to a boil, skimming. Reduce the heat to medium-low, cover, and simmer for 1½ hours. Keep checking the level of liquid, adding more cold water to keep it at the same level.

5. Add the reserved Italian sausage and the *linguiça* or kielbasa. Check the level of liquid, adding enough to cover the beans and the meats by 2½ inches. Continue cooking until the beans and all the meats are very tender, about 1 more hour.

6. In a large skillet, heat the remaining 2 tablespoons of the oil over medium heat. Add the onion and garlic and cook, stirring, until the onion is soft, about 7 minutes. With a slotted spoon remove about 2 cups of beans from the liquid in the pot and add them to the skillet. Mash the beans right in the skillet with a fork or potato ricer, and pour the contents of the skillet back into the pot. Add the cilantro and salt to taste (if necessary), and cook for another 20 minutes.

7. To serve, remove and discard the smoked bacon and the cilantro. With a slotted spoon remove all the meats from the pot. When cool enough to handle, cut the sausages into thick slices. Cut all the other meats into serving portions. Arrange all the meats on a large platter. Transfer the beans with some of their liquid to a large serving bowl.

8. Serve the beans and meats accompanied by bowls of rice, *farofa*, shredded kale, wedges of oranges, pickled chiles, and Piquant Sauce.

SERVES 10 TO 12

Farofa (Toasted Manioc Meal)

In a large skillet, melt the butter over medium heat. Add the *farofa* and stir for 2 minutes. Add the egg and keep stirring, breaking it up as much as possible, until the egg is set. Keep stirring until the *farofa* is crunchy and golden, about 5 minutes. Add salt to taste.

4½ TABLESPOONS UNSALTED BUTTER
2 CUPS *FAROFA* (AVAILABLE AT BRAZILIAN
    GROCERIES)
1 LARGE EGG, BEATEN
SALT TO TASTE

SERVES 10 TO 12 AS AN
ACCOMPANIMENT TO *FEIJOADA*

Poultry

Graffiti, Buenos Aires, Argentina.

Cap Ducal Restaurant,
Valparaíso, Chile.

Regulars
at the
San Telmo
Market,
Buenos
Aires,
Argentina.

EVERY LATIN cook will agree that for a Creole chicken dish to be *rico y sabroso* (flavorful and tasty), it has to be supremely well seasoned. Whether poultry is to be sautéed, stewed, or even boiled, most good recipes will begin with *para adobar el pollo*, "to season the chicken," then recommend a generous rub of pounded garlic, coarse salt, chiles, cumin, bay leaf, and oregano, and a nice sprinkling of sour orange, lemon or lime juice, vinegar, or white wine. Historically, the function of these spicy marinades, known as *adobos*, was not only to flavor the meat, but to tenderize and prevent it from spoiling in a hot tropical climate. The spicy, slightly acidic taste took hold and became the norm. To enhance the flavor still further, the bird can be simmered with various *sofritos*—piquant, fresh-tasting, cooked seasoning mixtures that are the base of most Latin American stews and boiled meals—and finished with an extra-fresh splash of vinegar or wine, capers or olives for a briny accent, a touch of annatto to add an appealing red hue, and a good dose of cilantro for freshness.

In Latin America and the Caribbean, poaching and braising are the preferred techniques, as fresh backyard chickens tend to be leaner and tougher than ours. Even for stews, the bird will often be poached first, and then finished in a well-spiced colorful sauce. Nourishing, colorful, and generous are the various soupy stews, *sancochos*, *ensopados*, and *guisos*, where the chicken simmers with a host of vegetables in a rich, deep-flavored, well-seasoned stock. Whole roast birds, not as economical as soupy stews, are usually reserved for fiestas and special occasions, as are European-influenced galantines and elaborate, painstakingly prepared, boned and stuffed chickens and turkeys.

No matter how you plan to cook it, a good-quality country chicken is of utmost importance. You will find that "ethnic" chickens often have better flavor. For boiled and soupy dishes, my choices are kosher or Chinatown birds—fatless, lean, and white. I also often buy my chickens at *halal* Indian and Middle Eastern butchers. For braised dishes, a stewing hen is also a good choice because it can sustain the long simmering without falling apart. A free-range chicken, while more expensive, is certainly worth it, as are the new breed of supermarket chickens, not fed on chemicals or preservatives. For roasting I like the large plump Perdue roasters, as long as you trim them of all fat.

Colored sands, Mendoza, Argentina.

Señora Sánchez's Roast Chicken with Plantain and Sausage Stuffing

(POLLO AL HORNO CON RELLENO DE MADUROS Y CHORIZO)

Señora Sánchez is the wife of my ebullient Colombian butcher. He noticed my interest in culinary matters (I am the only *gringa* on the block who buys pig's feet, dried meat, and his excellent *chorizo*) and introduced me to his wife, Soledad, a well-known cook in the Colombian community. "The *pollo* is so *sabroso,* and you won't find this 'formula' in any book," she exclaimed, proud of her invention. She was right, the plantains make a great stuffing for the bird. They have the right starchy, lush texture, which doesn't disintegrate with slow cooking, and a striking flavor, which combines excellently with smoked meats or sausages. The same stuffing will also work with turkey—just triple the amount. Serve this with Stir-Fried Greens with Chile and Annatto Oil (page 376).

1. To prepare the chicken: In a mortar and pestle, pound the garlic to a paste together with the salt. Whisk in the oil and orange juice. Rub the chicken all over with this mixture and let it stand while you prepare the stuffing.

CHICKEN

3 CLOVES GARLIC, CRUSHED THROUGH A PRESS

1 TEASPOON COARSE (KOSHER) SALT, OR TO TASTE

2 TABLESPOONS ANNATTO OIL (PAGE 376)

2 TABLESPOONS FRESH SOUR ORANGE JUICE (SEE PAGE 145) OR A COMBINATION OF LIME AND ORANGE JUICE

1 ROASTING CHICKEN (ABOUT 5 POUNDS) RINSED AND PATTED DRY

STUFFING

2 LARGE RIPE PLANTAINS, PEELED AS DIRECTED ON PAGE 379 AND CUT INTO ½-INCH SLICES

2 TABLESPOONS UNSALTED BUTTER, MELTED

1½ CUPS COARSELY CHOPPED ONIONS

2 SMALL *CHORIZO* SAUSAGES, SLICED

¼ CUP THINLY SLICED PITTED GREEN OLIVES

½ CUP CHICKEN STOCK (PAGE 372), CANNED LOWER-SALT CHICKEN BROTH, OR WATER

SALT TO TASTE

2. To make the stuffing: Boil the plaintains in salted water to cover until tender, about 10 to 15 minutes. Drain.

3. Preheat the oven to 350 degrees F.

4. In a large skillet, melt the butter over medium heat. Add the onions and cook, stirring, until wilted, about 5 minutes. Add the *chorizo* and cook until lightly browned. Pour off all but 2 tablespoons of the fat. Add the plaintains, olives, and stock, and cook for 10 minutes, stirring until the plaintains are soft. Season with salt to taste.

5. Stuff the cavity of the bird with the stuffing and truss the bird.

6. Place the chicken on a rack in a large roasting pan and roast until the juices run clear when you prick the thickest part of the thigh with a skewer, about 1½ hours.

7. Remove the stuffing from the chicken, transfer it to a bowl, and cover it with foil. Cover the chicken loosely with foil and let it stand for 10 minutes.

8. Carve the chicken and serve accompanied by the stuffing.

SERVES 4 TO 6

Chiles

"The uses of chile in the New World were not confined to food. When the Indians attacked the fort that Columbus built in Santo Domingo they lobbed calabashes full of wood ashes and ground chiles into the enclosure. Chile smoke was used as a fumigant, as well as a means of chemical warfare, and the Aztecs disciplined their recalcitrant offspring with it."

—Sophie Coe, *America's First Cuisines*

Just like Europeans, the indigenous peoples of South and Central America were given to religious rituals that included fasting and penitence. The first item they deprived themselves of during their fasts? Chiles.

Roast Chicken Adobo

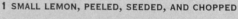

Adobo, a spicy marinade, appears in various forms throughout Latin America, Mexico, and the Caribbean. My version below is very versatile (and very hot!) and can be used with almost any roast or grilled poultry, meat, or fish.

1 SMALL LEMON, PEELED, SEEDED, AND CHOPPED

4 LARGE CLOVES GARLIC, CHOPPED

$^1/_3$ CUP FINELY CHOPPED CILANTRO LEAVES AND STEMS

1 TEASPOON DRIED OREGANO

1 TEASPOON GROUND CUMIN

$^1/_4$ TEASPOON GROUND CINNAMON

PINCH OF SUGAR

$1^1/_2$ TEASPOONS SALT

1 ROASTING CHICKEN (ABOUT $5^1/_2$ POUNDS), RINSED AND PATTED DRY

$1^1/_2$ TABLESPOONS OLIVE OIL

1 CUP CHICKEN STOCK (PAGE 372) OR CANNED LOWER-SALT CHICKEN BROTH

$^2/_3$ CUPS DRY WHITE WINE

1 SMALL DRIED ANCHO CHILE, SEEDED

4 DRIED ÁRBOL CHILES, SEEDED

1. In a dry, heavy skillet, toast the chiles over medium heat, stirring, until they become several shades darker, about $1^1/_2$ minutes. With scissors, cut the chiles into pieces. Place them in a small bowl and add hot water to cover. Let the chiles soak for 15 minutes. Drain, reserving 3 tablespoons of the soaking liquid.

2. In a blender, combine the chiles and their reserved soaking liquid with the lemon, garlic, cilantro, oregano, cumin, cinnamon, sugar, and salt and blend until pureed.

3. With your hands, loosen the skin on and around the legs and breast of the chicken. Rub some of the mixture under the skin of the chicken and spread the remaining mixture all over the chicken. Cover loosely with foil and refrigerate the chicken at least 2 hours or overnight.

4. Preheat the oven to 350 degrees F.

5. Place the chicken in a roasting pan and brush it with the oil. Roast for 30 minutes. Pour the stock and wine into the pan and continue roasting until the juices run clear when a skewer is inserted into the thickest part of the thigh, about $1^3/_4$ hours. Let the chicken stand, covered loosely with foil, for 15 minutes. Degrease the pan juices.

6. Carve the chicken and transfer it to a serving platter. Moisten with some of the pan juices and serve the rest on the side.

SERVES 6

Banana-Stuffed Chicken Breasts with Ginger Sauce

(PEITO DE FRANGO TROPICAL)

This recipe comes from the breathtakingly beautiful village of Olinda in the northeast of Brazil, where pristine Baroque churches are dramatically set against a backdrop of unimaginably lush tropical greenery. The recipe hails from the kitchen of Mauricio Andrade Carneiro, a European-trained chef who applies his classical skills to native tropical produce.

4 SKINLESS BONELESS CHICKEN BREAST HALVES (ABOUT 1½ POUNDS TOTAL), RINSED AND PATTED DRY

½ TEASPOON MILD PAPRIKA

LARGE PINCH OF CAYENNE

2 TEASPOONS FRESH LEMON JUICE

SALT AND FRESHLY GROUND BLACK PEPPER, TO TASTE

4-OUNCE LOG FRESH GOAT CHEESE

4 TEASPOONS MINCED FLAT-LEAF PARSLEY

1 LARGE BANANA, PEELED AND QUARTERED LENGTHWISE

3 TABLESPOONS UNSALTED BUTTER

1 SMALL ONION, FINELY CHOPPED

3 TABLESPOONS GRATED FRESH GINGER

½ TEASPOON GRATED ORANGE ZEST

⅓ CUP DRY WHITE WINE

1 CUP CHICKEN STOCK (PAGE 372) OR CANNED LOWER-SALT CHICKEN BROTH

½ CUP LIGHT CREAM

1. Preheat the oven to 375 degrees F.

2. Place the chicken breasts on a work surface. Remove the fillets (the finger-size muscle on the back of each breast) and save them for another use. Pound the chicken breasts with the flat side of a meat mallet until thin. Rub them with the paprika, cayenne, lemon juice, salt, and pepper.

3. Cut the cheese lengthwise into four pieces, shaping each one into a log. Lay the chicken breasts flat, and sprinkle the insides with parsley. Place a piece of banana and a piece of cheese lengthwise on each piece of chicken, trimming the ends of banana to fit the chicken, as necessary. Starting on a long side, roll up the chicken pieces, spring-roll fashion, tucking in the ends to enclose the filling completely. Secure them with toothpicks.

4. Place the chicken rolls, seam side down, in a shallow roasting pan. Cut 2 tablespoons of the butter into pieces and dot the rolls with the butter. Bake, basting frequently, until the chicken is golden and the juices run clear, about 25 to 30 minutes.

5. While the chicken is cooking, prepare the sauce. In a small skillet, melt the remaining tablespoon of butter over medium heat. Add the onion and sauté until wilted, about 5 minutes. Add the ginger and orange zest, and cook for another 2 minutes. Add the wine and reduce by half over high heat, about 3 to 4 minutes. Add the stock and cream and reduce by half again, about 10 minutes. Strain through a fine sieve and keep warm.

6. To serve, slice the rolls into 1-inch-thick rounds with a sharp knife. Arrange them decoratively on dinner plates and spoon some sauce around them.

SERVES 4 TO 6

Coconut-Crusted Chicken Nuggets

(POLLO ENROLLADO EN COCO)

In this Spanish-Caribbean recipe, the rum-and-lime-marinated chicken nuggets get a lush coating of coconut. Serve with Tamarind Ketchup (page 238) or Bahian Coconut-Peanut Dip (page 25).

1½ POUNDS SKINLESS, BONELESS CHICKEN
    BREASTS, RINSED AND PATTED DRY
1 TEASPOON MILD PAPRIKA
½ TEASPOON GROUND CUMIN
¼ TEASPOON GROUND TURMERIC
¼ TEASPOON CAYENNE
3 CLOVES GARLIC, CRUSHED THROUGH A PRESS
2 TABLESPOONS FRESH LIME JUICE
2 TABLESPOONS DARK RUM
1 CUP PLUS 1 TABLESPOON ALL-PURPOSE FLOUR
2 TEASPOONS BAKING POWDER
½ TEASPOON SALT
1 CUP CLUB SODA
PEANUT OIL, FOR DEEP FRYING THE CHICKEN
ABOUT 3 CUPS DRIED COCONUT

1. Rub the chicken with the paprika, cumin, turmeric, cayenne, and garlic. Place in a bowl and toss with the lime juice and rum. Cover with plastic wrap and chill for 2 to 6 hours.

2. Remove the chicken from the marinade and cut it into $1\frac{1}{2} \times \frac{1}{2}$-inch strips.

3. In a bowl, sift together the flour, baking powder, and salt. Whisk in the club soda and let stand for 10 minutes.

4. In a deep skillet, heat 1½ inches of the oil to 350 degrees F. over medium heat. Spread the coconut on a cutting board covered with wax paper. (You might want to use the coconut in batches.)

Working with a few pieces of chicken at a time, dip them in the batter, letting the excess drip off. Then roll them in the coconut, pressing with your fingers to help the coating adhere. Fry the chicken in batches until crisp and golden, about 4 to 5 minutes. Drain on paper towels and serve at once.

SERVES 6

Drunken Chicken with Papaya

(P O L L O   B O R R A C H O   C O N   P A P A Y A)

This chicken, inspired by the Spanish-Caribbean dish *pollo borracho*, is marinated in a mixture of lime, rum, and sugar, then baked with papaya.

1. To make the marinade: Combine all the marinade ingredients in a blender and process until smooth.

2. Prick the chicken all over with the tines of a fork and rub generously with salt and pepper. Place the chicken in a large glass or ceramic bowl and toss with the marinade. Cover with plastic wrap and refrigerate for 6 hours or overnight. Bring back to room temperature before baking.

3. Preheat the oven to 425 degrees F. Place the chicken in a large roasting pan, reserving the marinade. Brush the chicken with the oil and bake for 15 minutes until it begins to brown. Reduce the oven temperature to 350 degrees and bake another 10 minutes.

MARINADE

1/2 CUP FRESH LIME JUICE
1/2 CUP FRESH ORANGE JUICE
1/3 CUP DARK RUM
4 CLOVES GARLIC, CRUSHED THROUGH A PRESS
2 TEASPOONS GRATED LIME ZEST
2 TEASPOONS GRATED ORANGE ZEST
2 TABLESPOONS DISTILLED WHITE VINEGAR
2 1/2 TABLESPOONS LIGHT BROWN SUGAR

4 1/2 POUNDS CHICKEN DRUMSTICKS AND THIGHS, RINSED AND PATTED DRY
SALT AND FRESHLY GROUND BLACK PEPPER, TO TASTE
1 1/2 TABLESPOONS OLIVE OIL
1 SMALL PAPAYA, PEELED, SEEDED, AND DICED

4. Remove the chicken from the oven and add the papaya and the reserved marinade. Add salt to the sauce, if necessary. Return to the oven and bake, basting with the marinade, until the chicken is almost falling off the bone, about 30 minutes.

5. Transfer to a serving platter and spoon the papaya and sauce over the chicken.

S E R V E S   6   T O   8

Corn, Chicken, and Beef Pie with Olives and Raisins

(PASTEL DE CHOCLO)

This is a Chilean shepherd's pie of sorts, consisting of layers of spiced ground beef and smothered onions, bite-size pieces of chicken pepped up with raisins, olives, and chopped egg, and a magnificent cap of basil scented creamed corn. Traditionally, the *pastel* is baked in a clay *cazuela*, sprinkled with a generous amount of sugar, until the top caramelizes slightly. Even in my version, the dish is quite sweet, so you might want to reduce the amount of sugar to taste. In Chile you would not see *pastel de choclo*, even at commercial restaurants, when fresh tender young corn is not in season. However, I have tried the dish with pureed frozen corn kernels and found the results, if not dazzling, at least highly satisfying. The pie can be baked either in one large dish or in individual earthenware dishes.

7 CUPS FRESH OR FROZEN AND DEFROSTED
    CORN KERNELS
3½ TABLESPOONS OLIVE OIL
5 TEASPOONS FINELY MINCED GARLIC
1¼ CUPS MILK
2¼ TABLESPOONS SUGAR
3 TABLESPOONS SLIVERED FRESH BASIL LEAVES
3 TABLESPOONS UNSALTED BUTTER
3¼ CUPS CHOPPED ONIONS
1½ POUNDS GROUND BEEF SIRLOIN OR TOP
    ROUND
1½ TABLESPOONS MILD PAPRIKA
2 TEASPOONS GROUND CUMIN
2 TEASPOONS DRIED OREGANO
1½ CUPS BONED COOKED CHICKEN MEAT, CUT
    INTO BITE-SIZE PIECES
⅓ CUP CHICKEN STOCK (PAGE 372), CANNED
    LOWER-SALT CHICKEN BROTH, OR WATER
¾ CUP DARK RAISINS
¾ CUP SLICED CANNED PITTED BLACK OLIVES
SALT AND FRESHLY GROUND BLACK PEPPER, TO
    TASTE
3 HARD-COOKED EGGS, CHOPPED

1. Working in batches, process the corn in a food processor to a medium puree. In a large saucepan, heat 1 tablespoon of the oil over medium heat. Add 1½ teaspoons of the garlic and stir for 1 minute. Add the corn and cook, stirring, for 5 minutes. Add the milk, 1½ tablespoons of the sugar, and the basil, and cook over low heat, stirring, until the mixture thickens to porridge-like consistency, about 15 minutes. Set aside.

2. Preheat the oven to 350 degrees F.

3. In a large skillet, melt the butter in 1 tablespoon of the remaining oil over medium heat. Cook the onions and 2 teaspoons of the garlic, stirring, until softened but not browned, about 10 minutes. Add the beef, turn the heat to high, and cook, breaking it up with a fork, for 5 minutes. Add 1 tablespoon of the paprika, 1½ teaspoons of the cumin, and 1½ teaspoons of the oregano, and cook until the beef is no longer pink, about 5 to 7 minutes more.

4. In another skillet, heat the remaining 1½ tablespoons of the oil over medium heat. Add the remaining 1½ teaspoons of the garlic, and stir for 1 minute. Add the chicken, the remaining ½ tablespoon of paprika, ½ teaspoon of cumin, and ½ teaspoon of oregano, and cook, stirring, for 5 minutes. Add the stock, raisins, and olives and cook over low heat, stirring, for 5 to 7 minutes. Season the corn, the beef, and the chicken mixtures with salt and pepper.

5. To assemble the pie, place the beef in one layer in a deep clay or other ovenproof casserole, about 9 × 12 inches. Spread the chicken on top, and sprinkle with the chopped eggs. Spread the corn mixture evenly over all and sprinkle with the remaining ¾ tablespoon of the sugar.

6. Bake for 20 minutes. Increase the oven temperature to 450 degrees and bake until the top is well browned, about 10 to 15 minutes longer. Cut into squares and serve.

SERVES 6 TO 8

Panamanian Chicken Stew

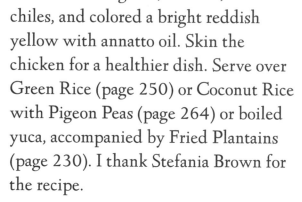

(POLLO GUISADO ESTILO PANAMEÑO)

This is a bracing, uncomplicated stew of chicken simmered in its own juices with the addition of a *sofrito*—a seasoning mixture of crushed garlic, cilantro, and chiles, and colored a bright reddish yellow with annatto oil. Skin the chicken for a healthier dish. Serve over Green Rice (page 250) or Coconut Rice with Pigeon Peas (page 264) or boiled yuca, accompanied by Fried Plantains (page 230). I thank Stefania Brown for the recipe.

SOFRITO

- 1 MEDIUM BUNCH CILANTRO, TRIMMED AND CHOPPED
- ⅓ CUP CHOPPED FLAT-LEAF PARSLEY
- 12 CLOVES GARLIC, CHOPPED
- 2 SWEET RED CHILES, SUCH AS FRESNO, OR 1 SMALL HOT CHILE AND ¼ CUP CHOPPED RED BELL PEPPER
- ½ SMALL GREEN BELL PEPPER, CORED, SEEDED, AND CHOPPED
- ½ TEASPOON SALT
- ¼ CUP DISTILLED WHITE VINEGAR

- 2 TABLESPOONS LIGHT OLIVE OIL
- 2 MEDIUM ONIONS, HALVED AND SLICED
- 3 POUNDS CHICKEN PIECES, RINSED AND PATTED DRY
- ½ CUP CHICKEN STOCK (PAGE 372), OR CANNED LOWER-SALT CHICKEN BROTH, OR WATER, AS NEEDED
- 5 RIPE PLUM TOMATOES, BLANCHED, PEELED, SEEDED, AND CHOPPED
- 1 TABLESPOON ANNATTO OIL (PAGE 376)
- SALT AND FRESHLY GROUND BLACK PEPPER, TO TASTE
- PINCH OF SUGAR, OR TO TASTE

1. To make the *sofrito*: In a blender using the on/off button, crush all the *sofrito* ingredients to a coarse paste. Set aside.

2. In a heavy, shallow casserole with a tight-fitting lid, heat the oil over medium-low heat. Add the onions and sauté until translucent, about 5 minutes. Raise the heat to medium, add the chicken, and cook, stirring, until it just begins to take on some color. Cover the casserole tightly and cook, shaking the pan occasionally, until the chicken throws off its liquid, about 10 minutes. Check the amount of liquid, and if there is not enough to barely cover the chicken, add some chicken stock or water. Stir in the *sofrito* mixture and the tomatoes, cover, and cook until the chicken is very tender, about 50 minutes, shaking the casserole occasionally. Periodically check the liquid, adding a little stock or water if the chicken looks dry.

3. Add the annatto oil, and check and correct the seasoning, adding enough sugar to take off the sour edge without making the dish sweet and sour. Cook, uncovered, for another 5 minutes.

SERVES 4

Tropical Root Vegetable and Chicken Stew

(SANCOCHO DE GALLINA)

Sancocho (which comes from the word *sancochar*, "to stew"), is a soupy dish, thick with meats or fish and filling tropical tubers. It is a classic one-dish meal in many Latin countries. This recipe comes from Eric Basulto, chef at SOB nightclub in New York, and is inspired by the *sancocho* prepared by his mother and grandmother. Meals at Eric's household were truly meal-in-a-pot affairs, Grandma dumping all her trimmings, rice, and salad straight into the stew pot. As *sancocho* is quite a thin stew, a good stock is the secret of its success. Eric's mother would start an oxtail stock in the morning and let it simmer pretty much all day. Here I use a rich, well-reduced chicken stock, made from scratch. If you have to use canned chicken broth, reduce it by one third before adding it to the stew ingredients. You should have 8 cups. Serve the *sancocho* in large soup plates with a serving of white rice added to each plate. You can skin the chicken, if you wish, for a healthier dish. The ingredient list is long, but the actual dish is very simple to prepare.

STOCK

4 POUNDS CHICKEN NECKS AND BONES, WELL RINSED AND PATTED DRY

12 CUPS WATER

1 ONION, QUARTERED

8 CLOVES GARLIC, SMASHED

2 STALKS CELERY

3 SMALL CARROTS, PEELED AND CUT INTO CHUNKS

8 SPRIGS FLAT-LEAF PARSLEY, TIED WITH A STRING

2 MEDIUM PLUM TOMATOES, QUARTERED

SALT AND FRESHLY GROUND BLACK PEPPER, TO TASTE

(continued)

1. To make the stock: Place all the stock ingredients in a large stockpot and bring to a boil, skimming off the froth that rises to the surface. Cook, covered, over low heat, for 2 hours. Strain the stock, return it to the pot, and cook, uncovered, over medium heat until the stock is reduced to about 8 cups, about 45 minutes.

2. While the stock is cooking, marinate the chicken: Prick the chicken all over with the tines of a fork. Rub the surface with garlic, salt, paprika, and cayenne. Cover with plastic, and let stand for about 1 hour.

3. In a deep, heavy saucepan, melt the butter over medium-low heat. Add the onions and minced garlic and sauté, stirring, for 5 minutes until wilted. Push the onion to the side of the saucepan. Add the chicken and cook, tossing and stirring, until the chicken is very lightly browned, about 10 minutes.

4. Add the stock, bring to a simmer, and simmer for 10 minutes. Add the yuca and *boniato* and simmer for another 15 minutes until half-cooked. Add the *calabaza* and plantain, and season with salt to taste. Cook, partially covered, until the chicken and vegetables are very tender, about 25 to 30 minutes.

5. Stir in the lime juice, hot sauce, sugar to taste, and cilantro and cook for 1 more minute. Serve in soup plates, accompanied by cooked rice.

CHICKEN AND VEGETABLES

3½ POUNDS CHICKEN PIECES, RINSED AND
   PATTED DRY
2 CLOVES GARLIC, CRUSHED THROUGH A PRESS
1 TEASPOON COARSE (KOSHER) SALT
2 TEASPOONS MILD PAPRIKA
½ TEASPOON CAYENNE
3 TABLESPOONS UNSALTED BUTTER
1½ CUPS THINLY SLICED ONIONS
1 TABLESPOON MINCED GARLIC
1½ POUNDS YUCA, PREPARED AS DIRECTED ON
   PAGE 79, AND CUT INTO 1½-INCH PIECES
½ POUND *BONIATO* (CUBAN WHITE SWEET
   POTATO) OR SWEET POTATO, PEELED AND CUT
   INTO 1½-INCH PIECES
½ POUND *CALABAZA*, PEELED, SEEDED, AND CUT
   INTO 1½-INCH PIECES
1 LARGE GREEN PLANTAIN (8 OUNCES), PEELED
   AS DIRECTED ON PAGE 379, BROKEN INTO
   1½-INCH SECTIONS, AND TOSSED WITH FRESH
   LEMON JUICE (2 TEASPOONS)
SALT, TO TASTE
2 TO 3 TABLESPOONS FRESH LIME JUICE
DASH OF HOT SAUCE OF YOUR CHOICE
PINCH OF SUGAR
1 SMALL BUNCH CILANTRO, TRIMMED AND
   MINCED
WHITE RICE (PAGE 247)

SERVES 6 TO 8

Chicken Vatapá

Vatapá is a masterpiece of the Afro-Brazilian Bahian repertoire—a coconut stew, thickened with nuts and/or bread, flavored with a mix of tomatoes, chiles, and ginger. Most often *vatapá* is prepared with seafood (and flavored with ground dried shrimp), but the chicken version is also delicious. *Dendê* (Brazilian palm oil) is a required ingredient in most Bahian dishes, but even if you manage to find it, it will certainly be an unfamiliar taste. Annatto oil, however, will do the job of adding a pleasing orange hue to the dish.

2 TABLESPOONS LIGHT OLIVE OIL OR PEANUT OIL

ONE 3½-POUND CHICKEN, CUT INTO SMALLISH SERVING PIECES, RINSED AND PATTED DRY

1 SMALL ONION, CHOPPED

3 CLOVES GARLIC, CHOPPED

4 LARGE PLUM TOMATOES, CHOPPED

1 SMALL GREEN BELL PEPPER, CORED, SEEDED, AND CHOPPED

1 SERRANO CHILE, CHOPPED

1-INCH KNOB FRESH GINGER, PEELED AND CHOPPED

2 CUPS CANNED COCONUT MILK, WELL STIRRED

1 CUP WATER

SALT AND FRESHLY GROUND BLACK PEPPER, TO TASTE

¾ CUP CUBED WHITE BREAD (CRUSTS REMOVED)

⅓ CUP GROUND CASHEW NUTS

HOT SAUCE, TO TASTE

1 TABLESPOON FRESH LEMON JUICE, OR MORE TO TASTE

1 TABLESPOON ANNATTO OIL (PAGE 376)

CILANTRO LEAVES, FOR GARNISH

WHITE RICE (PAGE 247)

1. In a large, heavy saucepan, heat the olive oil over medium heat, and lightly brown the chicken on all sides, about 5 minutes. Cover, and cook while preparing the next step, 5 to 7 minutes.

2. In a blender, process the onion, garlic, tomatoes, bell pepper, chile, and ginger to a paste. Add the processed mixture to the chicken and bring to a simmer over medium-low heat. Cook, stirring, for 10 minutes. Add 1½ cups of the coconut milk and the water. Season with salt and pepper, cover, and bring to a simmer. Cook until the chicken is tender, about 40 minutes.

3. In the meantime, soak the bread in the remaning ¹/₂ cup of the coconut milk. Process it in a food processor until smooth.

4. When the chicken is tender, add the pureed bread and the ground cashews to the saucepan. Simmer over low heat until the stew thickens, about 7 minutes. Add the hot sauce, lemon juice, and annatto oil, and cook for another minute. Serve, garnished with cilantro, accompanied by cooked white rice.

SERVES 4

Tamarind: Tart, Sweet, and Delicious

The tamarind tree—tall, shady, and beautiful—grows in many tropical climates, and the inhabitants of the Caribbean islands rely on it as a protection from hurricanes and strong winds. The tree bears brown pods, similar in size and appearance to fava bean pods. When you crack one open, it will reveal a sticky, light brown pulp, with a delightful sour-sweet taste (like an acidic date or prune), encasing several seeds. In the Latin kitchen, tamarind pulp is diluted with water and used mainly as a refreshing tart drink. In European and North American kitchens, some will recognize it as the "secret" ingredient in Worcestershire sauce. But it doesn't have to end there: the pulp is incredibly tasty when added to sweet-and-sour sauces, glazes, chutneys, stews, and marinades. In fact, it's one of my absolutely favorite tropical ingredients, and I urge you to try it as soon as you can.

While you can sometimes spot fresh tamarind pods in Hispanic groceries, most tamarind pulp in this country is sold dried, either as seedless concentrate, or in small rectangular blocks packaged in plastic. The best variety is from Thailand, and can be bought in most Asian groceries. Once opened, the tamarind pulp should be stored in small Ziploc bags, or wrapped tightly in plastic wrap. It will keep almost indefinitely.

To use the pulp (or the concentrate), soak it in boiling water for about 15 minutes to soften it, and pass the resulting thick liquid through a fine sieve to get rid of the fibers and seeds. Fresh pods should be cracked open, the flesh and the seeds scooped into a bowl, and then strained through a fine sieve. When a recipe calls for a small amount of tamarind, fresh lime or lemon juice, mixed with a bit of brown sugar or molasses, can be used as a substitute.

Grilled Chicken with Tamarind and Panela Glaze

(POLLO A LA BRASA CON GLASEADO DE TAMARINDO Y PANELA)

This recipe is typical of Nuevo Latino cooking—second-generation Latin chefs coining a new culinary style by drawing on the richness of their culinary traditions and the ingredients of their childhood. Unlike Southeast Asian cuisines, where tart tamarind pulp is used for flavoring savory dishes, Latin cuisines use it mostly as a base for a drink called *tamarindo*. Nevertheless, with its sweet-and-sour taste and sticky texture it is ideal for glazes and marinades, especially when mixed with the rich taste of the tropical cane sugar, *panela*.

4 TABLESPOONS TAMARIND PULP (AVAILABLE AT ASIAN OR HISPANIC GROCERIES)

2 DRIED ANCHO CHILES, BROKEN UP

3/4 CUP BOILING WATER

5 CLOVES GARLIC, CHOPPED

COARSE (KOSHER) SALT TO TASTE, PLUS ADDITIONAL FOR THE CHICKEN

1/3 CUP CHOPPED CILANTRO

3 TABLESPOONS DISTILLED WHITE VINEGAR

3 TABLESPOONS CRUSHED *PANELA* (*PILONCILLO*) OR PACKED LIGHT BROWN SUGAR

2 TABLESPOONS OLIVE OIL

4 POUNDS CHICKEN PIECES, RINSED AND PATTED DRY

1. Place the tamarind and chiles in a bowl and pour the boiling water over them. Soak for 30 minutes, mashing and breaking up the solids with a fork. Strain through a sieve, scraping the bottom of the sieve with a wooden spoon.

2. Combine the strained tamarind-ancho pulp, the garlic, salt, cilantro, vinegar, *panela*, and oil in a blender and puree.

3. Rub the chicken with salt and prick it all over with the tines of a fork. Place it in a large shallow bowl and pour the marinade over it. Cover with plastic wrap and marinate in the refrigerator for 6 hours or overnight, turning occasionally.

4. Preheat the broiler, or prepare coals for grilling. Grill the chicken, basting it with the marinade and turning it several times, until the juices run clear when you insert a skewer into the thickest part of the thigh, about 25 to 30 minutes. (The breasts will take less time to cook.) You can also bake the chicken in a 375-degree oven for 1 hour.

SERVES 4 TO 6

Pineapple: A Royal Favorite

When pineapple reached European shores, it was immediately received with unanimous acclaim. A native of South America, the pineapple was cultivated for centuries by pre-Columbian Indians. When the Spanish explorers first encountered it on the Caribbean islands, they thought it resembled a local pine cone and christened the fragrant fruit "piña." One of the reasons for its smashing success is that, unlike other New World fruits—which were transformed from ambrosia into a rotten mess by the months-long voyage from the newfound lands—the pineapple could be picked green and slowly ripened on the ship. It could also be compared in taste to the familiar European melon, peach, or muscat grape, which made a great difference to conservative Spanish taste buds.

According to an eyewitness, King Ferdinand of Spain, the monarch who dispatched Columbus on his momentous voyage, pronounced it "the best thing he's ever tasted." "None pleases my taste as does the pine," lauded George Washington centuries later, after sampling the fruit on the island of Barbados. In Europe, the new fruit had by then become a symbol of luxury and indulgence, of friendship and hospitality. In the eighteenth century, the British spared no expense constructing absurdly elaborate hothouses to grow this tropical fruit in their unwelcoming northern climate. But they certainly knew what they were doing: a single pineapple could be rented out at enormous cost to serve as a centerpiece for private banquets and state dinners!

Rum and Adobo Marinated Chicken with Pineapple Salsa

(POLLO A LA BRASA CON SALSA DE PIÑA)

This recipe comes from my friend Steven Raichlen, the author of a wonderful book called *Miami Spice*, and a great connoisseur of Latin food.

CHICKEN AND MARINADE

4 LARGE CHICKEN BREAST HALVES, PREFERABLY
    WITH BONE IN (ABOUT 2 POUNDS), RINSED
    AND PATTED DRY
½ CUP FRESH LIME JUICE
3 TABLESPOONS DARK RUM
3 TABLESPOONS PINEAPPLE JUICE
2 TABLESPOONS OLIVE OIL
3 CLOVES GARLIC, MINCED
1 TEASPOON GROUND CUMIN
1 TEASPOON DRIED OREGANO
SALT AND FRESHLY GROUND BLACK PEPPER, TO
    TASTE
1 TABLESPOON OLIVE OIL, FOR BRUSHING THE
    CHICKEN
PINEAPPLE SALSA (RECIPE FOLLOWS)

1. Place the chicken breasts in a glass baking dish. Combine the lime juice, rum, pineapple juice, olive oil, garlic, cumin, oregano, salt, and pepper in a blender and process until smooth. Pour the marinade over the chicken, cover with plastic wrap, and refrigerate for 4 to 6 hours, turning several times. Bring to room temperature before grilling.

2. Prepare the coals for grilling or preheat the broiler.

3. Drain the chicken and blot it dry. Brush each breast with oil and season with salt and pepper. Grill the chicken until cooked through but still moist, about 4 minutes per side. Slice the chicken and serve with the salsa on the side.

SERVES 4

Pineapple Salsa

For best results, the salsa should be made not more than 1 hour before serving.

Combine all the ingredients in a medium-size bowl and let stand for 15 to 30 minutes.

2 CUPS DICED FRESH PINEAPPLE

1/3 CUP DICED RED ONION

1/2 CUP DICED RED BELL PEPPER

1 SCOTCH BONNET CHILE, SEEDED AND MINCED

1/2 CUP CHOPPED CILANTRO

3 TABLESPOONS FRESH LIME JUICE

1 TABLESPOON BROWN SUGAR

MAKES ABOUT 2 1/2 CUPS

Chicken Wings with Guava Barbecue Sauce

(POLLO CON GLASEADO DE GUAYABA)

Slightly kitschy seventies' American dishes—like barbecued chicken wings—enjoy tremendous popularity in Puerto Rico, where they are often festively reinterpreted with local ingredients. Tinned guava paste comes in really handy when one is looking for an addictive, sticky, sweet-sour glaze—Goya is a good brand. Serve the wings with a dipping sauce such as Cilantro Dip (page 31).

3½ POUNDS CHICKEN WINGS (WING TIPS REMOVED), RINSED AND PATTED DRY
2 TEASPOONS MILD PAPRIKA
1 TEASPOON GROUND CUMIN
SALT AND FRESHLY GROUND BLACK PEPPER, TO TASTE
SLAB OF GUAVA PASTE, ABOUT 3 BY 2 INCHES
⅓ CUP RED WINE VINEGAR
FRESHLY SQUEEZED JUICE OF 1 LIME
2 TABLESPOONS TOMATO PASTE
1½ TABLESPOONS WORCESTERSHIRE SAUCE
3 CLOVES GARLIC, CRUSHED THROUGH A PRESS
1 SMALL DRIED RED CHILE, CRUMBLED

1. Rub the chicken with the paprika, cumin, salt, and pepper, and let stand while preparing the sauce.

2. In a medium-size nonreactive saucepan, melt the guava paste over medium-low heat, stirring, about 5 to 7 minutes. Add the vinegar, lime juice, tomato paste, Worcestershire sauce, garlic, and chile, and simmer for 10 minutes until thickened and a little reduced. Cool a little.

3. Preheat the oven to 425 degrees F.

4. Place the chicken wings in a foil-lined roasting pan and brush generously with the sauce. Bake, brushing twice more with the sauce, until the wings are cooked through and lightly charred, about 30 to 35 minutes.

SERVES 6

Duck and Potatoes in Beer and Peanut Sauce

(ALMENDRADO DE PATO)

Almendrado is a Spanish stew, usually made with chicken and a rich sauce thickened with pounded almonds. The Peruvians adopted this colonial dish, using ducks (which were cultivated by the Incas in pre-Columbian times) and their native peanuts. This is a good dish to prepare ahead, so that you can refrigerate it and skim off all the fat. Like so many Peruvian dishes, this stew is both simple and colorfully unusual, appropriate both for a festive occasion and for a family meal. Serve it with Red Rice with Toasted Cumin (page 248).

2 ANCHO CHILES, SEEDED AND CHOPPED
3 LARGE CLOVES GARLIC, CHOPPED
¼ TEASPOON SALT, PLUS MORE TO TASTE
1 DUCKLING (ABOUT 6 POUNDS)
2 TABLESPOONS PEANUT OIL
1½ CUPS CHOPPED ONIONS
4 MEDIUM TOMATOES, BLANCHED, PEELED, SEEDED, AND CHOPPED
2 TEASPOONS MILD PAPRIKA
½ TEASPOON *PALILLO* (A PERUVIAN SPICE) OR TURMERIC
½ TEASPOON GROUND CUMIN
1¼ CUPS DARK MALTY BEER
2¼ CUPS CHICKEN STOCK (PAGE 372) OR CANNED LOWER-SALT CHICKEN BROTH
FRESHLY GROUND BLACK PEPPER, TO TASTE
3 LARGE YUKON GOLD POTATOES, PEELED AND CUT INTO LARGE IRREGULAR CHUNKS
¼ CUP NATURAL SMOOTH PEANUT BUTTER
CILANTRO LEAVES, FOR GARNISH

1. Soak the chiles in hot water to cover for 15 minutes. Drain, seed to taste (more seeds means more heat), and chop into small pieces.

2. In a mortar and pestle, pound the soaked chiles with the garlic and ¼ teaspoon of the salt to a paste.

3. Remove the excess fat from the duckling, rinse, and pat it dry. Cut into small serving pieces.

4. Rub the duck pieces lightly with salt. Heat the oil in a large, heavy casserole. In batches, brown the duck pieces well over medium-high heat, 5

(continued)

Fiesta!
211

to 6 minutes. (If the duck throws off too much fat, tilt the casserole and pour it off.) With a slotted spoon, transfer the duck to drain on paper towels. Pat dry thoroughly.

5. Pour off all but 1 tablespoon of fat from the casserole. Add the onions and cook over medium heat, stirring, until it wilts, about 5 minutes. Add the chile paste, tomatoes, paprika, *palillo*, and cumin, and stir for 2 minutes. Add the beer and chicken broth, scraping the bottom of the casserole with a wooden spoon, and bring to a simmer. Replace the duck in the casserole, season it to taste with salt and pepper, and simmer over low heat until the duck is almost tender, about 45 minutes.

6. Add the potatoes and cook until they are almost tender, about 20 minutes longer. (If serving the duck right away, try to skim off as much fat as possible from the surface of the cooking liquid.) Just before serving, place the peanut butter in a bowl and whisk in about $1/3$ cup of the cooking liquid, stirring well to dissolve the peanut butter. Whisk the mixture back into the casserole and cook for 5 minutes longer.

7. Transfer to a serving bowl, and serve garnished with cilantro leaves.

SERVES 3 TO 4

Peanuts

The peanut was born in Bolivia and then traveled to other parts of South America. In Brazil it was noticed by Portuguese traders, who took it to West Africa and Southeast Asia in the 1600s. It was the African slaves who brought this crunchy legume to North America and the Caribbean. The peanut was a hit wherever it went, becoming a kitchen staple in all corners of the globe, from China to Africa, from Europe to the American South.

For the finicky Spaniards, however, it was not love at first sight. The poor peanut was accused of all kinds of vices, from causing headaches to making one faint. The Spanish warmed to the nut, however, when they compared it to the almond, which they so loved, discovering that it could be cooked in much the same way—used to thicken sauces, or to make Arab-influenced honey and nut confections. Not only that, but it could also be used to extract oil.

Today, peanuts are a popular snack throughout South America, and their culinary uses are myriad— from African-inspired sauces and ritual Yuruba dishes, to local variations of the almond-thickened Spanish sauces called *almendrados* and the chile-laden indigenous Indian creations of Peru and Ecuador.

Cutting a suckling pig with a plate at Candido's Restaurant, Segovia, Spain.

Farmer with olives, Évora Monte, Portugal.

Market, Santiago de Compostela, Spain.

Panadería (bakery), Tijuana, Mexico.

Saint's Day, Ayllón, Spain.

Llama at Fiesta de Santa Rosa
de Pelequén, Chile.

Fisherman's basket, near
Valparaíso, Chile.

Peppers, Haro, Spain.

Canapés and tapas, San Sebastián, Spain.

Chapter House window, Convent of Christ, Tomar, Portugal.

Meson Marinero fish restaurant, Castro Urdiales, Spain.

Candy faces, street fair, Chile.

Modern masks, street fair, Chile.

Figure in the Chincheros church, Peru.

Fiesta de Santa Rosa de Pelequén, Chile.

Fishing boats near Valparaiso, Chile.

House in La Boca, Buenos Aires, Argentina.

Cepes and olives at the market in San Sebastián, Spain.

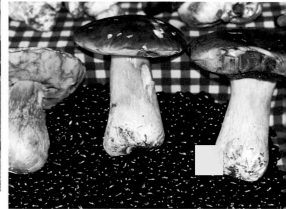

Coffee vendor, San Telmo Market,
Buenos Aires, Argentina.

Street vendor, Salvador (Bahia), Brazil.

Revelers having lunch at the Huassao Festival, Peru.

Ceramic mural of a meal in the Convento de
Serra Hotel, Serra d'Ossa, Portugal.

Ceramic tiles, Portugal.

Beauty queens, San Vicente de Cañete, Peru.

Follower of religious cult, near Brazília, Brazil.

Working with corn in a village in the Serra da Estrela, Portugal.

Dancers at the National Gastronomy Festival, Santarém, Portugal.

Baking at a fair, near Sintra, Portugal.

Statuette and "Money House Blessing" packs, San Juan, Puerto Rico.

Street mural of a festival, Olinda, Brazil.

Vegetables

VOLUMES COULD be written on the vegetable dishes of Iberia, and volumes more—perhaps even more fascinating—about those of Latin America. With Columbus's discovery of the New World, the Western diet was changed forever by the fertile agricultural exchange between the two cultures. The introduction of potatoes and maize into Europe not only altered the way we eat but also had a momentous social and economic impact on Western culture in general. No less than the precious metals that revolutionized the economies of Western Europe, New World crops—tomatoes, potatoes, squash, and maize—became the found-gold of Iberian cuisine. Who can imagine Spanish gastronomy without its famous *tortilla de patata* (potato omelet) or Portuguese cuisine without its rustic corn bread, pumpkin, or tomato sauces. And finally, where would our contemporary palates be without chiles, avocados, and tropical fruit? But besides their A-list New World exports—corn, potatoes, tomatoes, and squash—Latin America and the Caribbean boast another range of intriguing vegetables and roots. Today, with the popularity of ethnic cuisines on the rise and gastronomic imagination on the prowl, Western eaters are finally rediscovering yucas and plantains, *boniatos* and chayotes. Half a millennium after Columbus, another explosion of new flavors is on its way.

In this chapter, you will be introduced to the versatile yuca, so delicious just plain boiled, with a *picante* sauce to offset its pleasant blandness. When mashed, boiled yuca makes excellent pancakes and fritters. Cut into sticks and fried to a crisp, it can happily compete with french fries.

If you are not familiar with it already, you will love the Cuban white sweet potato called *boniato*, with a flavor less sweet and more interesting than its orange relative. In Cuba, it's made into a delicious sweet puree, called *boniatillo*, which is served for dessert, but it can also be treated much like a sweet potato, baked, mashed, or turned into chips, casseroles, and soufflés. Give it a try next Thanksgiving.

And who could ever tire of plantain, the sturdier, meatier cousin of the banana? Unlike the banana, however, it won't disintegrate when cooked, and its uses in the Latin kitchen are legion. When green, or semiripe (with black and yellow skin), it's cooked much like any other root vegetable: deep-fried as plump crunchy chips called *tostones*; cooked and pureed into creamy soups; added to stews to give them substance; mashed and transformed into sticky dough for tamales, *pasteles*, or empanadas; stuffed with meat or cheese and baked in the oven; mashed into a tasty nourishing puree; or turned into a delicious stuffing for poultry.

You will also be pleased to get acquainted with the Mexican-born squash called chayote (aka christophene), with a taste somewhere between a zucchini and a crunchy apple. Delicious when parboiled, stuffed with meat or bread crumbs, and baked in the oven (the preparation referred to as "old shoes"), it's also excellent steamed, deep-fried, or sautéed with a delicate sauce. Treat it as you would a zucchini, or other summer squash, bearing in mind that it will take slightly longer to cook.

Market, Barcelona, Spain.

On a more familiar note, what could be better than a simple plate of stir-fried greens accented with garlic and chile, or offset with raisins and pine nuts; tiny Portuguese baby potatoes tossed with fresh spearmint; or familiar mashed potatoes, given a new dimension by adding the smoky taste of chilpotle chiles?

The vegetables might be new or familiar, but the recipes in this chapter will certainly prove a discovery.

Stir-Fried Greens with Chile and Annatto Oil

(VERDURAS SALTEADAS CON ACHIOTE Y CHILES)

This is an excellent all-purpose side dish for almost any entree in this book. Use any green that strikes your fancy—collard greens, Swiss chard, mustard greens, spinach, or bok choy—or a combination.

1 DRIED RED CHILE, SUCH AS ÁRBOL OR
    JAPONÉS
3 TABLESPOONS ANNATTO OIL (PAGE 376)
7 CLOVES GARLIC, LIGHTLY SMASHED
1 CUP RED BELL PEPPER STRIPS
2 POUNDS GREENS (SEE HEADNOTE), TOUGH
    STEMS REMOVED, WASHED AND DRIED
SALT AND FRESHLY GROUND BLACK PEPPER, TO
    TASTE

1. Stem the chile and shake out the seeds. Using scissors, cut the chile into four pieces.

2. In a wok or a 12-inch skillet, heat the oil over low heat. Add the garlic and chile and sauté until the garlic is light golden, 2 to 3 minutes. With a slotted spoon, remove the garlic and chile to a bowl.

3. Turn the heat up to high and add the red pepper. Cook, stirring, for 2 minutes. Add the greens and cook, tossing and stirring, until they just wilt; the time will depend on the greens you have chosen, anywhere from 3 to 6 minutes.

4. Transfer the greens to a serving platter and garnish with the fried garlic and chile.

SERVES 4 TO 6

Basil-Scented Corn and Pumpkin Bake

(HUMITA)

This is one of the countless variations on *humita*, a marvelous South American dish of grated tender corn steamed in corn husks, much like tamales. In this Argentinian version, the corn is cooked with pumpkin and a tomato *sofrito* and finished in the oven.

1. In a food processor or blender, process the corn with the milk to a medium-fine puree.

2. In a large, heavy saucepan, melt the butter and sauté the onion, garlic, and bell pepper over medium heat, stirring, until the onion is translucent, about 5 minutes. Add the tomatoes and cook, stirring until they are reduced to a puree, about 10 minutes. Stir in the corn and pumpkin, and bring to a simmer. Cook over very low heat, stirring often with a wooden spoon, until the mixture begins to thicken, about 20 minutes.

3. Preheat the oven to 325 degrees F.

4. Transfer the mixture to a medium-size ovenproof casserole, preferably earthenware, and stir in the sugar, salt and pepper to taste, the basil, and the eggs. Bake for 20 minutes.

5. Raise the oven temperature to 425 degrees. Sprinkle the top with Parmesan, and bake until the top is light golden and bubbly, about 12 minutes.

5 CUPS FRESH TENDER CORN KERNELS (FROM ABOUT 3 MEDIUM EARS) OR BEST-QUALITY FROZEN AND THAWED CORN

2 CUPS WHOLE OR SKIM MILK

3½ TABLESPOONS UNSALTED BUTTER

1 CUP FINELY CHOPPED ONION

2 CLOVES GARLIC, MINCED

1 LARGE GREEN BELL PEPPER, CORED, SEEDED, AND FINELY CHOPPED

3 MEDIUM RIPE TOMATOES, BLANCHED, PEELED, SEEDED, AND FINELY CHOPPED

½ POUND FRESH PUMPKIN OR BUTTERNUT SQUASH, PEELED, CUT INTO CHUNKS, AND GRATED BY HAND OR IN A FOOD PROCESSOR

¾ TEASPOON SUGAR, OR MORE TO TASTE

SALT AND FRESHLY GROUND BLACK PEPPER, TO TASTE

3 TABLESPOONS SLIVERED FRESH BASIL LEAVES

2 LARGE EGGS, BEATEN

2 TABLESPOONS FRESHLY GRATED PARMESAN CHEESE

SERVES 4 TO 6

Mushrooms, Segovian-Style

(SETAS A LA SEGOVIANA)

From the town of Segovia comes this Castilian mushroom dish. *Setas*, the Spanish mushrooms used for this dish, are quite delicate, so you shouldn't substitute varieties that are dark and woody, such as portobellos.

1 POUND DELICATE WILD MUSHROOMS, SUCH AS OYSTER, CHANTERELLE, OR SHIITAKE, OR A COMBINATION, TRIMMED

4 STRIPS BACON, FINELY CHOPPED

3 TABLESPOONS VIRGIN OLIVE OIL, PREFERABLY SPANISH, OR MORE AS NEEDED

4 CLOVES GARLIC, CHOPPED

⅓ CUP CHOPPED ONION

⅓ CUP DICED SERRANO HAM OR PROSCIUTTO

LARGE PINCH OF DRIED THYME

LARGE PINCH OF GOOD, SMOKY MILD PAPRIKA, PREFERABLY SPANISH

3 TABLESPOONS WHITE WINE

½ TEASPOON SHERRY VINEGAR

SALT AND FRESHLY GROUND BLACK PEPPER, TO TASTE

MINCED FLAT-LEAF PARSLEY, FOR GARNISH

1. Wipe the mushrooms clean with a damp paper towel and cut them into thick slices, leaving the smaller mushrooms whole.

2. In a large skillet, cook the bacon until it is crisp and has rendered its fat, about 6 minutes. Remove the cracklings to drain on paper towels and discard the fat from the skillet.

3. Wipe the skillet, add the olive oil and the garlic, and heat over low heat for 3 to 4 minutes until fragrant but not browned. Add the onion and ham and cook another 3 minutes, stirring. Raise the heat to medium-high, add the mushrooms, the reserved cracklings, the thyme and paprika, and cook until the mushrooms are cooked through and lightly colored, 7 minutes or more. Add a little more olive oil if the skillet looks dry during cooking. Add the wine and cook over high heat until it evaporates, 2 to 3 minutes. Stir in the vinegar, season the dish with salt and pepper, and stir in the parsley.

SERVES 4 TO 6 AS A SIDE DISH

Portuguese New Potatoes with White Wine and Spearmint

(BATATAS À MODA PORTUGUESA)

This is a very traditional potato dish from Portugal in which tiny cooked new potatoes are smashed lightly until just cracked, then fried in olive oil with garlic, a touch of white wine, and wild spearmint. If you can't find spearmint, use regular fresh mint. Good-quality dried mint works very nicely too. There are versions of this recipe in which the potatoes are roasted instead of boiled.

2 POUNDS SMALL NEW POTATOES (RED OR WHITE), SCRUBBED
¼ CUP OLIVE OIL
5 CLOVES GARLIC, SMASHED
⅓ CUP DRY WHITE WINE
SALT TO TASTE
3 TABLESPOONS FINELY JULIENNED FRESH SPEARMINT OR REGULAR MINT, OR 1 TABLESPOON GOOD-QUALITY DRIED MINT

1. Cook the potatoes in boiling salted water to cover until tender, about 15 minutes or more, depending on the size. (Alternatively, drizzle them with virgin olive oil, sprinkle with coarse salt, and bake in a 375 degree F. oven until tender, about 30 minutes.) Drain well and gently pat dry with paper towels. Place a potato on a work surface and crush it lightly with the back of a cleaver until it is slightly "cracked."

2. In a large, heavy skillet, heat the oil with the garlic over medium heat. Remove the garlic and turn the heat up to high. In batches, add the potatoes and cook until lightly browned on all sides, about 5 minutes, removing the browned ones to a bowl as they are done. Replace all the potatoes in the skillet and add the wine. Raise the heat to high and cook until the wine is almost evaporated, about 6 minutes, gently shaking the skillet and tossing the potatoes. Add salt to taste and the mint, and cook for another 2 minutes.

SERVES 4 TO 6

Argentinian Sweet Potato Gnocchi

(ÑOQUIS DE CAMOTE)

It would not be an exaggeration to say that, along with beef, Italian classics such as cannelloni and gnocchi and fried breaded meats called *milanesa* are considered by Argentinians to be their national dishes. Here then is a typically Argentinian recipe from the kitchen of Chef Francis Mallmann from Buenos Aires, who makes his gnocchi with sweet potatoes, a typical Creole touch.

1 POUND SWEET POTATOES, WITH SKIN ON, SCRUBBED WELL

1 LARGE EGG, BEATEN

1 CUP PLUS 2 TABLESPOONS FLOUR, PLUS MORE FOR FLOURING THE SURFACE

2 CLOVES GARLIC, CRUSHED THROUGH A GARLIC PRESS

1 TEASPOON SUGAR

1 TEASPOON DRIED CRUMBLED ROSEMARY

SALT AND FRESHLY GROUND BLACK PEPPER, TO TASTE

1 TABLESPOON OLIVE OIL

3 TABLESPOONS UNSALTED BUTTER, MELTED

FRESHLY GRATED PARMESAN CHEESE, FOR SPRINKLING THE GNOCCHI AND FOR SERVING

1. Preheat the oven to 375 degrees F. Roast the potatoes in their skins until soft when tested with the tip of a sharp knife, about 45 minutes. When cool enough to handle, peel them, cut them into chunks, and pass them through a ricer or a food mill.

2. In a large bowl, combine the potatoes with all the remaining ingredients except the olive oil, butter and cheese, and knead with your hands until smooth. The dough will be somewhat sticky. Divide the dough into six parts and turn it out onto a well-floured surface. Roll each piece of dough into a $3/4$-inch-thick rope, sprinkling the surface with just enough flour to stop the dough from sticking. Cut each rope into 1-inch pieces.

3. Bring a large pot of salted water to a boil and add the olive oil. Drop the gnocchi into the water and cook until they float to the surface, about 45 seconds. Drain in a colander.

4. Preheat the oven to 400 degrees.

5. Place the gnocchi in an ovenproof serving dish and toss with the butter. Sprinkle generously with the Parmesan and bake until the tops are light golden, about 10 minutes. Serve with additional Parmesan.

SERVES 4 AS A SIDE DISH

Masks, Buenos Aires, Argentina.

Castilian Potato and Rib Stew

(GUISO DE PATATAS CON COSTILLA DE CERDO)

In true Castilian fashion, this peasant stew of potatoes and pork ribs derives its superb flavor from excellent olive oil and good smoky paprika. The pork ribs are here to boost the flavor, and you can omit them if you are a vegetarian—in which case add the potatoes and all the liquid in step 1, and cook until the potatoes are very tender, about 30 minutes. This recipe comes from the venerable Luis Monje from the restaurant of the Parador in Segovia, where you can find some of the best regional cuisine in the city.

1 POUND MEATY, LEAN, CHINESE-STYLE PORK SPARERIBS, SEPARATED INTO RIBLETS

2 TABLESPOONS BEST-QUALITY SMOKY MILD PAPRIKA, PREFERABLY SPANISH

½ CUP FRUITY VIRGIN OLIVE OIL, PREFERABLY SPANISH

6 CLOVES GARLIC, SLICED

1½ CUPS DICED ONIONS

1½ CUPS DICED RED BELL PEPPERS

1½ CUPS DICED RIPE TOMATOES

1½ TEASPOONS CRACKED BLACK PEPPERCORNS

3 BAY

2 SPRIGS FRESH THYME, OR 1½ TEASPOONS DRIED THYME

2 CUPS DRY WHITE WINE

SALT TO TASTE

7 MEDIUM YELLOW POTATOES, PREFERABLY YUKON GOLD (ABOUT 3 POUNDS TOTAL), PEELED

3 TO 3½ CUPS WATER

3 TABLESPOONS MINCED FLAT-LEAF PARSLEY

1. Rub the pork ribs with 1 tablespoon of the paprika and set aside. In a large heavy saucepan, heat the oil with the garlic over medium-low heat. Add the onions and cook, stirring, until golden, about 7 minutes. Stir in the bell peppers and tomatoes, and cook, stirring frequently, until the tomatoes are cooked down to a paste, about 10 minutes. Stir in the ribs and cook, stirring, until browned, for 7 minutes. Stir in the peppercorns, bay leaves, thyme, and wine and bring to a simmer. Cook over low heat, partially covered, for about 45 minutes, stirring occasionally.

2. Break the potatoes into irregular 2-inch chunks by inserting a sharp knife halfway into a piece of potato and then twisting it to break off a chunk. Stir the potatoes and the remaining 1 tablespoon of paprika into the saucepan with the ribs. Add enough water to barely cover the meat and potatoes and bring to a boil. Add salt to taste. Simmer, partially covered, over low heat until the ribs and potatoes are tender, about 30 minutes.

3. Transfer to a serving dish, remove the bay leaf, and serve, sprinkled with the parsley.

SERVES 4 TO 6

Market, Barcelona, Spain.

Peruvian Potato Pâté with Shrimp and Avocado

(CAUSA RELLENA CON CAMARONES Y PALTA)

Causa, a kind of potato pâté, is one of the jewels of Peruvian gastronomy, with dozens of regional variations. In Spanish *causa* means "cause," though historians suggest that the name of this dish derives from the Quechua *kausac*, "that which feeds" or "sustains." In the early nineteenth century, during Peru's fight to overthrow Spanish rule, the dish became a revolutionary symbol of sorts—its name now implying the heated *causa de independencia*, the "crusade for independence."

The version below is a cosmopolitan contemporary *causa*, made from yellow potatoes flavored with marinated onions, and stuffed with a light shrimp and avocado salad. Serve it as a light main course, a first course, or as part of a buffet, and have copies of the recipe handy. Guests will be sure to ask!

FOR THE POTATOES

1 MEDIUM ONION, FINELY CHOPPED

¼ CUP FRESH LEMON JUICE

1 TABLESPOON WHITE WINE VINEGAR

2 LARGE CLOVES GARLIC, CRUSHED THROUGH A
    PRESS

2 TEASPOONS MINCED MILD FRESH CHILES, SUCH
    AS ANAHEIM OR POBLANO

¼ CUP OLIVE OIL

6 MEDIUM YELLOW POTATOES, SUCH AS YUKON
    GOLD (ABOUT 2¾ POUNDS TOTAL), PEELED
    AND CUT INTO CHUNKS

SALT AND FRESHLY GROUND BLACK PEPPER, TO
    TASTE

(continued)

1. To make the potatoes: In a small bowl, toss together the onion, lemon juice, vinegar, garlic, chiles, and oil, and let stand for 30 minutes.

2. Boil the potatoes in salted water to cover until tender, about 18 minutes. Drain and puree the potatoes until smooth with a potato ricer, working in the onion mixture. Season with salt and pepper and set aside to cool.

3. To make the filling: In a medium-size bowl, toss together the shrimp, avocado, onion, and tomatoes. In another bowl, whisk together the mayonnaise, water, and lemon juice. Reserve 1 tablespoon of the dressing for garnish and toss the rest with the shrimp mixture. Add salt and pepper to taste.

4. To assemble the pâté, line an 8-inch square baking pan with plastic wrap, leaving a 4-inch overhang on two sides. Spread half of the potato mixture on the bottom, patting it down with your hands. Spread the filling evenly on top and sprinkle with cilantro. Spread the other half of the potato mixture evenly over the filling and pat it down with your hands. Lift up the plastic overhang and cover the pâté with it. Chill the pâté for at least 2 hours.

5. To serve, unwrap the pâté and invert it onto a serving platter. Remove the plastic and spread the top and sides of the pâté with the reserved mayonnaise mixture. Decorate the top with the hard-cooked egg slices, olives, and pimiento strips. Cut into squares and serve.

FOR THE FILLING

10 OUNCES COOKED SHRIMP (ANY SIZE),
   CHOPPED MEDIUM-FINE
1 MEDIUM HAAS AVOCADO, PEELED, PITTED, AND
   CUT INTO SMALL DICE
1/3 CUP CHOPPED RED ONION
3/4 CUP CHOPPED SEEDED RIPE TOMATOES
7 TABLESPOONS MAYONNAISE (LOW-FAT IS FINE)
1 1/2 TABLESPOONS WATER
4 TABLESPOONS FRESH LEMON JUICE
SALT AND FRESHLY GROUND BLACK PEPPER, TO
   TASTE

3 TABLESPOONS CHOPPED CILANTRO
SLICES OF HARD-COOKED EGG, SLICES OF BLACK
   OR GREEN OLIVES, AND PIMIENTO STRIPS,
   FOR GARNISH

**SERVES 8 AS AN APPETIZER,
4 AS A LIGHT MAIN COURSE**

The Ancient Cuisine of Peru

The inhabitants of pre-Columbian Peru were certainly not blessed by nature. Yet in the rugged Andean sierras—with their bitter night frosts and fierce afternoon sun—and in the scarcely irrigated oases of the arid coastal deserts, farmers of the great Inca Empire (as well as pre-Incan civilizations) accomplished feats of agriculture and miracles of distribution that made their culture a legend. They also laid the foundation for what was to become one of the world's great (though still little-known) culinary cultures.

In the freezing highlands, farmers not only managed to cultivate various species of potatoes but developed a miraculous technique for dehydrating them so that they could be stored for several years. But if the hardy potato was sustenance for the peasant highlanders, corn—cultivated on the skillfully constructed terraces of the Andean slopes—was the food of the aristocracy, the stuff of worship and legends, and the "bread" of the Empire.

These two essentials were supplemented by fish on the coast and meat of Andean cameloids (llama, alpaca, and vicuña) in the mountains; as well as wild ducks, deer, and guinea pigs (*cuy*). Before the Spaniards introduced rice, healthful quinoa was the staple grain. Indigenous root vegetables such as oca, olluco, yuca, and camote (sweet potato) were abundant—often roasted in underground ovens or cooked in stews called *chupes* and *rocros*, versions of which can still be found throughout South America. For fruit, there were subtropical delicacies like fragrant cherimoyas, guavas, and passion fruit. Aromatic herbs and a variety of chiles (*ajíes*) seasoned the food. And on ceremonial occasions the nobility indulged in *chicha*, a filling fermented corn beer, prepared by the Chosen Women of the Inca Court.

As you travel through the remote Andean villages of today, things don't seem to have changed all that much. Often the only markers of the present are the bubbling cauldrons of "*espaguetis*" or bright ads for Nestlé's milk or Fleishmann's yeast. No money is exchanged at the vibrant Indian markets, where Quechua-speaking *campesinos* (the politically correct way to refer to Indians) from the central valley barter bags of corn with Aymara Indians from Lake Titicaca for dehydrated potatoes. There you can taste ancient dishes like *olluquito con charqui*, shredded Andean tuber with sun-dried meat of alpaca; *cuy chactado*, local guinea pig cooked between two hot stones; or *pachamanca*, a feast of maize, tubers, and meats cooked over hot stones in underground earth ovens.

On Sundays and during fiestas, *chicha* still flows freely at the village markets—as well as in *chicherías* and *picanterías*, the campesino equivalent of pubs. To accompany the *chicha*, there are rustic snacks, usually simple slices of cold yellow potato enlivened by a piquant sauce.

The Spanish introduced a variety of meats, wheat, rice, olive oil, cheese, and milk, among other foodstuffs. While their pork initially made the Indians violently ill, today it's the most popular meat in the country.

The pre-Columbian *rocros* (stews) married with the Spanish one-dish meals to evolve into a stunning variety of soupy stews that skillfully blend European meats with ancient corn, pumpkin, potatoes, and other root vegetables.

The cold Humbolt current of Peru's Pacific coast produces some of the world's most extraordinary seafood. Delicate *corvina* (white sea bass), delicious scallops from the Bay of Nazca (one of the richest scallop deposits in the world), pearlescent langoustines, black clams, and enormous crabs are only some of the coastal delicacies. Other waterways contribute tender pink trout, giant meaty fish, and lobster-like freshwater prawns. *Cebiche*, a tangy mixture of raw fish marinated in the juice of the fragrant local lime, red onion, and chiles, is a Peruvian passion and certainly the best way to enjoy its seafood.

The cuisine of Peru is creamier and milder than that of its culinary rival, Mexico. But chiles, nevertheless, are consumed in great profusion. Local varieties include the large, red *rocoto*, used either as seasoning, or stuffed with a mixture of beef, raisins, and peanuts. When *rocotos* are dried, they become the smoky *pancas*. *Mirasol* (literally "look at the sun"), which come in a riot of colors, are large, tapered, and quite mild. The mild orange-yellow *ají amarillo* imparts most Peruvian dishes with a characteristic sunny hue, also achieved by adding a local herb called *palillo*.

Rich confections such as nougats (*turrones*) and marzipans, airy sponge cakes soaked in syrup, delicate cookies, and unbelievably rich custards are the highlights of Peruvian desserts.

If *chicha* is worshipped by the *campesinos* the upper classes indulge in *pisco*, a potent *aguardiente* (distilled liquor) manufacture in the city of Pisco south of Lima. The *pisco* sour, a frothy cocktail of *pisco*, lime juice, sugar, and beaten egg white—often accompanied by elaborate *piqueos* (snacks)—is a whole lifestyle in itself.

And talking of lifestyles, the restaurants of Lima offer a mind-boggling cocktail of the cosmopolitan and the traditional, the basic and the extravagantly luxurious. Choose from among a fascinating New World branch of Chinese cuisine called *chifa*; sparkling sushi prepared by Japanese immigrants; elaborate Creole cuisine served in sumptuous colonial settings; jet-set waterfront restaurants boasting $50 lobster dishes; or the hypertrendy Nuevo Andino cooking, a contemporary style that blends indigenous ingredients and European presentation.

Garlic and Chilpotle Mashed Potatoes

(PURÉ DE PATATAS CON CHILPOTLES)

A hot Latin fantasy on the perennial theme of mashed potatoes. The best chilpotles (large, smoky Mexican chiles) for this dish are the canned ones, packed in *adobo* sauce. If you can find only dried chilpotles, stem, seed, and soak them in warm water to cover for 1 hour before beginning the recipe.

6 LARGE BAKING POTATOES (ABOUT 3 POUNDS), PEELED AND CUBED

2 LARGE CANNED CHILPOTLE CHILES, SEEDED AND CHOPPED (SEE HEADNOTE)

1/3 CUP WARM MILK

3 CLOVES GARLIC, CRUSHED THROUGH A PRESS

3 TABLESPOONS VIRGIN OLIVE OIL

SALT AND FRESHLY GROUND BLACK PEPPER, TO TASTE

1. In a large saucepan, combine the potatoes, chilpotles, and water to cover, and cook, covered, until the potatoes are soft, about 15 minutes. With a slotted spoon remove the potatoes from the liquid, discarding the chilpotle pieces.

2. Pass the potatoes through a ricer into a bowl and stir in the milk and garlic. Whisk in the oil and season with salt and pepper. Transfer to a serving dish and serve.

SERVES 6

Spinach with Pine Nuts, Raisins, and Garlic

(ESPINACA CON PIÑONES Y PASAS)

This delicate Spanish dish will make an excellent accompaniment to a whole range of main courses, from roasts to stews to seafood.

1. In a small bowl, cover the raisins with hot water and let them stand for 20 minutes. Drain and pat dry with paper towels.

2. In a small skillet, toast the pine nuts over medium heat, stirring frequently, until deep golden, 2 to 3 minutes.

3. In a large, heavy skillet, heat the oil with the garlic over medium heat. When the garlic is deep golden, remove the garlic with a slotted spoon to drain on paper towels. Add the spinach to the oil and cook until it just wilts, about 2 to 3 minutes. Add the raisins, pine nuts, and garlic, and toss to combine.

4. Season with salt and pepper, transfer to a serving platter, and serve at once.

3 TABLESPOONS GOLDEN RAISINS

3 TABLESPOON PINE NUTS

3 TABLESPOONS FRUITY VIRGIN OLIVE OIL, PREFERABLY SPANISH

6 SMALL CLOVES GARLIC

2 BUNCHES SPINACH (ABOUT 1½ POUNDS TOTAL), STEMMED, RINSED, AND DRIED

SALT AND FRESHLY GROUND BLACK PEPPER, TO TASTE

SERVES 4

Plantain and Black Bean Torta

(TORTA DE PLÁTANOS Y FRIJOLES NEGROS)

Spiced black beans baked in a terrine between layers of mashed sweet plantains make one of the most striking and tasty dishes I know. It's a filling and exciting vegetarian entree, or a side dish that will steal the show from any main course. I am not a big fan of canned black beans, but in a pinch you can just about get away with it here. Choose plantains with blackened skin but not overripe. They should feel firm to the touch.

4 LARGE RIPE PLANTAINS (ABOUT 2 POUNDS TOTAL), PEELED AS DIRECTED ON PAGE 379

1 TABLESPOON OLIVE OIL

2 MEDIUM CLOVES GARLIC, CRUSHED THROUGH A PRESS

1 SMALL ONION, FINELY CHOPPED

1½ CUPS BASIC BLACK BEANS (PAGE 374), PLUS 2 TABLESPOONS OF THEIR COOKING LIQUID RESERVED SEPARATELY

LARGE PINCH OF GROUND CUMIN

½ TEASPOON DRIED OREGANO

1 TEASPOON MILD PAPRIKA

3 TABLESPOONS UNSALTED BUTTER, MELTED

SALT, TO TASTE

½ CUP GRATED *QUESO BLANCO* (HISPANIC WHITE CHEESE) OR MOZZARELLA CHEESE

3 TABLESPOONS CHOPPED CILANTRO

2 TABLESPOONS FRESHLY GRATED PARMESAN CHEESE

1. Cut the plantains into 2-inch chunks, place them in a saucepan with enough water to cover them by 1½ inches, and cook over medium heat until soft, about 20 minutes. Leave the plantains in the liquid until ready to use. Do not prepare them more than 15 minutes ahead of time.

2. In a medium-size skillet, heat the oil over medium heat, and sauté the garlic and onion until the onion wilts, about 5 minutes. Add the drained beans, cumin, oregano, and paprika, and cook, stirring, for about 7 minutes. Mash the beans with

a fork, so that about half of them are crushed. Add the bean cooking liquid, and cook for another 3 to 4 minutes.

3. Preheat the oven to 350 degrees F.

4. With a slotted spoon, remove the plantains to a large bowl and add ⅓ cup of the plantain cooking liquid and the butter. Quickly mash the plantains with a fork until they are smooth. Do not overwork them, or they will become gluey. Add salt to taste.

5. Line a 9 × 5-inch loaf pan with foil, shiny side down, leaving a 2-inch overhang on two sides. Spread half the plantain mixture in the bottom of the pan, patting it down with your hands. Spread the bean filling evenly on top and sprinkle with the *queso blanco* and the cilantro. Top with an even layer of plantains, patting it down with your hands. Bake for 15 minutes.

6. Turn the oven temperature to 500 degrees. Remove the *torta* from the oven and carefully invert it onto a heatproof serving dish, removing the foil. Sprinkle the top with Parmesan and return it to the oven until the top is golden brown, about 10 minutes. Cut in slices and serve.

SERVES 4 AS A VEGETARIAN MAIN COURSE
OR 6 AS A SIDE DISH

Fried Plantains

(M A D U R O S   F R I T O S)

3 LARGE RIPE PLANTAINS (ABOUT 1½ POUNDS TOTAL), PEELED AS DIRECTED ON PAGE 379

PEANUT OIL FOR DEEP-FRYING

Few dishes are more pleasing than a plate of *maduros*, sweet, ripe, yellow plantains, cooked until soft and luscious. Choose yellow plantains whose skin is almost blackened—that way you'll know they are ripe. You can cut them either into ½-inch slices or into long strips.

1. Slice the plantains diagonally into ¼-inch-thick slices, or cut them in half crosswise and then slice lengthwise into ¼-inch-thick slices.

2. In a deep-fryer, heat 1 inch of oil to 360 degrees F. Working in batches, fry the plantains until soft and golden, 2 to 3 minutes on each side. Transfer the cooked plantains to drain on paper towels.

S E R V E S   6

Afro-Cuban Plantain Mash

(FUFÚ DE PLÁTANO)

The development of Spanish-Caribbean cuisine owes a great deal to the cooking of African slaves. It was they who introduced the islanders to nourishing mashes (*fufú*) made from various vegetables or tubers. *Fufú de plátano*, a mash of plantain enriched with garlic and savory bacon cracklings became a Cuban classic. The only trick is to mash and serve the plantain while it is still very hot, as it tends to harden as it cools. If you want to omit the bacon, use 1 tablespoon of olive oil to sauté the garlic.

6 MEDIUM (ABOUT 3 POUNDS IN TOTAL) SEMIRIPE PLANTAINS (WITH BLACK AND YELLOW SKIN), PEELED AS DIRECTED ON PAGE 379

8 SLICES BACON, DICED

3 LARGE CLOVES GARLIC, CRUSHED THROUGH A PRESS

1 1/2 TABLESPOONS FRESH SOUR ORANGE JUICE (SEE PAGE 145) OR A COMBINATION OF FRESH ORANGE AND LIME JUICE

1. Cut the plantains into 1-inch chunks, place them in a saucepan with enough water to cover them by 1 1/2 inches, and cook over medium heat until soft, 15 to 20 minutes. Leave the plantains in the liquid until ready to use. Do not prepare them more than 15 minutes ahead of time.

2. While the plantains are cooking, cook the bacon in a heavy skillet over medium heat until it is crispy and renders its fat, 8 to 10 minutes. Remove the bacon to drain on paper towels and discard all but 1 tablespoon of the fat.

3. Add the garlic to the skillet and cook, stirring, for 30 seconds. Remove from the heat and stir in the sour orange juice and 2/3 cup of the liquid from cooking the plantains.

4. Drain the plantains and return them to the saucepan. Mash them with a fork into a coarse puree, working in the garlic mixture and the bacon bits. Serve at once.

SERVES 6

Chayote

Chayote, also known as christophene, mirlitone, or vegetable pear, is a native of Mexico. It is a lovely vegetable, crisp and juicy, with a sweetish, almost apple-like taste. And you won't have a problem finding it. It's carried by most ethnic groceries and many supermarkets. The variety most commonly found here is pale green, with a shape similar to a pear, weighing $1/2$ to 1 pound. The small, sweet chayotes one finds in Mexico can be eaten raw but the ones available here should be peeled, cored, and cooked.

I love chayote cut into wedges or diced, and simply boiled and tossed with some herbed lemon butter before serving. You can add pieces of it to vegetable soups, or puree cooked chayote with a bit of cream and a touch of lemon zest and ginger to make excellent cream soups. Or you can treat it as you would zucchini or other summer squash: peel it, cut it into sticks, and stir-fry or sauté it; or roll it in beaten egg and bread crumbs and deep-fry it. Another favorite preparation, often referred to in South America as *chancletas*, "old shoes," is to parboil halves of chayote, scoop out some of the flesh, stuff it with a mixture of cooked minced meat and/or bread crumbs, raisins, and almonds, and bake it in the oven for about 10 minutes.

The cooking will take longer than chayote's tender-looking flesh might suggest. Figure on about 15 to 20 minutes for boiling or sautéing medium-size chunks over medium heat.

Chayote with Lemon and Dill Sauce

This recipe is inspired by a dish I tasted at a beautiful restaurant in Salvador, Bahia, called Caterina de Pargauaçú, where the chayote's delicate texture was accented by a lemony sauce and a touch of dill. It makes a simple, delicious, and surprising side dish for Ropa Nueva (page 160) or Roast Chicken Adobo (page 192).

2 TABLESPOONS UNSALTED BUTTER
2 LARGE CHAYOTE (ABOUT 1¼ POUNDS TOTAL), PEELED, CORED, AND CUT INTO 2- BY ½-INCH STICKS
2 CLOVES GARLIC, CRUSHED THROUGH A GARLIC PRESS
2 TABLESPOONS DRY WHITE WINE
½ CUP CHICKEN STOCK (PAGE 372) CANNED LOWER-SALT CHICKEN BROTH, OR WATER
2 TABLESPOONS FRESH LEMON JUICE
1 TABLESPOON FINELY CHOPPED FRESH DILL
PINCH OF SUGAR, OR TO TASTE
SALT AND FRESHLY GROUND BLACK PEPPER, TO TASTE

1. In a large, nonstick skillet, melt the butter over medium heat. Add the chayote and garlic and sauté, stirring, for 5 minutes. Add the wine, stock, and lemon juice, reduce the heat to low, cover, and simmer, stirring occasionally, until the chayote is tender but still slightly crunchy, about 25 minutes.

2. Turn the heat up to high and cook, shaking the skillet occasionally, until the liquid has evaporated, about 3 minutes. Stir in the dill, sugar, and salt and pepper to taste and cook for 1 more minute. Transfer to a serving bowl, and serve at once.

SERVES 4

Stir-Fried Garlicky Kale

(COUVE À MINEIRA)

In Brazil, this shredded kale is one of the traditional accompaniments to the *feijoada* dinner, but it also makes an excellent all-purpose side of greens. It is a simple dish, but the trick is to shred the kale by hand as thinly as possible. It takes a bit of time but the resulting dish is ethereally light and delicious. You will probably want to double this recipe if serving as an accompaniment for *feijoada* which serves 10–12.

2 POUNDS KALE, RINSED AND DRIED
ABOUT 3 TABLESPOONS OLIVE OIL (IN TOTAL)
2 TABLESPOONS FINELY MINCED GARLIC
SALT TO TASTE

1. To shred the kale, roll up a few kale leaves and then, using a chef's knife, shred them into very thin ribbons.

2. Working in batches, heat 2 teaspoons of oil in a large skillet over medium-high heat. Add some kale, some garlic, and some salt, and cook, stirring, until the kale turns bright green, about 2 to 3 minutes. Transfer the kale to a bowl and continue until all the kale, oil, and garlic are used up. Serve at once.

SERVES 4 TO 6

Roasted Eggplant with Parsley Sauce

(BERENJENAS ASADAS EN SALSA VERDE)

The parsley sauce here is a variation on *salsa verde*, a traditional Spanish sauce used mainly for seafood. This is a sprightlier version than the original, made without any flour, and it provides an excellent piquant foil for the eggplants.

Untraditionally, I use the slender, light purple Asian eggplants, which are sweet, tender, and do not need salting. This can be served as an appetizer or as a cold side dish.

ABOUT 2½ POUNDS CHINESE OR JAPANESE EGGPLANTS (CHOOSE THE SLIGHTLY LARGER ONES)
SALT, TO TASTE
OLIVE OIL, FOR BRUSHING THE EGGPLANTS

PARSLEY SAUCE
¾ CUP PACKED MINCED FLAT-LEAF PARSLEY
1 LARGE CLOVE GARLIC, MINCED
2 TABLESPOONS MINCED ONION
½ TEASPOON MINCED GREEN CHILE, SUCH AS JALAPEÑO
⅓ CUP WATER
⅓ CUP FRUITY VIRGIN OLIVE OIL
1 TABLESPOON FRESH LEMON JUICE
2 TABLESPOONS RED WINE VINEGAR
SMALL PINCH OF SUGAR, TO TASTE
SALT AND FRESHLY GROUND BLACK PEPPER, TO TASTE

1. Preheat the oven to 475 degrees F.

2. Stem the eggplants and halve them lengthwise. Place them on an oiled baking sheet, cut side up, rub with salt, and brush generously with the olive oil. Bake the eggplants, turning once, until golden and cooked through, about 15 minutes total. Brush them again with the oil during cooking if they look dry.

3. While the eggplants are cooking, make the sauce: In a food processor or blender, process the parsley, garlic, onion, and chile with the water until minced but not pureed. Scrape the mixture into a bowl and whisk in the remaining sauce ingredients.

4. Place the eggplants on a serving platter and drizzle the sauce over them while they are still warm. Cool, cover with plastic wrap, and refrigerate for at least 2 hours to allow the eggplant to marinate lightly in the sauce. The eggplants will keep for at least 5 days.

SERVES 4

Yuca Fries with Tamarind Ketchup

(YUCA FRITA CON SALSA DE TAMARINDO)

The delicious ketchup here, flavored with tart and sweet tamarind pulp, is great to have at hand as a dipping sauce or a glaze for grilled or roast poultry or meat. It will keep for about 3 weeks refrigerated in a clean jar, and would make a great food gift. However, the yuca fries are also sensational with regular ketchup.

TAMARIND KETCHUP

3/4 CUP TAMARIND PULP (AVAILABLE AT ASIAN OR
    HISPANIC GROCERIES)
1 1/2 CUPS BOILING WATER
3 TABLESPOONS TOMATO PASTE
2 1/2 TABLESPOONS UNSULFURED MOLASSES
1 1/2 TEASPOONS RED WINE VINEGAR, OR MORE
    TO TASTE
2 TEASPOONS WORCESTERSHIRE SAUCE
2 CLOVES GARLIC, CRUSHED THROUGH A PRESS
1 TEASPOON MILD PAPRIKA
1/4 TEASPOON GRATED FRESH GINGER
1/4 TEASPOON GROUND CUMIN
1/4 TEASPOON HOT RED PEPPER FLAKES
SALT, TO TASTE
1/4 CUP FINELY CHOPPED CILANTRO

YUCA FRIES

2 POUNDS PEELED YUCA (THAWED, IF FROZEN),
    PEELED AS DIRECTED ON PAGE 79 AND CUT
    INTO 2 1/2-INCH LENGTHS
VEGETABLE OIL, FOR DEEP FRYING
GARLIC SALT

1. To make the ketchup: Soak the tamarind pulp in the boiling water for 15 minutes. When just cool enough to handle, rub the pulp with your fingers to release the flesh. Strain it through a fine sieve, pressing on the solids and scraping the bottom of the sieve with a wooden spoon. Discard the solids.

2. In a small, nonreactive saucepan, combine the strained tamarind liquid with the tomato paste and molasses, and simmer for 20 minutes, stirring occasionally until it thickens somewhat. Off the heat, stir in the remaining ingredients except the cilantro. The ketchup will keep in the refrigerator for up to 3 weeks, stored in a clean, tightly covered jar. Stir in the cilantro right before serving.

3. In a large saucepan, combine the yuca with salted water to cover by 2 inches, and bring to a boil. Simmer over low heat until the yuca is tender, about 25 minutes. With a slotted spoon, remove the yuca to a bowl and let it cool until manageable.

4. Pat the yuca dry with paper towels and cut it into ½-inch sticks. As you are cutting the yuca, remove the tough stringy fibers with a small sharp knife.

5. Heat 1½ inches of oil to 360 degrees F. in a deep-fryer or a deep skillet. Working in small batches, deep-fry the yuca until light golden, about 4 to 5 minutes per batch. Add a large pinch of garlic salt to each batch when the yuca is almost done. With a slotted spoon transfer each cooked batch to drain on paper towels. Serves at once, accompanied by Tamarind Ketchup, or regular ketchup.

SERVES 4 AS A SIDE DISH, APPETIZER, OR SNACK

Sugarcane.

Boiled Yuca with Salsa Cruda

(Y U C A   S A N C O C H A D A   C O N   S A L S A   C R U D A)

In many ways, boiled yuca is an even more satisfying a side dish than boiled potatoes, its texture being more buttery and fluffy. As boiled yuca is rather bland and readily absorbs other flavors, in South America and the Caribbean it's usually offered with a piquant sauce. The sauce I suggest, made of crushed fresh tomatoes with garlic, cilantro, chile, and vinegar, is both refreshing and visually pleasing.

SALSA CRUDA

1 TABLESPOON FINELY CHOPPED GARLIC

¼ CUP FINELY CHOPPED RED ONION

4 MEDIUM RIPE PLUM TOMATOES, BLANCHED,
    PEELED, SEEDED, AND CHOPPED

1 LARGE MILD CHILE, SUCH AS ANAHEIM,
    SEEDED AND CHOPPED

¼ CUP CHOPPED CILANTRO LEAVES

2 TABLESPOONS FRESH LEMON JUICE

1 TABLESPOON RED WINE VINEGAR

1½ TABLESPOONS VIRGIN OLIVE OIL

SALT, TO TASTE

2 POUNDS YUCA, PEELED AS DIRECTED ON PAGE
    79 AND CUT INTO 2-INCH LENGTHS

1. To make the *salsa cruda*: Using a mortar and pestle, and working in batches, crush the garlic, onion, tomatoes, chile, and cilantro to a coarse paste. This can also be done in a blender, using the on/off button. Transfer the mixture to a bowl, add the lemon juice, vinegar, oil, and salt to taste, and let stand for 30 minutes.

2. In a large saucepan, combine the yuca with enough salted water to cover it by 1½ inches, and bring to a boil. Simmer over low heat until the yuca is tender, about 25 minutes. Let the yuca cool a little in the liquid. When just cool enough to handle, drain and cut the yuca in half lengthwise. As you are cutting the yuca, remove the tough stringy fibers with a small sharp knife.

3. Place the yuca on a serving platter and pour the sauce over it. Serve at once.

SERVES 4

Gingered Boniato and Coconut Mash

(PURÉ DE BONIATO CON LECHE DE COCO Y JENGIBRE)

Boniato is a white Cuban sweet potato with a flavor that is less sweet than its orange cousin. Coconut and ginger are flavors typical of northern Brazil, and combined with the *boniato* they produce an exotic silky puree, excellent as a side dish with any main course for which you would normally serve regular mashed potatoes.

2 POUNDS *BONIATO*, PEELED AND CUT INTO
    1-INCH CUBES
2 QUARTS COLD WATER
2 TABLESPOONS UNSALTED BUTTER
1 SMALL ONION, CHOPPED
1 TABLESPOON GRATED FRESH GINGER
1/3 CUP CHICKEN STOCK (PAGE 372), LOWER-
    SALT CANNED CHICKEN BROTH, OR WATER
1/3 CUP CANNED UNSWEETENED COCONUT MILK,
    WELL STIRRED
GRATING OF FRESH NUTMEG
SALT AND FRESHLY GROUND WHITE PEPPER, TO
    TASTE

1. In a large saucepan, combine the *boniato* with the water and bring to a boil. Simmer over low heat until the *boniato* is tender, about 15 minutes.

2. While the *boniato* is cooking, melt the butter in a medium skillet over medium-low heat. Add the onion and cook until softened, about 7 minutes. Add the ginger and cook for another minute. Add the stock and coconut milk and simmer for 5 minutes.

3. Drain the *boniato* and place it in a bowl. Mash the *boniato* into a medium-fine puree. Gradually stir in the coconut mixture until the puree is smooth. Add the nutmeg and salt and pepper to taste.

SERVES 4 TO 6

Bright Red Pickled Onion

(ENCURTIDO DE CEBOLLA)

In Latin America, meals—especially grills—are often accompanied by some sort of pickled vegetable condiment designed to cut through the richness of the food. These sweet-and-sour onion rings, colored bright red with beets, make a tasty, tangy, all-purpose relish for soups, rich tropical stews, grills, or sandwiches. If you want to keep these for a long time, or give them as a gift, pack them in a sterilized jar.

2 MEDIUM SPANISH ONIONS (ABOUT 1 ½ POUNDS
    IN TOTAL), HALVED AND SLICED
1 ¼ CUPS CIDER VINEGAR
⅓ CUP WATER
⅓ CUP SUGAR
1 SMALL BEET, PEELED AND CUT INTO THICK
    WEDGES
8 LARGE CLOVES GARLIC, LIGHTLY CRUSHED
1 TABLESPOON LIGHTLY CRUSHED CORIANDER
    SEEDS

1. Blanch the onions in boiling water to cover for 30 seconds. Drain and refresh under cold water.

2. In a medium-size nonreactive saucepan, combine the vinegar, water, sugar, beet, garlic, and coriander and bring to a simmer, over medium heat, stirring to dissolve the sugar. Simmer for 5 to 7 minutes.

3. Pack the onions into a clean 1-quart jar. Pour the marinade and the beets over them. Remove the beets after a few hours or keep them with the onions, as you wish. The onions will keep, refrigerated, for up to 2 weeks, and in a sterilized jar for several months.

MAKES ONE 1-QUART JAR

Beans, Rice, and All Things Nice

Anya von Bremzen and local revelers, Juli, Peru.

Lake Titicaca, Peru.

Indio Amazónico (Amazon Indian) Botánica, Jackson Heights, New York.

As MARILYN Monroe is to Western sex appeal, so rice and beans are to Latin food. Whether the extravagant *paellas* of Valencia and Catalonia, the robust fava bean stews of Asturias, the rich Portuguese baked rice casseroles, the famous Cuban black bean soup, a simple Colombian dish of soupy red beans, or the ubiquitous pan-Latin *arroz con pollo*—rice and beans, together and apart, are the compelling *pas de deux* of Latin eating.

In the New World and on the Iberian Peninsula, beans always offered, and still provide, a major source of nutrition and sheer culinary pleasure. The Iberians historically subsisted on fava beans, chickpeas, and lentils, while kidney, lima, and lupini beans, black-eyed peas, black beans, and pigeon peas were the mainstays of Latin America and the Caribbean.

So central are black beans to Cuban cuisine that preparing them to perfection is considered the first measure of a cook's culinary skill. In Colombia, you will sample a bowl of soupy red beans cooked with a little bacon, a spicy *sofrito*, and some diced plantain for a nice velvety texture. In Peru and Ecuador, along with the rainbow of other beans, one finds soups and stews prepared with large buttery lima and lupini beans. In Brazil, black beans are the base for the country's national dish, *feijoada*, but you will also savor delicious rustic dishes prepared with black-eyed peas. A favorite dish in Chile is *porotos granados*, a sweet mellow casserole of fresh cranberry beans simmered with pumpkin and corn. In Puerto Rico the islanders relish musky-colored pigeon peas (*gandules*), which they mix with rice or cook up with *calabaza* and spicy sausage.

But perhaps no other nation in the world prepares beans with as much reverence and skill as the Spanish. Like precious wines or boutique olive oils, beans are awarded prizes and denominations of origin. All over the country there are bean-harvesting fiestas, bean-cooking contests, and bean competitions for farmers. They are cooked slowly and lovingly with fragrant olive oil (instead of the lard or pork fat used in other cuisines) together with a flavorful piece of smoked ham, country sausages, or unctuous pig's feet, to give the finished dish the required depth of flavor. And during Lent the beans are paired with salt cod or shellfish, a typically Iberian combination.

The same skills and obsessions are invested in the preparation of rice. While the classic *paella* is undoubtedly a triumph of world grain cookery, the Iberian rice repertoire is certainly not limited to this culinary masterpiece. Throughout Spain and Portugal there is a whole spectrum of innumerable rice dishes, red from tomatoes or paprika, yellow from saffron, or black from squid ink. The rice can be *seco* (dry), *caldoso* (soupy), or *meloso* (syrupy and sticky); it can be baked, simmered, or cooked over charcoal; and it can join forces with spectacular coastal seafood, or more humble salt cod, country sausages and bacon, game, chicken, seasonal vegetables, or sturdy beans and turnips. Whatever the dish, the preferred rice is of the short-grain variety, valued for its ability to soak up and absorb other flavors.

Rice was introduced into Latin America by the colonists, and its various preparations throughout the continent bear a strong Iberian influence. Without doubt, the most popular Latino rice dish is *arroz con pollo*, a take-off on *paella*, made zesty with a flavorful tomato-based sauce, olives, and capers. Any soupy bean dish or stew will come with a huge plate of rice, either white rice, cooked until the grains are moist but separate, or yellow rice, brightly colored with saffron or achiote. Often the rice will be placed in a ring mold and ceremoniously presented as a centerpiece for the meal.

To make foolproof rice, choose a brand you like and a capacious pot with a tight-fitting lid, and stick with them. Consistency is your key to successful rice. With long-grain rice, another important tip, practiced religiously by many Latin cooks, is to wash the rice thoroughly in several changes of water to get rid of excess starch, which can make the rice sticky when cooked. (Short-grain rice, on the other hand, is valued for its starchiness and should not be washed.) I like sautéing the rice briefly in butter or oil, perhaps with some onions or garlic, as this gives rice extra flavor. The longer you allow the rice to stand covered after you take it off the heat, the drier it will become. To allow it sufficient time to rest, do not put the rice to cook at the last minute. In fact, it can even be prepared as much as 1 hour ahead of time, and kept warm in a very low oven.

White Rice

(ARROZ BLANCO)

To produce moist but fluffy rice, I rinse it carefully to get rid of excess starch, bring the rice and liquid to a boil, and cook it *uncovered*, until the liquid is almost absorbed. Then I cover it, reduce the heat to very low, and let it steam until done. If you increase the amount of rice, the amount of liquid does not necessarily increase proportionately. For large quantities of rice, make sure the liquid covers it by 1 inch, about a knuckle. To this recipe you can add diced carrots, celery, zucchini, red pepper, peas, or corn. Add them in step 3.

1½ CUPS LONG-GRAIN RICE, PREFERABLY GOYA
2 TABLESPOONS GOOD OLIVE OIL
⅔ CUP CHOPPED ONION
2¾ CUPS HOT WATER, CANNED LOWER-SALT CHICKEN BROTH, OR CHICKEN STOCK (PAGE 372)
SALT, TO TASTE
1 CUP FINELY DICED VEGETABLES (SEE HEADNOTE), OR A COMBINATION, OPTIONAL

1. Place the rice in a fine sieve and rinse it in several changes of lukewarm water, running your fingers through the rice, until the water runs clear. Leave it in the sieve, set over a bowl, and let drain for about 20 minutes.

2. In a large, heavy saucepan with a tight-fitting lid, heat the oil over medium heat. Add the onion and cook, stirring, until limp, about 5 minutes. Add the rice and stir until the grains are translucent and coated with oil, about 2 minutes.

3. Stir in the water and salt and bring to a boil. Cook, uncovered, over medium-low heat, stirring once, until the liquid is almost level with the rice and small air bubbles appear on its surface, 5 to 7 minutes. Gently stir in the vegetables, if using them. Cover tightly, reduce the heat as low as possible, and steam the rice until all the liquid has been absorbed, about 12 minutes. Remove from the heat and let stand, covered, for at least 15 minutes.

4. To serve, fluff the rice gently with a fork and transfer it to a serving platter.

SERVES 4 TO 6

Red Rice with Toasted Cumin

(ARROZ ROJO)

This rice is gently flavored with tomato, jalapeño, cilantro, and toasted cumin, which give it an interesting dimension of taste. The jalapeño does produce some heat, so for a milder dish, seed it. The rice makes a tasty two-step with red or black beans.

1½ CUPS LONG-GRAIN RICE, PREFERABLY GOYA

1 TEASPOON CUMIN SEEDS

2 LARGE RIPE TOMATOES, COARSELY CHOPPED

2 TABLESPOONS CHOPPED ONION

2 CLOVES GARLIC, CHOPPED

ABOUT 2¼ CUPS WATER, CHICKEN STOCK (PAGE 372), OR CANNED LOWER-SALT CHICKEN BROTH

2 TABLESPOONS PEANUT OR CANOLA OIL

½ TABLESPOON TOMATO PASTE

SALT, TO TASTE

1 SMALL JALAPEÑO CHILE, SEEDED AND HALVED LENGTHWISE

2 LARGE SPRIGS CILANTRO

1. Place the rice in a fine sieve and rinse it in several changes of lukewarm water, running your fingers through the rice, until the water runs clear. Leave it in the sieve, set over a bowl, and let it drain for about 20 minutes.

2. In a small skillet, stir the cumin seeds over medium heat for 2 minutes. When cool enough to handle, crumble the seeds with your fingers and set aside.

3. Puree the tomatoes, onion, and garlic in a blender until smooth. Measure the tomato puree. You should have about ½ cup. Then separately measure the amount of water or stock to be added to the rice. Together, they should make 2¾ cups. Adjust the amount of water accordingly. Do not combine the tomato puree with the liquid.

4. In a large, heavy saucepan with a tight-fitting lid, heat the oil over medium heat. Add the rice and stir until the grains are translucent and coated with oil, about 2 minutes. Add the tomato paste, and keep stirring for about 2 minutes.

5. Add the pureed tomato mixture and cook, stirring, until it is almost absorbed, about 5 minutes. Add the water or stock and bring to a boil over medium heat. Add salt to taste. Cook, uncovered, over medium-low heat, stirring once, until the liquid is almost level with the rice and small air bubbles appear on its surface, 5 to 7 minutes.

6. Gently stir the cumin, jalapeño, and cilantro sprigs into the rice. Cover tightly, reduce the heat as low as possible, and steam the rice until it is tender and all the liquid has been absorbed, about 12 minutes. Remove from the heat and let stand, covered, for at least 15 minutes.

7. To serve, fluff the rice gently with a fork and transfer it to a serving platter.

SERVES 4 TO 6

Green Rice

(ARROZ VERDE)

This, and the red rice recipe (page 248), come from my friend Bertha Palenzuela, who is of Cuban-Mexican-Lebanese extraction. The rice takes its color and unique flavor from a combination of tomatillos and cilantro. But if you find the taste of cilantro too assertive, substitute parsley. This rice has a lot of individuality, and is best next to a simple entree, perhaps a roast or a grill.

1½ CUPS LONG-GRAIN RICE, PREFERABLY GOYA

4 TOMATILLOS, HUSKS REMOVED, COARSELY CHOPPED

¾ CUP CHOPPED CILANTRO LEAVES

1 CUP CHOPPED SPINACH LEAVES

2 CLOVES GARLIC, CHOPPED

ABOUT 2¾ CUPS WATER, CHICKEN STOCK (PAGE 372), OR CANNED LOWER-SALT CHICKEN BROTH

2 TABLESPOONS PEANUT OR CANOLA OIL

⅓ CUP CHOPPED ONION

SALT, TO TASTE

1. Place the rice in a fine sieve and rinse it in several changes of lukewarm water, running your fingers through the rice until the water runs clear. Leave it in the sieve, set over a bowl, and drain for about 20 minutes.

2. In a blender, puree the tomatillos, cilantro, spinach, and garlic with ½ cup of the water until very smooth. Strain through a sieve. Measure the puree. Then measure the amount of water or stock to be added to the rice. Together, they should make 2¾ cups. Adjust the amount of stock accordingly. Do not combine the tomatillo puree with the liquid.

3. In a large, heavy saucepan with a tight-fitting lid, heat the oil over medium heat. Add the onion and cook, stirring, until limp, about 5 minutes. Add the rice and stir until the grains are translucent and coated with oil, about 2 minutes.

4. Add the pureed mixture and cook, stirring, until it is almost absorbed, about 5 minutes. Add the remaining water and bring to a boil over medium heat. Add salt to taste. Cook, uncovered, over medium-low heat, stirring once, until the liquid is almost level with the rice and small air bubbles appear on its surface, 5 to 7 minutes. Cover tightly, reduce the heat as low as possible, and steam the rice until it is tender and all the liquid has been absorbed, about 12 minutes. Remove from the heat and let stand, covered, for at least 15 minutes.

5. To serve, fluff the rice gently with a fork and transfer it to a serving platter.

SERVES 4 TO 6

Hat store, Buenos Aires, Argentina.

Wagon-Riding Gaucho's Rice

(ARROZ DE CARRETEIRO)

This is a dish of the wagon-riding cowboys of Argentina (*carreteros*) and southern Brazil (*carreteiros*), traditionally made with bits and pieces of dried meats and other chance ingredients that could be thrown together on the road. The thing that gives the rice its unique smoky taste is dried beef, for which you can substitute jerked beef. If that's not to be found either, use very dry salami. The resulting dish is somewhat like a Chinese fried rice, deeply flavored, and studded with delicious bits and pieces, with a scrambled egg stirred in at the end.

2 TO 3 OUNCES DRIED BEEF (*TASAJO*), BEEF JERKY STICKS, OR DRIED SALAMI (SEE HEADNOTE)

1 ½ CUPS LONG-GRAIN RICE

1 TABLESPOON PLUS ½ TEASPOON LIGHT OLIVE OIL

1 ½ CUPS DICED ONION

3 CLOVES GARLIC, MINCED

⅔ CUP FINELY DICED *LINGUIÇA* OR KIELBASA SAUSAGE

1 SMALL RED BELL PEPPER, CORED, SEEDED, AND FINELY DICED

1 CUP FRESH OR FROZEN AND THAWED CORN KERNELS

2 ¾ CUPS WATER

2 LARGE EGGS, BEATEN

2 MEDIUM TOMATOES, CUT INTO SMALL DICE

2 ½ TABLESPOONS MINCED FLAT-LEAF PARSLEY

1. If using dried beef, soak it in cold water to cover for at least two hours or overnight. Drain. Cook over medium heat in water to cover for 30 minutes. Drain and cut into fine dice. If using beef jerky or salami, cut them into fine dice.

2. Place the rice in a fine sieve and rinse in several changes of lukewarm water, running your fingers through the rice, until the water runs clear. Leave it in the sieve, and let it drain for 20 minutes.

3. In a large, heavy saucepan, heat 1 tablespoon of the oil over medium heat. Add the onion and garlic and cook, stirring, for 5 minutes. Add the dried beef, sausage, and pepper and cook for another 5 minutes. Stir in the corn and cook for 1 minute more. Add the rice and stir until the grains are translucent. Add the water and bring to a boil over medium heat. Cook until small air bubbles appear on the surface of the rice, about 7 minutes. Cover tightly, reduce the heat to low, and simmer until the rice is tender and all the liquid has been absorbed, about 12 minutes. Remove from the heat and let stand, covered, for 15 minutes.

4. While the rice is standing, heat the remaining $1/2$ teaspoon of the oil in a nonstick skillet. Stir in the eggs and cook, stirring with a wooden spoon, as you would scrambled eggs, until set.

5. Transfer the rice to a large mixing bowl and fluff it with a fork. With two forks, stir in the scrambled egg until it is broken into small pieces. Stir in the tomatoes and parsley. Transfer to a serving bowl and serve.

SERVES 4 TO 6 AS A SIDE DISH OR
3 TO 4 AS A LIGHT MAIN COURSE

Arroz con Pollo

Without doubt, one of the most popular dishes throughout the Latin world is *arroz con pollo*, chicken and rice. Essentially it's a simplified version of *paella*, but with the added zest of capers and olives. Each country and each cook have a slightly different recipe. To me, the most important distinction is the actual texture—the classic Iberian and Cuban versions are done with short-grain, Valencia-type rice and are quite soupy, while in Latin America the dish is often prepared with long-grain rice, cooked until dry. Both are good in their own way but here I offer a simpler variant with long-grain rice and a flavorful sauce of *sofrito* and beer. After the rice is almost cooked, it is covered with a banana leaf, which imparts a wonderful tropical flavor to the dish, and finished in the oven. The banana leaf, of course, is optional, and you can still have a great *arroz* without it. You can substitute a large pinch of pulverized saffron threads for the annatto oil, adding it to the chicken braising liquid. To make a festive island meal of it, serve this with Fried Plantains (page 232) and Cuban Black Beans with a Touch of Chocolate (page 272).

3 CLOVES GARLIC, MINCED

½ TEASPOON SALT, PLUS MORE TO TASTE

½ TEASPOON MILD PAPRIKA

3 POUNDS CHICKEN PIECES (BREASTS CUT INTO SERVING-SIZE PIECES), RINSED WELL AND PATTED DRY

2 TABLESPOONS OLIVE OIL

1 TABLESPOON ANNATTO OIL (PAGE 376)

1 DRY *CHORIZO* SAUSAGE, CUT INTO FINE DICE

4 CLOVES GARLIC, CRUSHED THROUGH A PRESS

1 CUP CHOPPED ONION

1 MEDIUM RED BELL PEPPER, CORED, SEEDED, AND DICED

3 LARGE RIPE TOMATOES, BLANCHED, PEELED, AND CHOPPED

1 TEASPOON GROUND CUMIN

1 TEASPOON DRIED OREGANO

2 TABLESPOONS SMALL CAPERS

¼ CUP SLICED PITTED GREEN OLIVES

1 CUP BEER

2 CUPS LONG-GRAIN RICE

2½ CUPS WATER

(continued)

1. In a mortar and pestle, pound the minced garlic, ½ teaspoon salt, and the paprika to a paste. Rub the chicken with this mixture and refrigerate it for at least 2 hours or overnight.

1 LARGE FROZEN BANANA LEAF, THAWED AND SOFTENED AS DIRECTED ON PAGE 380, OPTIONAL

¾ CUP FRESH OR FROZEN AND THAWED GREEN PEAS

½ CUP DICED ROASTED RED PEPPER STRIPS (PAGE 375), OR ¼ CUP DICED PIMIENTOS

2. In a large, ovenproof saucepan heat the olive oil over medium-high heat. Brown the chicken, in batches, on all sides and transfer it to drain on paper towels.

3. Add the annatto oil to the saucepan and heat over medium heat. Add the *chorizo* and cook, stirring, for 2 minutes. If there seems to be too much oil in the saucepan, remove all but about 2 tablespoons. Add the onion and pepper, and cook, stirring, until softened, about 5 minutes. Add the tomatoes, cumin, and oregano, cover, and cook over low heat, stirring, until the tomatoes are reduced to a paste, about 10 minutes. Replace the chicken in the saucepan and add the capers and olives. Stir in the beer, bring to a simmer, and cook over low heat, covered, stirring occasionally, until the chicken is almost cooked through, about 20 minutes.

4. Preheat the oven to 325 degrees F.

5. Stir in the rice, water, and salt to taste and bring to a boil over medium-low heat. Cook until the water is almost level with the rice and air bubbles appear on the surface of the rice, about 5 to 7 minutes.

6. Using scissors, cut the banana leaf to fit the saucepan. Stir in the peas and cover the top with the banana leaf. Cover the saucepan tightly, transfer it to the oven, and cook until the rice is tender and all the liquid has been absorbed, about 20 minutes. Remove from the heat and let stand, covered, for at least 15 minutes.

7. Transfer to a serving platter, fluffing the rice with a fork, and serve garnished with roasted pepper strips or pimientos.

SERVES 6 AS A MAIN COURSE, 8 AS PART OF A BUFFET

Catalan "Paella"

(ARRÒS PARELLADA)

A true Valencian *paella*, worthy of its name, has to be prepared with a particular variety of short-grain rice, has to include rabbit and snails, and must be cooked in a proper *paella* pan, over a wood fire, which imparts a slightly smoky taste. In Spain, anything that's not a proper *paella* is often simply referred to as *arroz con* . . . "rice with . . ." And this *arroz*, called *Parellada* after a legendary Catalan gourmand, is certainly a lavish one—rice studded with sausage, cubes of pork, vegetables, and several kinds of seafood. As this dish was invented in an elegant restaurant, all the meats and fish are boned, shelled, and cut into neat pieces before they go into the pan. It's an elaborate dish, indeed, but it will crown any festive table, and much of the work can be done ahead of time.

The *sofregit*—a base of tomatoes and onions cooked down until it acquires a rich, concentrated flavor, and a dark brownish color—is a crucial element of many Catalan dishes. The *sofregit* for this recipe can be made up to 3 days ahead and refrigerated.

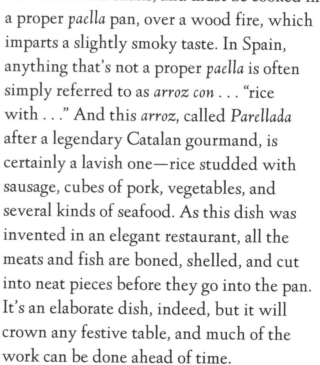

2 LINKS GOOD FRESH PORK SAUSAGE (ABOUT 1/2 POUND)

1 POUND SMALL MUSSELS, BEARDED AND SCRUBBED RIGHT BEFORE USING

5 LARGE CLOVES GARLIC, CHOPPED

2 TABLESPOONS CHOPPED FLAT-LEAF PARSLEY

1/8 TEASPOON SAFFRON THREADS

3 TABLESPOON PLUS 2 TEASPOONS OLIVE OIL

1 POUND BONED CHICKEN THIGHS (BONED WEIGHT), CUT INTO SMALL PIECES

1/2 POUND BONELESS CENTER-CUT PORK CHOPS, CUT INTO 3/4-INCH CUBES

8 FROZEN ARTICHOKE HEARTS, THAWED AND QUARTERED

1 MEDIUM RED BELL PEPPER, DICED

SOFREGIT (RECIPE FOLLOWS)

2 CUPS SHORT-GRAIN RICE

4 CUPS SIMMERING CHICKEN STOCK (PAGE 372), CANNED LOWER-SALT CHICKEN BROTH, OR MORE AS NEEDED

SALT, TO TASTE

1/2 CUP FRESH OR FROZEN AND THAWED GREEN PEAS

(continued)

1. Prick the sausage in several places with the tip of a small knife. Blanch it in boiling water for 1 minute. Pat dry with paper towels, and cut into thick slices.

2. Steam open the mussels in a colander set over boiling water. Discard any that don't open. When they are cool enough to handle, remove and discard the top shell. Cover the mussels with plastic wrap so they don't dry out, and set them aside until ready to use.

³/₄ POUND CLEANED SQUID BODIES, RINSED, DRIED THOROUGHLY, AND CUT INTO BITE-SIZE PIECES
16 JUMBO SHRIMP, SHELLED AND DEVEINED, TAILS LEFT ON
6 TO 8 LEMON WEDGES

3. In a mortar and pestle, pound the garlic, parsley, and saffron to a paste. Set aside.

4. Heat 3 tablespoons of the oil over medium heat in a *paella* pan or a heavy, deep, ovenproof 12-inch skillet. Add the sausage slices and cook, stirring, for 5 minutes. Remove with a slotted spoon. Add the chicken, pork, artichokes, and red pepper, raise the heat to high, and cook, stirring, until the chicken is lightly browned, about 4 minutes. (The *paella* can be prepared ahead up to this point.) Return the sausage to the skillet and add the *sofregit*.

5. Stir the rice into the skillet and reduce the heat to medium. Add 4 cups of the stock, the garlic mixture, and salt to taste. Cook, uncovered, stirring gently from time to time, until most of the liquid has been absorbed but the rice is still slightly wet, 8 to 10 minutes. At this stage the rice should taste almost cooked, but al dente. If it is still too hard to the bite, add ¹/₂ cup more stock and cook for another 5 minutes. (Different varieties of short-grain rice might require different amounts of liquid.)

6. Preheat the oven to 325 degrees F.

7. Gently stir the peas into the rice with two forks. Cover the skillet loosely with foil, transfer the pan to the oven, and bake until cooked through but still a little soupy, about 8 minutes. If the rice is still too hard, add another ¹/₂ cup liquid and cook 5 minutes more.

8. While the rice is baking, in a large skillet, heat 1 teaspoon of oil over high heat. Add the

(continued)

squid and cook until it is just tender, about 1½ minutes. Remove from the skillet, add the remaining 1 teaspoon of oil, and cook the shrimp until they just turn pink, about 3 minutes.

9. Remove the rice from the oven and, using two forks, stir in the shrimp, squid, and the reserved mussels. Turn the oven temperature up to 400 degrees, return the rice to the oven, and cook another 5 minutes. The rice should look fairly dry.

10. Remove the rice from the oven and let it stand, covered with foil, for 10 minutes. Squeeze some lemon juice over the *paella*, and serve with additional lemon wedges on the side.

SERVES 6 TO 8

Sofregit

⅓ CUP SUN-DRIED TOMATOES, PACKED IN OIL,
    OR 4 TABLESPOONS SUN-DRIED TOMATO
    PASTE
2½ TABLESPOONS GOOD OLIVE OIL
1 MEDIUM ONION, CHOPPED
4 LARGE CLOVES GARLIC, CHOPPED
4 MEDIUM RIPE TOMATOES, PEELED, SEEDED,
    AND CHOPPED

In many good Catalan restaurants, the *sofregit* is prepared in large quantities and simmered so long it acquires a caramelized, almost smoky taste. To re-create this smokiness in a home kitchen, I add some sun-dried tomatoes.

1. If using whole sun-dried tomatoes, puree them in a food processor, and set aside.

2. In a medium-size skillet, heat the oil over medium-low heat. Add the onion and garlic and cook, stirring from time to time, until the onion is soft, about 7 minutes. Add the processed sun-dried tomatoes or sun-dried tomato paste and the fresh tomatoes and cook, stirring, until the tomatoes are slightly darkened and reduced to a pulp, adding water a tablespoon at a time, if they begin to stick to the skillet. This should take 20 to 25 minutes. Leave the *sofregit* in the skillet if using it immediately, or transfer it to an airtight container and refrigerate until ready to use.

Yellow Rice with Carrots and Orange Zest

(ARROZ AMARILLO)

Slowly cooked grated carrots, orange zest, and a touch of saffron impart a lovely yellow hue and a mellow sweet flavor to this rice. It makes a versatile side dish with any entree. Although they are more Arab than Spanish, for a nice sweet touch you can add some slivered dry apricots or a handful of raisins to the carrot mixture as it cooks.

1 TABLESPOON UNSALTED BUTTER
2 TABLESPOONS VEGETABLE OIL
1 CUP GRATED CARROTS
1 TEASPOON MILD PAPRIKA
1/8 TEASPOON PULVERIZED SAFFRON THREADS
1½ TABLESPOONS GRATED ORANGE ZEST
1½ CUPS LONG-GRAIN RICE
3 CUPS HOT WATER, CHICKEN STOCK (PAGE 372), OR CANNED LOWER-SALT CHICKEN BROTH
SALT, TO TASTE

1. In a large, heavy saucepan with a tight-fitting lid, heat the butter and oil over medium-low heat. Add the carrots and cook, stirring until softened, about 10 minutes. Add a tablespoon of water if the carrots look dry. Add the paprika, saffron, orange zest, and rice, and stir until the grains are translucent and coated with the oil, about 2 minutes.

2. Add the liquid and salt and bring to a boil. Reduce the heat as low as possible, cover, and simmer until the rice is tender and all the liquid has been absorbed, about 20 minutes. Remove from the heat and let stand, covered, for 15 minutes.

3. To serve, fluff the rice gently with a fork and transfer it to a serving platter.

SERVES 4 TO 6

Music: Cuba's Greatest Export

Forget sugarcane and tobacco—music is Cuba's greatest export and its most unique contribution to world culture! It's simply astonishing how an island so small could produce such an incredible concentration of great musicians and such a rich, intricate bounty of musical styles. Here is a look at some of them.

The Sound of Son

Son—one of founding genres of Cuban music and the direct ancestor of salsa—is considered to be the first musical style actually invented in Cuba. It is of rural stock, having originated in the mountainous, multiethnic Cuban province of Oriente (famous for its red beans and its countryside), where the descendants of black slaves and freemen lived side by side with *guajiros*—tobacco farmers of Spanish origin—influencing each other's music and culture. In *son* lyrical Spanish songs for guitar and voice blended with the complex polyrhythms of Africa to produce a sound that was to define Cuban music.

Son traveled westward, reaching Havana in the 1910s where the original simple, rustic instrumentation expanded into ensembles known as *sextetos* (and later *septetos*), adding the sound of the coronet and the string bass to the voice, *tres* (the six-stringed *Criollo* guitar), maracas, and bongo, and the grounding rhythmic clack of the *clave* sticks. The *típico* sound of early *son* is a melodious song, at times sad, at times humorous and feisty, sung by slightly crackling, nasal male voices. Despite its strong African heritage, the feel of *son* is very Iberian, with its characteristic guitar and haunting, melancholy melodies that tell of love, rural life, and, later, witty social commentaries. The best examples of classic early son are the recordings of Septeto Nacional, led by the great bassist/composer Ignacio Piñero.

New generations brought major innovations to the genre. Arsenio Rodríguez, the blind Congolese *tres* player, became the godfather of modern Cuban dance music by adding conga drums to the horns and piano, cutting loose on the improvised rhythmic workout known as the *montuno* portion of the *son—son montuno*. Arsenio immigrated to America, where he died in relative obscurity, but his musical innovations were rediscovered by later generations, becoming a giant force on the Cuban-American musical scene. The beloved mambo king, *sonero* Beny Moré, who developed his singing career in Mexico with the famous orchestra leader Pérez Prado, expanded the style further by adding an Afro-Cuban percussion section to the American jazz orchestra—style lineup. In the 1940s and 1950s, son and other Cuban rhythms were worked into the idiom of American big bands and jazz outfits (also influencing classical composers like Aaron Copland and George Gershwin), whose brassy accents, in turn, shaped the sound of Cuban music. Mambo, which took over the dance floors of the 1940s, is essentially a faster, jazzier *son*, a glamorous mulatto child of American and Afro-Cuban sounds.

In recent years *son* has had its ups and downs, eclipsed in this country by its giant brat-baby, salsa. But it's still alive and well, and a major force in the musical landscape of contemporary Cuba, where many musicians resist the "American" umbrella designation of salsa.

Rumba: A Riot of Percussion

The real rumba is to its nightclub-Hollywood version as beans and rice are to lobster thermidor. Like the samba of Brazil and American blues, rumba is the musical and poetic idiom of black slaves, who were brought to Cuba from Nigeria, Cameroon, Benin, and the Congo to work on the sugar plantations. In the late nineteenth century, soon after the abolition of slavery in Cuba, the black population who migrated to the cities began to organize into *cabildos*—a type of social and religious organization—that united blacks from different parts of Africa. It was in these *cabildos* that rumba was fused from the various West African folk and religious dances that had been furtively danced in slave barracks into a recognizable form of artistic expression, becoming a symbol for black unity and identity.

Of all the Cuban styles, rumba, with its percussive sound and complex polyrhythms typical of African music, has the most distinctly African sound. Rumba is a real riot of percussions, including at least seven instruments ranging from spoons and wooden boxes for salt cod, to the obligatory conga and bongo drums, sticks called *claves*, and an iron shaker called a *maruga*, among others. The dance is an extraordinary reenactment of the sexual mating game, the male and female dancers pursuing and seducing each other through a series of choreographed gestures, the most characteristic of which is the famous male pelvic thrust known as *vacuno*. There are three distinct kinds of rumba: *yambu*—a slow dance for couples; *columbia*—a showy male dance, and the popular *guaguancó*—a faster, more social style that was orchestrated for dance floors and often reworked and transformed by salsa bands after it was exported to America.

While rumba is considered a secular style, *santería* (the syncretic Afro-Caribbean religion) is where the roots of rumba lie. And an especially electrifying rumba performance arouses among its participants the same ecstatic trance as a *santería* ceremony. A truly all-encompassing genre, rumba is not about dance-hall maneuvers or concert music. In fact, it's always more than just music—it's a collective feast of song, dance, poetry, religion, socializing, and drink that celebrates Cuba's African heritage.

His Majesty, Danzón

Danzón might have found its most enthusiastic following in the Mexican seaside city of Veracruz, but it's a pure Cuban dance, or rather, an Afro-Cuban rendition of a European country dance, the *contradanza*, which arrived in Cuba via the white French colonists who fled Haiti after the revolution. In fact, *danzón*, in Cuba during the 1870s, was a way of designating a specific way of dancing the *contradanza*, until the first formal *danzón* was composed by Miguel Falide in 1879. Unlike the wild, ecstatic rumba and the swaying-hip *son*, *danzón* is a "polite society" dance—white bourgeois music performed by all classes. It's slow, formal, elegant, and stately, replete with fans for ladies and white gloves for men—danced by elderly couples with almost comical seriousness to the old-fashioned sound of coronet-led bands. His majesty, *danzón* (as a Cuban historian describes it), "is a dance to dance on a single tile."

Félix de Jesús' Incredible Black Beans and Rice

(ARROZ CON FRIJOLES DE FÉLIX)

I have many Cuban friends, and they all cook rice and beans, but no one makes a more spirited dish of it than Félix de Jesús, the pride and joy of the New York Latin dance circuit. Besides having a body that can move to five different beats at once, Félix is a dandy, a poet, and an artist, and his beans and rice are as wild and complex as the beat he dances to. In his recipe—a version of the famous *moros y cristianos* (Moors and Christians)—the rice and beans are flavored with an incredibly zesty *sofrito*, which includes three kinds of meat, olives, capers, wine, vermouth, and lots of spices. The recipe comes from Félix's grandmother, *abuelita* Amelia Roque. The dish is certainly substantial enough to make a light party meal, especially when accompanied by The Latino Big Salad (page 115).

8 OUNCES DRIED BLACK TURTLE BEANS,
   PREFERABLY GOYA
8 CUPS WATER
1 HEAD GARLIC, PEELED AND CUT IN HALF
   CROSSWISE
2 BAY LEAVES

S O F R I T O
4 STRIPS BACON, CHOPPED
2 MEDIUM ONIONS, FINELY CHOPPED
6 LARGE CLOVES GARLIC, MINCED
2 DRY *CHORIZO* SAUSAGES (ABOUT 6 OUNCES
   TOTAL), CUT INTO MEDIUM DICE
6 OUNCES GOOD-QUALITY HAM, CUT INTO
   MEDIUM DICE
6 OUNCES CORNED BEEF, IN 1 PIECE, CUT INTO
   MEDIUM DICE
1 LARGE GREEN BELL PEPPER, CORED, SEEDED,
   AND DICED
1 RED BELL PEPPER, CORED, SEEDED, AND
   DICED
1 TABLESPOON MILD PAPRIKA
1 TABLESPOON CHILI POWDER

(continued)

1. In a large saucepan, combine the beans, water, head of garlic, and bay leaves, and bring to a boil. Reduce the heat to low, cover, and simmer the beans until tender, about 1½ hours.

2. While beans are cooking, make the *sofrito*: In a large, deep skillet, cook the bacon over medium heat until it renders its fat. Drain off all but 2 tablespoons of the fat, add the onions and minced garlic and cook, stirring until the onion is soft, about 7 minutes. Push the onions to the side of the skillet and add the *chorizo*, ham, corned beef, and the green and red peppers. Cook, stirring, until the meats are lightly browned, about 7 minutes, adding a little water if the mixture begins to stick. Mix in the onions from the side of the pan, add the paprika, chili powder, cumin, oregano, ground bay leaf, and salt and pepper, and stir for 1 minute. Add the olives with their brine, the vinegar, wine, and brandy and bring to a boil over medium-high heat. Cook for 5 minutes. Set aside until ready to use.

1 TABLESPOON GROUND CUMIN

1½ TABLESPOONS DRIED OREGANO

1 TABLESPOON GROUND BAY LEAF (AVAILABLE FROM GOYA), OPTIONAL

SALT AND FRESHLY GROUND BLACK PEPPER, TO TASTE

⅓ CUP SLICED PIMIENTO-STUFFED GREEN OLIVES, PLUS 2 TABLESPOONS OF THEIR BRINE

1 TABLESPOON DISTILLED WHITE VINEGAR

⅓ CUP DRY WHITE WINE

3 TABLESPOONS BRANDY OR VERMOUTH

2 CUPS LONG-GRAIN RICE

SALT, TO TASTE

CILANTRO LEAVES, FOR GARNISH, OPTIONAL

3. When the beans are ready, drain them into a colander set over a large bowl. Measure and reserve 3¼ cups of the liquid and discard the rest, or save it for soup. Discard the garlic and bay leaves.

4. Preheat the oven to 325 degrees F.

5. Rinse the rice well in several changes of cold water. Combine the rice with the beans in a large ovenproof saucepan with a tight-fitting lid. Add the reserved bean liquid and bring to a boil. Add salt to taste and simmer, uncovered, over medium-low heat until most of the liquid has been absorbed and small bubbles appear on the surface of the rice, 5 to 7 minutes.

6. Working with two forks, gently stir the *sofrito* into the rice and beans until well distributed, adding more salt if necessary. Cover, and place in the oven for 30 minutes. Remove from the heat and let stand, covered, for 15 minutes. Transfer to a serving dish and serve, garnished with cilantro if desired.

SERVES 8 AS A SUBSTANTIAL SIDE DISH OR A LIGHT PARTY MEAL

Coconut Rice with Pigeon Peas

(ARROZ CON GANDULES Y LECHE DE COCO)

Pigeon peas (*gandules*), which look like musky green peas, are a staple on a number of Caribbean islands, including Puerto Rico and the Dominican Republic. Combined with rice, they form the cornerstone of the island diet. Pigeon peas are now available in many forms at Latin markets and supermarkets, and sometimes you can even spot them fresh, still on the vine. Next to fresh, frozen *gandules* are the best option, though in a pinch, you can use Goya canned *gandules*. Don't attempt to make this recipe with canned coconut milk; it is too oily for the rice to absorb.

1½ CUPS LONG-GRAIN RICE
2½ CUPS DRIED COCONUT
3 CUPS BOILING WATER
½ CUP FINELY CHOPPED ONION
2 CLOVES GARLIC, MINCED
⅓ CUP DICED GREEN BELL PEPPER
½ CUP CHOPPED RIPE TOMATO
2 SWEET CHILES, SUCH AS FRESNO, SEEDED AND
    DICED (IF UNAVAILABLE, SUBSTITUTE
    ¼ TEASPOON CAYENNE)
1 TABLESPOON OLIVE OIL
1¼ CUPS FROZEN AND THAWED PIGEON PEAS
SALT AND FRESHLY GROUND BLACK PEPPER, TO
    TASTE

1. Place the rice in a fine sieve and rinse in several changes of lukewarm water, running your fingers through the rice, until the water runs clear. Leave in the sieve, set over a bowl, to drain for about 20 minutes.

2. Combine the coconut and boiling water in a blender and blend for 3 minutes. Transfer the contents of the blender to a bowl and let stand for 15 minutes. Strain through a fine sieve, pressing hard on the solids to extract as much liquid as possible.

3. In a mortar and pestle, crush the onion, garlic, bell pepper, tomato, and chiles to a coarse paste. Alternatively, you can do this in a blender with quick on/off pulses.

4. Heat the oil over medium-low heat in a heavy medium-size saucepan. Add the crushed mixture and cook, stirring, for 5 minutes. Add the rice and pigeon peas and stir until the grains are translucent, about 1 minute. Add the coconut milk and bring to a boil. Add salt and pepper to taste, reduce the heat to low, cover, and cook until all the liquid has been absorbed and the rice is tender, about 20 minutes. Remove from the heat and let the rice stand, covered, for at least 15 minutes.

5. Fluff the rice with a fork and transfer it to a serving platter.

SERVES 4 TO 6

Royal Palace Lima Beans

(JUDIONES DEL REAL SITIO CON CHORIZO)

Only a Castilian cook can make a lowly bean stew taste like an ethereal soufflé. One of the secrets is the use of good olive oil instead of the lard or bacon fat that is often used in other cultures. The other secret is the beans themselves. Spain is probably the only country where beans have as many quality grades and denominations of origin as precious wines. This melt-in-your-mouth dish of delicate lima beans simmered for a long time with serrano ham and pig's feet comes from Real Sitio, a former royal palace and town just outside of Segovia, Spain. The beans are cooked for a long time, with cold water added periodically to stop the boiling. This keeps the beans meltingly tender but intact. The pig's feet and ears give the dish a special unctuousness, but you can omit one of them if you wish. Serve the beans as a first course or a light meal.

1 PIG'S FOOT, SPLIT IN HALF

2 PIG'S EARS

2 FRESH *CHORIZO* SAUSAGES

1 POUND DRIED BABY LIMA BEANS

3/4 CUP DICED CARROT

3/4 CUP DICED ONION

3/4 CUP DICED GREEN BELL PEPPER

3/4 CUP DICED TOMATO

8 LARGE CLOVES GARLIC, LIGHTLY SMASHED

2 BAY LEAVES

ONE 4-OUNCE SLAB SERRANO HAM, PROSCIUTTO, OR GOOD SMOKY BACON

10 CUPS WATER

2 TABLESPOONS VIRGIN OLIVE OIL

1 TABLESPOON BEST-QUALITY MILD PAPRIKA

SALT, TO TASTE

1. Place the pig's foot and ears (or whichever one you are using) in a medium-size saucepan and add cold water to cover. Bring to a boil, reduce the heat to low, and simmer for 15 minutes. Prick the *chorizos* in several places with the tip of a small knife. Add them to the saucepan and simmer until opaque for another 10 minutes. Drain and reserve.

2. In a large, heavy saucepan, combine the beans with the pig's foot and ears, and half the carrot, onion, bell pepper, and tomato. Reserve the rest of the vegetables. Add the garlic, bay leaves, ham, and 8 cups of the water, and bring to a boil, skimming. Simmer, covered, over medium heat for 1 hour until the beans are half-cooked. Add 1 cup of cold water, and simmer for another half hour.

3. Slice the *chorizo* into thick slices. Add it to the beans along with another cup of cold water. Uncover, and simmer for another half hour.

4. In a medium-size saucepan, heat the oil over medium heat and sauté the reserved vegetables, stirring, until softened, about 7 minutes. Transfer the cooked vegetables to a food processor and add about $1/2$ cup of the beans. Process to a coarse puree and stir this mixture back into the beans. Add the paprika and salt to taste and cook for another 10 minutes to thicken.

5. With a slotted spoon remove and discard the ham and the bay leaves, and the pig's foot and ears. Serve the beans in rustic earthenware bowls.

SERVES 6 TO 8 AS A FIRST COURSE
OR A LIGHT MEAL

Cranberry Beans with Pumpkin

(POROTOS GRANADOS)

A Chilean national bean dish, this is an irresistibly suave combination of mellow New World flavors—fresh cranberry beans, pumpkin, and corn—scented with fresh basil. If fresh cranberry beans are unavailable, substitute $1^{1}/_{2}$ cups dried beans, soaked overnight and drained.

4 CUPS SHELLED FRESH CRANBERRY BEANS, OR
    $1^{1}/_{2}$ CUPS DRIED CRANBERRY BEANS
8 CUPS WATER (IF USING DRIED BEANS)
2 TABLESPOONS LIGHT OLIVE OIL
1 LARGE ONION, CHOPPED
$1^{1}/_{2}$ TEASPOONS MINCED GARLIC
1 TEASPOON MILD PAPRIKA
1 POUND PUMPKIN OR WINTER SQUASH, PEELED
    AND CUT INTO 1-INCH CUBES
1 CUP DRAINED CHOPPED CANNED TOMATOES
$^{3}/_{4}$ CUP FRESH OR FROZEN AND THAWED CORN
    KERNELS
$^{1}/_{2}$ CUP CHICKEN STOCK (PAGE 372) OR CANNED
    LOWER-SALT CHICKEN BROTH, OR WATER
2 TABLESPOONS LIGHT CREAM
$^{1}/_{4}$ CUP SLIVERED FRESH BASIL
SALT AND FRESHLY GROUND BLACK PEPPER, TO
    TASTE

1. In a large pot, cover the fresh beans with 2 inches of water. Bring to a boil, reduce the heat to low, and simmer until the beans are almost tender, about 35 minutes. If using dried beans, simmer them, covered, in 8 cups of water until tender, about $1^{1}/_{4}$ hours.

2. While the beans are cooking, heat the oil over medium-low heat in a large, heavy ovenproof saucepan. Sauté the onion and garlic, stirring, until the onion is soft, about 7 minutes. Stir in the paprika and cook for 1 more minute. Add the pumpkin and tomatoes and cook, stirring, for 5 minutes.

3. Preheat the oven to 350 degrees F.

4. Drain the liquid from the beans, reserving $2^{1}/_{4}$ cups, and discard the rest. Add the beans and the reserved liquid to the pumpkin mixture. You can

bake the dish in the same saucepan, or in an ovenproof earthenware casserole, if you have one. Cover, and bake for 1 hour, stirring occasionally. The beans and pumpkin should be soft.

5. In a food processor, puree the corn with the stock. Stir the pureed mixture and the cream into the beans and cook, uncovered for 15 minutes longer.

6. Add the basil and salt and pepper to taste. Serve in soup bowls as a first course, or over rice as a vegetarian entree or a light meal.

**SERVES 6 AS A FIRST COURSE OR
A LIGHT MAIN COURSE**

Cap Ducal Restaurant, Valparaíso, Chile.

Lenten White Beans with Clams

(POCHAS CON ALMEJAS)

There are few dishes more Spanish than *pochas con almejas*, an unspeakably delicious stew of white beans and clams. Traditionally, beans were flavored with a piece of salt pork and sausage, but during the Easter Lent, clams or salt cod would replace the pork. The combination of flavors took hold and the dish became a classic in its own right. Choose a saucepan large enough to accommodate the beans and clams and attractive enough to go from stove to table.

1 POUND WHITE BEANS, SUCH AS GREAT NORTHERN

1 MEDIUM LEEK

1 GREEN ITALIAN (FRYING) PEPPER, CORED AND SEEDED

1 SMALL DRIED RED CHILE, SEEDED

1 SMALL ONION PLUS ½ CUP CHOPPED ONION

1 CARROT

2 LARGE RIPE TOMATOES

3 CLOVES GARLIC, LIGHTLY SMASHED, PLUS 1 TABLESPOON CHOPPED GARLIC

5 TABLESPOONS VIRGIN OLIVE OIL, PREFERABLY SPANISH

8 CUPS WATER

2 TEASPOONS BEST-QUALITY MILD PAPRIKA

SALT, TO TASTE

3 DOZEN SMALL CLAMS, SUCH AS LITTLENECKS, WELL SCRUBBED

½ CUP DRY WHITE WINE

2 TABLESPOONS CHOPPED FLAT-LEAF PARSLEY

1. In a heavy saucepan large enough to accommodate the beans and clams, combine the beans, leek, pepper, chile, whole onion, carrot, tomatoes, smashed garlic, 3 tablespoons of the oil, and the water. Bring to a boil, skimming. Simmer, covered, over low heat, stirring occasionally, until the beans are tender, about 1½ hours.

2. With a slotted spoon, remove the leek, onion, carrot, pepper, tomatoes, and about ¾ cup of the beans, and puree in a food processor. Stir the pureed mixture back into the beans and add the paprika and salt to taste. Return to a simmer while preparing the clams.

3. In a large saucepan with a lid, heat the remaining 2 tablespoons of the oil over medium heat. Add the chopped onion and chopped garlic and sauté, stirring, until the onion wilts, about 5 minutes. Add the clams and wine. Cover the saucepan and cook, shaking the saucepan occasionally, until the clams have opened, about 5 to 7 minutes. Discard any clams that don't open. Stir the clams and other contents of the saucepan gently into the beans. Sprinkle with the parsley and serve.

SERVES 6 AS A LIGHT MAIN COURSE

Beans: To Soak or Not to Soak?

I say don't. After many experiments with almost all kinds of beans, I've come to the conclusion that soaking doesn't add many extra benefits. True, it reduces cooking time, but usually by no more than 30 to 40 minutes. The extra hassle of setting the beans to soak hours before or overnight is not worth the time you save on cooking. Why plan ahead when you don't have to?

What does help in cooking beans is adding a little cold water from time to time as you cook them, which prevents the beans from bursting, keeping them soft but not mushy.

Cuban Black Beans with a Touch of Chocolate

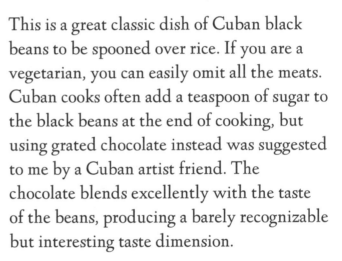

1 POUND DRIED BLACK TURTLE BEANS,
    PREFERABLY GOYA

8 CUPS WATER

1 MEATY HAM BONE

1 HEAD GARLIC, PEELED AND HALVED
    CROSSWISE, PLUS 8 CLOVES GARLIC,
    CRUSHED THROUGH A PRESS

2 BAY LEAVES

1 TABLESPOON ANNATTO OIL (PAGE 376)

1 DRY *CHORIZO* SAUSAGE, DICED

3 SLICES BACON, CHOPPED

1 MEDIUM ONION, FINELY CHOPPED

1 RED OR GREEN BELL PEPPER, CORED, SEEDED,
    AND DICED

2 TEASPOONS DRIED OREGANO

1 TEASPOON GROUND CUMIN

1 TABLESPOON MILD PAPRIKA

1 TEASPOON CAYENNE

12 PIMIENTO-STUFFED GREEN OLIVES, SLICED

¼ CUP DRY WHITE WINE OR DRY SHERRY

ONE 16-OUNCE CAN TOMATOES, CHOPPED,
    LIQUID RESERVED

1 SMALL BUNCH CILANTRO, TIED

(continued)

This is a great classic dish of Cuban black beans to be spooned over rice. If you are a vegetarian, you can easily omit all the meats. Cuban cooks often add a teaspoon of sugar to the black beans at the end of cooking, but using grated chocolate instead was suggested to me by a Cuban artist friend. The chocolate blends excellently with the taste of the beans, producing a barely recognizable but interesting taste dimension.

1. In a large saucepan, combine the beans, water, ham bone, garlic, and bay leaves, and bring to a boil, skimming off the froth. Reduce the heat to low, cover, and simmer until the beans are almost tender, about 1¼ hours.

2. Heat the oil in a large skillet over medium heat. Add the *chorizo* and bacon and cook, stirring, for 3 to 4 minutes, until the bacon renders most of its fat. Drain off all but 2 tablespoons of the fat from the skillet. Add the onion, crushed garlic, and pepper

and cook, stirring, until the onion is soft, about 7 minutes. Add the oregano, cumin, paprika, and cayenne and stir for 1 minute. Add the olives and the wine, and cook for 10 minutes.

1 ½ TABLESPOONS DISTILLED WHITE VINEGAR
1 ½ TABLESPOONS GRATED BITTERSWEET
    CHOCOLATE
SALT, TO TASTE
WHITE RICE (PAGE 247)

3. Add the contents of the skillet to the beans, along with the tomatoes and their reserved juice and the cilantro. Cook over low heat, stirring once or twice, for 20 minutes. Add the vinegar, chocolate, and salt to taste. Cook, stirring, for 1 minute.

4. Remove the cilantro and the ham bone from the beans and discard the cilantro. When the ham is cool enough to handle, remove the meat from the bone. Cut the meat into bite-size pieces, and return it to the beans. Remove the bay leaves from the beans and serve the beans over the rice.

SERVES 8 TO 10

Catalan Noodles with White Beans and Seafood

(FIDEUS AMB PEIX I MONGETES BLANQUES)

This is a typically Catalan dish, both earthy and sophisticated, combining thin vermicelli called *fideos,* with sausage, shrimp, and white beans, cooked until soft and delicious. (Unlike the Italians, Catalans like their pasta "well done.") *Fideos* are available at Hispanic sections of most supermarkets or at any Latin grocery. You can also use *cabello de ángel,* angel-hair pasta. Ideally, this dish should be cooked and served in an earthenware *cazuela,* but if you don't own one, cook it in a glazed enamel ovenproof skillet. The recipe can easily be doubled when cooking for a crowd.

8 LITTLENECK CLAMS, WELL SCRUBBED

8 MUSSELS, WELL SCRUBBED

1 TABLESPOON SALT

2 TABLESPOONS VIRGIN OLIVE OIL, PREFERABLY SPANISH

3 LARGE CLOVES GARLIC, CHOPPED

⅓ CUP THINLY SLICED GOOD-QUALITY DRY *CHORIZO* SAUSAGE

½ CUP DRAINED COOKED OR CANNED WHITE BEANS

2 CUPS *FIDEOS* OR ANGEL-HAIR PASTA, BROKEN INTO 1-INCH LENGTHS

2¾ CUPS BOILING CHICKEN STOCK (PAGE 372) OR CANNED LOWER-SALT CHICKEN BROTH

12 MEDIUM SHRIMP, PEELED AND DEVEINED

SALT AND FRESHLY GROUND BLACK PEPPER, TO TASTE

2 TABLESPOONS FINELY MINCED FLAT-LEAF PARSLEY

1. Place the clams and the mussels in a large bowl and add cold water to cover by 2 inches and the 1 tablespoon of salt. Soak for 1 hour, then drain. Scrub the clams under cold running water and debeard and clean the mussels.

2. Preheat the oven to 400 degrees F.

3. In an earthenware *cazuela* or a deep, medium-size ovenproof skillet, heat the oil with the garlic over medium heat, until the garlic is fragrant but not browned, about 3 minutes. Add the *chorizo* and cook, stirring, for 3 minutes. Add the beans and cook for 2 more minutes. Add the pasta and 2¼ cups of the broth and bring to a boil. Cook over medium-high heat, stirring gently, until most of the liquid has been absorbed, 7 to 8 minutes. At this stage the noodles should be fully cooked but still a little al dente. Stir in the remaning ½ cup of broth and the clams. Cover and cook for 5 more minutes.

4. Stir in the shrimp and mussels. Cover and cook until the clams and mussels open, shaking the pan occasionally, about 5 minutes. Discard any clams that don't open. Season with salt and pepper.

5. Place the skillet in the oven for 5 to 7 minutes. It should look fairly dry. Stir in the parsley, and serve at once.

SERVES 2 AS A MAIN COURSE, OR 4 AS A FIRST COURSE

Market, Barcelona, Spain.

Baked Orzo with Peas, Olives, and Cheese

(ORZO AL HORNO CON GUISANTES, ACEITUNAS, Y QUESO)

This is a side dish I serve often with Latin food, substituting fluffy, plump orzo instead of the more traditional rice for a richer, homier dish.

2½ TABLESPOONS VIRGIN OLIVE OIL

1 TABLESPOON MINCED GARLIC

1½ TEASPOONS MILD PAPRIKA

1 TEASPOON DRIED OREGANO

¾ CUP CHOPPED DRAINED CANNED PLUM TOMATOES, PLUS ⅔ CUP OF THEIR LIQUID

3 TABLESPOONS FINELY CHOPPED FRESH BASIL

1 POUND ORZO

1 CUP FRESH OR FROZEN AND THAWED GREEN PEAS

⅓ CUP SLICED PITTED BLACK OLIVES

SALT AND FRESHLY GROUND BLACK PEPPER, TO TASTE

⅓ CUP GRATED *QUESO BLANCO* (HISPANIC WHITE CHEESE)

1. In a small saucepan, heat the oil with the garlic over medium-high heat for about 2 minutes. Add the paprika and oregano and stir for 1 minute. Add the tomatoes, the reserved juice, and the basil, and cook over low heat until the tomatoes are reduced to a puree, about 10 minutes. Set aside.

2. Bring a large pot of salted water to a boil and cook the orzo until slightly al dente, about 5 minutes or more. Drain.

3. Preheat the oven to 375 degrees F.

4. Place the orzo in an ovenproof dish, preferably earthenware, and stir in the tomato mixture, peas, and olives. Season to taste with salt and pepper. Sprinkle with the cheese, and bake for 12 minutes, until the top is bubbly.

SERVES 6

Desserts

"El Rey Fritas," Calle Ocho, Miami.

Cigar factory, Miami.

Hat store, San Telmo Market, Buenos Aires, Argentina.

THE IBERIAN dessert repertoire was shaped by two cultures, Arab and Catholic. From the Arabs (who played a prominent role in the development of Iberian gastronomy) came silky-smooth stove-top puddings and custards thickened with starch or rice flour (which were modified into the famous *natilla* or *arroz con leche*), as well as marzipan, nougat, candied fruit, rich and intricate honey and nut sweets, and fritters served in a pool of syrup perfumed with orange peel and cinnamon. Many of these, along with the renowned Iberian egg yolk sweets, were then perfected in the convents, where the nuns supported themselves (sometimes it was their only source of income) by selling cakes, cookies, and confections. Egg yolk "conventual" sweets became an art form in the convents of Andalusia that were located in proximity to the *jerez*-making centers. At that time, egg whites were used to clarify the *jerez*. The leftover yolks were given to nuns, who made them into every conceivable kind of sweet. The nuns also baked delicate crumbly cookies, using up the lard that was left over from the *matanzas*, the famous November ritual slaughtering of the pigs. These traditions are very much alive today, and the nuns continue to perfect their centuries-old recipes, which are zealously guarded within the convent walls. It is almost a mystical experience to knock on the window of a convent, and wait for the thin hand in a black sleeve to silently hand you a packet of tiny custard cakes, ethereal biscuits, or an almond tart. You walk away overcome with a feeling of sweet piety.

Later, in the eighteenth and nineteenth centuries, came the penchant for lavishly decorated French-style sponge cakes, bombes, meringues, éclairs, and napoleons. The French also contributed the caramel, which, in combination with the rich puddings and custards, became a hallmark of Iberian desserts.

In Spain, Portugal, and Latin America, you won't often find yourself devouring a chocolate cake or a rich pastry puff after a filling meal. Most likely the finale will be a simple flan, a bowl of fresh seasonal fruit, or a glass of dessert wine. But sweets—little cakes, cookies, pound cakes, sponge cakes, and bonbons of all sorts—will be offered to you at afternoon tea or second breakfast. During fiestas and celebrations, sweet fritters and crullers are sold at street fairs, and bakery windows come alive with buns, marzipans, and nougats.

The desserts of South America are treasure houses of tradition. Some are inherited from Spain and Portugal, others brought over by more recent immigrants from Austria, Germany, and Italy. As with so many other classic European recipes, these are often miraculously transformed into tropical fantasies by the use of coconut, cane sugar, or by the fragrant, flamboyant taste of tropical fruit. In my research, I have leafed through dozens of family notebooks, their pages yellowed by time, finding recipes for fanciful cakes with elaborate names to match, often marked with exclamation points or singled out as "¡*delicioso!*" These sweet family heirlooms are reborn with each birthday or Christmas, often lovingly prepared by an elderly grandmother or a loyal family retainer.

Passion Fruit Mousse Cake

(BÔLO DE MARACUJÁ)

Strolling through a riotous street fair in Bahia, I stumbled upon a row of ladies in ruffled dresses, selling some of the most spectacular cakes I have ever seen. Many of them looked like edible sculptures of chocolate, marzipan, coconut, and exotic fruit. There was even a cake depicting a soccer match between Brazil and Argentina! My favorite, however, was an ethereal, vibrantly flavored passion fruit mousse cake. It certainly was the simplest in appearance, but the taste was truly exquisite, worthy of the best French patisserie. The name of its creator was Maria-Isabel, and she scribbled the recipe for me on a syrup-soaked napkin. Unfortunately, the syrup rendered the cake part of the recipe illegible, so I am offering a traditional genoise base, which tastes pretty close to the original. If you are not in the mood for making a cake base at all, the mousse is spectacular on its own.

For the glaze I use Goya-brand mango jelly, available at many supermarkets and Hispanic groceries. In a pinch, you can substitute good-quality apricot jam, which should be strained in step 8, if it is lumpy.

CAKE

4 LARGE EGGS

⅔ CUP SUGAR

1 TEASPOON VANILLA EXTRACT

¼ CUP MELTED BUTTER, KEPT SLIGHTLY WARM

⅔ CUP ALL-PURPOSE FLOUR

½ TEASPOON SALT

SYRUP

½ CUP FRESH ORANGE JUICE

3 TABLESPOONS SUGAR

2 TABLESPOONS WHITE RUM

PASSION FRUIT MOUSSE (RECIPE FOLLOWS)

GLAZE

3 TABLESPOONS WATER

1 TEASPOON UNFLAVORED GELATIN

⅔ CUP MANGO JELLY (SEE HEADNOTE)

3 TABLESPOONS UNSWEETENED PASSION FRUIT
   PULP (SEE PAGE 323), THAWED IF FROZEN

1. Preheat the oven to 350 degrees F. Line the bottom of a 9-inch springform pan with wax paper. Butter the wax paper and dust it lightly with flour, shaking off the excess.

2. To make the cake: Combine the eggs and sugar in a large metal bowl. Set the bowl over a large pan filled with simmering water and whisk until it is warm and the sugar is dissolved. Remove the bowl from the heat and beat the mixture with an electric mixer until tripled in volume, about 7 minutes.

3. Add the vanilla and the butter to the egg mixture. Sift the dry ingredients together and gently fold them into the egg mixture until just combined.

4. Pour the batter into the prepared pan and smooth the top with a spatula. Bake in the middle of the oven until the top is golden and a cake tester comes out clean, about 35 minutes. Remove from the oven and let stand for 5 minutes. Remove the sides of the pan, invert the cake onto a plate, and carefully remove the wax paper. Cool the cake on a cake rack.

5. To make the syrup: Combine the syrup ingredients in a small nonreactive saucepan and bring to a boil, stirring, until the sugar is dissolved, about 5 minutes. Let cool to room temperature.

6. With a large serrated knife, cut off a thin layer of the cake.

7. Place the remaining cake layer in the springform pan, cut side up, and brush it with the syrup. Pour all the mousse over the cake and smooth the top with a spatula. Refrigerate until set, about 4 hours.

8. To make the glaze: In a small bowl, sprinkle 3 tablespoons of water over the gelatin and let it soften for 3 minutes. In a small saucepan, combine the mango jelly with the passion fruit pulp. Bring to a boil, stirring, and cook for 1 minute. Remove from the heat, add the gelatin mixture and stir until dissolved. Cool slightly.

9. Pour the glaze evenly all over the top of the cake, cover the pan with plastic wrap, making sure it doesn't touch the top of the cake, and refrigerate until the glaze is set, about 1 hour. Carefully remove the sides of the springform pan and place the cake on a cake platter.

Passion Fruit Mousse

If you can't find passion fruit, try 2 cups of fresh mango puree. You will need much less sugar—adjust to taste.

2 TABLESPOONS WHITE RUM

2 TABLESPOONS WATER

2 PACKETS UNFLAVORED GELATIN (ABOUT
    2 TABLESPOONS)

ONE 14-OUNCE BAG (ABOUT 1 1/2 CUPS) FROZEN
    UNSWEETENED PASSION FRUIT PULP, THAWED
    (PAGE 323)

1/2 CUP ORANGE JUICE

3 TABLESPOONS SUGAR

1/2 CUP CONDENSED MILK

1 1/2 CUPS CHILLED HEAVY CREAM

FRESH BERRIES OF YOUR CHOICE, FOR GARNISH,
    OPTIONAL

1. In a small saucepan, pour the rum and water over the gelatin and let it soften for 5 minutes. Then heat the mixture over low heat, stirring, until the gelatin is dissolved, about 2 minutes.

2. In a medium-size nonreactive saucepan, heat the passion fruit pulp, orange juice, and sugar over medium heat, stirring, until the sugar is dissolved, about 5 minutes. Stir in the dissolved gelatin mixture and heat, stirring, for another 3 minutes. Cool completely.

3. In a blender, combine the passion fruit mixture with the condensed milk and blend until smooth. Transfer to a bowl and chill until the mixture just begins to set, about 1 hour.

4. Whip the cream until soft peaks form and gently fold it into the passion fruit mixture. Pour the mousse into the springform pan as directed in step 7 of the previous recipe. If serving the mousse by itself, pour it into a glass serving bowl, or individual dessert bowls or ramekins, and chill until set, about 4 hours. Serve the mousse, garnished with fresh berries, if you wish.

THE MOUSSE WILL SERVE 8 TO 10 BY ITSELF

Olive Oil and Honey Cake

(BÔLO DE MEL À ALENTEJANA)

This is a Portuguese cake from the central province of Alentejo, famous for its rich rustic sweets. With its generous quantity of beaten egg whites, this cake is light and fluffy, more like a chiffon cake than the Middle European–influenced American honey cake—and it is baked in a tube pan. The cake will improve on standing, so plan to make it a day ahead. It's excellent served with Castilian Christmas Compote (page 363).

1. Preheat the oven to 325 degrees F. Butter and flour a loose-bottomed 10-inch nonstick tube pan.

2. In a large bowl, beat the egg yolks and the ³⁄₄ cup granulated sugar with an electric mixer until fluffy and pale yellow, about 5 minutes. Beat in the oil, then the honey and brandy.

3. In a second large bowl, sift the flour with the baking powder, lemon zest, cinnamon, and salt. With a wooden spoon fold the flour into the yolk mixture, 1 cup at a time, mixing well after each addition.

4. With clean dry beaters, beat the egg whites until they form soft peaks. Fold in the remaining 2 tablespoons of granulated sugar and continue beating

(continued)

9 EGGS, SEPARATED

³⁄₄ CUP PLUS 2 TABLESPOONS GRANULATED SUGAR

1¹⁄₂ CUPS FRUITY OLIVE OIL, PREFERABLY PORTUGUESE

1¹⁄₂ CUPS HONEY

¹⁄₄ CUP BRANDY

3¹⁄₄ CUPS ALL-PURPOSE FLOUR

1 TEASPOON BAKING POWDER

GRATED ZEST OF 2 MEDIUM LEMONS

4 TEASPOONS GROUND CINNAMON

¹⁄₄ TEASPOON SALT

30 WHOLE TOASTED ALMONDS

CONFECTIONERS' SUGAR, FOR SPRINKLING THE CAKE

until stiff. With a wooden spoon, fold one third of the whites into the batter, then gently fold in the rest. Drop the almonds into the batter.

5. Pour the batter into the prepared tube pan and bake until a cake tester inserted into the center of the cake comes out clean, about 1 hour and 20 minutes. Remove the cake from the oven and let it cool in the pan for 10 minutes. Loosen the sides of the pan with a knife and remove the bottom of the pan. Invert the cake onto a plate and remove the center core. Reinvert it onto a cake rack and cool completely. Cover the cake with plastic wrap and let it stand for at least 6 hours or overnight.

6. Transfer to a serving platter and sprinkle with confectioners' sugar just before serving.

SERVES 10 TO 12

Chocolate: The Nectar of Gods

To the Aztec aristocracy of pre-colonial days, chocolate was an elixir of the gods—a holy beverage to be sipped from golden goblets during grand religious celebrations. The beans were such a precious commodity that they were used as small change; sacks of beans were considered an acceptable form of tax payment. Christopher Columbus, who first encountered cocoa during his 1502 voyage, was in for a shock when he saw Indians drop a few almond-like beans to the ground. They panicked so completely that he thought "their eyes had fallen out."

The chocolate discovered by the Spanish *Conquistadores* when they landed in Mexico in the 1500s was a far cry from the rich sweet drink enjoyed in Spain today. The Aztec *tchocolatl*, a bitter, frothy, tongue-biting mixture (often mixed with ground chiles), assaulted the colonial taste buds. Some early accounts presumed that it was an alcoholic beverage that made Aztec nobility drunk if taken in large doses; others credited it with magical healing powers, or saw it as a source of fat.

Presumably it was the Spanish nuns—those zealous guardians of the Iberian dessert tradition in the New World—in the convents of Oaxaca, who first began mixing the bitter ground cocoa with sugar to produce a drink the Spaniards grew to relish so much over the centuries. However, for nearly a century after its discovery, chocolate remained Spain's best-kept secret. Meanwhile, according to an Italian trader named Antonio Carletti—who introduced chocolate to Florence at the turn of the sixteenth century—the Spaniards back in Mexico (especially ladies and clergy) became so addicted to the new potion that "their strength failed them if they did not have it at their accustomed hour."

Chocolate finally conquered the courts of Europe when it was served at the lavish wedding of the

French King Louis XIII. The rest is history. Just as it was in the Aztec courts, so in its new homeland, chocolate once more became the domain of the elite, a status symbol and a valued currency, used by kings and nobility as a precious gift and bribe. Seventeenth-century dandies squandered small fortunes on the new luxury. Offering a lady a cup of chocolate was considered the surest way to win her affection—even more so when it was accompanied by candied fruit, dainty sponge cakes, marzipan, and nougat. Scientific treatises were produced on the medicinal benefits of chocolate, attributing to it the power to cure anything from stomach ailments to nervous disorders. It was also credited with powerful aphrodisiac properties, causing the British to express serious concerns about its effects on the chastity of the population.

Originally, cocoa beans were cleaned, dried, and ground into the finest of powders to be taken as a drink, which could either be enjoyed straight or flavored with precious aromatics like vanilla, citron, musk, or jasmine. Later, chocolate-makers began solidifying the ground beans into tablets, which could be dissolved in hot water or melted and added to all kinds of confections. By the eighteenth century one could feast on chocolate mousses, ice creams, marzipans, wafers, and truffles.

Around the period of the French Revolution, consumption of chocolate went into a brief decline, as it came to symbolize the excesses and indulgences of the aristocracy. But it was revived half a century later as advances were made in its production technology. Ways were discovered of making fat-free chocolate, milk chocolate, and chocolate bars studded with fruit and nuts. Not that chocolate could ever become mundane, but it became a small luxury of the people.

Today, few pleasures are more quintessentially Spanish than visiting a *chocolatería* to indulge in a luscious hot chocolate accompanied by puffy sugar-coated crullers called *churros*. Spanish hot chocolate is very thick and very sweet, almost a meal in itself—the perfect restorative, in the wee hours of the morning, after a long night of wine drinking and tapa tasting.

Truffle Cake Mesón Marinero

(TARTA DE TRUFAS, DE MESÓN MARINERO)

At a fantastic seafood restaurant called Mesón Marinero on Spain's Cantabrian coast, I enjoyed a delicious cake of whipped cream and truffle mousse nestled between layers of light sponge, which the chef, Don Esteban Modino, referred to as *tarta de trufas*. Here is his recipe.

CAKE

3 LARGE EGGS, SEPARATED, PLUS 1 WHOLE EGG
$1/2$ CUP PLUS 1 TABLESPOON SUGAR
$2/3$ CUP CAKE FLOUR
1 TEASPOON VANILLA EXTRACT

CHOCOLATE FILLING

$1 1/4$ CUPS HALF AND HALF
3 LARGE EGG YOLKS, BEATEN
7 OUNCES BITTERSWEET CHOCOLATE, BROKEN
   INTO SMALL PIECES
4 TABLESPOONS UNSALTED BUTTER, CUT INTO
   PIECES

$1 1/4$ CUPS HEAVY CREAM, CHILLED
1 TABLESPOON SUGAR

1. To make the cake: Preheat the oven to 350 degrees F. Line an 18 by 12-inch baking sheet with parchment. Butter and flour the parchment.

2. In a large bowl, beat the egg yolks, whole egg, and $1/2$ cup sugar until pale yellow and fluffy, about 2 minutes. Beat in the flour. Add the vanilla.

3. With clean dry beaters beat the egg whites with the 1 tablespoon of sugar until stiff peaks form. Fold one third of the whites into the egg yolk mixture and then gently fold in the rest. Spread the batter evenly on the parchment. Bake in the middle of the oven until golden and springy to the touch, about 15 minutes. When cool enough to handle, invert the cake onto a rack and gently peel off the parchment. Cut the cake crosswise into three equal rectangles and set aside.

4. To make the filling: Heat the half and half in the top of a double boiler set over simmering water. Place the beaten egg yolks in a bowl and whisk in some of the hot half and half. Carefully whisk the mixture back into the double boiler and cook over low heat, stirring, until the mixture thickens to a custardlike consistency, 5 to 7 minutes. Stir in the chocolate, a few pieces at a time, and cook, stirring, until it melts. Off the heat, whisk in the butter, one piece at a time. Cool the mixture, then refrigerate until it's almost set but is still spreadable, about 1 hour.

5. Whip the cream with the sugar until it holds stiff peaks. Reserve $1/2$ cup of the whipped cream for decorating the cake.

6. To assemble the cake: Reserve $1/3$ cup of the chocolate mixture for decorating the cake. Place a layer of cake on a serving platter. Top it with half the chocolate mixture and then with half the whipped cream. Top with another layer of cake, the remaning chocolate mixture, and the remaining whipped cream. Top with the last layer of cake. With a large sharp knife trim the edges of the cake. Using a rubber spatula, spread the top and sides of the cake with the reserved chocolate mixture. Refrigerate the cake for at least 2 hours or overnight.

7. Place the reserved whipped cream in a pastry bag with a decorative tip. Pipe it in an attractive pattern around the rim of the cake.

SERVES 8

Guava and Cheese Roulade

(ROCAMBOLE COM GOIABADA E QUEIJO)

Guava paste and fresh white cheese make one of South America's most beloved dessert combinations. So popular is this culinary two-step that a Brazilian saying goes: *Goiabada sem queijo e como amor sem beijo* ("*Goiabada* without cheese is like love without a kiss"). Here, they join forces as a filling for a luscious Brazilian jelly roll called *rocambole*. In Spanish-speaking countries, this type of jelly-roll cake is referred to as "*brazo de gitano*," or gypsy's arm. Tins of guava paste are available at all Hispanic groceries and many supermarkets.

CAKE

4 LARGE EGGS, SEPARATED, WHITES AT ROOM
    TEMPERATURE
¼ CUP GRANULATED SUGAR
1 TEASPOON VANILLA EXTRACT
⅓ CUP ALL-PURPOSE FLOUR, SIFTED
2 TABLESPOONS CORNSTARCH

FILLING

10½ OUNCES GUAVA PASTE (HALF A 21-OUNCE
    TIN)
1 TABLESPOON WATER
3 TABLESPOONS DARK RUM
3 TABLESPOONS FRESH LEMON JUICE
6 OUNCES CREAM CHEESE (LOW-FAT IS FINE),
    SOFTENED
½ CUP HEAVY CREAM
1½ TABLESPOONS GRANULATED SUGAR

CONFECTIONERS' SUGAR, FOR SPRINKLING THE
    CAKE

1. To make the cake: Line a 15 by 11-inch jelly-roll pan with cooking parchment. Grease the parchment and dust it gently with flour. Preheat the oven to 375 degrees F.

2. In a large bowl, with an electric beater, beat the egg yolks with the sugar and vanilla extract until they are pale yellow and form a ribbon when the beaters are lifted. Gradually add the flour and the cornstarch and beat until blended.

3. In another large bowl, with clean, dry beaters, beat the egg whites until they hold stiff peaks. Fold one third of the beaten whites into the yolks and then, gently, fold in the rest.

4. Spread the batter evenly in the pan and bake, without disturbing, until the cake is gently colored and springy to the touch, 12 to 15 minutes. Let it cool for several minutes and then invert it onto a large kitchen towel sprinkled generously with confectioners' sugar. Carefully peel off the parchment and roll up the cake in the towel, starting with the long side. Let the cake cool on a rack for at least 1 hour.

5. While the cake is resting, make the filling: Cut the guava paste into pieces and place it in a heavy saucepan along with the water and rum. Heat over medium-low heat, stirring, until the guava is melted, 5 to 7 minutes. Stir in the lemon juice and set aside.

6. In a food processor, process the cream cheese, cream, and sugar until smooth.

7. Unroll the cake gently and spread it with the guava paste. Spread the cream cheese on top and reroll the cake (without the towel). Carefully transfer it onto a cake board and trim the edges neatly. Cover it with plastic wrap and refrigerate for 1 hour to firm up the cream cheese.

8. Remove the jelly roll from the refrigerator and bring it back to room temperature. Sprinkle generously with confectioners' sugar and serve, cut into thick slices.

SERVES 8

Donha Dorothea's Coconut-Yuca Cake

(BÔLO DE MANDIOCA E COCO, DONHA DOROTHEA)

Dorothea Elman-Winston is a magnificent cook, a food writer, and the organizer of culinary adventure tours to her native Brazil. Among her vast repertoire of Brazilian cakes (*bôlos*), she is particularly fond of this deliciously moist recipe combining Brazil's favorite tropical ingredients: coconut and yuca. For peeling and cleaning yuca, see page 79.

½ CUP ALL-PURPOSE FLOUR

1 TABLESPOON DOUBLE-ACTING BAKING POWDER

¼ TEASPOON SALT

½ CUP (1 STICK) UNSALTED BUTTER, MELTED

2 CUPS SUGAR

½ CUP CANNED COCONUT MILK, WELL-STIRRED

4 LARGE EGGS, BEATEN

4 CUPS FINELY GRATED FRESH YUCA (ABOUT 1½ POUNDS)

1 CUP FRESHLY GRATED COCONUT (SEE PAGE 10) OR UNSWEETENED DRIED SHREDDED COCONUT

1. Preheat the oven to 350 degrees F. Butter and lightly flour a rectangular 13- by 9- by 2-inch pan.

2. In a bowl, sift together the flour, baking powder, and salt.

3. In a food processor, process the butter, sugar, and coconut milk. Slowly add and blend in the dry ingredients. Transfer the batter to a bowl and stir in the eggs, yucca, and shredded coconut. Mix well.

4. Pour the mixture into the pan and bake in the middle of the oven until the top is deep golden and a cake tester comes out clean, about 55 minutes. Cool on a cake rack. Serve warm or at room temperature.

SERVES 8

Sweet Masterpieces

In Latin America cake decorating is an art unto itself, with the windows of cake shops displaying edible Disneylands made out of dough, marzipan, or colored cream. The soccer motif seems to be most in demand, and I will never forget a huge Brazilian cake made for the last World Cup—a football field with marzipan figurines of each player, their faces bearing an uncanny resemblance to their living counterparts. The more traditional cakes might be adorned with cowboys and horse-drawn carriages, frivolous circus clowns, and young ladies in communion gear, set amid bright green, pink, and orange meringue hills. Less traditionally, you will find cakes featuring unclothed Barbie dolls nestled among miniature champagne bottles, Disney characters suspended among wavy clouds of brightly colored cream, or Rolls-Royces and Maseratis careening down chocolate slopes surrounded by miniature plastic road signs.

Walnut-Caramel Torte with Dulce de Leche

(QUEQUE DE NUECES RELLENO CON MANJAR)

This cake is unmistakably and deliciously South American—a moist walnut torte (inherited from Austrian and German immigrants) filled with a classic milk custard. You can either make the filling yourself from scratch (page 328), or buy it under the name *dulce de leche* or *manjar* at a good Latin grocery. The cake is best when made a day ahead, (though you should ice it not too long before serving) and is delicious with a dollop of Toasted Coconut Ice Cream (page 316) or Coconut-Caramel Custard Sauce (page 326). Because the cake is rather sweet, I prefer a simple icing of whipped cream. However, for those who share South America's wicked sweet tooth, I also offer a very sweet but wonderful *panela* (raw sugar) icing.

6 LARGE EGGS, SEPARATED

¾ CUP SUGAR

1 TABLESPOON BRANDY

1¾ CUPS GROUND WALNUTS

¼ CUP UNFLAVORED BREAD CRUMBS

½ TO ⅔ CUP HOMEMADE MILK CUSTARD (PAGE 328) OR PURCHASED *DULCE DE LECHE* (SEE HEADNOTE)

1 CUP HEAVY CREAM, CHILLED, OR *PANELA* CARAMEL ICING (RECIPE FOLLOWS)

1. Preheat the oven to 350 degrees F. Butter and flour a 10-inch springform pan.

2. In a large bowl, beat the egg yolks with the sugar until pale yellow and fluffy, about 3 minutes. Stir in the brandy.

3. With clean dry beaters, beat the egg whites until they form stiff peaks. Gently fold one third of the egg whites into the yolks. Fold in one third of the ground walnuts. Continue folding in the egg whites, alternating with the walnuts and the bread crumbs, until all the ingredients are well combined.

4. Pour the batter into the prepared pan and bake in the middle of the oven until the top is golden brown and a cake tester comes out clean, 35 to 40 minutes.

5. Allow the cake to cool on a rack in the pan. Then remove the sides of the pan and, using a large serrated knife, cut the cake into two layers.

6. Place one cake layer on a work surface, cut side up, and spread the milk custard over it. Cover with the other cake layer, cut side down.

7. If using whipped cream icing: In a large bowl whip the cream until it forms stiff peaks. Spread the cream around the sides of the cake with a rubber spatula. Pipe out the rest of the cream on the top of the cake from a pastry bag fitted with a decorative tip. If using Panela Caramel Icing: Spread it on the top and sides of the cake and let stand for about 1 hour.

SERVES 8

Panela Caramel Icing

In a medium-size, heavy saucepan, melt the butter over low heat. Add the sugar and milk, raise the heat to medium, and cook the mixture, stirring, until the sugar melts, 2 to 3 minutes. Remove from the heat and cool until barely warm. Beat in the confectioners' sugar, making sure there are no lumps. Spread the icing on the cake at once.

5 TABLESPOONS UNSALTED BUTTER
1/2 CUP GRATED DARK CANE SUGAR (*PANELA* OR *PILONCILLO*) OR DARK BROWN SUGAR
1 1/2 TABLESPOONS MILK
1 CUP CONFECTIONERS' SUGAR

ENOUGH FOR A 10-INCH CAKE

Papaya Cake with Lime–Cream Cheese Frosting

(BIZCOCHO DE PAPAYA EXQUISITO)

I tasted this lovely cake with tropical overtones at a community bake sale in Puerto Rico. Its creator, a young woman named María Cristina, described it as her version of American carrot cake, which, along with a whole range of classic American desserts, enjoys tremendous popularity on the island. If you have access to a good Latin grocery, you can also try this cake with frozen and thawed *mamey* pulp puree instead of the papaya.

2 CUPS MASHED RIPE PAPAYA

2 LARGE EGGS

2 TABLESPOONS FRESHLY SQUEEZED LIME JUICE

1 TABLESPOON DARK RUM

1 CUP (2 STICKS) UNSALTED BUTTER, AT ROOM TEMPERATURE

1½ CUPS TIGHTLY PACKED BROWN SUGAR

2 TEASPOONS GRATED LEMON ZEST

1 TEASPOON VANILLA EXTRACT

2½ CUPS ALL-PURPOSE FLOUR

2 TEASPOONS BAKING POWDER

½ TEASPOON BAKING SODA

1 CUP CHOPPED WALNUTS

¾ CUP FINELY DICED DRIED PAPAYA OR APRICOTS

LIME–CREAM CHEESE FROSTING (RECIPE FOLLOWS)

SLIVERED LIME ZEST AND DRIED PAPAYA, FOR DECORATING THE CAKE

1. Preheat the oven to 350 degrees F. Butter and flour a 9-inch springform pan.

2. In a food processor, process the mashed papaya, eggs, lime juice, and rum until thoroughly combined.

3. In a large bowl using an electric mixer, beat the butter with the brown sugar just until pale yellow and fluffy. Beat in the papaya mixture until combined. Add the lime zest and vanilla extract.

4. In another large bowl, sift the flour with the baking powder and baking soda. Stir in the walnuts

and dried papaya. In small batches stir the dry mixture into the butter mixture until well combined.

5. Pour the batter into the prepared pan and bake in the middle of the oven until the top is golden brown and a cake tester comes out clean, about 50 minutes. Cool the cake on a rack in the pan. Then remove the sides and the bottom of the springform pan. Spread the frosting on the top and sides of the cake. Cover loosely with plastic wrap and refrigerate for at least 2 hours or overnight. Before serving, decorate the cake with the lime zest and slivered papaya.

SERVES 8

Lime-Cream Cheese Frosting

In a large bowl, beat the cream cheese, butter, lime zest, and juice with an electric beater at low speed until light and fluffy. Gradually beat in the sugar.

ENOUGH FOR ONE 9-INCH CAKE

6 OUNCES PHILADELPHIA CREAM CHEESE, AT
    ROOM TEMPERATURE
4 TABLESPOONS ($\frac{1}{2}$ STICK) UNSALTED BUTTER,
    AT ROOM TEMPERATURE
1 TABLESPOON FINELY GRATED LIME ZEST
2$\frac{1}{2}$ TABLESPOONS FRESHLY SQUEEZED LIME
    JUICE
1$\frac{1}{4}$ CUPS SIFTED CONFECTIONERS' SUGAR

Caramel-Pineapple Cheesecake

(FLAN DE QUESO Y PIÑA)

This Spanish dessert is not strictly a cheesecake but rather a sweet cheese custard baked in a caramel-lined mold. Cream cheese makes a good enough substitute for the Spanish fresh curd cheese called *requesón*. And the pineapple flavor makes the whole thing just heavenly. Make sure to drain the fresh pineapple well, otherwise it will throw off too much liquid into the custard. Make the caramel before you prepare the custard. If it becomes too hard, reheat it gently over low heat until it is of pourable consistency.

6 OUNCES CREAM CHEESE, AT ROOM
   TEMPERATURE
3 LARGE EGGS
4 LARGE EGG YOLKS
¼ CUP SUGAR
1 CUP CONDENSED MILK
1½ CUPS WHOLE MILK
⅓ CUP THAWED FROZEN PINEAPPLE JUICE
   CONCENTRATE
1 CUP FINELY DICED FRESH RIPE PINEAPPLE
   (WELL DRAINED AND PATTED DRY)
1 RECIPE CARAMEL (PAGE 330)

1. Preheat the oven to 325 degrees F. Bring a kettle of water to a boil.

2. In a blender, combine the cream cheese, eggs, egg yolks, and sugar until smooth. Add the condensed milk, whole milk, and the pineapple concentrate and blend, using the on/off button, until just smooth. Transfer to a mixing bowl and stir in the fresh pineapple.

3. Pour the caramel into a 9-inch square baking pan or a ring mold. Swirl the pan to cover the entire bottom and part of the sides with caramel. Pour the cream cheese mixture into the prepared pan and cover the top tightly with foil. Set the pan in a larger pan and carefully pour enough boiling water into the outer pan to reach halfway up the sides of the smaller pan. Bake until the flan is set, about 1 hour and 25 minutes. (Test it with a toothpick, though, after 1

hour, as the exact baking time depends on the thickness of your pan and the quality of the egg yolks.)

4. Let the flan cool in the pan; then carefully unmold it onto a serving platter. If the caramel on the bottom of the pan has begun to solidify, place the pan on a burner and gently reheat it until it is pourable. Pour the caramel all over the custard and chill the flan for at least 2 hours.

SERVES 8

Breads,
Pontevedra Market,
Spain.

Coconut Blancmange with Prune Sauce

(MANJAR BRANCO COM MÔLHO DE AMEIXAS)

This is a classic Brazilian dessert. A sublime just-like-mother-used-to-make version was presented to me by Maria Lemos, who owns Rice and Beans, a tiny Brazilian eatery in midtown Manhattan. She served the *manjar* with stewed prunes, but it will also taste spectacular with Red and Black Berry Sauce (page 327) or Passion Fruit Sauce (page 324).

ONE 13-OUNCE CAN COCONUT MILK, WELL
   STIRRED
3½ CUPS MILK
3½ TABLESPOONS SUGAR
3 TABLESPOONS CORNSTARCH, MIXED WITH
   3 TABLESPOONS COLD WATER

PRUNE SAUCE
ONE 16-OUNCE BOX PITTED PRUNES
1½ CUPS WATER
4 TABLESPOONS SUGAR, OR MORE TO TASTE
1½ TABLESPOONS COGNAC

1. In a medium-size, heavy saucepan, combine the coconut milk, milk, and sugar and bring to a simmer. Slowly drizzle in the cornstarch mixture. Simmer over low heat, stirring, until the mixture thickens to a custardlike consistency, about 25 to 30 minutes.

2. Meanwhile, prepare the prunes. Combine the prunes, water, and sugar in a saucepan, bring to a simmer, and cook over low heat, stirring occasionally, until the prunes are soft and the cooking liquid has thickened, about 20 minutes. Stir in the cognac and cook 5 more minutes.

3. Pour the custard mixture into six 1-cup soufflé or custard cups. Cover with plastic wrap and chill until set, 4 to 6 hours.

4. To serve, carefully but firmly invert the custards onto dessert plates. They will be much softer than regular mousses, but should just about hold their shape. Spoon the prunes and their liquid around the custards and serve.

SERVES 6

Rice Pudding

(ARROZ CON LECHE)

Recipes for *arroz con leche* abound, but I am especially partial to this one. It is scrumptious by itself, and even better with a spoonful of Coconut-Caramel Custard Sauce (page 326) or some diced mangoes.

1. In a small saucepan, heat the anise liqueur and raisins. Set aside and let stand while the pudding is baking.

2. Preheat the oven to 325 degrees F.

3. In a medium-size saucepan, heat the rice, milk, sugar, cinnamon stick, and lemon zest, stirring, until the sugar is dissolved, about 5 minutes. Do not bring to a boil. Stir the rice well, breaking up any lumps that might have formed.

¼ CUP ANISE LIQUEUR, SUCH AS SAMBUCA OR ANISETTE
½ CUP WHITE RAISINS
½ CUP SHORT-GRAIN RICE, SUCH AS VALENCIA, RINSED
6 CUPS WHOLE MILK
½ CUP SUGAR
ONE 3-INCH CINNAMON STICK, BROKEN INTO 2 PIECES
ZEST OF 1 LEMON, IN 1 PIECE
1 CUP CANNED COCONUT MILK, WELL STIRRED
GROUND CINNAMON, FOR DUSTING THE PUDDING

4. Transfer the rice mixture to a deep 8- to 9-inch square or round baking dish, preferably earthenware or ovenproof glass, and bake for 1½ hours, until thickened and the rice is very soft, stirring and removing the crust that forms on the milk every 20 minutes or so. Add the coconut milk and raisins and bake for 30 minutes more. The rice should be very soft and creamy.

5. Remove the baking dish from the oven and remove the cinnamon stick and lemon zest. Let the pudding cool a little and transfer to a glass serving bowl, or individual glass dessert bowls. Place some lightly buttered wax paper on the surface of the rice, and cool until warm, or chill in the refrigerator if you prefer your rice pudding cold. Remove the wax paper and dust the pudding generously with cinnamon before serving.

SERVES 6

Caramel Orange Bread Pudding

(B U D Í N   D E   N A R A N J A)

After flan, bread pudding runs a tight race with *arroz con leche* as the second-favorite dessert of the Spanish-speaking world. My favorite recipe is the one below, which comes from Cuarta Esquina, a wonderful *taberna* in the Spanish province of Navarra. Serve it with Passion Fruit Sauce (page 324), or Red and Black Berry Sauce (page 327).

3 CUPS WHOLE MILK

4 LARGE EGGS, BEATEN

⅓ CUP SUGAR

½ CUP GOOD-QUALITY BITTER ORANGE
    MARMALADE

6 CUPS (12 TO 14 OUNCES) CUBED DAY-OLD
    EGG BREAD (CRUSTS REMOVED)

CARAMEL (PAGE 330)

1. Preheat the oven to 350 degrees F. Bring a kettle of water to a boil.

2. In a large bowl, whisk together the milk, eggs, sugar, and marmalade. Mix the bread in with your hands, crumbling it into small pieces as you mix. Working in two batches, puree the mixture in a food processor or blender.

3. Pour the caramel into an 8-inch square baking pan. Swirl the pan to cover the entire bottom and part of the sides with caramel.

4. Pour the bread mixture into the caramel-covered pan. Place the pan in a larger roasting pan and add enough boiling water to reach halfway up the sides of the smaller pan. Bake in the center of the oven until the pudding is set and amber, about 1 hour and 10 minutes. If the top of the pudding begins to brown too much, cover the pan loosely with foil.

5. When the pudding is cool enough to handle, carefully run a knife around the sides of the mold, then invert the pudding onto a serving platter, spooning the caramel over it. Let it cool to room temperature, then refrigerate until chilled, about 2 hours. Cut into squares and serve.

SERVES 8

Carmen Miranda

Old World European sweets such as meringues, trifles, and custards are the backbone of the South American family dessert repertoire. Often these are studded with tropical fruits and, in the old French tradition, given fancy names such as "fantasy," "surprise," or "queen such and such." This is one such recipe, given to me by a cake vendor in a São Paulo park. The name? Carmen Miranda, she blurted out cheerfully. The dessert proved as flamboyant as its namesake: layers of champagne biscuits (for which I have substituted ladyfingers), soaked in *cachaça* (Brazilian "white lightning"), luscious tart custard, and a cornucopia of tropical fruit. The recipe's creator specified Philadelphia Cream Cheese, which is a huge hit in South America. This is a wonderful party dessert, and the recipe can easily be doubled if you are serving a large crowd.

4 LARGE EGG YOLKS

1 CUP SUGAR

12 OUNCES CREAM CHEESE, AT ROOM TEMPERATURE

1½ CUPS HEAVY CREAM, CHILLED

1 CUP *CACHAÇA* OR WHITE RUM

ONE AND A HALF 7-OUNCE PACKAGES LADYFINGERS

2 CUPS DICED RIPE MANGOES, PLUS MORE FOR GARNISH

2 CUPS DICED RIPE PINEAPPLE, PLUS MORE FOR GARNISH

2 CUPS DICED RIPE PAPAYAS, PLUS MORE FOR GARNISH

1. In a large bowl, beat the egg yolks with ⅔ cup of the sugar until light and pale yellow, about 2 minutes. Transfer the mixture to the top of a double boiler set over simmering water, and simmer, whisking constantly, until it is thick enough to coat the back of a spoon, about 5 minutes. Remove from the heat and let cool.

2. In a food processor, combine the yolk mixture with the cream cheese and process until fluffy and blended.

(continued)

3. With clean beaters, whip the cream until it forms stiff peaks. Fold this into the cream cheese mixture.

4. In a small saucepan, bring the *cachaça* to a simmer with the remaining $1/3$ cup of sugar, stirring to dissolve the sugar, about 5 minutes. Cool a little and transfer to a bowl.

5. Dipping them in the *cachaça* as you work, place one third of the ladyfingers in the bottom of a 9-inch glass bowl. Cover with the diced mangoes and then with one third of the cream cheese mixture. Cover with another third of the ladyfingers, the pineapple, and one third of the cream cheese mixture. Repeat, using the remaining lady fingers, the papaya, and finishing with the remaining cream cheese. Chill for at least 2 hours or overnight. Serve garnished with diced fruit.

SERVES 8

Spiced Café con Leche Mousse

(MOUSSE DE "CAFÉ CON LECHE")

This dessert was inspired by my morning *café con leche*, at a neighborhood Chino-Latino lunch counter. There, the Chinese-Cuban Mr. Elías Chee Chung—using a 1950s Italian espresso machine bought in Cuba by his father—prepares a great cup of strong espresso with hot milk, spicing it up liberally with freshly grated nutmeg and cinnamon. I also add a suggestion of star anise, a heady spice introduced to Cuba by Chinese immigrants. If you don't have a spice grinder, use 1 teaspoon ground cinnamon and ³/₄ teaspoon ground cardamom, and omit the star anise.

1 SMALL STICK CINNAMON (PREFERABLY MEXICAN *CANELA*), BROKEN INTO PIECES

1 SMALL STAR ANISE, BROKEN INTO POINTS (SEE HEADNOTE)

SEEDS FROM 8 CARDAMOM PODS

1½ CUPS EVAPORATED MILK

1¼ CUPS VERY STRONG BREWED HISPANIC COFFEE, SUCH AS CAFÉ BUSTELO, PICO, OR GOYA, OR ESPRESSO

3 LARGE EGG YOLKS

³/₄ CUP SUGAR

½ TEASPOON FRESHLY GRATED NUTMEG

1 ENVELOPE UNFLAVORED GELATIN

3 TABLESPOONS DARK RUM

1²/₃ CUPS HEAVY CREAM, CHILLED

GOOD-QUALITY COCOA POWDER, FOR GARNISH

1. In a spice grinder or a well-cleaned coffee grinder, grind the cinnmon, star anise, and cardamom seeds to a fine powder.

2. In a small saucepan, combine the evaporated milk and the coffee, and heat, stirring, until small bubbles appear around the edges of the saucepan, about 7 minutes. Remove from the heat.

3. In a large bowl, whisk the egg yolks with the sugar until pale yellow and fluffy, about 2 minutes. Slowly whisk in the hot milk. Transfer the mixture to the top of a double boiler set over simmering water and cook, stirring constantly without letting it boil, until thick enough to coat the back of a spoon, 6 to 7 minutes. Transfer to a bowl and add the ground spices and nutmeg.

(continued)

4. In a small saucepan, sprinkle the gelatin over the rum and soften for 3 minutes. Place over low heat and heat, stirring, until the gelatin is dissolved. Stir the dissolved mixture thoroughly into the hot custard. Refrigerate the mixture until it begins to set, about 45 minutes.

5. Whip the cream until soft peaks form. Reserve ½ cup of the whipped cream. Fold the remaining cream into the chilled mousse mixture. Divide the mixture among six coffee cups and chill for at least 4 hours.

6. Garnish each portion with a dollop of the reserved whipped cream and dust with cocoa powder.

SERVES 6

Peruvian Pumpkin Doughnuts

(PICARONES)

One of the great delights of traveling through Peru—and there are many—is stumbling across a vendor loudly hawking *picarones:* light, puffy doughnuts that are soaked in a spiced raw sugar syrup. This recipe comes from such a vendor in the village of Carmen, near Cañete, a great center in Peru for black music and culture. In traditional Peruvian villages the dough is fermented with *chicha,* a fizzy Andean corn beer, but yeast makes a fine substitute.

This recipe makes quite a large amount. Make as many doughnuts you wish, and keep the rest of the dough in the refrigerator, covered with plastic wrap, so that you can whip up a batch for an improvised breakfast or *merienda* ("afternoon tea"). The dough will keep for up to 4 days.

¼ CUP LUKEWARM WATER (110 TO 115 DEGREES F.)
1 TEASPOON PLUS 1½ TABLESPOONS SUGAR
2 TEASPOONS ACTIVE DRY YEAST
¼ CUP MILK
1 LARGE EGG, BEATEN
LARGE PINCH OF SALT
2 TABLESPOONS UNSALTED BUTTER, MELTED
½ CUP PUREED COOKED SWEET POTATO (ABOUT 1 SMALL)
1 CUP SOLID-PACKED PUMPKIN PUREE
2¾ TO 3 CUPS ALL-PURPOSE FLOUR, OR MORE AS NEEDED
PEANUT OR CANOLA OIL, FOR DEEP FRYING
PANELA SYRUP (PAGE 69)

1. In a large mixing bowl, stir together the water, 1 teaspoon of sugar, and the yeast, and let stand until foamy, about 5 minutes.

2. Add the milk, the remaining 1½ tablespoons of sugar, the egg, salt, butter, sweet potato, and pumpkin, and whisk until the mixture is smooth. Add 2¾ cups of the flour, 1 cup at a time, mixing well after each addition, until you have a soft, slightly sticky dough. If the dough

(continued)

is too sticky, add another $^1/_4$ cup of the flour. Transfer the dough to a well-floured surface and knead until smooth. If the dough keeps sticking to your hands, add more flour, a little at a time.

3. Shape the dough into a ball and place it in a large buttered bowl. Turn to coat with the butter, cover loosely with plastic wrap, and let rise in a warm draft-free place until doubled in bulk, about 1 hour.

4. Punch the dough down and let it stand for 10 minutes. Break off a piece of dough the size of a large walnut. On a well-floured surface, roll the dough into a thin rope. (The dough will be somewhat sticky, so keep adding a little flour to the surface until the dough just stops sticking.) Bring the ends of the rope together to form a circle. Repeat with the rest of the dough, making as many doughnuts as you need.

5. Line two large baking sheets with a double layer of paper towels. In a deep fryer, a large skillet, or a wok, heat 2 inches of oil to 360 degrees F. The oil is ready when a piece of dough dropped in it sizzles and puffs up. Reduce the heat to medium-low and drop several doughnuts into the oil. Fry until they are golden brown and puffed, about $2^1/_2$ minutes per batch. It is important to keep the oil at the correct temperature: If it is too cool, the doughnuts won't puff; if it is too hot, they will brown too quickly but won't be cooked through. Keep watching and regulating the heat; you'll get it right after one or two batches. Transfer the fried doughnuts to drain on the paper towels. Repeat the process with the rest of the shaped doughnuts. Keep the finished doughnuts warm in a low oven.

6. To serve, place several doughnuts on a plate, and pour the syrup over and around them.

MAKES ABOUT 4 DOZEN

Flan

Undisputably, flan is the king of desserts in the Spanish-speaking world. And it is not hard to understand why—the combination of silky smooth custard and its burnt sugar foil is one of the most successful inventions in culinary history. Below is an excellent basic flan recipe, certainly delicious in its own right, followed by three variations on this classic theme. The recipe below will make eight individual flans or one 9-inch flan.

6 LARGE EGG YOLKS
3 LARGE EGGS
1 CUP SUGAR
2 CUPS MILK
1 CUP HEAVY CREAM
1 CUP EVAPORATED MILK
1 TEASPOON VANILLA EXTRACT
CARAMEL (PAGE 330)

1. Preheat the oven to 325 degrees F. Bring a kettle of water to a boil.

2. In a large bowl, whisk the egg yolks, whole eggs, and sugar together, then whisk in the milk, cream, evaporated milk, and vanilla. This can also be done in a blender.

3. Divide the caramel among eight ³/₄-cup ramekins, coating the bottom and part of the sides evenly. (Or pour it into a 9-inch round or square baking pan or a flan mold.)

4. Place the ramekins (or baking pan) in a larger baking pan and add enough boiling water to reach halfway up the sides of the ramekins. Cover the flans loosely with foil and bake in the middle of the oven until set (when a skewer inserted in the middle comes out clean), about 40 minutes. (The flan will take longer to set if you are using a 9-inch baking pan or a flan mold.)

5. Remove the ramekins from the water and let the flans cool to room temperature. Then place them in the refrigerator and chill for at least 4 hours.

(continued)

6. To serve, run a knife around each flan and invert it onto a dessert plate. Pour any caramel remaining in the ramekin over the flan.

SERVES 8

Coconut and Raw Sugar Flan

1½ CUPS RAW SUGAR (*PANELA* OR *PILONCILLO*), BROKEN INTO PIECES WITH A HAMMER OR A HEAVY-DUTY KNIFE

½ CUP WATER

6 LARGE EGG YOLKS

3 LARGE EGGS

1½ CUPS EVAPORATED MILK

2 CUPS CANNED COCONUT MILK, WELL-STIRRED

3 TABLESPOONS COFFEE LIQUEUR

1 RECIPE CARAMEL (PAGE 330)

This is a very unusual flan with the deep, intriguing flavor of raw sugar, the sweet mellow taste of coconut, and a touch of coffee liqueur, which you can also add to the caramel when you make it.

1. In a heavy, medium saucepan, combine the raw sugar and water and cook, stirring, over medium heat until the sugar is completely dissolved, about 7 minutes. Strain through a fine strainer.

2. In a large bowl, whisk the sugar together with all the remaining ingredients except the caramel. Continue to make the flan as directed in the main recipe on page 307.

SERVES 8

Mango Flan

6 LARGE EGG YOLKS

3 LARGE EGGS

ONE 7-OUNCE CAN SWEETENED CONDENSED MILK

2 CUPS MILK

2 CUPS PUREED MANGO FLESH (ABOUT 4
    MEDIUM MANGOES)

ORANGE JUICE CONCENTRATE, THAWED (IF
    NEEDED)

CARAMEL (PAGE 330)

Choose ripe, intensely flavored mangoes for this flan. Taste the puree, and if it tastes watery, add a few tablespoons of orange juice concentrate. I like this flan with Red and Black Berry Sauce (page 327).

In a blender, blend together the egg yolks, eggs, and the condensed milk until smooth. Add the milk and the mango puree and blend to combine. Continue to make the flan as directed in the main recipe on page 307.

SERVES 8

Port Flan

6 LARGE EGG YOLKS

3 LARGE EGGS

1 CUP SUGAR

2 CUPS MILK

1½ CUPS HEAVY CREAM

½ CUP TAWNY PORT

CARAMEL (PAGE 330)

This is a recipe famous in Portugal, the country of birth of port wine. It is excellent served with stewed figs or Castilian Christmas Compote (page 363).

In a large bowl, whisk together all the ingredients except the caramel. Continue to make the flan as directed in the main recipe on page 307.

SERVES 8

Nuria's Quince-Filled Purses

(PASTELITOS DE MEMBRILLO DE NURIA)

This recipe was given to me by a young Barcelona pastry chef called Nuria. After training with Alain Ducasse, she returned to Barcelona to work at her father's renowned restaurant, Cal'Isidre. The dessert is a combination of old and new. Nuria begins with a dark fragrant caramelized quince compote, which is a very traditional Catalan family recipe, and stuffs it into fashionable phyllo purses. She suggests mascarpone cheese or whipped cream as an accompaniment.

1½ CUPS SUGAR

4 MEDIUM QUINCES (ABOUT 2 POUNDS), PEELED, CORED, AND CUT INTO 1½-INCH CHUNKS

¼ CUP WATER, PLUS MORE AS NEEDED

ZEST OF 1 LEMON, IN 1 PIECE

ONE 3-INCH BEST-QUALITY CINNAMON STICK

JUICE OF 1 LARGE LEMON

ABOUT ½ POUND PHYLLO DOUGH, THAWED

½ CUP (1 STICK) UNSALTED BUTTER, MELTED

CONFECTIONERS' SUGAR, FOR SPRINKLING THE PURSES

MASCARPONE CHEESE, OR WHIPPED CREAM, FOR SERVING

1. In a heavy saucepan, combine the sugar, quinces, and water and heat over medium-low heat, stirring, until the sugar is dissolved, about 10 minutes. Add the lemon zest and cinnamon stick and continue to cook over very low heat, stirring often, until the quince is soft and deep-caramel in color, 1½ to 2 hours. Add more water, about 3 tablespoons at a time, if the quince begins to stick to the bottom of the saucepan. Watch it closely so that it doesn't burn. Remove the lemon zest and cinnamon stick, add the lemon juice, and mash the quince a little with a fork. Cool completely before proceeding to the next step.

2. Preheat the oven to 350 degrees F.

3. Cover the phyllo sheets with a damp towel and let stand for 10 minutes. Place a sheet of phyllo on a work surface and brush with melted butter. Stack four more sheets of phyllo on top, brushing each layer with butter. With a sharp knife, trim about $1^{1}/_{2}$ inches off the phyllo sheets along the length of the rectangle. Cut the sheets in half lengthwise, and then cut them crosswise into three equal sections. You should end up with six squares about 5 by 5 inches.

4. Place a heaping tablespoon of the cooled quince mixture in the middle of a phyllo square. Fold the four corners toward the center, envelope-fashion, pressing them together until they stick. Repeat the procedure with the rest of the squares, transferring the finished "purses" to a large baking sheet, folded sides up, and keeping them covered with a slightly damp towel to prevent them from drying out.

5. Repeat the whole procedure twice more with the remaining phyllo sheets. You should have eighteen finished pastries in total. Brush each pastry with melted butter and bake them until deep golden, about 12 to 15 minutes.

6. Transfer the pastries to a serving platter and sprinkle them with confectioners' sugar. Serve warm, with mascarpone or whipped cream.

MAKES 18 PURSES

Almond Crescents

In the Spanish countryside, for months after the *matanza* (the November slaughtering of the pigs), everyone enjoys *mantecadas*, crumbly cookies made with good, homemade lard. These are flavored with almonds and anise liqueur and shaped into half-moons. While lard definitely produces the very best texture, if you are vehemently against it, substitute butter.

1¾ CUPS ALL-PURPOSE FLOUR, SIFTED
⅓ CUP CONFECTIONERS' SUGAR, PLUS MORE FOR SPRINKLING THE COOKIES
PINCH OF SALT
¾ CUP (1½ STICKS) CHILLED GOOD-QUALITY LARD OR UNSALTED BUTTER, CUT INTO SMALL PIECES (YOU CAN ALSO USE ½ CUP BUTTER AND ¼ CUP LARD)
⅔ CUP GROUND LIGHTLY TOASTED ALMONDS
2 TABLESPOONS ANISE-FLAVORED LIQUEUR, SUCH AS SAMBUCA OR ANISETTE

1. Combine the flour, ⅓ cup of the confectioners' sugar, and salt in a food processor. Add the lard or butter and process in pulses until the pastry resembles coarse crumbs. Blend in the almonds, add the liqueur, and process for several pulses more, until the dough just begins to come together. It should not form into a ball.

2. Transfer the mixture to a large bowl and press it into a ball. (If the pastry is still too crumbly to stick together, wait a few minutes until the butter softens just a little.) Cover the ball with plastic wrap and refrigerate it for at least 1½ hours.

3. Line two cookie sheets with baking parchment. Break off walnut-size pieces of dough and briefly roll them between your palms to form 3-inch ropes. Bend the ropes into crescent shapes and place them on the cookie sheets. Place the cookie sheets in the refrigerator for 15 minutes.

4. Preheat the oven to 350 degrees F.

5. Place the cookie sheets in the middle of the oven and bake until the crescents are light golden, 12 to 15 minutes.

6. Cool the cookies on a wire rack. To serve, arrange them on a large platter and sprinkle them with confectioners' sugar. You can store the *mantecadas* in an airtight container in a cool place for up to a week.

MAKES ABOUT 4 DOZEN COOKIES

Market, Pontevedra.

Fiesta!
313

Coco-Cocoa Squares

(PASTEIZINHOS DE COCO E CACAU)

I tasted these rich, fluffy, brownie-like pastries in the Brazilian state of Bahia, which is rich in coconut and cocoa plantations. Use the best-quality unsweetened cocoa powder you can find.

1/3 CUP UNSWEETENED COCOA POWDER

4 TABLESPOONS UNSALTED BUTTER, MELTED

2 LARGE EGGS

1 1/4 CUPS SUGAR

1/3 CUP VEGETABLE OIL

1/3 CUP PLUS 1 TABLESPOON ALL-PURPOSE FLOUR

3/4 TEASPOON BAKING POWDER

PINCH OF SALT

1 1/4 CUPS FRESHLY GRATED COCONUT (SEE PAGE 10) OR UNSWEETENED DRIED SHREDDED COCONUT

1. In a small bowl, stir together the cocoa and butter. In another bowl whisk the eggs and sugar until pale yellow and frothy. Stir in the cocoa mixture and the oil.

2. In a bowl, sift together the flour, baking powder, and salt. Stir the dry ingredients into the egg mixture until thoroughly combined. Stir in the coconut.

3. Preheat the oven to 350 degrees F.

4. Pour the batter into a buttered 8-inch square baking pan. Bake in the middle of the oven until the top is crusty and browned, about 25 minutes.

5. Remove from the oven and cool on a rack in the pan. Cut into 2-inch squares. Serve slightly warm.

MAKES 16 SQUARES

Passion Fruit Sorbet

Passion fruit makes hauntingly delicious, tart, refreshing desserts. This sorbet is excellent on its own, or as an accompaniment to rich custards and chocolate cakes.

1. In a small saucepan, combine the water, sugar, and corn syrup and cook over medium-low heat, stirring until the sugar is dissolved, about 5 minutes. In a large bowl, combine the passion fruit pulp with the syrup and stir well. Chill until very cold, 2 to 3 hours.

2. Freeze in an ice cream maker according to the manufacturer's instructions.

MAKES ABOUT 1 1/4 QUARTS

1 1/4 CUPS ORANGE JUICE
2/3 CUP SUGAR
1/4 CUP LIGHT CORN SYRUP
ONE 14-OUNCE BAG (ABOUT 1 1/2 CUPS) FROZEN,
    UNSWEETENED PASSION FRUIT PULP, THAWED
    (PAGE 323)

Toasted Coconut Ice Cream

(HELADO DE COCO)

When toasted in a dry skillet, coconut acquires a rich nutty flavor, which infuses this unusual ice cream. Serve it on its own or with Coconut-Caramel Custard Sauce (page 326).

½ CUPS DRIED SHREDDED COCONUT OR
   UNSWEETENED COCONUT FLAKES
1½ CUPS MILK
1½ CUPS HALF AND HALF
¾ CUP (TIGHTLY PACKED) LIGHT BROWN SUGAR
5 LARGE EGG YOLKS
1 TABLESPOON CREAM OF COCONUT SUCH AS
   COCO LÓPEZ, WELL-STIRRED

1. In a dry skillet, toast the coconut over medium heat, stirring constantly, until dark golden, 2 to 3 minutes.

2. In a medium-size saucepan, combine the toasted coconut with the milk, half and half, and sugar, and heat, over medium heat, stirring until the sugar is dissolved, about 5 minutes. Remove from the heat and let stand for 2 hours for the flavors to develop.

3. Strain through a fine sieve, pressing on the solids to extract as much liquid as possible, and reheat to warm.

4. In a large bowl, whisk the egg yolks until light and pale yellow, about 3 minutes. Gradually whisk in the milk mixture.

5. Transfer the mixture to the top of a double boiler set over simmering water. Cook, stirring constantly without allowing it to boil, until the mixture is thick enough to coat the back of a spoon, about 7 minutes. Strain through a sieve. Stir in the coconut cream and chill until very cold, 2 to 3 hours.

6. Freeze the custard in an ice cream maker according to the manufacturer's instructions.

MAKES ABOUT 1 QUART

Tamarind-Rum Ice

Island flavors blend into an intriguing taste of something tart, cool, and unexpected. Tamarind nectar (made from the tart pulp of tamarind pods), available in Goya or Iberia brands, can be found at most Latin groceries.

1 CUP SUGAR
1 CUP WATER
$^2/_3$ CUP DARK RUM
3 CUPS TAMARIND NECTAR (SEE HEADNOTE)
MINT SPRIGS, FOR GARNISH

1. In a small saucepan, combine the sugar and water and cook over medium-low heat, stirring until the sugar is dissolved, about 5 minutes.

2. In a small saucepan, boil the rum until reduced to $^1/_2$ cup, about 5 minutes.

3. In a large bowl, stir together the tamarind nectar, sugar syrup, and rum. Chill until very cold, 2 to 3 hours.

4. Freeze in an ice cream maker according to the manufacturer's instructions.

5. Transfer to a plastic container and freeze for at least 3 hours more. The ice will be soft. Scoop into martini or champagne glasses and serve, garnished with mint.

MAKES ABOUT 5 CUPS

Guanábana Frozen Yogurt

(HELADO DE GUANÁBANA Y YOGURT)

Guanábana (soursop), like cherimoya, is a member of the *anona* family, which produces fruit with fragrant custardy white flesh. It's hard to find fresh

guanábanas here, but if you see one, you will recognize it as a heart-shaped, olive-green fruit covered with small bumps. Like many new, expensive tropical fruits, your best bet is to look for it in a good Latin grocery, where it's sold frozen, packaged in plastic bags. Puree it in a blender until completely smooth, then mix it with milk or yogurt and a touch of honey to make tangy, mouthwatering, tropical shakes, sorbets, ice creams, or mousses.

1 PACKAGE UNFLAVORED GELATIN
3 TABLESPOONS COLD WATER, PLUS 1 CUP WATER
1/3 CUP SUGAR
1/3 CUP HONEY
ONE 14-OUNCE BAG FROZEN *GUANÁBANA* PULP, THAWED (SEE HEADNOTE)
2 3/4 CUPS PLAIN YOGURT

1. In a small saucepan, soften the gelatin in 3 tablespoons of cold water. Heat, stirring, until the gelatin is dissolved.

2. In a small saucepan, combine the 1 cup water, the sugar, and the honey, and cook over medium-low heat, stirring, to dissolve the sugar, about 5 minutes. Thoroughly stir in the dissolved gelatin. Cool completely.

3. In a food processor, puree the *guanábana* pulp with the syrup-gelatin mixture until smooth. Strain through a medium sieve into a large bowl and stir in the yogurt. Chill until cold, but not set, about 1 hour.

4. Freeze in an ice cream maker according to the manufacturer's instructions.

MAKES ABOUT 1 1/4 QUARTS

Mango Magic

Mango is everything one looks for in a tropical fruit: soft, fragrant, vibrantly colored, and lusciously sensuous. Mango is a darling in many parts of the globe—according to production numbers, it's the third favorite fruit in the world. And recently, its magic is beginning to catch on in this country—so much so that the only problem in getting a mango is choosing one. Imported from different tropical countries and grown domestically in Florida, mangoes come in many varieties, with subtle and not-so-subtle variations in color, shape, and flavor. My favorite is the Kent variety, with firm sweet flesh and a deep orange-yellow color.

Choose a mango as you would an avocado, by touching it. To be eaten straightaway, it has to be firm but slightly yielding to the touch, with a sweet, fragrant aroma around the stem, and tight unblemished skin. A slightly overripe mango is hard to cut up neatly, but it still might be delicious mashed or pureed. If you see such mangoes on sale, puree them in a food processor and freeze the puree to use in desserts and sauces. To get a mango to the perfect point of ripeness, choose a slightly hard fruit and ripen it at home at room temperature, tucked in a paper bag together with some banana peel. The flavor of the fruit might vary from spectacularly sweet and concentrated to thin and watery. If the mango is not great, I add a touch of orange juice concentrate, as well as some extra lime juice and/or sugar, then puree it for a mousse or ice cream. One large mango will yield about 1 cup of puree.

Mango can be enjoyed diced into chicken, seafood, and vegetables salads. It can be made into a bright salsa with a bit of lime, red onion, and cilantro; pureed into cold soups, mousses, ice creams, cocktails, and dessert toppings; and eaten expertly diced as a simple dessert or snack.

In my Latin neighborhood, the moment good mangoes come in season, a huge line forms around Fernando's little fruit stall. He carves them into neat slices and packs them into small plastic bags. "*Un peso*," he chants, as my Mexican, Colombian, Peruvian, and Argentinian neighbors hand him one-dollar bills in exchange for a neat plastic bag filled with expertly sliced mango—which they consume on the spot with a sprinkling of lime juice and chili powder.

Frozen Mango-Orange Soufflés

(SOUFFLÉS DE MANGO Y NARANJA CONGELADOS)

Choose ripe, soft mangoes for these soufflés, otherwise the taste might be somewhat thin. Taste the soufflé mixture and if the flavor lacks depth, add some more orange juice concentrate.

2 LARGE EGG YOLKS
$^1/_4$ CUP PLUS 2 TABLESPOONS SUGAR, PLUS MORE FOR SPRINKLING THE SOUFFLÉ DISHES
2 CUPS PUREED RIPE MANGO (SEE HEADNOTE), PLUS 1 FIRM MANGO, PEELED, PITTED, AND DICED
$^1/_3$ CUP ORANGE JUICE CONCENTRATE, THAWED
2 TABLESPOONS FRESHLY SQUEEZED LIME JUICE
2$^1/_4$ CUPS CHILLED HEAVY CREAM
3 LARGE EGG WHITES, AT ROOM TEMPERATURE
PINCH OF CREAM OF TARTAR

1. In a stainless steel bowl set over simmering water, whisk the egg yolks with $^1/_4$ cup of the sugar until the mixture is thick and pale, about 5 minutes. Scrape the mixture into a large bowl and let it cool.

2. In a second bowl, stir together the mango puree, orange juice concentrate, and lime juice.

3. Lightly butter six $^1/_2$-cup soufflé dishes and sprinkle them with sugar. Tear off strips of wax paper long enough to wrap around the dishes and fold them in half lengthwise. Using rubber bands or Scotch tape, secure the strips around the dishes so that they form a collar extending 2 inches above the rim.

4. Whip the cream until it holds soft peaks. Reserve $^1/_2$ cup of whipped cream.

5. With clean dry beaters, beat the egg whites with the cream of tartar until they hold soft peaks. While beating, sprinkle in 2 tablespoons of sugar and beat until glossy, 30 seconds more.

6. Gently but thoroughly fold the egg white mixture into the yolk mixture. Gently but thoroughly fold in the cream and the mango mixture.

7. Divide the soufflé mixture among the prepared soufflé dishes and chill them in the freezer until completely frozen, about 4 hours.

8. To serve, remove the wax paper strips from the frozen soufflés, and top each soufflé with some diced mango and a dollop of the reserved whipped cream.

MAKES 6 SOUFFLÉS

Cherimoya:
The Secret of the Andes

Cherimoya (sometimes called custard apple) was originally cultivated by Indian fruit farmers in the highlands of Ecuador, Chile, and Peru, and its name means "black seed" in Quechua, the language of the Andean Indians. Today domestically grown cherimoyas can be spotted more and more often at supermarkets and better grocery stores during their season, from August to November. If you see one, grab it! It's a heart-shaped fruit, the size of a large pear, with a thick olive-green shell covered with neat thumbprint-like indentations. The pulp is granular, white, and custardy, with large black, shiny seeds. The taste of a fully ripe cherimoya is exquisite, with hints of vanilla, pineapple, mango, and wild strawberries. Most cherimoyas found in this country will either be over- or underipe. Choose fruit that is slightly hard, clear green, and blemish free, and allow it to ripen at room temperature in a paper bag. A ripe fruit should yield to finger pressure as much as a perfectly ripe avocado. Once ripe, cherimoyas won't keep well and should be refrigerated as soon as possible.

In its Andean homelands, cherimoyas are put to all sorts of imaginative uses in the kitchen—for custards, pies, tarts, ice cream, and fruit salads. One of my favorite Chilean desserts is a sweetened mashed cherimoya mold topped with a cap of meringue. Here, however, the best way to appreciate this delicate and pricey fruit is to eat it on its own, scooped out of its shell with a spoon, or diced and served with a sprinkling of fresh orange juice.

Cherimoya Alegre

1 LARGE CHERIMOYA (ABOUT 1 POUND), PEELED AND CUT INTO CHUNKS (THE SEEDS ARE EDIBLE)

2½ CUPS FRESHLY SQUEEZED ORANGE JUICE

4 TABLESPOONS COINTREAU (ORANGE LIQUEUR), OPTIONAL

MINT SPRIGS, FOR GARNISH

If you dine out in Chile, you are likely to conclude your meal with this simple but delicious dessert (which translates as "happy cherimoya").

Divide the cherimoya among four small glass bowls or large wineglasses. Divide the orange juice and Cointreau equally among them. Chill for 1 hour and serve garnished with mint sprigs.

SERVES 4

Market, Santiago, Chile.

Passion Fruit:
What's in a Name

To my mind, passion fruit is the most beguiling of all the hot-zone fruits, lending a magically exotic, concentrated, tart, fragrant flavor to desserts, cocktails, sauces, and salad dressings. One can certainly de-

velop an obsession with this amazing fruit, but its name has nothing to do with the baser passions. Unlike many other New World exports, from avocado to cacao, it was never claimed to be an aphrodisiac. Quite the opposite! It was named *pasiflora* by the zealously devout early missionaries, who compared the intricate cross shape of its flower to the Crucifixion.

The Spanish names for this tropical gem are *maracuyá*, *parcha*, and *granadilla*, depending on the country you're in. From the outside, it is a crinkly purplish or yellow ball, the size of a small plum, which promises anything but the ambrosial tart pulp, dotted with crunchy black seeds, that is found inside. Fresh passion fruit are expensive and rare, but you can sometimes find them in gourmet groceries and some supermarkets, during their short season, which runs from December to February. Choose a wrinkled fruit that feels heavy for its size. Cut it in half, and scoop out the pulp with a spoon to sprinkle on ice creams, mousses, and cakes.

Otherwise, scour Latin groceries for plastic bags of frozen passion fruit pulp imported from Colombia or the Dominican Republic. It's an incredibly good buy! Thaw the pulp and use it as you would fresh orange juice or pureed mango: in

Anya von Bremzen, Calle Ocho Marketplace, Miami.

vinaigrettes, *beurres blancs*, and other savory sauces. Cook it with a bit of cornstarch to make a lovely dessert sauce (see page 324); add it to custards, mousses, and crèmes anglaises (but be careful not to curdle the milk or cream); fold it into cheesecake batter, or make it into ice creams and sorbets.

Passion Fruit Sauce

(SALSA DE MARACUYÁ)

This sauce is very simple to make, provided you can find frozen passion fruit pulp, and it can transform any dessert—be it a scoop of ice cream or a simple piece of pound cake—into a memorable and exotic confection. I especially like this sauce with rich chocolate desserts, which, to me, literally beg for a touch of fragrance and acidity.

ONE 14-OUNCE BAG (ABOUT 1½ CUPS) FROZEN
UNSWEETENED PASSION FRUIT PULP, THAWED
(SEE PAGE 323)
⅓ CUP SUGAR, OR MORE TO TASTE
2 TEASPOONS CORNSTARCH MIXED WITH
1 TABLESPOON COLD WATER

1. In a medium-size nonreactive saucepan, bring the passion fruit pulp and sugar to a simmer, over medium-low heat stirring to dissolve the sugar, about 7 minutes. Slowly drizzle in the cornstarch mixture and cook the sauce, stirring, until thickened, about 2 minutes.

2. Transfer to a pitcher or serving bowl and chill.

MAKES ABOUT 1½ CUPS

Papaya-Coconut-Lime Sauce

(SALSA DE PAPAYA, COCO, Y LIMÓN)

This is a lovely silky Caribbean sauce for your ice creams, custards, and cakes. I especially like it with a simple cheesecake.

1. Puree the papaya with the lime juice and cream of coconut in a blender until smooth.

2. Transfer the puree to a saucepan and add the rum, water, and sugar. Simmer over medium heat for 5 minutes, stirring to dissolve the sugar. Transfer to a serving bowl or pitcher and chill.

MAKES ABOUT 2 $\frac{1}{2}$ CUPS

3 CUPS DICED FRESH PAPAYA

3½ TABLESPOONS FRESHLY SQUEEZED LIME JUICE

2 TABLESPOONS CREAM OF COCONUT, SUCH AS COCO LÓPEZ, WELL STIRRED

2 TABLESPOONS DARK RUM

¼ CUP WATER

3 TABLESPOONS SUGAR, OR MORE TO TASTE

Coconut-Caramel Custard Sauce

(SALSA DE CARAMELO CON COCO)

Caramel is one of the flavors beloved by the Latin sweet tooth, and I love it with a tropical touch of coconut. You can serve it with chocolate or nut cakes, ice cream, or flan.

$\frac{1}{3}$ CUP, PLUS 3 TABLESPOONS SUGAR

$\frac{1}{2}$ CUP HALF AND HALF

1 CUP MILK

$\frac{1}{2}$ CUP CANNED COCONUT MILK, WELL STIRRED

1 $\frac{1}{2}$ TABLESPOONS CREAM OF COCONUT, SUCH AS
      COCO LÓPEZ, WELL STIRRED

2 LARGE EGGS

$\frac{1}{2}$ TEASPOON GROUND CINNAMON

1. In a small, heavy saucepan, cook $\frac{1}{3}$ cup of the sugar over medium heat until it is melted and turns a deep caramel color, about 8 minutes. Remove from the heat and stir in the half and half, standing back as the mixture might splatter. Return the pan to the heat and cook over low heat, stirring, until the caramel is dissolved, about 3 minutes. Set aside.

2. In a saucepan, heat the milk, coconut milk, and coconut cream over low heat until small bubbles begin to form around the edges.

3. In a large bowl, whisk the eggs with the remaining 3 tablespoons of the sugar. Whisk in the warm milk in a slow steady stream and add the caramel mixture.

4. Transfer the sauce to a heavy saucepan and cook over low heat, stirring constantly without allowing it to boil, until it reaches custard consistency, about 7 minutes. Strain through a fine sieve into a serving bowl or pitcher, and stir in the cinnamon. Place a piece of plastic wrap directly on the surface of the sauce to prevent a skin from forming and cool it to the desired temperature.

MAKES ABOUT 2 CUPS

Red and Black Berry Sauce

(SALSA DE FRAMBUESAS, FRESAS, Y MORAS)

This sauce is particularly delicious with yellow tropical fruit (such as mango, papaya, or passion fruit) ice creams and sorbets, with simple pound cakes, or spooned around a flan. I use frozen berries here because they release more juice and have a more concentrated flavor when cooked. One of my favorite quick desserts is this sauce spooned over purchased pound cake, in a pool of tart Passion Fruit Sauce (page 324).

Combine all the ingredients in a medium-size saucepan and bring to a simmer, over medium heat, stirring. Cook, over medium-low heat, stirring gently with a wooden spoon, until the berries burst and release their juices, about 10 minutes. Cool before serving.

1 CUP PARTIALLY THAWED FROZEN
    BLACKBERRIES
1 CUP PARTIALLY THAWED FROZEN RASPBERRIES
1 CUP SLICED PARTIALLY THAWED FROZEN
    STRAWBERRIES
1/4 CUP WATER
1/2 CUP SUGAR, OR MORE TO TASTE

MAKES ABOUT 1 1/2 CUPS

Homemade Milk Custard

(DULCE DE LECHE CASERO)

No sweet is more adored in South America than *dulce de leche* (also called *manjar*), a silky, creamy, caramel-colored condensed milk with a fudge-like taste. Its uses are myriad—as a filling for cakes, crepes, pastries, and cookies; as a topping for ice creams and custards; or just spread on bread or eaten straight out of a jar. While ready-made *dulce de leche* can easily be found at Latin markets in this country, nothing compares to the homemade taste. Making *dulce de leche* is a time-consuming proposition, as it has to be stirred almost continuously for its several-hour cooking time. However, a pastry chef, Jorje Massey from Buenos Aires, offered me an ingenious solution, practiced by his family cook: a heatproof plate is placed in the pot with the milk. As the plate moves and rattles during cooking, it takes the place of stirring until the milk begins to thicken. According to Jorje, the baking soda gives the milk a rich brown color, while the water adds a bit of shine.

3 CUPS MILK
1²/₃ CUPS SUGAR
¹/₃ CUP WATER
1 VANILLA BEAN, SPLIT IN HALF LENGTHWISE
LARGE PINCH OF BAKING SODA

1. In a heavy, 2-quart saucepan, combine the milk, sugar, water, and the vanilla, and bring to a boil, skimming off the foam and stirring constantly. Choose a heatproof glass dessert or salad plate, and lower it into the pot. Add the baking soda and simmer, uncovered, over medium-low heat, until the milk begins to thicken, about 45 minutes. Stir it every 10 minutes.

2. As soon as the milk begins to thicken, reduce the heat to very low, carefully remove the plate from the pot, and begin stirring constantly with a wooden spoon. Stir until the mixture is

the consistency of condensed milk and is light amber in color. This should take 10 to 15 minutes. Do not stop stirring, or the milk and bottom of your pot will scorch. Remove the vanilla bean and transfer the *dulce de leche* to a clean jar. If you use a sterilized jar, the milk will keep for several months on the lowest shelf of a refrigerator.

MAKES ABOUT 1 ¹/₂ CUPS

Funerary relief, Recoleta Cemetery, Buenos Aires, Argentina.

Caramel

This is the caramel recipe used for flans, bread puddings, and other Latin custards. Depending on the main recipe, you can add a tablespoon or so of orange liqueur, such as Grand Marnier or Cointreau, or coffee or chocolate liqueur, such as Kahlúa or Tía María.

4 TABLESPOONS WATER
1 ¼ CUPS SUGAR

Remember that the caramel will continue cooking after you've turned off the heat. To avoid burning it, either pour it immediately into the container you are using for the main recipe, or place the saucepan with the hot caramel in a shallow pan filled with cold water to stop the cooking. Should your caramel happen to solidify before you've used it, reheat it over low heat. Use boiling water to wash the hardened caramel off your saucepan. And remember that caramel gets very hot, so use a bit of caution!

Pour the water into a heavy saucepan (copper is best), add the sugar and stir well. Cook over high heat, stirring, until the sugar dissolves, brushing down the sides of the saucepan as necessary with a wet brush. Reduce the heat to medium-high and cook without stirring until the mixture is caramel brown, about 7 minutes. If the caramel colors unevenly, swirl the saucepan gently to redistribute the syrup. Remove it from the heat as soon as it is done (see Headnote).

MAKES ENOUGH TO COAT A 9-INCH SQUARE OR ROUND PAN

Fiesta

Festival at Juli, Peru.

IN THE colorful cycle of the Latin year, hardly a day goes by without some kind of party or celebration. With the recipes in this chapter, you will be able to partake in the revelry and joy that make Latin fiestas so unforgettable.

You can prepare a traditional Madrileño Christmas Eve feast of baked fish, savory braised red cabbage with pine nuts, and a scrumptious, velvety pumpkin pudding. On a more elegant note, your festival table will sparkle with a pistachio-stuffed pheasant in pomegranate sauce, Argentinian roast pork loin with apricots and beer, or the Catalan Christmas turkey.

Those searching for new ways to prepare Easter lamb, will certainly be pleased with my favorite recipe from Portugal—a whole leg of lamb roasted under an aromatic crust of mint and peppercorns, and served slathered with a rich red wine sauce. And before Easter, why not enjoy a delicious Lenten Galician empanada stuffed with a melting mixture of salt cod, raisins, and red pepper.

Fiesta!

If you want to throw a fun party for a crowd, put on a salsa tape, and cook up a whole fresh roast ham with cracklings—unless it's a very special occasion, which would call for a whole crispy suckling pig.

To capture the joyous, boisterous atmosphere of a Spanish or Portuguese street fair, fry up some *churros* or *sonhos*, those *flores de la sartén* ("flowers of the skillet"), to enjoy with coffee and hot chocolate; or transform leftover bread into festival *torrijas*, the delicious, Spanish-style French toast.

I never go to a Christmas party without bringing a Venezuelan *pan de jamón*, a spectacular holiday bread stuffed with smoked ham, raisins, and olives; and I love making Luis Irizar's brandied prunes to give away as a gift.

If you want to make a surprise for your children just when they thought Christmas was over, throw a costume party for Three Kings' Day (January 6) to choose the next year's king or queen, and bake a Three Kings' Wreath, with a special secret inside.

Festival at Juli, Peru.

Holiday Punch

Here is a festive soul-warming Catalan hot wine and fruit punch to welcome guests to your holiday party.

2 MEDIUM APPLES, CORED WITH A FRUIT CORER,
    PEELED AND CUT INTO RINGS
3 BOTTLES (750 L) FRUITY DRY RED WINE
2 CINNAMON STICKS
1 SMALL ORANGE, STUCK WITH CLOVES
1¾ CUPS SUGAR, OR MORE TO TASTE
2 CUPS DRIED FIGS
1 CUP BRANDY
1 CUP DARK RUM

1. Sear the apple rings in a nonstick skillet over medium-high heat.

2. In a nonreactive saucepan large enough to accommodate all the liquid, combine the wine, apples, cinnamon sticks, orange, sugar, and figs and bring to a simmer over medium heat. Simmer over low heat until the figs are soft, about 20 to 25 minutes.

3. Raise the heat to high and add the brandy and rum. Bring to a boil, reduce the heat to low, and ignite the liquor with a match, letting it burn until the flames die down naturally.

4. Transfer to a large punch bowl and serve.

SERVES 12

Catalan Christmas Turkey with Dried Fruit and Sausage Stuffing

(PAVO ROSTIT FARCIT)

In Catalonia the traditional Christmas Day meal always begins with *escudella i carn d'olla*, an elaborate boiled dinner containing oxtail, pig's feet, ham bones, sausages, various meats, vegetables, and large meatballs, called *pilota*. The *escudella* is served in two courses, first the stock from cooking the meats, served with large pasta shells, and then the meats and vegetables. But the meal does not end there. As if anyone has room for more food, the lunch proceeds to a spectacular roast turkey, stuffed with sausages, fruit, and pine nuts. As if in anticipation of an ample amount of leftovers, December 26 brings yet another feast, San Esteban, for which leftover turkey is mixed with béchamel and stuffed into Catalan *canelones*. The turkey is best if marinated in herbs and lemon juice overnight. However, if you start at the last minute, you can rub it with the marinade right before roasting.

(continued)

1 FRESH TURKEY (12 TO 14 POUNDS)
6 CLOVES GARLIC, CHOPPED
2 TEASPOONS COARSE (KOSHER) SALT
2 TABLESPOONS CRACKED BLACK PEPPERCORNS
1 1/2 TEASPOONS DRIED ROSEMARY
2 LARGE BAY LEAVES, CRUMBLED
4 TABLESPOONS VIRGIN OLIVE OIL
1/4 CUP FRESH LEMON JUICE

STUFFING

5 LINKS (ABOUT 1 1/4 POUNDS) SWEET ITALIAN
     SAUSAGE
1 1/4 CUPS DRY OR MEDIUM-DRY SHERRY
1 CUP PITTED DRIED CHERRIES (SUCH AS
     MICHIGAN SOUR)
1 CUP CHOPPED PITTED PRUNES
1 CUP COARSELY CHOPPED DRIED PEARS
3 TABLESPOONS OLIVE OIL
2 1/4 CUPS COARSELY CHOPPED ONIONS
3 CLOVES GARLIC, SLICED
2 LARGE QUINCES OR 3 MEDIUM APPLES,
     PEELED, CORED, AND DICED

(continued)

½ CUP TURKEY GIBLET STOCK (RECIPE
    FOLLOWS), CHICKEN STOCK (PAGE 372), OR
    CANNED LOWER-SALT CHICKEN BROTH
2 TEASPOONS MILD PAPRIKA
1 SMALL BAY LEAF, CRUMBLED
1 LARGE SPRIG DRIED THYME, CRUMBLED, OR
    1½ TO 2 TEASPOONS DRIED THYME
1 CINNAMON STICK, BROKEN INTO 2 PIECES
⅔ CUP TOASTED PINE NUTS
SALT AND FRESHLY GROUND BLACK PEPPER, TO
    TASTE

1 LARGE SPRIG DRIED ROSEMARY, CRUMBLED OR
    1 TEASPOON DRIED ROSEMARY
10 LARGE UNPEELED CLOVES GARLIC, SMASHED
2 CUPS TURKEY GIBLET STOCK (RECIPE
    FOLLOWS) OR CHICKEN STOCK (PAGE 372),
    PLUS MORE AS NEEDED
1 CUP DRY WHITE WINE, PLUS MORE AS NEEDED

1. Rinse the turkey thoroughly inside and out and pat it dry with paper towels. Reserve the giblets and remove the wing tips to make the stock (recipe follows). In a mortar and pestle, pound the chopped garlic, salt, pepper, rosemary, and bay leaves to a paste. Work in the oil and the lemon juice. Rub the turkey inside and out with the marinade, cover it with plastic wrap, and refrigerate it for at least 8 hours or overnight. Bring back to room temperature before roasting.

2. To make the stuffing: Prick the sausages all over with the tip of a sharp kinfe and blanch them in boiling water to cover for 1 minute. Drain. When cool enough to handle, cut the sausages into medium slices.

3. In a large saucepan, bring the sherry to a boil. Add the dried cherries, prunes, and pears, remove from the heat, and let stand, tossing occasionally, until plump, about 30 minutes.

4. In a large skillet, heat the oil over low heat. Add the onions and garlic and cook, stirring until the onion wilts, about 5 minutes. Add the quinces or apples and the sliced sausage and cook, stirring often until it softens a little, about 10 minutes (5 minutes if using apples). Add the soaked fruit with its liquid, the stock, paprika, bay leaf, thyme, and cinnamon stick, and cook another 5 minutes. Transfer to a bowl and add the pine nuts, and salt and pepper to taste.

5. Preheat the oven to 425 degrees F.

6. Stuff the cavity and the neck of the turkey loosely with the stuffing. Fold the neck skin under the turkey and secure it with a skewer. Truss the turkey.

7. Place the turkey on a rack in a large roasting pan and roast for 30 minutes.

8. Reduce the oven temperature to 325 degrees. Remove the turkey briefly from the oven and add the rosemary, smashed garlic, stock, and wine to a pan. Cover the turkey loosely with foil and roast, basting it every 20 minutes with the pan juices, until the juices run clear when the fleshiest part of the thigh is pricked with a skewer, about 3 hours. Add more stock and wine to the pan periodically to maintain the same level of liquid. If the turkey skin is not crisp when the turkey is done, raise the heat to 450 degrees and roast it for 10 minutes more to crisp up, removing the foil if it has been covered. The internal temperature of the thigh should be 180 degrees.

9. Transfer the turkey to a carving board, cover it loosely with foil, and let it stand for 15 minutes. Scoop out the stuffing onto a serving plate. Degrease the pan juices and remove the garlic and rosemary, if you wish. Transfer the pan juices to a sauceboat. Carve the turkey and moisten it with the pan juices. Serve the turkey with the stuffing and the pan juices.

SERVES 8 TO 10

Turkey Giblet Stock

Place all the ingredients in a medium-size saucepan and bring to a boil, skimming the foam. Cook over medium heat, partially covered, for 30 minutes. Strain, discarding the solids.

MAKES ABOUT 4 CUPS

GIBLETS AND WING TIPS FROM ONE 12- TO
    14-POUND TURKEY, WASHED AND TRIMMED
    OF ALL FAT
5 CUPS WATER
$\frac{1}{3}$ CUP MEDIUM-DRY SHERRY
1 SMALL ONION, SLICED
1 SMALL CARROT, PEELED AND CUT INTO 3
    SECTIONS
1 BAY LEAF
1 SMALL STALK CELERY
SALT AND FRESHLY GROUND BLACK PEPPER, TO
    TASTE

Fiesta!
337

Pork Loin and Apricots with Beer-Mustard Sauce

(LOMO DE CERDO AL HORNO CON OREJONES)

This is a typical middle-class European-Argentinian family dish, which would be served at a cattle ranch for Christmas (as a break from grilled beef) or another festive occasion. This recipe comes from an old family recipe book of my friend Señora Shaw.

1 PORK LOIN (ABOUT 4 POUNDS), TIED WITH
    KITCHEN STRING

SALT TO TASTE

3 TABLESPOONS CRACKED BLACK PEPPERCORNS

1 TABLESPOON MILD PAPRIKA

4 TABLESPOONS TIGHTLY PACKED BROWN SUGAR

3 TABLESPOONS DIJON-STYLE MUSTARD

4 CUPS LAGER-STYLE BEER

1 LARGE ONION, SLICED

1½ CUPS DRIED APRICOTS, PREFERABLY
    CALIFORNIA

2 TEASPOONS APRICOT PRESERVES

⅔ CUP CHICKEN STOCK (PAGE 372) OR CANNED
    LOWER-SALT CHICKEN BROTH

2 TEASPOONS KETCHUP

2 TEASPOONS WORCESTERSHIRE SAUCE

2 TEASPOONS CORNSTARCH, DILUTED IN
    1 TABLESPOON COLD WATER

1. Preheat the oven to 350 degrees F.

2. Rub the roast generously with the salt, pepper, and paprika.

3. Spread the sugar on a cutting board. Spread the mustard over the pork and roll it in the sugar. Place the roast in a roasting pan and add 1½ cups of the beer, the onion, and the apricots. Roast for 45 minutes. Pour the rest of the beer into the pan and continue roasting until the juices run clear when tested with a skewer and the internal temperature reads 150° to 160°F, about 45 minutes more.

4. Remove the pork from the roasting pan and cover it loosely with foil, leaving the pan juices in the pan.

5. Place the pan with the pan juices on a burner and add the apricot preserves, stirring to dissolve. Add the stock, ketchup, and Worcestershire sauce, and cook over medium-high heat until a little reduced, about 5 minutes, scraping the bottom of the pan with a wooden spoon. Reduce the heat to low and drizzle in the cornstarch mixture. Cook until the sauce thickens, about 2 minutes. Transfer it to a sauceboat.

6. Slice the meat into thin slices and serve accompanied by the sauce.

SERVES 8

Accordionist,
San Telmo Market,
Buenos Aires,
Argentina.

Mint-Crusted Easter Lamb with Wine Sauce

(CARNEIRO DE PASCOA À ALENTEJANA)

Roast lamb is a symbol of Easter pretty much all over the Catholic world. One of my favorite Easter lamb recipes is this one from central Portugal, where the lamb is roasted under a crust of black peppercorns and dried local spearmint, and served with a rich garlicky red wine sauce. In Portuguese villages the *almoço de Páscoa* (Easter lunch) often begins with a rich soup made from the trimmings and tougher parts of the spring lamb, followed by the more tender meat, baked in earthenware in a rustic bread oven until it is so tender it's almost falling off the bone. I have reduced the cooking time to produce more contemporary-style rare meat. For the crust I like dried mint, used for brewing mint tea, which I buy at Middle Eastern groceries.

3 TABLESPOONS BLACK PEPPERCORNS

1 TABLESPOON WHITE PEPPERCORNS

3 TABLESPOONS CRUMBLED DRIED MINT (SEE HEADNOTE)

1 TABLESPOON MILD PAPRIKA, PREFERABLY SPANISH

1/2 TEASPOON HOT RED PEPPER FLAKES, OR MORE TO TASTE

1 TABLESPOON COARSE (KOSHER) SALT

1/3 CUP FRUITY OLIVE OIL

3 TABLESPOONS RED WINE VINEGAR

1 LEG OF LAMB (7 TO 8 POUNDS)

6 LARGE CLOVES GARLIC, SLIVERED, PLUS 12 LARGE WHOLE CLOVES GARLIC, LIGHTLY SMASHED

1 LARGE CARROT, PEELED AND CUT INTO CHUNKS

1 LARGE ONION, CHOPPED

2 CUPS BEEF STOCK (PAGE 373), CHICKEN STOCK (PAGE 372), OR CANNED LOWER-SALT CHICKEN BROTH

2 CUPS GOOD RED WINE, PREFERABLY FROM THE PORTUGUESE REGIONS OF THE DÃO OR RIBATEJO

1. In a spice grinder or a clean coffee grinder, grind the black and white peppercorns with the mint to a coarse powder. In a bowl, whisk the ground mixture with the paprika, red pepper flakes, salt, oil, and vinegar.

2. With the tip of a small knife, make deep slits all over the lamb. Coat several garlic slivers with the pureed mixture and stuff them into the slits. Continue until all the slivered garlic is used up.

3. Rub the remaining pureed mixture all over the lamb. Place the lamb in a large shallow dish, cover it loosely with plastic wrap and marinate it in the refrigerator for at least 4 hours or overnight. Bring the lamb to room temperature before roasting.

4. Preheat the oven to 425 degrees F.

5. Scatter the carrot, onion, and smashed garlic in a large roasting pan. Place the lamb on a rack in the roasting pan, and roast for 30 minutes. Reduce the oven temperature to 350 degrees. Pour the stock and 1 cup of the wine into the pan. Roast the lamb for 1 hour. (If the crust begins to brown too much, cover it loosely with foil.) Pour the remaining wine into the pan and roast for another $1^{1}/_{4}$ hours for medium meat.

6. Raise the oven temperature to 450 degrees, and cook the lamb for 15 minutes more to crisp up the crust, removing the foil if lamb has been covered.

7. Remove the lamb from the pan and let stand, covered loosely with foil, for 15 minutes.

8. Degrease the pan juices and pass the solids through a vegetable mill or fine sieve into a saucepan. Add the liquid and reduce it over high heat for 5 minutes. Transfer the sauce to a gravy boat.

9. Carve the lamb and serve accompanied by the sauce.

SERVES 10 TO 12

Fiesta!
341

Latin Party Roast Fresh Ham with Cracklings

(JAMÓN DE FIESTA CON CHICHARRONES)

After whole suckling pig, this fresh ham—larded with a spicy *adobo* mixture of olives, capers, herbs, spices, and vinegar—is the best thing for a sizzling Latin fiesta. My Dominican neighbors might keep the building awake with their wild *merengue* parties, but those who get to taste their roast ham never complain! Here is their recipe. For a true fiesta, serve it with Félix de Jesús' Incredible Black Beans and Rice (page 262), and Watercress and Hearts of Palm Salad (page 113), and be sure to play a Wilfredo Vargas *merengue* tape.

1 FRESH HAM (SHANK END OF LEG OF PORK) (10 TO 12 POUNDS)

STUFFING MIXTURE

$^1/_3$ CUP FINELY CHOPPED ONION

12 CLOVES GARLIC, MINCED

$^1/_2$ CUP MINCED CILANTRO LEAVES

$^1/_3$ CUP CHOPPED PIMIENTO-STUFFED GREEN OLIVES

$^1/_4$ CUP DRAINED CAPERS

2 JALAPEÑO PEPPERS, CORED, SEEDED, AND CHOPPED

1 TABLESPOON DRIED OREGANO

3 TABLESPOONS DISTILLED WHITE VINEGAR

1 TABLESPOON COARSE (KOSHER) SALT

(continued)

1. With a large, sharp knife score four deep slits across the entire ham, and two slits down its length. Carefully cut the skin off the ham and reserve it. Trim all but a $^1/_4$-inch layer of fat from the ham.

2. Preheat the oven to 450 degrees F.

3. Place all the stuffing ingredients in a large mortar or in a wooden bowl and crush them with a pestle or the bottom of a cup to a coarse paste. This can also be done in a blender or food processor, using the on/off button, until the ingredients are crushed but not pureed. With a sharp knife, make long, $1^1/_2$-inch-deep slits all over the ham. Stuff some stuffing mixture into each slit, pushing it in as deeply as you can with a handle of a knife or fork.

4. Combine all the spice rub ingredients in a small bowl and stir well. Rub the ham with the spice rub, reserving about 1 tablespoon for the cracklings.

5. Set the ham on a rack in a roasting pan and pour 2 cups of water into the pan. Roast for 15 minutes. Reduce the oven temperature to 325 degrees and roast the ham until a meat thermometer inserted into the thickest part of its flesh registers 170 degrees. The total roasting time should be about 4 hours or slightly longer, depending on the exact weight of the ham. Baste it with the pan juices every 30 minutes, and add water periodically to keep a consistent level of liquid in the pan.

6. Two and a half hours into the cooking, rub the reserved ham skin with the reserved spice rub and place it in a shallow baking pan, rind side up. Place it in the oven and roast it with the ham until the ham is cooked and the skin is crackling-crisp. Remove the skin from the oven once or twice during cooking and pour off the fat that accumulates in the pan. Don't forget to replenish the liquid in the ham pan.

7. Remove the meat and the cracklings from the oven and cover the meat loosely with foil. Let it stand for 15 minutes. When the skin is cool enough to handle, break it or cut it with scissors into 1-inch pieces. Place it on a plate and cover it loosely with foil.

8. Skim off the fat from the juices in the ham pan and add enough water to make 3 cups. Bring to a boil, scraping the bottom of the pan with a wooden spoon. Transfer the pan juices to a saucepan set over medium heat, and stir in the mustard, vinegar, and raisins. Cook over medium-high heat, until a little reduced, about 10 minutes. Slowly drizzle in the cornstarch mixture and cook, stirring, until the gravy thickens, about 1 minute. Transfer it to a sauceboat.

9. Slice the meat into thin slices across the grain. Transfer it to a serving platter and place the cracklings on a separate plate. Serve with the gravy.

SERVES 10

SPICE RUB

2½ TABLESPOONS MILD PAPRIKA

1 TABLESPOON COARSE (KOSHER) SALT

2½ TABLESPOONS GARLIC POWDER

2 TABLESPOONS DRIED OREGANO

1 TABLESPOON GROUND CUMIN

¼ CUP OLIVE OIL

2 CUPS WATER, PLUS MORE AS NEEDED

1 TABLESPOON DIJON-STYLE MUSTARD

2 TEASPOONS DISTILLED WHITE VINEGAR

½ CUP DARK RAISINS

2 TEASPOONS CORNSTARCH, DISSOLVED IN
   1 TABLESPOON COLD WATER

Roast Suckling Pig

(LECHÓN ASADO)

At a Latin fiesta, *lechón* is king. Come Chrismastime, you will see golden-brown, crisp-roasted baby pigs gleefully grinning at you from the windows of restaurants and butcher shops. Spain, Portugal, and each Latin American country has its own special way of roasting the pig—but the goal is always the same: achieving a super-crispy skin and tender, juicy, melt-in-your-mouth flesh. (In the Castilian town of Segovia, the pig is so tender that it's cut into portions with nothing more than a dinner plate!) My own favorite preparation is in the style of Bairrada, an otherwise nondescript town in central Portugal that attracts gastronomic pilgrims from all over the country because of its famous suckling pig, traditionally accompanied by the region's superb sparkling rosé wine. The six-week-old piglets of a very particular breed are spit-roasted in large brick ovens traditionally used for making *broa*, the local corn bread. Before roasting, the pig is marinated in a mixture of pounded garlic, coarse salt, and crushed black peppercorns. During roasting, it's sprinkled with the local white wine to prevent the skin from wrinkling and bursting open. Serve the pig with a very dry sparkling white or rosé, or with the excellent red wine of Bairrada. The pig has to marinate for 12 to 24 hours, so start a day ahead.

1. In a food processor, combine the garlic, peppercorns, salt, 1/3 cup of the wine, 1/3 cup of the oil, and the cilantro and process, using the on/off button, to a medium-coarse paste. Do not overprocess.

2. Wash the pig thoroughly inside and out under cold running water, and pat it dry with paper towels. Rub the pig all over with half of the marinade, and rub the pig's cavity with the remaining marinade. Place the pig in a large baking pan, cover it loosely with plastic wrap or foil, and refrigerate it for 12 to 24 hours. Bring it back to room temperature before roasting.

3. Preheat the oven to 350 degrees F.

4. Wrap pieces of foil loosely around the pig's ears and tail so that they don't burn during the cooking. Prop the mouth open with a tiny apple or tinfoil. Brush the pig with the remaining oil and set it on a rack in a large roasting pan. Roast for 1 hour. Remove from the oven and brush it with a pastry brush in white wine. Continue roasting for another 2 1/2 hours, brushing it with wine in the same fashion every 30 minutes.

5. Raise the oven temperature to 450 degrees. Remove the foil from the ears and tail, and continue roasting the pig for another 20 to 30 minutes, until the skin is crispy and the juices run clear when you prick the pig with a skewer.

6. Remove the pig from the oven and carefully transfer it to a serving platter decorated with orange wedges and cilantro sprigs. To carve, cut the pig lengthwise along the backbone. Cut each half crosswise between the ribs into five to six pieces.

2 LARGE HEADS GARLIC, SEPARATED INTO CLOVES, CHOPPED

1/4 CUP CRUSHED BLACK PEPPERCORNS

1 TABLESPOON COARSE (KOSHER) SALT

1/3 CUP DRY WHITE WINE, PLUS MORE FOR BASTING THE PIG

1/3 CUP PLUS 3 TABLESPOONS VIRGIN OLIVE OIL

1 SMALL BUNCH CILANTRO, STEMMED AND CHOPPED

1 SUCKLING PIG (12 TO 14 POUNDS)

ORANGE WEDGES AND CILANTRO SPRIGS, FOR GARNISH

SERVES 10

Fiesta!

345

Flamenco Fire

It was in Libertad 8, a tiny smoky neighborhood bar in Madrid, just off the graceful Art Nouveau Gran Vía that I had my first real encounter with the true spirit of flamenco. Not that it was anything more than drunken brothers, actors from Cádiz, and their black-clad philosophy-student niece, enjoying a night off. But I have seen nothing like it onstage: no frilly skirts, no rattle of the castanets, no dramatic stamping of the heels. One of the brothers suddenly broke out in a chant (which the Spanish call *cante jondo*, "deep song"), haunting and strange, a lone, pained monologue punctuated by the perfectly placed *castañeteos* ("snaps of the fingers"), and the nervous clapping of cupped hands. The niece made a few *pasos*, the brothers shouted something, and that was it. But it was astounding in its melancholy force, the seemingly formless improvisation so amazingly combined with the intricacy and control of its rhythms. The experience was heart-wrenching—exactly the effect a true flamenco performance is designed to achieve, for it expects an intense emotional response from the audience, a response that is actually inscribed into the texture of the music, and has a name—*duende*.

North African, Pakistani, Indian, Jewish, and Arab influences, among others, mingled together to create flamenco, one of the most idiosyncratic and powerful musical forms in the world. Perhaps it was the Gypsies who brought this strange, tragic music to southern Spain in the fifteenth century. Perhaps not. But it was certainly the Gypsy clans who perfected and preserved the tradition in Spain. The origin of the name is just as ambiguous. It could be derived from the name given to the Spanish Jews who escaped the Inquisition and settled in Flanders; or it might be a corruption of the Arab phrase *felag mengu*, "fugitive peasant."

The music was traditionally performed on the streets at town fiestas, at private parties, and in small bars, as well as in flamenco clubs called *tablaos*. The classic flamenco sound is a duet between a singer (and often dancers) and the spontaneous, improvising sound of the guitar, which controls the rhythmic structure of each piece, and is allowed brief solos during the pauses in the songs. The atmosphere is created by the *paleo*, an audience participation which consists of clapping, finger-snapping, and shouting at the right moment in the song. In a great flamenco performance there is always room for improvisation, which is usually determined by the mood set by the audience.

Flamenco had its heyday in the nineteenth century. In this century, especially during the rule of Franco, true flamenco—aside from the kitsch tourist version that (along with mushy *paella*), became an official tourist emblem of Spain—went into a decline. Its revival as a widely popular music form dates back to the 1950s, and owes its success to the emergence of *nuevo flamenco*, a genre that blends the classic style with other popular influences, such as rumba, salsa, jazz, rock, and blues. This commercial success created a renewed interest in the authentic sounds, and you are likely to see young performers today returning to flamenco's classic roots.

Venezuelan Christmas Ham Bread

(PAN DE JAMÓN)

Although probably few people outside of Venezuela have heard of, let alone tasted, *pan de jamón*, the *Venezolanos* consider it their national contribution to the culinary world. *Pan de jamón* is certainly a handsome bread—a huge loaf that can easily feed ten, stuffed with a colorful sweet and piquant mixture of smoked ham, raisins, and sliced olives. One legend credits its invention to an Italian immigrant baker, one Pietrolucchio Pancaldi, in the 1940s. Pietrolucchio was known to drink one too many, and when intoxicated, he would go back to the bakery late at night and experiment with various breads. Once, around Christmastime, he returned from a bar in an especially creative mood and started a traditional Italian ham roll, except this one was supposed to be of particularly enormous proportions. In the middle of it, he ran out of ham. He reached for the jar of olives, and when they were finished too, he began adding goodies normally reserved for his famous *pannetone*: raisins, candied fruit, and nuts. When he tasted the results, he didn't care for the nuts and candied fruit but the general idea pleased him. News of his new invention spread all over Caracas, and the bread became a holiday pièce de résistance.

Since I discovered *pan de jamón* in a tiny Venezuelan restaurant in New York, I bring it to all the Christmas parties I attend—much to everybody's delight.

(continued)

1¼ CUPS LUKEWARM MILK (110 TO 115
    DEGREES F.)
1½ TABLESPOONS SUGAR
1 PACKAGE ACTIVE DRY YEAST (ABOUT
    2¼ TEASPOONS)
4½ CUPS ALL-PURPOSE FLOUR, PLUS MORE AS
    NEEDED
7 TABLESPOONS BUTTER, MELTED
2 LARGE EGGS, BEATEN
2 TEASPOONS SALT
¾ CUP DARK RAISINS
¾ CUP WHITE RAISINS
½ POUND DOMESTIC PROSCIUTTO, SLICED
1 CUP SLICED PIMIENTO-STUFFED OLIVES
1 EGG YOLK, BEATEN WITH 1 TEASPOON MILK,
    FOR THE EGG WASH

1. In a large bowl, combine the milk, sugar, and yeast. Stir and let stand until foamy, about 5 minutes. Whisk in 1 cup of the flour and set this sponge to rise in a warm place for about 1 hour.

2. Whisk in 4 tablespoons of the butter, the eggs, and the salt. Add 2 cups of the flour and mix well. Continue to add flour, mixing well after each addition with a wooden spoon, until you have soft, slightly sticky dough. Transfer the dough to a lightly floured work surface and knead until it is smooth and elastic, about 8 minutes, kneading in more flour if the dough is still sticky.

3. Shape the dough into a ball and place it in a large buttered bowl. Turn to coat it with the butter, cover it loosely with plastic wrap, and let it rise in a warm, draft-free place until doubled in bulk, about 1 hour.

4. In a large bowl, soak the raisins in hot water to cover until plump, about 15 minutes. Drain well.

5. On a lightly floured surface, roll out the dough into an 18- by 14-inch rectangle.

6. Brush the rectangle all over with the remaining melted butter. Layer the entire surface evenly with the sliced ham. Sprinkle evenly with the raisins and olives. Starting on the long side, roll it up, jelly-roll style, into a log. Carefully transfer the bread, seam side down, to a large, lightly buttered baking sheet. Cover it with a clean kitchen towel and let it rest for 15 minutes.

7. Preheat the oven to 350 degrees F.

8. Brush the bread with the egg wash and bake until golden brown, about 45 minutes to 1 hour. Remove from the oven, cover with a damp kitchen towel and let cool for about 15 minutes.

SERVES 10

Christmas Baked Fish

(BESUGO AL HORNO DE NOCHEBUENA)

Baked *besugo* (porgy), associated with St. Peter in Iberian Catholic mythology, is one of the most ritualistic offerings of the Christmas Eve supper in many parts of Spain, especially Madrid. I suggest substituting bass or red snapper. Christmas Eve Red Cabbage (page 353) is the customary accompaniment.

2 SEA BASS OR RED SNAPPER (ABOUT 2 POUNDS EACH), CLEANED BUT WITH THE HEAD AND TAIL LEFT ON
1 TEASPOON COARSE (KOSHER) SALT
2 TABLESPOONS CRACKED BLACK PEPPERCORNS
5 TABLESPOONS FRESHLY SQUEEZED LEMON JUICE
1 SMALL DRIED CHILE, SEEDED
5 TABLESPOONS VIRGIN OLIVE OIL
1 LARGE ONION, THINLY SLICED
4 LARGE CLOVES GARLIC, CHOPPED
2 TABLESPOONS FRESHLY CHOPPED FLAT-LEAF PARSLEY, PLUS MORE FOR GARNISH
1/2 CUP DRY WHITE WINE
1/3 CUP FISH STOCK (PAGE 371) OR WATER

1. Rub the fish with 1/2 teaspoon of the salt, the pepper, and 2 tablespoons of the lemon juice, refrigerate for 30 minutes. Bring to room temperature before roasting.

2. Soak the chile in hot water to cover for 20 minutes. Drain and chop fine.

3. Preheat the oven to 400 degrees F.

4. In a large ovenproof skillet or shallow, ovenproof earthenware dish, heat 3 tablespoons of the oil over medium heat. Add the onion and cook, stirring, until wilted, about 5 minutes. Push the onion to the side of the skillet and sear the fish on both sides, one at a time, for about 1 minute on each side.

5. Place both fish in the skillet, side by side on top of the onion, and bake in the oven for 10 minutes.

(continued)

6. While the fish is baking, in a mortar and pestle pound the chile, garlic, parsley, and the remaining ½ teaspoon of the salt to a paste. Work in the remaining 2 tablespoons of the oil and 2 tablespoons of the wine.

7. Turn the fish on the other side and spread the pounded mixture on the fish. Bake until the fish is browned on top and the flesh flakes easily when tested with a fork, about 15 minutes.

8. Remove the fish from the oven and carefully transfer it to a serving platter. Cover loosely with foil. To the skillet add the remaning lemon juice, wine, and the fish stock and reduce over high heat for 5 minutes.

9. Pour the sauce over the fish and sprinkle with parsley.

SERVES 6 AS A FIRST COURSE, OR 4 AS A MAIN COURSE

![Market, Barcelona, Spain]

Market, Barcelona, Spain.

Lenten Salt Cod and Raisin Empanada

(EMPANADA DE BACALAO DE SEMANA SANTA)

Bacalao (salt cod) is a staple in Latin cooking, but at no time does it enjoy so much of the spotlight as during Lent, when eating meat is strictly forbidden. In many regions of Spain, Portugal, and Latin America, some kind of salt cod pie features in the holy week festivities (*semana santa*). I particularly like this Galician empanada, a large rectangular pie with a filling of sweet, slowly sautéed onions and peppers, raisins, olives, and salt cod. The salt cod has to soak overnight or longer, so start ahead.

1. Rinse the salt cod and pat it completely dry with paper towels. Shred the salt cod by hand into bite-size pieces.

2. In a large skillet, heat the oil over low heat. Add the onions and garlic and cook until the onion wilts, about 5 minutes. Add the bell pepper, tomatoes, bay leaf, and paprika, and sauté, stirring occasionally, until the vegetables are soft and sweet, about 20 minutes. Transfer the vegetables to a colander set over a bowl, and allow the oil to drain for about 10 minutes. Reserve the oil.

(continued)

¾ POUND BONELESS SALT COD (PREFERABLY CENTER-CUT), SOAKED AS DIRECTED ON PAGE 377

½ CUP FRUITY VIRGIN OLIVE OIL, PREFERABLY SPANISH

2 CUPS THINLY SLICED ONIONS

3 CLOVES GARLIC, MINCED

1 LARGE RED BELL PEPPER, CORED, SEEDED, AND SLICED

4 TO 5 CANNED TOMATOES, DRAINED AND FINELY CHOPPED

1 SMALL BAY LEAF, CRUMBLED

2 TEASPOONS GOOD SMOKY MILD PAPRIKA, PREFERABLY SPANISH

¼ CUP DRY WHITE WINE

5 TABLESPOONS WHITE RAISINS

½ CUP SLICED WELL-DRAINED PIMIENTO-STUFFED OLIVES

SALT, AS NEEDED

1 RECIPE QUEEN OF EMPANADA DOUGH (PAGE 52)

3 TABLESPOONS MINCED FLAT-LEAF PARSLEY

1 LARGE EGG YOLK, MIXED WITH 1 TEASPOON MILK, FOR THE EGG WASH

3. Heat the wine in a nonreactive saucepan. Off the heat, add the raisins and let them soak in the wine while you prepare the next step.

4. In a large skillet, heat 3 tablespoons of the oil drained from the vegetables over low heat (discarding the rest of the oil). Add the salt cod and sauté slowly, gently breaking it up with a fork, until cooked through and flaky, about 7 minutes.

5. Transfer the drained vegetables to a large bowl and, with two forks, gently stir in the salt cod. Add the raisins and their soaking liquid, the olives, and salt if needed. Let the filling cool.

6. Preheat the oven to 350 degrees F.

7. On a lightly floured surface, roll out half the empanada dough to a 13- by 9-inch rectangle. Drape it over a rolling pin and transfer it to a large buttered baking sheet. Spread the filling evenly over the dough and sprinkle it with parsley. Roll out another rectangle, roughly the same dimensions, from the other half of the dough. Drape it over a rolling pin and transfer it to cover the filling. Fold about $^1/_2$ inch of the edge upward and pinch to close. Press with the tines of a fork to seal. With the tip of a small knife, make several slits in the pastry to allow the steam to escape. Brush the dough with the egg wash.

8. Bake the empanada in the middle of the oven until the top is golden brown, about 45 minutes. Remove from the oven, cover with a damp kitchen towel, and let rest for 15 minutes. Serve warm or at room temperature, cut into squares.

SERVES 10

Christmas Eve Red Cabbage with Apples and Pine Nuts

(LOMBARDA)

This red cabbage, braised with serrano ham and apples, is the traditional Madrileño Christmas Eve dish to accompany the Christmas Baked Fish (page 349). The recipe is from the Christmas menu of Chef Francisco Rubio of the Palacio Hotel in Madrid.

1. In a small skillet, toast the pine nuts over medium heat, stirring frequently, until golden, about 3 to 5 minutes. Set aside.

2. In a large, heavy saucepan, heat the oil over medium heat. Add the ham and onion, and cook, stirring, until the onion is soft, about 7 minutes. Add the cabbage and apple and sauté, stirring, for 5 minutes. Stir in the broth and simmer, covered, over low heat, until the cabbage is soft, 35 to 40 minutes, adding more broth, a little at a time, if the mixture looks dry.

3. Stir in the vinegar and sugar, season with salt and pepper, and cook for 5 more minutes. Transfer to a serving bowl and sprinkle with the parsley and pine nuts.

3 TABLESPOONS PINE NUTS

2 TABLESPOONS OLIVE OIL

⅓ CUP DICED SERRANO HAM OR PROSCIUTTO

1 MEDIUM ONION, FINELY CHOPPED

ONE 2-POUND RED CABBAGE, CHOPPED

1 LARGE TART GREEN APPLE, PEELED, CORED, AND CHOPPED

⅓ CUP CHICKEN STOCK (PAGE 372), CANNED LOWER-SALT BROTH OR WATER, OR MORE AS NEEDED

1 TABLESPOON BEST-QUALITY RED WINE VINEGAR

LARGE PINCH OF SUGAR

SALT AND FRESHLY GROUND BLACK PEPPER, TO TASTE

FINELY CHOPPED FLAT-LEAF PARSLEY, FOR GARNISH

SERVES 4 TO 6

Stuffed Pheasant with Pomegranate Sauce

(FAISANA RELLENA CON SALSA DE GRANADA)

You will love this special-occasion Spanish dish, with its intriguing blend of Moorish and French influences. It's a roast pheasant stuffed with a mixture of pistachios, ground veal, dark grapes, wild mushrooms, and muscatel, served in a refreshing tart and sweet pomegranate and red wine sauce. Try to choose small juicy pomegranates which have very red seeds. The dish can also be prepared with Rock Cornish hens. You will need four 1¼-pound hens, instead of the two pheasants, and they should roast for about 35 to 40 minutes at 350 degrees F.

STUFFING

4 TABLESPOONS UNSALTED BUTTER

1½ CUPS COARSELY CHOPPED ONIONS

2 SMALL CARROTS, PEELED AND FINELY DICED

1 SMALL STALK CELERY, DICED

4 OUNCES FRESH SHIITAKE MUSHROOMS, STEMMED AND SLICED

12 OUNCES LEAN GROUND VEAL

¼ CUP MUSCATEL WINE

¼ CUP BRANDY

1½ CUPS DARK SEEDLESS GRAPES, EACH GRAPE HALVED LENGTHWISE

⅔ CUP UNSALTED PISTACHIO NUTS, LIGHTLY TOASTED

1 LARGE EGG, BEATEN

SALT AND FRESHLY GROUND BLACK PEPPER, TO TASTE

3 TABLESPOONS MINCED FLAT-LEAF PARSLEY

(continued)

1. To make the stuffing: In a large skillet, melt the butter over medium heat. Add the onions, carrots, celery, and mushrooms and sauté, stirring, until the vegetables are soft, about 10 minutes. Raise the heat to high and add the veal. Cook, breaking it up with a fork, until no longer pink, about 5 minutes. If the veal throws off too much liquid, tilt the skillet and pour it off. Add the muscatel and brandy and reduce over high heat for 5 minutes.

2. Transfer the stuffing to a bowl and let it cool a little. Stir in all the remaining stuffing ingredients.

3. Preheat the oven to 425 degrees F.

4. Rub the pheasants inside and out with salt and pepper. Divide the stuffing in half and place half in each pheasant's cavity. Truss with trussing skewers. Place the pheasants on a rack in a large roasting pan and pour the wine and port into the pan. Roast for 10 minutes.

5. Reduce the oven temperature to 350 degrees. Dip two pieces of cheesecloth into the melted butter and drape them over the pheasants. Continue roasting the pheasants, basting twice with the pan juices, for 30 minutes, until the juices run clear. The pheasants will be cooked to medium. Transfer them to a carving board and let them stand for 15 minutes, covered loosely with foil.

6. Transfer the pan juices to a medium saucepan and add the pomegranate seeds, sugar, and cinnamon stick. Cook over medium heat, crushing the seeds with the back of a fork, for 10 minutes. Strain through a fine strainer, pressing hard on the solids to extract all the juices from the pomegranate seeds. Discard the solids, return the liquid to the saucepan and cook over high heat until the mixture is reduced by one third, about 7 minutes.

7. Scoop out the stuffing into a serving bowl. Carve the pheasants, and serve, accompanied by the sauce.

2 PHEASANTS (ABOUT 2½ POUNDS EACH), WELL RINSED AND PATTED DRY

SALT AND FRESHLY GROUND BLACK PEPPER, TO TASTE

1½ CUPS FRUITY DEEP-FLAVORED DRY RED WINE

¼ CUP PORT WINE

8 TABLESPOONS (1 STICK) UNSALTED BUTTER, MELTED

3 CUPS POMEGRANATE SEEDS (FROM ABOUT 4 TO 5 SMALL POMEGRANATES)

1 TO 2 TEASPOONS SUGAR, OR MORE TO TASTE

ONE 1-INCH PIECE CINNAMON STICK

SUGAR TO TASTE, DEPENDING ON THE TARTNESS OF THE POMEGRANATES

SERVES 6

Dreams

(S O N H O S)

Sonhos, or dreams, are light puffy Portuguese doughnuts traditionally served at holiday time. While spiced sugar syrup is a classic accompaniment to these, Mrs. Silvina Barroso, who gave me this recipe, suggests the following dried apricot sauce. For an even more formal presentation, she serves the dreams with the apricot sauce and a crème anglais.

½ CUP WATER

½ CUP MILK

4 TABLESPOONS UNSALTED BUTTER

1 TABLESPOON GRATED LEMON ZEST

1 TEASPOON VANILLA EXTRACT

PINCH OF SALT

1 CUP ALL-PURPOSE FLOUR

4 LARGE EGGS

LIGHT OLIVE OIL, FOR DEEP FRYING THE DREAMS

⅓ CUP SUGAR

2 TEASPOONS GROUND CINNAMON

APRICOT SAUCE (RECIPE FOLLOWS)

1. In a heavy, medium-size saucepan, bring the water, milk, and butter to a boil over medium-low heat with the lemon zest, vanilla, and salt. Off the heat, vigorously stir in the flour. Return the pan to the heat and cook over low heat, stirring, until the mixture starts pulling away from the bottom of the saucepan, about 2 minutes.

2. Remove from the heat and, using an electric mixer, beat in the eggs, one by one, beating well after each addition. Don't worry if the mixture looks curdled.

3. Line a large baking sheet with a double layer of paper towels. In a deep fryer, a large skillet, or a wok, heat 2 inches of oil to 360 degrees F. over medium-high heat. The oil is ready when a piece of batter dropped in it sizzles and puffs up. Reduce the heat to medium-low. Between two soup spoons, shape about ¾ tablespoon of the mixture into balls as round as possible. Drop the shaped balls into the hot oil in batches of six, and fry them until puffed and golden brown on all sides, about 4 to 5 minutes. It is important to keep the oil at the correct temperature: If it is too cool, the doughnuts won't puff. If it is too hot, they will brown too

quickly but won't be cooked through. Keep watching and regulating the heat; you'll get it right after one or two batches. Transfer the fried doughnuts to drain on the paper towels. Repeat with the rest of the dough, keeping the finished doughnuts warm in a low oven.

4. Mix the sugar and cinnamon and spread it on a plate. Roll the warm *sonhos* in the mixture and serve at once, with the warm Apricot Sauce.

MAKES 18 TO 20 DREAMS

Apricot Sauce

1. In a medium saucepan, combine the apricots, water, and sugar and bring to a boil, stirring to dissolve the sugar. Simmer over low heat until the apricots are soft, about 15 minutes.

2. Puree the apricots with their liquid in a food processor until smooth. Return to the heat, add the brandy, lemon juice, and more sugar, if desired, and heat for 2 to 3 minutes. Cool to warm to serve with the *sonhos*.

³/₄ CUP CHOPPED DRIED APRICOTS, PREFERABLY CALIFORNIA

2¹/₂ CUPS WATER

2 TABLESPOONS SUGAR, OR MORE TO TASTE

1 TABLESPOON BRANDY

1 TABLESPOON FRESH LEMON JUICE

MAKES ABOUT 2 ¹/₂ CUPS

Spanish Crullers

(C H U R R O S)

One of the enchantments of being in Spain is an early morning (or late night, if you're on the party circuit) plate of these famous Spanish crullers dipped into a cup of thick, sweet Spanish chocolate. But *churros* are also the star attraction at *verbenas* (various saint's days), which are celebrated with boisterous street fairs, running of the bulls, religious processions, and block parties. Serve the crullers with hot chocolate, if you wish.

1 CUP WATER
8 TABLESPOONS (1 STICK) UNSALTED BUTTER,
    CUT INTO PIECES
ZEST OF 1 LEMON, IN 1 PIECE
PINCH OF SALT
1 1/2 CUPS FLOUR
VEGETABLE OIL, FOR DEEP FRYING THE *CHURROS*
SUGAR, FOR SPRINKLING THE *CHURROS*

1. In a medium-size, heavy saucepan, combine the water, butter, lemon zest, and salt, and bring to a boil over medium heat.

2. Remove the lemon zest, and, with the pan still on the heat, immediately add the flour, all at once, stirring vigorously with a wooden spoon until the mixture is completely smooth. Transfer it to a large bowl.

3. Line a large baking sheet with a double layer of paper towels. In a deep fryer, a large skillet, or a wok, heat 2 inches of oil to 375 degrees F. over medium-high heat. The oil is ready when a piece of dough dropped into it sizzles and puffs up. Place about 1/2 cup of the dough in a sturdy pastry bag fitted with a 1/2-inch star tip. Pipe out several 4- to 5-inch-long ribbons directly into the oil (be very careful; the oil might splatter). Reduce the heat to medium-low and fry the *churros* until golden brown, turning once, about 4 minutes total. It is important to keep the oil at the correct temperature: If it is too cool, the *churros* won't puff up. If it is too hot, they will brown too quickly but won't be cooked through. Keep watching and regulating the

heat; you'll get it right after one or two batches. Transfer the fried *churros* to drain on the paper towels. Repeat with the rest of the dough, keeping the finished *churros* warm in a low oven.

4. Sprinkle the warm *churros* generously with sugar and serve.

MAKES ABOUT 18 *CHURROS*

Cheeses, Pontevedra Market, Spain.

Christmas French Toast

(TORRIJAS)

Few people revere bread as do the Spaniards. For simple occasions, yesterday's bread might be turned into a gazpacho or garlic soup, while at holiday times it's soaked in wine or milk, dipped into beaten egg, fried in olive oil, and sprinkled with generous amounts of cinnamon and sugar. Few desserts are more humble, but I promise you, there isn't a household in Spain at Easter or Christmas that's not enjoying *torrijas*—either as a dessert or as an afternoon snack with a cup of hot chocolate. The *torrijas* have to be fried in very hot oil so that they are soft and pillowy inside and nice and golden on the outside. As is traditional in some Spanish households, sweetened red or white wine can be used instead of the milk, and you can serve the *torrijas* accompanied by Castilian Christmas Compote (page 363) or stewed figs or prunes.

3 CUPS MILK

¾ CUP SUGAR, PLUS MORE FOR SPRINKLING THE *TORRIJAS*

ZEST OF 1 LEMON

3 TABLESPOONS ANISE-FLAVORED LIQUEUR (OPTIONAL)

12 SLICES DAY-OLD ITALIAN BREAD (¾ INCHES THICK AND ABOUT 3 INCHES IN DIAMETER)

3 LARGE EGGS

LIGHT OLIVE OIL, FOR DEEP FRYING

GROUND CINNAMON, FOR SPRINKLING THE *TORRIJAS*

1. In a medium saucepan, bring the milk to a boil with the ¾ cup sugar, lemon zest, and liqueur. Let stand until cool and strain into a shallow dish that will accommodate all the bread slices in one layer.

2. Add the bread to the milk and soak it for 2 minutes. Turn it over and soak for 2 more minutes.

3. Beat the eggs in a large, shallow bowl.

4. In a large skillet, heat 1 inch of oil over medium heat to 375 degrees F. Working in batches, dip the bread slices into the beaten egg and fry them until golden brown, about 3 minutes per side. Transfer the finished batches to drain on paper towels.

5. Place the *torrijas* on a serving platter and sprinkle on both sides with sugar and cinnamon. Serve warm.

SERVES 6

Christmas Eve Pumpkin Pudding

(BUDÍN DE CALABAZA DE NOCHEBUENA)

For Christmas Eve, Francisco Rubio, chef at the fabled turn-of-the-century Palacio Hotel in Madrid, prides himself on preparing a lavish feast. For dessert he cooks up this pumpkin flan generously spiked with brandy and Grand Marnier.

1 POUND PUMPKIN OR WINTER SQUASH, PEELED
   AND CUT INTO LARGE CHUNKS
3 TABLESPOONS TIGHTLY PACKED BROWN SUGAR
$^1/_2$ CUP BRANDY
$^1/_3$ CUP GRAND MARNIER
$3^1/_2$ CUPS HALF AND HALF
$^3/_4$ CUP GRANULATED SUGAR
7 LARGE EGGS
2 TEASPOONS GROUND CINNAMON
$^1/_2$ TEASPOON GROUND CARDAMOM
1 TEASPOON VANILLA EXTRACT
WHIPPED CREAM, FOR SERVING, OPTIONAL

1. Preheat the oven to 375 degrees F. Place the pumpkin in a baking dish, sprinkle it with the brown sugar, and pour the brandy and Grand Marnier over it. Cover with foil and bake, tossing the pieces occasionally, until the pumpkin is soft, 50 minutes or more. When cool enough to handle, puree the pumpkin in a blender with 1 cup of the half and half until smooth. Leave the oven on but reduce the temperature to 350 degrees.

2. In a large mixing bowl, whisk together the granulated sugar, the remaining half and half, and eggs. Stir in the pumpkin puree, cinnamon, cardamom, and vanilla, and stir until the mixture is smooth.

3. Pour the mixture into a 6- to 7-cup soufflé dish. Place the soufflé dish in a deep baking pan and add enough hot water to the outer pan to reach halfway up the sides of the soufflé dish. Carefully place the pan in the center of the oven and bake until the pudding looks set, about $1^1/_2$ hours.

4. Serve warm or cool, with whipped cream if desired.

SERVES 8 TO 10

Castilian Christmas Compote

(COMPOTA CASTELLANA NAVIDEÑA)

This is a typical family recipe—passed on to me by Señora Zulema Martín from Burgos—for a delicious spiced compote of dried and fresh fruit, spiked with red wine and cognac, much enjoyed in Castile during Christmastime. The better the wine, the more delicious the compote. Try a good Rioja or better, a Duero, and buy good dried fruit at a Middle Eastern shop or a health food store.

In a large, nonreactive saucepan, bring the wine to a boil with the sugar, cloves, and cinnamon stick, stirring to dissolve the sugar. Add all the fruit and simmer, covered, over low heat until soft, 25 to 30 minutes. Stir in the cognac and cook for another 5 minutes. Chill the compote until ready to serve.

4 CUPS GOOD FRUITY DRY RED WINE
$3/4$ CUP SUGAR, OR MORE TO TASTE
4 CLOVES
TWO 3-INCH CINNAMON STICKS
$1 1/2$ CUPS DRIED PEACHES
$3/4$ CUP DARK RAISINS
$1 1/2$ CUPS PITTED DRIED CHERRIES (SUCH AS MICHIGAN SOUR)
2 SMALL APPLES, PEELED, CORED, AND CUT INTO $1 1/2$-INCH CHUNKS
2 SMALL PEARS, PEELED, CORED, AND CUT INTO $1 1/2$ INCH CHUNKS
$1/3$ CUP COGNAC

SERVES 6

Three Kings' Day in Spain

For Spanish children, winter festivities are certainly not over on Christmas Day. In fact, Christmas—celebrated with a mass, family visits, and an enormous meal—marks only the beginning of a fortnight of merrymaking in anticipation of the real event, Three Kings' Day, celebrated on the night of January 6. While most Catholic cultures observe this date (the Epiphany) in one way or another, Spain is unique in that the role of gift-giving is assigned not to Santa or Papa Noel on Christmas Eve, but to the Three Kings or *tres reyes*.

The occasion is marked with a splendid parade, the culmination of which is the appearance of the Three Magi—the elderly Melchior with a long white beard, the more sprightly Gaspar, and the make-believe Moor Balthazar, sporting a turban—riding on camels or horseback, clothed in magnificently colorful robes, with crowns on their heads. That night the kings will make house visits, delivering presents for the children, who, in turn, leave drinks and *turrón* (nougat) for the eagerly awaited guests, as well as straw and water for their camels and horses.

The traditional Three Kings' sweet is *roscón de reyes*, a spectacular sugar-coated wreath with a secret. The secret is a dried bean (or a little doll), baked into the bread. When everyone is assembled, the *roscón* is cut into as many pieces as there are guests, then the platter is covered with a napkin and spun around, so that everyone gets to choose a piece at random. The lucky person who finds the bean is crowned "Bean King" for the coming year.

This curious custom dates back to ancient Roman times. During winter celebrations, known as Saturnalias, the Romans baked a round cake that included figs, honey, and dates. Inside a bean was hidden—to which the Romans attributed magical and erotic powers. Pieces of the cake were handed out to slaves and plebeians, and the lucky person who found the bean was declared "king of kings," and got to exercise unlimited power for the duration of the festivities.

Three Kings' Wreath

(ROSCÓN DE REYES)

1. In a large bowl, combine the yeast, 1 teaspoon of the sugar, and the milk. Let the mixture stand until foamy, about 5 minutes. With a sturdy wire whisk, whisk in 2 cups of the flour and stir until smooth. Cover the bowl with plastic wrap and let it stand in a warm draft-free place until the sponge has doubled in bulk, about 1 hour.

2. While the sponge is rising, heat the brandy until very hot in a medium-size saucepan over medium heat. Off the heat, add the raisins and let them soak until plump, about 30 minutes. Drain the raisins, reserving the soaking liquid. Toss the raisins lightly with some flour.

3. In a large bowl, with an electric beater, beat the butter with the remaining ²/₃ cup sugar until light and fluffy. Beat in the eggs, one by one, and then stir in the reserved brandy, the orange flower water, and the orange and lemon zests.

4. Stir the butter mixture, raisins, and 1 cup of the candied fruit into the risen sponge. Sift the remaining flour with the salt and stir it into the sponge, ¹/₂ cup at a time, until you have a soft, workable dough. Transfer the dough to a lightly floured surface and knead until smooth and elastic, about 7 minutes, adding more flour if the dough feels sticky. Knead in the figurine or bean.

(continued)

2 PACKAGES ACTIVE DRY YEAST

1 TEASPOON SUGAR PLUS ²/₃ CUP

1¹/₂ CUPS LUKEWARM MILK (110 TO 115 DEGREES F.)

5¹/₂ CUPS UNBLEACHED ALL-PURPOSE FLOUR, PLUS MORE AS NEEDED

¹/₂ CUP BRANDY

1 CUP DARK RAISINS

9 TABLESPOONS UNSALTED BUTTER, AT ROOM TEMPERATURE

3 LARGE EGGS

1 TABLESPOON ORANGE FLOWER WATER (AVAILABLE AT GOURMET GROCERIES AND MIDDLE EASTERN MARKETS)

2 TEASPOONS GRATED ORANGE ZEST

2 TEASPOONS GRATED LEMON ZEST

1 CUP BEST-QUALITY CANDIED FRUIT, PLUS ABOUT ²/₃ CUP FOR DECORATING THE CAKE

1 TEASPOON SALT

SMALL FIGURINE OR DOLL, BEAN, OR COIN

1 LARGE EGG YOLK, BEATEN WITH 1 TEASPOON MILK, FOR THE EGG WASH

¹/₄ CUP SLIVERED ALMONDS

5. Shape the dough into a ball and place it in a large well-buttered bowl. Turn to coat with the butter, cover it loosely with plastic wrap and let it stand in a warm, draft-free place until doubled in bulk, about $1^{1}/_{2}$ hours.

6. Punch the dough down, knead it briefly, cover it with plastic wrap, and let it rest for 10 minutes. Shape the dough into a log about 32 inches long and 4 inches thick. Shape the log into a ring and press the edges together to seal them. Carefully transfer the dough to a buttered baking sheet, cover it with a clean kitchen towel, and let it rest for 15 minutes.

7. Preheat the oven to 375 degrees F.

8. Brush the dough all over with the egg wash and decorate the top with candied fruit and slivered almonds, pressing them lightly into the dough. Place it in the middle of the oven and bake until golden brown, about 35 to 40 minutes. If the ring darkens too quickly, cover it loosely with foil.

9. Remove from the oven and cool on a rack for 10 minutes. To serve, make sure to cut as many pieces of the *roscón*, as there are guests, and tell everyone to look out for the suprise.

SERVES 10 TO 12

Brandied Prunes

(C I R U E L A S   A L   C O Ñ A C)

In Spain, Christmas is the time to exchange lavish gift baskets, full of traditional homemade or boutique-bought food conserves. Prunes in cognac is one such holiday favorite. They are used to fill pies and tarts, or simply as a topping for vanilla ice cream or custards. They make a wonderful gift, and one that is also very simple to prepare. The only trick (shared with me by the Basque cooking teacher Luis Irizar) is to bake the prunes to open their pores before packing them into the brandy-filled jars. Unlike the sweetened American brandied fruit, these prunes contain no sugar. Using a good cognac will make the gift truly luxurious.

3½ TO 4 CUPS PITTED PRUNES, PREFERABLY ORGANIC
ABOUT 2 CUPS GOOD BRANDY OR COGNAC

1. Preheat the oven to 350 degrees F.

2. Spread the prunes on a baking sheet and bake for 10 minutes.

3. Pack the prunes tightly into a 1-quart mason-type jar and shake the jar to compress the prunes. Pour enough brandy into the jar to cover the prunes completely. If you plan to keep the prunes without opening them for more than 2 months, sterilize the jar before filling it. Otherwise, cover tightly, and store on a the lowest shelf of the refrigerator. The prunes are ready to eat after 2 to 3 days.

MAKES ONE 1-QUART JAR

Basic
Recipes

Indio Amazónico
(Amazon Indian)
Botánica, Jackson
Heights, New York.

Fish Stock

(CALDO DE PESCADO)

To make the fish stock richer, I like to use whole small sweet fish, such as smelts, in addition to the fish trimmings. Whenever I have shrimp and lobster shells, I save and freeze them to add to my fish stock later on.

1. Melt the butter in a heavy soup pot over medium heat. Add the onion, garlic, carrots, chile, fish trimmings, and fish. Stir, cover, and steam for about 7 minutes, shaking the pot from time to time.

2. Add all the remaining ingredients and bring to a boil. Skim off the foam as it rises to the top. Reduce the heat to low, cover, and simmer for 20 minutes.

3. Strain through a fine sieve, pressing on the solids with the back of a spoon to extract as much liquid as possible. Cool and refrigerate the stock until ready to use. It will keep for 3 to 4 days in the refrigerator. Freeze it for longer storage.

MAKES ABOUT 9 CUPS

2½ TABLESPOONS UNSALTED BUTTER

1 CUP SLICED ONION

7 CLOVES GARLIC, SLICED

2 CARROTS, DICED

1 LONG GREEN CHILE, SUCH AS ANAHEIM, CUT IN HALF LENGTHWISE AND SEEDED, OPTIONAL

2 POUNDS FISH TRIMMINGS, SUCH AS HEADS, TAILS, AND CARCASSES, WELL RINSED

1 POUND INEXPENSIVE SMALL FISH, SUCH AS SMELTS, UNSKINNED, GILLS REMOVED

10 CUPS WATER

½ CUP DRY WHITE WINE

1 TABLESPOON FRESHLY SQUEEZED LEMON JUICE

1 BUNCH PARSLEY, TIED

1 TEASPOON BLACK PEPPERCORNS, LIGHTLY CRUSHED

SALT, TO TASTE

Market, Barcelona, Spain.

Chicken Stock

(C A L D O   D E   P O L L O)

Adding turkey wings and giblets to the chicken, or using only turkey, will give you a stronger, more savory stock, excellent for many one-dish soups and stews in this book.

3 TO 4 POUNDS CHICKEN BACKS, NECKS, AND
   WINGS, OR TURKEY WINGS, OR A
   COMBINATION, WELL RINSED

3 QUARTS WATER

SALT, TO TASTE

1 CARROT, HALVED

2 MEDIUM ONIONS, UNPEELED AND QUARTERED

1 TURNIP, PEELED AND QUARTERED

1 BUNCH PARSLEY, TIED

8 UNPEELED CLOVES GARLIC, SMASHED

2 TEASPOONS BLACK PEPPERCORNS, LIGHTLY
   CRUSHED

1 BAY LEAF

1 SPRIG FRESH OR DRIED OREGANO, OPTIONAL

1. Place the chicken pieces and water in a large soup pot and bring to a boil. Skim off the foam as it rises to the surface.

2. Add all the remaining ingredients, reduce the heat to low, cover, and simmer, skimming occasionally, for 2 hours.

3. Strain the stock, cool, and refrigerate. Degrease the stock before using it. It will keep for 3 to 4 days in the refrigerator. Freeze it for longer storage.

MAKES ABOUT 2 QUARTS

Beef Stock

(CALDO DE CARNE)

Oxtails give this stock a rich unctuousness. I rarely roast the bones for making stock, but in this case, roasting the bones at 500 degrees F. for about an hour certainly does add depth. Also, if you plan to use the stock for one of the multi-ingredient Latin stews, try adding a ham hock—it will give the finished dish just the right, slightly smoky flavor.

1. Place the bones (roasted if you wish), oxtails, and water in a large soup pot and bring to a boil. Skim off the foam as it rises to the surface.

2. Add all the remaining ingredients, reduce the heat to low, cover, and simmer, skimming occasionally, for 3 hours.

3. Strain the stock, cool, and refrigerate. Degrease the stock before using it. It will keep for 3 to 4 days in the refrigerator. Freeze it for longer storage.

MAKES ABOUT 2 QUARTS

3 POUNDS BEEF STEWING BONES WITH MARROW, ROASTED IF DESIRED (SEE HEADNOTE)

2 POUNDS OXTAILS

3 QUARTS WATER

2 LEEKS, WELL RINSED AND HALVED LENGTHWISE

2 STALKS CELERY, WITH LEAVES, HALVED

2 PARSNIPS, PEELED AND HALVED

6 UNPEELED CLOVES GARLIC, SMASHED

2 SCALLIONS, SMASHED

1 SMALL BUNCH PARSLEY, TIED WITH KITCHEN STRING

4 CLOVES

1 TABLESPOON BLACK PEPPERCORNS

Basic Black Beans

Boiling a pot of beans is so simple a proposition that there's really no need to resort to cans. After experimenting with countless bean dishes, I have come to the conclusion that soaking them overnight or quick-soaking them in boiling water, is really a redundant step: The cooking time is only marginally shorter. Beans tend to vary quite considerably in quality from brand to brand, and the cooking time fluctuates accordingly. It also depends on the age of the beans. Of the easy-to-find brands, Goya is my favorite, producing tender cooked beans that still retain their shape. I start with 4 cups water per cup of beans, plus some additional cold water to add during cooking to prevent the beans from breaking and becoming mushy.

1 CUP BLACK TURTLE BEANS, OR MORE AS
   NEEDED, WELL RINSED AND PICKED OVER
4 CUPS WATER, PLUS MORE AS NEEDED
2 BAY LEAVES
6 UNPEELED CLOVES GARLIC, LIGHTLY SMASHED
SALT, TO TASTE

In a large saucepan, combine the beans, water, bay leaves, and garlic and bring to a boil, skimming. Reduce the heat to low, cover, and cook until the beans are very tender. This should take $1\frac{1}{2}$ to 2 hours, depending on the beans. Add about $\frac{1}{3}$ cup of cold water every 25 minutes or so. Add salt to taste in the last 5 minutes of cooking. Remove and discard the garlic and bay leaves before serving.

MAKES ABOUT $2\frac{1}{2}$ CUPS COOKED BEANS

Roasted Red Pepper Strips

(PARA ASAR PIMIENTOS ROJOS)

These can be used as a tasty, colorful garnish for many of the stews or vegetable dishes.

1. Preheat the broiler or prepare the coals for grilling. Grill as many peppers as you wish, about 3 inches away from the heat, turning them once, until charred and soft, about 15 minutes. Carefully transfer the peppers to a sturdy plastic bag. Close the bag tightly and wrap it in a kitchen towel. Let stand for 15 minutes. Remove the peppers from the bag and peel off the skins.

LARGE MEATY RED BELL PEPPERS, CORED AND SEEDED

2. Cut the peppers into $1/4$-inch-wide strips. They will keep in the refrigerator for up to 5 days. To keep for up to 10 days, cover the peppers with good virgin olive oil.

1 LARGE PEPPER WILL YIELD ABOUT 1 CUP
OF PEPPER STRIPS

Annatto Oil

(A C E I T E   D E   A C H I O T E)

Many Latin dishes are prepared with an appealing red-hued oil infused with annatto seeds. If you don't have any annatto oil on hand, it can be made quickly by infusing the desired amount of oil with annatto seeds as described below. The proportion is about $1\frac{1}{2}$ teaspoons of annatto seeds for each tablespoon of oil. Annatto seeds are available at all Latin groceries and corner *bodegas*, and in many supermarkets in areas with large Hispanic populations.

2 CUPS LIGHT OLIVE, PEANUT, OR CANOLA OIL
1 CUP ANNATTO SEEDS

In a medium skillet, heat the oil with the annatto seeds over medium-high heat for 5 minutes. Remove the oil from the heat and let it cool completely, about 25 minutes. Strain through a double layer of cheesecloth into a clean bottle. Store in a cool place. It will keep as long as any other oil.

MAKES 2 CUPS

Handling Salt Cod

(PARA PREPARAR EL BACALAO)

When reconstituted properly, salt cod is full of wonderful flavor and not at all salty. The only inconvenience is having to plan ahead, as it needs plenty of soaking time. It's hard to say exactly how much soaking time is needed, as it largely depends on the brand and the thickness of the cut. The minimum is 24 hours, though in my experience, 36 hours, or even two days, is more like it. I try to stick with the same brand and cut of salt cod, since after one or two experiences, I know how much time it will take to de-salt it. After 24 hours of soaking, break off and taste a little piece—if it tastes *very* salty, soak it some more.

Once soaked, salt cod can be drained, wiped thoroughly with paper towels, and frozen until ready to use. I don't like frozen salt cod for main dishes, but it's certainly fine for making puffs, croquettes, and for filling empanadas.

Many Latin cooks simmer the salt cod in water and/or milk before proceeding with a recipe. I find that if the cod is soaked properly this step isn't necessary unless a dish specifically calls for boiled cod. If cooking salt cod in liquid, make sure it never comes to a boil, otherwise the fish will get tough and stringy. If frying the salt cod (which I particularly like), do it in plenty of oil over low heat. Drain it on paper towels after frying. And if the recipe calls for shredding the salt cod, do so only by hand, as metal produces an unpleasant aftertaste.

(continued)

CENTER-CUT BONELESS SALT COD, PREFERABLY
¾ INCH THICK

1. Place the salt cod in a large nonmetallic bowl and cover it with cold water. Cover the bowl tightly with plastic wrap and soak the cod in the refrigerator for at least 24, but preferably 36 hours, changing water at least every 4 hours. After 24 hours, break off a small piece of salt cod and taste it for doneness. It shouldn't taste unbearably salty.

2. Remove the salt cod from the soaking liquid, gently pat it dry with paper towels, and, using tweezers, remove any bones that might have remained in the fish. The salt cod is now ready to use.

NOTE: If the salt cod is still salty, place it in a skillet or saucepan and add enough cold milk to cover it by 1 inch. Bring to a simmer without allowing the milk to boil, and simmer for 10 minutes. The milk should draw out the final salt from the cod. Drain and rinse the cod and proceed with the recipe. If the recipe calls for *cooked* salt cod, cook it as directed above, replacing the milk with water.

Market, Barcelona, Spain.

Handling Plantains

(PARA PREPARAR LOS PLÁTANOS)

Slice the ends off the plantain. With a small knife, make two continuous slits along the length of the plantain, one inside and one outside the curve. Make another continuous slit in the middle around the periphery of the plantain. Under cold running water, insert your thumbs under the skin and pry it away from the flesh, working around the periphery. The skin of green plantains doesn't come off as easily as that of ripe plantains.

If you are not planning to use the peeled plantains immediately, soak them in a bowl of ice water until ready to use. Because of their high starch content, cooked plantains tend to get dry and hard when exposed to the air. If you need to make them ahead of time, keep them in their cooking liquid until ready to use. This way they can be prepared up to 1 hour ahead.

Handling Banana Leaves

(PARA PREPARAR HOJAS DE PLÁTANO)

Food wrapped in banana leaves acquires a unique green tropical flavor. Banana leaves can be found frozen at most Hispanic and some Asian markets. The frozen packaged leaves are often already pre-cut and all you have to do is thaw them and soften them until pliable. If they are not pre-cut, cut them to the desired dimension, using scissors, before softening.

To soften banana leaves, wipe each one with a damp paper towel. The most traditional way to soften the leaves is to pass them over a gas flame until soft, about 15 seconds per side. Alternatively, the leaves can be blanched in boiling water for about 20 seconds, then refreshed under cold running water. You can also iron them with a regular iron, set on low.

INDEX